Patently Innovative

Biohealthcare Publishing Series on Pharma, Biotech and Biosciences: Science, Technology and Business

Volumes in the Series

1. *Clinical Research in Asia*. U. Sahoo (ISBN 9781907568008).
2. *Outsourcing Biopharma R&D to India*. P.R. Chowdhury (ISBN 9781907568084).
3. *Practical Leadership for Biopharmaceutical Executives*. J. Chin (ISBN 9781907568060)
4. *A Biotech Manager's Handbook*. M. O'Neill (ed.) (ISBN 9781907568145).
5. *RNA Interference*. T. Novobrantseva et al. (ISBN 9781907568169).
6. *Therapeutic Protein Formulation*. B. Meyer (ed.) (ISBN 9781907568183).
7. *Patent Litigation in the Pharmaceutical and Biotechnology Industries*. G. Morgan (ISBN 9781907568206).
8. *Matlab® in Bioscience and Biotechnology*. L. Burstein (ISBN 9781907568046).
9. *Clinical Research in Paediatric Psychopharmacology*. P. Auby (ISBN 9781907568244).
10. *Concepts and Techniques in Genomics and Proteomics*. N. Saraswathy and P. Ramalingam (ISBN 9781907568107).
11. *An Introduction to Biotechnology*. W.T. Godbey (ISBN 9781907568282).
12. *The Application of SPC in the Pharmaceutical and Biotechnology Industries*. T. Cochrane (ISBN 9781907568336).
13. *Patently Innovative: How Pharmaceutical Firms Use Emerging Patent Law to Extend Monopolies on Blockbuster Drugs*. R. Bouchard (ISBN 9781907568121).
14. *Therapeutic Antibody Engineering*. W.R. Strohl and L.M. Strohl (ISBN 9781907568374).
15. *Ultrafiltration for Bioprocessing*. H. Lutz (ISBN 9781907568466).
16. *Therapeutic Risk Management of Medicines*. A.K. Banerjee (ISBN 9781907568480).
17. *21st Century Quality Management and Good Management Practices: Value Added Compliance for the Pharmaceutical and Biotechnology Industry*. S. Williams (ISBN 9781907568503).
18. *An Introduction to Pharmaceutical Sciences*. J. Roy (ISBN 9781907568527).
19. *Pharmaceutical Licenses: Valuation and Execution*. S. Mayhew and I. Walker (ISBN 9781907568565).
20. *CAPA in the Pharmaceutical and Biotech Industries*. J. Rodriguez (ISBN 9781907568589).
21. *Commercialising the Stem Cell Sciences*. O. Harvey (ISBN 9781907568602).
22. *Process Validation for the Production of Biopharmaceuticals: Principles and Best Practice. Applied Strategies*

for Bioprocess Development and Manufacture. A. Newcombe et al. (ISBN 9781907568640).

23. *Clinical Trial Management. An Overview*. A.U. Sahoo et al. (ISBN 9781907568664).

24. *Annotating New Genes: From In Silico to Validations by Experiments*. S. Uchida (ISBN 9781907568688).

25. *Impact of Regulation on Drug Development*. H. Guenter Hennings (ISBN 9781907568701).

26. *The Design and Manufacture of Medical Devices*. J. Paulo Davim (ISBN 9781907568725).

Biohealthcare Publishing Series on Medical and Health Science, Technology and Policy

Volumes in the Series

1. *Medical Education, Training and Care Delivery in a Virtual World*. K. Kahol (ISBN 9781907568039).

2. *Allergens and Respiratory Pollutants*. M. Williams (ed.) (ISBN 9781907568541).

Biohealthcare Publishing Series on Bioinformatics

Volumes in the Series

1. *In Silico Protein Design*. C.M. Frenz (ISBN 9781907568268).

2. *Bioinformatics for Computer Science*. K. Revett (ISBN 9781907568329).

3. *Gene Expression Analysis in the RNA World*. J.Q. Clement (ISBN 9781907568305).

4. *Computational Methods for Finding Inferential Bases in Molecular Genetics*. Q.-N. Tran (ISBN 9781907568398).

5. *Computer-Aided Vaccine Design*. T.J. Chuan and S. Ranganathan (ISBN 9781907568411).

6. *Bioinformatics for Biomedical Science and Clinical Applications*. K.-H. Liang (ISBN 9781907568442).

7. *Deterministic Versus Stochastic Modelling in Biochemistry and Systems Biology*. P. Lecca et al. (ISBN 9781907568626).

This book is dedicated to my wife Patricia Barker without whom none of the long nights and work that have gone into this book, or the patience to hang in there during difficult circumstances, would have come about.

Patently Innovative

How pharmaceutical firms use emerging patent law to extend monopolies on blockbuster drugs

Ron A. Bouchard

Biohealthcare
PUBLISHING (OXFORD) LIMITED
Oxford · New York

Biohealthcare Publishing (Oxford) Limited

Hexagon House
Avenue 4
Station Lane
Witney
Oxford OX28 4BN, UK
Tel: +44 (0) 1865 59 8888; Fax: +44 (0) 1865 884448
Email: info@biohealthcarepublishing.com
Website: www.biohealthcarepublishing.com

First published in 2011 by Biohealthcare Publishing (Oxford) Limited
ISBN: 978 1 907568 12 1

British Library Cataloguing-in-Publication Data: a catalogue record for this book is available from the British Library.

Typeset by Domex e-Data Pvt. Ltd.
Printed in the UK and USA
Cover design by Hutchins Creative

Cover image courtesy of R.A. Bouchard and Ian Hutchins

Contents

Acknowledgements

I am grateful to many of my colleagues in scholarship, government, and the intellectual property bar for their input and mentorship over the course of the last four years. Thanks are especially due to Richard Hawkins, Joel Lexchin, Alex Stack, Ed Hore, Harry Radomski, David Vaver, Wayne Giles, Tim McTiernan, David Lee, Maurica Maher, Robert Clark, Aiden Hollis, and Paul Grootendorst. I am also thankful to my colleagues in the Consortium Study of Global Pharmaceutical Linkage for their collaboration and comments during our work together thus far, including Dan Cahoy, Joel Lexchin, Aidan Hollis, Bengt Domeij, Graham Dutfield, Tom Faunce, Paul Jones, Feroz Ali Khader, Heesob Nam, and Juan Luis Serrano. Also requiring immense thanks are Monika Sawicka, Jamil Sawani, Chris McLelland, Kirsten Burrows, Dan Meeking, and Cam Sklar for their excellent research assistance at varying stages of the work, and for continually pushing me to grow as a scholar and an individual. I am also grateful to the federal and provincial agencies that funded the work described in this book. In particular, I thank the Alberta Heritage Foundation for Medical Research (AHFMR) for a career establishment award and the Canadian Institutes for Health Research (CIHR) for supporting my ongoing work through a New Investigator Award. I also wish to thank the Editors of the journals that have published my work over the last few years, including the leading intellectual property and science and technology law reviews published by Berkeley, Marquette, Minnesota, Northwestern, McGill, Santa Clara, and Boston schools of law. Finally, I am deeply grateful to my wife Patricia. Without her encouragement, and that of our beautiful children Naomi, Zoe, and Rhael, this book would not have come about.

List of figures and tables

Figures

Tables

List of abbreviations

ANDS	Abbreviated New Drug Submission
ATC	Anatomic Therapeutic Class
CDER	Center for Drug Evaluation and Research
CER	Cost Effectiveness Research
CHMP	Committee for Medicinal Products for Human Use
CIPO	Canadian Intellectual Property Office
CPR	Canadian Patent Register
CPRY	Cumulative Patents Registered per Year
CPY	Cumulative Patents per Year
DIN	Drug Identification Number
EC	European Commission
EMEA	European Medicines Agency
ER	Expedited Review
EU	European Union
FDA	Food and Drug Administration
FTA	Free Trade Agreement
GAO	Government Accountability Office
GATT	General Agreement on Tariffs and Trade
GOC	Government of Canada
HTA	Health Technology Assessment
IOM	Institute of Medicine

IPR	Intellectual Property and Regulatory [rights]
MA	Marketing Authorization
MI	Most Innovative
NAFTA	North American Free Trade Agreement
NAS	New Active Substance
NCE	New Chemical Entity
NDS	New Drug Submission
NIH	National Institutes of Health (US)
NOC	Notice of Compliance
NOC/c	Notice of Compliance with Conditions
OB	Orange Book
OECD	Organization for Economic Cooperation and Development
PCT	Patent Cooperation Treaty
PLF	Progressive Licensing Framework
PMPRB	Patented Medicine Prices Review Board
PY	Patent per Year
RIAS	Regulatory Impact Analysis Statement
rTPL	regulated Therapeutic Product Lifecycle
S&T	Science and Technology
SANDS	Supplemental Abbreviated New Drug Submission
SNDS	Supplemental New Drug Submission
TRIPS	Trade Related Aspects of Intellectual Property Rights
USPTO	US Patent and Trademark Office
WHO	World Health Organization
WTO	World Trade Organization

About the author

Dr Ron A. Bouchard is a health law and policy and intellectual property scholar and lawyer, specializing in innovation, government regulation, and litigation of medical research and commercial products. His career has focused on the science, law, policy, regulation, and commercialization of medical technologies. He started as a medical scientist, completing a PhD and Postdoctoral Fellowship in the field of ion channel biophysics and Ca^{2+} imaging. He shifted focus to obtain a law degree specializing in pharmaceutical and biotechnology law and has been involved in the prosecution, acquisition, financing, distribution, and litigation of intellectual property rights. Dr Bouchard has appeared before the Federal Court of Canada and the Supreme Court of Canada. He has consulted with firms, universities, governments, and international organizations on legal, regulatory, and policy issues. He worked with the Government of Canada on its platforms for lifecycle-based drug approval and public-private partnerships in technology commercialization. His research has been funded by federal and provincial funding agencies and private endowments. His current research is focused on the clinical, regulatory, and intellectual property aspects of therapeutic product development, including global aspects of medical research, technology commercialization, patenting, licensing, and regulatory approval. A particular interest of the lab is to elucidate the manner in which intellectual property, innovation, public health, and economic law and policy interact as a single complex adaptive health system, with a focus on the empirical assessment of the impact of government regulation on innovation and affordable medicine in the life sciences sector. He lives in Canada, with his wife Patricia, daughters Naomi, Zoe, and Rhael, and dog Kiva.

The author may be contacted via the publishers.

1

Introduction

Abstract. Global linkage regulation of pharmaceutical products has emerged under intense political pressure to balance effective patent enforcement over new and innovative drugs with the timely market entry of lower-priced generic competitors. The United States was the first jurisdiction to institute linkage in 1984, following which time pressure was brought to bear on other countries to do so through inclusion of linkage terms in various free-trade agreements. Canada was the second jurisdiction to bring in linkage as part of its perceived obligations under NAFTA and TRIPS. It has now been over two decades since the regulations were enacted and to date there has been little objective assessment as to whether the regulations have, in fact, stimulated innovation and timely generic entry. This book describes the public health implications of the evolution of pharmaceutical linkage worldwide, with a particular focus on empirical studies of the scope of linkage between drug approval and drug patenting. A major goal of the work was to probe in detail the specific legal nexus between the innovative character of new and follow-on drugs approved by domestic regulators, the scope of intellectual property protection afforded to these drugs under the linkage regulations, the effect of linkage on the timing of generic entry, and the impact of linkage on public health. The implications of the data for the legal legitimacy of pharmaceutical linkage as an emerging intellectual property paradigm are discussed in light of the public policy goals to stimulate new and innovative drug development while also facilitating the timely entry of generic products as well as leading patent law jurisprudence.

Keywords: introduction, pharmaceutical linkage, drug approval, drug patenting, innovation, access to essential medications

Prompt and affordable access to essential medicines is a significant component of most domestic and global models of public health, and is central to the goal of ensuring value for money regarding drug costs and expenditures. The availability and costs of new and generic drugs is a function both of traditional patent law incentives and emerging linkage regulations in conjunction with food and drug laws.

Patent law is a well described,[1] if controversial,[2] policy lever for stimulating the development of new drugs.[3] Linkage regulations tie generic drug availability to existing drug patents by connecting approval to the resolution of patent validity or infringement.[4] All patents listed by a brand manufacturer on a patent register must be demonstrated in litigation to be either invalid or not infringed by the generic drug in order for market entry to occur. This can result in long and costly litigation, the costs of which are ultimately borne by consumers.[5] The alternative is that generics do not gain market entry, and that brand firms continue to enjoy patent monopolies on products until all relevant patents expire, thus reducing access to affordable essential medications in both developing and developed nations.

The patent system has been in operation for about 500 years, with early patent laws in Italy and the United Kingdom.[6] By contrast, the linkage regime has only been in existence for about 25 years following the passage of Hatch-Waxman in the United States in 1984[7] and the Canadian Patented Medicines (Notice of Compliance) Regulations in 1993.[8] Up until recently, North America was the only economic region where generic entry and drug access were explicitly tied to existing brand-name drugs through linkage regulations. In both jurisdictions, the linkage regime was brought in explicitly to balance the competing policy goals of stimulating the development of new and innovative drugs and the timely entry of generic drugs.[9]

1.1 The emergence of global pharmaceutical linkage

As discussed above, compared with the patent system, the linkage regime represents a novel and emerging intellectual property paradigm for protecting pharmaceutical inventions. Nevertheless, by 2010, we were witnessing a rapid spread of the linkage regime on a global level. This is due to a growing number of Free Trade Agreements (FTAs) involving the US.[10] Recent agreements include Trade Related Aspects of Intellectual Property Rights (TRIPS), [11] as well as narrower multilateral and bilateral agreements with Canada and Mexico,[12] Australia,[13] and Korea,[14] among others.[15] The latter agreements require participating nations to incorporate linkage and other intellectual property provisions in their patent systems in exchange for preferential trade terms[16] and are increasingly negotiated outside the purview of the World Trade Organization (WTO). As these provisions provide stronger intellectual property protection for drugs than provided for by TRIPS, they are referred to as 'TRIPS-Plus.'[17] Indeed, the European Commission (EC) has recently reported numerous instances where member nations have attempted to institute pharmaceutical linkage regimes even though EU law prohibits the same.[18]

The implications of pharmaceutical linkage for global public health are potentially immense. For example, recent empirical work has shown that the Canadian linkage regime can extend cumulative patent terms for high-value pharmaceuticals by as much as twofold.[19] This is consistent with early predictions of the potential impact of pharmaceutical linkage by Schondelmeyer,[20] based on his work with the US Hatch-Waxman linkage regime.[21] An additional concern is that the extension of market exclusivity on brand drugs (and thus prolonged monopoly pricing) occurs even though up to 50–75% of the patents challenged in Canada and the US may be either invalid or not infringed by the generic equivalent when challenged on the merits.[22] A related issue is that costs of prolonged litigation are known to be passed on to consumers,[23] with differential costs to governments and the public in accordance with their system of drug reimbursement,[24] public health,[25] public-private discourse,[26] and health equity.[27] This creates a conflicting system where governments with linkage regimes that limit the timely appearance of generics also depend on these firms to produce cost savings and limit the growth in pharmaceutical expenditures.

Considerations such as these must be balanced against the need for innovative drugs in developed and developing nations, the presumption favoring the validity of patents in most developed nations,[28] and data suggesting that enhanced national research and development activities can increase national productivity and prosperity,[29] as well as the idea that if the state grants a party an exclusive right, in this case an intellectual property right, it cannot turn around and grant a third party permission to invade that right without just cause.

In addition to shaping the marketplace for brand and generic drugs, intellectual property protection for pharmaceuticals has become a controversial cog in the global machine of providing individuals with essential medications, in both developed[30] and developing[31] nations. Canada, like a host of developed nations, has attempted to play a key role in the global effort to provide underserved populations with essential medications through its Access to Medicines Regime,[32] but with less success than anticipated to date.[33] Moreover, and perhaps more importantly, up to this point effort has been focused primarily on the limits of traditional patent law,[34] with emerging forms of patent law such as pharmaceutical linkage receiving considerably less attention.

A related observation is that while the concept of pharmaceutical linkage is relatively new compared to the patent system, there is already significant pressure to broaden it beyond drug approval to include linkage between patent rights and other regulatory aspects of drug approval and marketing.[35] As such, the perceived success of drug approval-drug patenting linkage may operate as a 'template' for the expansion of the concept of linkage. In this regard, the basket of a given nation's global trade obligations clearly represents an expansive notion of linkage compared to the relatively discrete nexus envisioned between drug patents and the marketed products against which they are listed when linkage first came into force.[36]

For example, the EC Pharmaceutical Sector Inquiry[37] recently articulated a broad basket of pharmaceutical linkage practices, including linkage of patent status to formal legal proceedings between parties; patent settlements; and interventions before national drug regulators regarding market approval, drug pricing, and reimbursement.[38] An evolving landscape such as this raises the question of whether the pharmaceutical industry is using linkage as an expansive stepping stone in its efforts to reach across global borders. Moreover, a growing number of legal disputes have been reported whereby countries without linkage regulations have attempted to import or export drugs and the shipments have been seized by other nations alleging that these shipments are in violation of domestic patent laws linked to international trade instruments[39] such as TRIPS or other FTAs.[40]

In addition to being extended beyond the drug approval nexus, the linkage regime may also be serving as a model for the development of other systems of intellectual property protection. For example, the legal mechanism currently being developed for the regulation of follow-on biologics[41] appears to be a hybrid of traditional patent law, pharmaceutical linkage regulation, and data exclusivity regimes.[42]

Linkage regulations in respect of therapeutic products have therefore quietly emerged as a key driver of public health costs and medical product regulation on the global stage.

1.2 Canadian pharmaceutical linkage regulations

The Patented Medicines (Notice of Compliance) Regulations ('NOC Regulations')[43] came into force in 1993 as part of Canada's perceived obligations under TRIPS and NAFTA to support the domestic pharmaceutical industry.[44] The original policy intent of the regulations, as outlined in successive government Regulatory Impact Analysis Statements (RIAS), was to encourage the development of new and innovative drugs and facilitate the timely market entry of generic drugs, and thus to balance the goals and objectives of food and drug law with those of patent law. Prior to the linkage regime coming into force, drug regulation and drug patenting represented distinct goals and policy objectives.[45] This balancing exercise is a familiar one to the intellectual property bar owing to the quid pro quo of the traditional patent bargain. Thus, under the terms of the linkage regime, there must be a specific functional nexus between approved drugs and patent protection for those drugs pursuant to the NOC Regulations.

As appreciated in the early literature on the topic,[46] it was not output metrics but a combination of lobbying by the US pharmaceutical industry, their hopeful domestic university funding partners, and a federal government bent on harmonizing the Canadian system of intellectual property with that of the US that led to enactment of the NOC Regulations. Once the domestic US policy environment was recalibrated away from nascent support for a Canadian-based system of price controls and towards preventing nations such as Canada from what was deemed to be 'rights piracy,'[47] stronger patent protection in Canada was inevitable. However, with one notable exception,[48] few independent observers would have guessed during the debate on patent reform that the linkage regime would potentially tip so far to the rights-protection end of the spectrum.

It has now been almost two decades since the regulations were enacted subsequent to Canada's perceived obligations under NAFTA and TRIPS. Given the continuing public debate over high drug prices,[49] the large fraction of research and development carried out by publicly funded institutions that is ultimately enveloped within commercialized products,[50] and wide criticism of the failings of the patent system to promote innovation,[51] it is an excellent time to assess whether the NOC Regulations have satisfied the twin policy goals of encouraging new and innovative drug development and the timely market entry of generic drugs. The author's research group has chosen as the vehicle of our investigation the growing field of empirical legal research. This approach was taken, at least in part, owing to the author's many years as a bench scientist prior to entering law.

The empirical work reviewed and discussed is this book was designed specifically to investigate whether and how the NOC Regulations have encouraged the development of new and innovative drugs while also facilitating the timely entry of generics since being enacted. The importance of empirical studies to assessing the efficiency and effectiveness of policy levers such as intellectual property law and regulations cannot be overstated. As noted by some of the most prominent economists, innovation scholars, and patent scholars,[52] robust conclusions regarding the consequences for technological innovation of changes in patent law and policy are few and far between. This is due primarily to a fundamental lack of relevant empirical data. Important to the present project, the same principle also applies in reverse, as governments have specific legal and policy goals in mind when drafting law and regulations that are reviewable by the courts in judicial review or other statutory interpretation proceedings.

1.3 Organization

The remainder of the book reviews data from our recent empirical studies, analyzes this data in terms of the original policy intent underpinning the regulations in Canada and the United States and associated Supreme Court jurisprudence, and concludes with a series of testable hypotheses for future research and a brief review of the global spread of pharmaceutical linkage and the implications of this spread for global and domestic public health.

Chapter 2 provides a broad overview of the domestic requirements for drug approval and operation of the NOC Regulations. It is necessary to understand in some detail the different types of drug approval pathways for brand-name and generic drugs, whether drugs are new or follow-on in nature, and what characteristics certain drugs have that render them potentially high-value drug candidates from the regulator's point of view. This information can in turn be used to evaluate the innovative character of a given drug. Chapter 2 also provides an overview of the Canadian linkage regulation regime, how it operates in tandem with the traditional patent law system and food and drug law, and how it can be used to extend market exclusivity for high value pharmaceuticals that are nearing the point of expiration of early patent(s) associated with a given drug. The chapter ends with a discussion of the tensions between public health policy and economic policy when they are forced to cohabit under the roof of pharmaceutical linkage.

Chapters 3–5 review three empirical studies our group recently published that were intended to provide empirical data for analysis of whether the NOC Regulations, in operation, are consistent with the original policy intent underpinning the regulations to effectively and efficiently balance the goals of patent law with those of food and drug law. Chapter 3 focuses on the types of new and follow-on drugs approved by Canadian regulators between 2001 and 2008. In particular we studied trends over the eight-year test period for new drug submissions, supplemental, or line extension-type, submissions, generic submissions, drugs that underwent some form of priority review (with or without post-market reporting obligations), and drugs that contained a new active substance (previously referred to as new chemical entities), were first in class or were me-too drugs. We studied a total of 608 drugs that received 2,122 regulatory approvals over the test period. The year 2001 was taken as our starting point, as this was the date when substantial amendments to Canadian drug regulation were made that affected both the mechanisms and speed of approval.

Chapter 4 extends the analysis in Chapter 3 by quantifying the level of innovation for the cohort of 2,122 approvals and additionally focuses on the legal nexus between drug approval and drug patenting in a subgroup of the most profitable drugs sold in Canada.[53] Our aim was to quantify patenting, patent listing, and patent litigation patterns associated with these drugs under the NOC Regulations and to investigate the manner in which patent terms on already approved blockbuster drugs were extended via operation of the linkage regime. We also characterized case law associated with the extension of market exclusivity.

Chapter 5 focuses on patenting patterns associated with a more fully developed cohort of 95 high-value pharmaceuticals and 3,850 related patents. A number of different groups were analyzed: the entire cohort of drugs, most profitable drugs by sales, drugs approved via an expedited approval process without significant post-market conditions, drugs approved via expedited approval with significant post-market conditions, and drugs approved via a combination of the two pathways. Drugs were thus split into categories representing products already vetted by the market to be blockbuster in nature and those that were granted expedited review status by regulators in the hope they would be. We analyzed the number of patents per drug, the number of patents listed on the patent register, and the timing of these metrics to one another and the date of drug approval. We conducted tests on the statistical nature of the trends in patenting before and after the NOC Regulations came into force. In addition, we analyzed patents and approved drugs in terms of the World Health Organization Anatomic Therapeutic Class (ATC) in order to identify therapeutic areas in which firms are focusing their drug development activities. We also developed an independent patent classification scheme in order to analyze the type of patents associated with approved drugs.

Chapter 6 reviews the empirical data from these studies with the goal of analyzing the results in light of the original policy intent underpinning the Canadian and American linkage regimes to balance the competing goals of stimulating the production of new and innovative drugs while also facilitating the timely entry of generic drugs. The data are also assessed through the lens of relevant Supreme Court of Canada jurisprudence, which expressly provides for a 'patent-specific' analysis of cases under the NOC Regulations. A final component of the analysis is to view the data in light of principles of statutory interpretation holding that judicial review of legislation should allow for assessment of a given law 'in operation.' A major goal of Chapter 6 is to probe the value of empirical legal research for assessment of the *vires* of legislation viewed with an eye to judicial review proceedings, particularly jurisprudence directed to statutory interpretation of intellectual property law.

Chapter 7 concludes the discussion on linkage by offering a glimpse into our group's current and future research directions, including articulating several testable hypotheses underpinning a theory of cluster-based drug development and providing a description of a new structure-function analysis being undertaken by a group of global scholars studying pharmaceutical linkage worldwide.

The review of law, policy, and accompanying data in this book provides substantial evidence for a linkage-based theory of innovation focused on the development of 'product clusters.' These clusters are specifically enabled by specific provisions of linkage laws, and are comprised of one or a small number of innovative drugs, surrounded by a halo of patents that are all interconnected between products. The possibility is discussed that it is the sum of drugs and patents in these clusters that most effectively chills generic entry under linkage regulations. Chapter 7 finishes with a commentary on the manner in which pharmaceutical linkage regulations are rapidly spreading worldwide, and the implications of this development for domestic and global public health. Indeed, while it is generally understood that linkage is being increasingly seeded into domestic intellectual property frameworks via TRIPS and other FTAs, very little is known about how the regulations work and impact on drug costs and expenditures in developed nations let alone how they might impact on domestic public health systems across international borders. The goal of this portion of Chapter 7 is to provide an overview of the structural and functional aspects of global linkage regulations, and their relationship to drug availability costs and expenditures on one hand and incentives for innovation and protection of intellectual property rights on the other.

Notes

1. Kenneth Arrow, *Economic Welfare and the Allocation of Resources for Invention* (Rand Corporation, 1959); Kenneth Arrow, 'Economic Welfare and the Allocation of Resources for Innovation,' in Richard R. Nelson (ed.), *The Rate and Direction of Inventive Activity* (Universities-National Bureau, 1962) 609–26; Robert P. Merges and Richard R. Nelson, 'On the Complex Economics of Patent Scope,' 90 *Colum. L. Rev.* (1990) 839; Dan L. Burk and Mark A. Lemley, 'Policy Levers in Patent Law,' 89 *Va. L. Rev.* 157 (2003); David Vaver, *Intellectual Property Rights: Critical Concepts in Law* (Routledge, 2006). For an account of the relationship between patents and drug discovery, development, and marketing from the earliest days of the industry to the present, see Graham Dutfield, *Intellectual Property Rights and the Life Science Industries: Past, Present and Future* (World Scientific, 2009); Bengt Domeij, *Pharmaceutical Patents in Europe* (Kluwer Law International, 2000); Bengt Domeij, 'Initial and Follow-on Pharmaceutical Inventions in Europe,' in Ove Granstrand (ed.), *The Economics and Law of Intellectual Property* (Kluwer Law International, 2003) 177–98.

2. Sheldon Krimsky, *Science in the Private Interest: Has the Lure of Profits Corrupted Biomedical Research?* (Rowman & Littlefield, 2003) [Krimsky (2003)]; Michele Boldrin and David K. Levine, *Against Intellectual Monopoly* (Cambridge University Press, 2008); James Bessen and Michael J. Meurer, *Patent Failure: How Judges, Bureaucrats, and Lawyers Put Innovators at Risk* (Princeton University Press, 2008); Adam B. Jaffe, 'The U.S. Patent System in Transition: Policy Innovation and the Innovation Process,' 29 *Research Policy* 531 (2000) [Jaffe (2000)]; Roberto Mazzoleni and Richard R. Nelson, 'The Benefits and Costs of Strong Patent Protection: A Contribution to the Current Debate,' 27 *Research Policy* 273 (1998) [Mazzoleni and Nelson (1998)]; Marcia Angell, *The Truth About the Drug Companies: How They Deceive Us and What to Do About It* (Random House, 2004); Kevin Outterson, 'Pharmaceutical Arbitrage: Balancing Access and Innovation in International Prescription Drug Markets,' *Yale Journal of Health Policy, Law and Ethics*, December (2004); Michele Boldrin and David K. Levine, 'The Economics of Ideas and Intellectual Property,' 102 *Proceedings of the National Academy of Sciences of the United States of America* 1252 (2005) [Boldrin and Levine (2005)]; Keith Pavitt, 'National Policies for Technical Change: Where Are the Increasing Returns to Economic Research?' 93 *Proceedings of the National Academy of Sciences of the United States of America* 126 (1996).
3. R.A. Bouchard, 'Should Scientific Research in the Lead-Up to Invention Vitiate Obviousness Under the Patented Medicines (Notice of Compliance) Regulations: To Test or Not to Test?' 6(1) *CJLT* 1–27 (2007) [Bouchard (2007a)]; R.A. Bouchard, 'Living Separate and Apart Is Never Easy: Inventive Capacity of the PHOSITA as the Tie that Binds Obviousness and Inventiveness,' 4(1) *University of Ottawa Law and Technology Journal* 1–57 (2007) [Bouchard (2007b)]; R.A. Bouchard, '*KSR* v. *Teleflex* Part 1: Impact of U.S. Supreme Court Patent Law on Canadian Intellectual Property and Regulatory Rights Landscape,' 15(1) *Health L.J.* 222–46 (2008); T.A. Faunce and J. Lexchin, '"Linkage" Pharmaceutical Evergreening in Canada and Australia,' *Australia and New Zealand Health Policy* 4(1) (2007) at 8; Paul Jones, '*KSR* and the Supreme Court: The Silence Is Deafening,' 53 *Antitrust Bulletin* 849 (2008).
4. For a review of Canadian linkage regulations, see: R.A. Bouchard, 'I'm Still Your Baby: Canada's Continuing Support of U.S. Linkage Regulations for Pharmaceuticals,' 15(1) *Marquette Intellectual Property Review* 1–52 (2011); R.A. Bouchard et al., 'Empirical Analysis of Drug Approval-Drug Patenting Linkage for High Value Pharmaceuticals,' 8(2) *Northwestern Journal of Technology and Intellectual Property* 174–227 (2010) [Bouchard (2010)]; R.A. Bouchard et al., 'The Pas de Deux of Pharmaceutical Regulation and Innovation: Who's Leading Whom?' 24(3) *Berkeley Tech. L.J.* 1461–522 (2009) [Bouchard (2009)]; M. Sawicka and R.A. Bouchard, 'Empirical Analysis of Drug Approval Data 2001–2008: Are Canadian Pharmaceutical Players "Doing More With Less"?' 3(1) *McGill Journal of Law & Health* 49–84 (2009); J. Lexchin, 'After Compulsory Licensing: Coming Issues in Canadian Pharmaceutical Policy and Politics,' 40(1) *Health Policy* 69–80 (1997).

5. Boldrin and Levine (2005), *supra* note 2.
6. Jean O. Lanjouw and William Jack, 'Trading Up: How Much Should Poor Countries Pay to Support Pharmaceutical Innovation?' 4(3) *Center for Global Development Brief* 1–8 (2004).
7. 21 USC § 355(j)(7)(A) (establishing a list of 'Approved Drug Products with Therapeutic Equivalence' commonly known as the 'Orange Book'). For a description of US linkage laws see: Gerald Mossinghoff, 'Overview of the Hatch-Waxman Act and Its Impact on the Drug Development Process,' 54 *Food & Drug L.J.* 187–94 (1999); Andrew A. Caffrey and Jonathan M. Rotter, 'Consumer Protection, Patents and Procedure: Generic Drug Market Entry and the Need to Reform *The Hatch-Waxman Act*,' 9 *Va. J.L. & Tech.* 1, 4–7 (2004) [Caffrey and Rotter (2004)]; Rebecca S. Eisenberg, 'Patents, Product Exclusivity, and Information Dissemination: How Law Directs Biopharmaceutical Research and Development,' 72 *Fordham L. Rev.* 477, 483 (2003); Jeremy Bulow, *The Gaming of Pharmaceutical Patents*, National Bureau of Economic Research (NBER) Paper (2003) [Bulow (2003)]; Richard Epstein and Bruce Kuhlik, *Navigating the Anticommons for Pharmaceutical Patents: Steady the Course on Hatch-Waxman*, University of Chicago Law & Economics Working Paper No. 209; Mathew Avery, 'Continuing Abuse of the Hatch-Waxman Act by Pharmaceutical Patent Holders and the Failure of the 2003 Amendments,' 60 *Hastings L.J.* 171 (2008) [Avery (2008)].
8. Patented Medicines (Notice of Compliance) Regulations amend. SOR. /93-133 (NOC Regulations). For early descriptions of Canadian linkage law see, for example: Robert Tancer, 'Foreign Investment in North America and the Pharmaceutical Industry in Canada,' 39(2) *The International Executive* 283–97 (1997) [Tancer (1997)]; Christopher Scott Harrison, 'Protection of Pharmaceuticals as Foreign Policy: The Canada–U.S. Trade Agreement and Bill C-22 Versus the North American Free Trade Agreement and Bill C-91,' 26 *N.C. Int'l L. & Com. Reg.* 457–528 (2001) [Harrison (2001)]; Edward Hore, 'A Comparison of United States and Canadian Laws as They Affect Generic Pharmaceutical Market Entry,' 55 *Food & Drug L.J.* 373 (2000).
9. Avery (2008), *supra* note 7; Bouchard (2010), *supra* note 4.
10. Carlos María Correa, 'Bilateral Free Trade Agreements and Access to Medicines,' 84 *Bulletin of the World Health Organization* 399–404 (2006) [Correa (2006)]; Judit Rius Sanjuan, *Patent-Registration Linkage*, CPTech, April 3, 2006, online: CPTech <http://www.cptech.org/publications/CPTechDPNo2Linkage.pdf>; Finston Consulting, LLC, 'Overview on Patent Linkage' (August 7, 2006), online: <http://www.finstonconsulting.com/version03/files/Overview.pdf> (UK Consulting Report).
11. *Agreement on Trade Related Aspects of Intellectual Property (TRIPS) 1994*, October 30, 1947, 58 UNTS 187, Can. T.S. 1947 No. 27 (negotiated as part of the Uruguay Round (1986–1994) of the World Trade Organization's General Agreement on Tariffs and Trade (GATT)).
12. North American Free Trade Agreement Between the Government of Canada, the Government of Mexico, and the Government of the United States, December 17, 1992, Can. T.S. 1994 No. 2, 32 ILM 289 (entered into force January 1, 1994).

13. HR 4759: United States–Australia Free Trade Agreement Implementation Act, online <http://www.govtrack.us/congress/bill.xpd?bill=h108-4759>.
14. Korea–US Free Trade Agreement [KorUS FTA], signed June 30, 2007, online: Office of the United States Trade Representative <http://www.ustr.gov/trade-agreements/free-trade-agreements/korus-fta>.
15. Correa (2006), *supra* note 10.
16. Faunce (2006); T.A. Faunce and K. Shats, 'Bilateral Trade Agreements as Drivers of National and Transnational Benefit from Health Technology Policy: Implications of Recent US Deals for Australian Negotiations with China and India,' 62(2) *Australian Journal of International Affairs* 196–213 (2008).
17. Correa (2006), *supra* note 10.
18. European Commission Pharmaceutical Sector Inquiry Final Report, 8 July 2009 [European Commission Pharmaceutical Sector Inquiry Final Report (2009)] at 23. This theme is developed extensively in the European Commission Pharmaceutical Sector Inquiry Preliminary Report, 28 November 2008 [European Commission Pharmaceutical Sector Inquiry Preliminary Report (2008)] at 14 and 113.
19. Bouchard (2010), *supra* note 4.
20. Dr Stephen Schondelmeyer, a pharmacologist and health economist, gave evidence before the House of Commons to the effect that it is not the term of single patents that mattered most, but rather how patents add cumulatively to extend market exclusivity, a claim the government at the time vigorously denied. Compare the testimonies of Dr Stephen Schondelmeyer (Professor, University of Minnesota) and Dr Kay Dickson (Director General, Department of Industry, Science and Technology). Parliament of Canada, 33:7, *Minutes of Proceedings and Evidence of the Legislative Committee on Bill C-22* (December 1, 1992) 7:65–7:96 and 33:8; (September 2, 1992) 8:37–8:40.
21. Lara J. Glasgow, 'Stretching the Limits of Intellectual Property Rights: Has the Pharmaceutical Industry Gone Too Far?' 41 *Idea* 227 (2001), citing data from a US study at note 27: The Gale Group, 'Intellectual Property Rules: A Delicate Balancing Act for Drug Development,' 23 *Chain Drug Review* (2001) RX13.
22. Federal Trade Commission 2002 Study, *Generic Drug Entry Prior to Patent Expiration: An FTC Study*, online: Federal Trade Commission <http://www.ftc.gov/os/2002/07/genericdrugstudy.pdf> [FTC Study (2002)]; Ed Hore, 'Patently Absurd: Evergreening of Pharmaceutical Patent Protection under the Patented Medicines (Notice of Compliance) Regulations of Canada's Patent Act 5, 11 (2004), online: <http://www.canadiangenerics.ca/en/news/docs/patently_absurd_04.pdf>; Caffrey and Rotter (2004), *supra* note 7. It should be noted, however, that these data are now somewhat old and require updating in both the US and Canada following amendments to the respective linkage regimes over the last half decade. For an update of these numbers, see generally, *Pharmaceuticals: Analyzing Litigation Success Rates*, RBC Capital Markets, Industry Comment, January 15, 2010; C. Scott Hemphill and Mark A. Lemley, *Earning Exclusivity: Generic Drug Incentives and the Hatch-Waxman Act*, Stanford Law and Economics Olin Working Paper No. 405, Columbia Law and Economics Working Paper No. 391, 2011, available at <http://papers.ssrn.com/sol3/papers.

cfm?abstract_id=1736822>. For a discussion of parallel rates of litigation and findings of invalidity in the EU, see European Commission Pharmaceutical Sector Inquiry Final Report, July 8, 2009 and the European Commission Pharmaceutical Sector Inquiry Preliminary Report, November 28, 2008.

23. Boldrin and Levine (2005), *supra* note 2; Bulow (2003), *supra* note 7.
24. Colleen Flood, Mark Stabile, and Carolyn Tuohy (eds), *Exploring Social Insurance: Can a Dose of Europe Cure Canadian Health Care Finance?* (McGill-Queen's University Press, 2008); C. Flood, J. Downie, and T. Caulfield (eds), *Canadian Health Law and Policy*, 3rd edn (LexisNexis, 2007).
25. Philip J. Hilts, *Protecting America's Health: The FDA, Business, and One Hundred Years of Regulation* (Alfred A. Knopf, 2003) [Hilts (2003)]; Jerry Avorn, *Powerful Medicines: The Benefits, Risks, and Costs of Prescription Drugs* (Alfred A. Knopf, 2004) [Avorn (2004)]; Marcia Angell, *The Truth About the Drug Companies: How They Deceive Us and What To Do About It* (Random House, 2004) [Angell (2004)]; Jay S. Cohen, *Overdose: The Case Against the Drug Companies* (Penguin, 2001) [Cohen 2001)]; Ray Moynihan and Alan Cassels, *Selling Sickness: How the World's Biggest Pharmaceutical Companies Are Turning Us All Into Patients* (Nation Books, 2005).
26. E. Wiktorowicz, 'Emergent Patterns in the Regulation of Pharmaceuticals: Institutions and Interests in the United States, Canada, Britain and France,' 28 *J. Health Pol.* 615 (2003).
27. Trudo Lemmens, 'Leopards in the Temple: Restoring Scientific Integrity to the Commercialized Research Scene,' 32 *J.L. Med. & Ethics* 641 (2004); Trudo Lemmens, 'Piercing the Veil of Corporate Secrecy about Clinical Trials,' 34(5) *Hastings Center Report* 14 (2004). See also: World Health Organization, *Integrating Intellectual Property Rights and Development Policy*, Report of the Commission on Intellectual Property Rights (2002) <http://www.iprcommission.org/graphic/documents/final_report.htm>; Kevin Outterson, 'Should Access to Medicines and TRIPS Flexibilities Be Limited to Specific Diseases?' 34(2–3) *Am. J.L. & Med.* 123–37 (2008).
28. Mark A. Lemley and Douglas Lichtman, 'Rethinking Patent Law's Presumption of Validity,' 60 *Stan. L. Rev.* 45 (2007).
29. *Reinventing Innovation and Commercialization Policy in Ontario*, Institute for Competitiveness and Prosperity Working Paper No. 6. (2004); Brian Guthrie and Trefor Munn-Venn, Conference Board of Canada, *Six Quick Hits for Canadian Commercialization: Leaders' Roundtable on Commercialization* (2005); Canadian Government, Rotman Expert Panel on Commercialization, *People and Excellence: The Heart of Successful Commercialization* (2006); Erika Fitzpatrick, *Innovation America: A Final Report* (National Governors Association, 2002); Council on Competitiveness, *Innovate America: Thriving in a World of Challenge and Change* (2006); Council on Competitiveness, *Five for the Future* (2007).
30. S. Kesselheim and J. Avorn, 'Biomedical Patents and the Public's Health: Is There a Role for Eminent Domain?' 295(4) *Journal of the American Medical Association* 434–7 (2006).

31. World Health Organization, *Public Health: Innovation and Intellectual Property Rights*, Report of the Commission on Intellectual Property Rights, Innovation and Public Health (May 5, 2006); Graham Dutfield, Delivering Drugs to the Poor: Will the TRIPS Amendment Help?' 34(2–3) *Am. J.L. & Med.* 107–24 (2008); Aaron Kesselheim, 'Think Globally, Prescribe Locally: How Rational Pharmaceutical Policy in the US Can Improve Global Access to Essential Medicines,' 34(2–3) *Am. J.L. & Med.* 83–91 (2008).
32. Canada's Access to Medicines Regime was established by the Government of Canada. It allows Canada to enact compulsory licenses, despite provisions in the Patent Act to the contrary, in order to export essential medicines to countries without the capacity to manufacture them. The popular front for this effort was the 2004 Act to amend the Patent Act and the Food and Drugs Act, also known as the 'Jean Chrétien Pledge to Africa Act.' See, for example, online: <http://www.camr-rcam.gc.ca/intro/context_e.html>.
33. J.C. Kohler et al., 'Canada's Access to Medicines Regime: Promise or Failure of Humanitarian Effort,' 5(3) *Healthcare Policy* 40–8 (2010).
34. Peter Drahos, 'Intellectual Property and Pharmaceutical Markets: A Nodal Governance Approach,' 77(2) *Temp. L. Rev.* 401–24 (2004); Jillian Clare Cohen, Patricia Illingworth, and Udo Schulenk (eds), *The Power of Pills: Social, Ethical and Legal Issues in Drug Development, Marketing and Pricing Policies* (Pluto Press, 2006).
35. European Commission Pharmaceutical Sector Preliminary Inquiry Report (2008) and European Commission Pharmaceutical Sector Inquiry Final Report (2009), *supra* note 18.
36. Caffrey and Rotter (2004), *supra* note 7; Hore (2001); Bouchard (2009), *supra* note 4.
37. European Commission Pharmaceutical Sector Inquiry Final Report, *supra* note 18. At p. 23 of the Executive Summary, the EC states:

> The Commission will continue to strictly enforce the applicable Community law and, for instance, act against patent linkage, as according to Community legislation, marketing authorisation [MA] bodies cannot take the patent status of the originator medicine into account when deciding on marketing authorisations of generic medicines.

In the 2008 Preliminary Report, the EC stated (at p. 14) more specifically that patent-linkage is considered unlawful under Regulation (EC) No 726/2004 and Directive (EC) No 2001/83. At p. 113, further elaboration is provided to the effect that:

> Patent linkage refers to the practice of linking the granting of MA, the pricing and reimbursement status or any regulatory approval for a generic medicinal product, to the status of a patent (application) for the originator reference product. Under EU law, it is not allowed to link marketing authorisation to the patent status of the originator reference product.

38. European Commission Pharmaceutical Sector Inquiry Preliminary Report (2008), *supra* note 18, at 22–3 (para. 9). At para. 895, the report states:

> ... including intervention before regulatory bodies. Interventions before regulatory bodies (marketing authorisation authorities and pricing and reimbursement bodies) appear to be a standard tool in originator companies' toolbox. Although contacting the health authorities may address legitimate concerns, it can also be used to delay or block the marketing authorisation or the pricing or reimbursement status of the generic product. In particular, by suggesting that the generic product is less efficient or safe or is not equivalent, raising patent infringement issues concerning the generic product in question and alleging that any decision favourable to the generic company would make the authorities liable to patent infringement damages (patent linkage), originator companies gain time and can create delays in granting marketing approval for the generic product and its entry into the market.

39. *North American Free Trade Agreement Between the Government of Canada, the Government of Mexico, and the Government of the United States*, December 17, 1992, Can. T.S. 1994 No. 2, 32 ILM 289 (entered into force January 1, 1994). *Agreement on Trade Related Aspects of Intellectual Property (TRIPS) 1994*, 30 October 1947, 58 UNTS 187, Can. T.S. 1947 No. 27 (negotiated as part of the Uruguay Round (1986–1994) of the World Trade Organization's General Agreement on Tariffs and Trade (GATT)).
40. A potential example of how linkage may be expanding with time beyond the narrow nexus of drug approval-drug patenting is provided by increasing reports of border disputes involving drugs and patent law. For example, a 2008 shipment of the anti-HIV drug abacavir was confiscated by Dutch Customs authorities. The shipment was from an Indian company bound for Nigeria. It was paid for by UNITAID, the drug-purchasing arm of the WHO, and was meant to be distributed by the William J. Clinton Foundation. The reasons provided by the Dutch Customs authorities for confiscation was that the drugs were counterfeit and violated patent law. (See, for example, Indian Patent Oppositions: Abacavir Hemisulfate. Indian pre-grant opposition documents, online: <http://indianpatentoppositions.blogspot.com/2007/11/abacavir-hemisulfate-indian-pre-grant.html>; EUR-Lex-32003R1383-EN, <http://eur-lex.europa.eu/LexUriServ/LexUriServ.do?uri=CELEX:32003R1383:EN:HTML>.
41. Follow-on biologics, or biosimilars, are biotechnology products near the end of their patent protection and which may become subject to a form of genericization. See, for example: <http://www.bio.org/healthcare/followonbkg/>. In Canada, see: *Consultation on the Regulatory Framework for Subsequent Entry Biologics – Summary Report*, online: Health Canada <http://www.hc-sc.gc.ca/dhp-mps/pubs/biolog/2008-consult-seb-pbu-rep-rap/index-eng.php>.
42. Henry Grabowski, 'Follow-on Biologics: Data Exclusivity and the Balance Between Innovation and Competition,' 7 *Nature Reviews Drug Discovery* 479–88 (2008).

43. Patented Medicines (Notice of Compliance) Regulations amend. SOR /93-133 (NOC Regulations).
44. Tancer (1997) and Harrison (2001), *supra* note 8.
45. In *AstraZeneca Canada Inc.* v. *Canada (Minister of Health)*, 2006 SCC 49 (at para. 12) the Supreme Court of Canada acknowledged that until 1993, the two regulatory systems for drug approval and drug patenting were largely 'kept distinct and separate.' Indeed, as late as 2003, Robert Peterson, Director General of the Therapeutics Product Directorate of Health Canada, stated before the Standing Committee on Industry, Science and Technology that the purpose of the drug submission structure was '... to support drug review. It was not designed with the aim of safeguarding intellectual property rights.' Regarding confusion over the precise nature of the approval-patenting nexus, Dr Peterson stipulated 'this in our view is one reason why the linkage aspects of the patented medicines NOC regulations are so hard to grapple with ...' For a detailed discussion of the political climate leading up the NOC Regulations, see: Michael C. Jordan, *The Politics of Drug Patenting in Canada*, Master of Arts Thesis (University of Saskatchewan, 2005) [Jordan (2005)] at 102.
46. Tancer (1997) and Harrison (2001), *supra* note 8.
47. This position was strongly advocated by numerous Canadian politicians, particularly those in the governing Conservative Party. See, generally, Harrison (2001), *supra* note 8, Jordan (2005), *supra* note 45, and the Parliamentary debates leading up to Bill C-91 (see, generally, Parliament of Canada, 33:7, Minutes of Proceedings and Evidence of the Legislative Committee on Bill C-22. Tuesday, December 1, 1992, 7:65–7:96). For example, Harvie Andre, Minister for Consumer and Corporate Affairs under Prime Minister Brian Mulroney, referred to the 1969 bill authorizing compulsory licensing as 'legalized theft' and that repeal of same will indicate that Canada would not be 'taking a free ride at the expense of the rest of the world' (cf. Alan Story, 'Drug Wars: Does Anyone Really Know the Price Tag?' *Toronto Star* (December 20, 1986). See also Harrison (2001), *supra* note 8, at 513.
48. As detailed more extensively in Chapter 6, Stephen Schondelmeyer, a pharmacologist and health economist, gave evidence before the House of Commons to the effect that it is not the term of single patents that mattered most, but rather how patents add cumulatively to extend market exclusivity, a claim the government at the time vigorously denied. Compare the testimony of Dr Stephen Schondelmeyer (Professor, University of Minnesota) and Dr Kay Dickson (Director General, Department of Industry, Science and Technology). Parliament of Canada, 33:7, Minutes of Proceedings and Evidence of the Legislative Committee on Bill C-22. Tuesday, December 1, 1992, 7:65–7:96; and 33:8 Wednesday, September 2, 1992, 8:37–8:40.
49. Hilts (2003), *supra* note 25; Avorn (2004), *supra* note 25; Angell (2004), *supra* note 25; Cohen (2001), *supra* note 25.
50. Krimsky (2003), *supra* note 2; Ron A. Bouchard, 'Balancing Public and Private Interests in the Commercialization of Publicly Funded Medical Research: Is

There a Role for Compulsory Government Royalty Fees?' 13 *B.U.J. Sci. & Tech. L.* 120, 158–64 (2007); Ron A. Bouchard and Trudo Lemmens, 'Privatizing Biomedical Research – A Third Way,' 26 *Nat. Biotechn.* 31 (2008).

51. Boldrin and Levine (2008), *supra* note 3; Krimsky (2003), *supra* note 2.
52. Jaffe (2000), *supra* note 2. Jaffe notes that it is possible that the R&D boom in the late 1970s and early 1980s would not have been so large or lasted so long without enhanced IPR rights, and that it is 'disquieting, however, that there is so little empirical evidence that what is widely perceived to be a significant strengthening of intellectual property protection had significant impact on the innovation process' (ibid.). Jaffe further observes:

> Overall, there is a noticeable gap between the highly developed theoretical literature on patent scope and the limited empirical literature. This is due partially to the infrequency of changes in patent regimes like the one examined by Sakakibara and Branstetter. Part of the difficulty also lies in the weakness of the connection between the model constructs and quantifiable aspects of a patent regime. (Ibid. at 588)

Finally, Jaffe comments:

> This limited success is due partially to the difficulty of measuring the parameters of patent policy, and partly due to the difficulty of discerning statistically significant effects when many things have been changing at the same time. But it should surely be viewed as a challenge to researchers to try to do more. (Mazzoleni and Nelson (1998), *supra* note 2)

The authors state, at 554, that:

> The range of arguments about the positive social value of patents is obviously much wider than the area of strong empirical studies explored to date. An analyst, citing earlier studies that appear to show limited value, obviously is vulnerable to the argument that those studies do not provide evidence on some of the possibly most important functions patents serve. We cannot present here an empirically supported and intellectually persuasive argument on this broad question. The important empirical research that needs to be done in order to map out the basic facts simply has not been done yet . . . (Ibid.; Boldrin and Levine, *supra* note 2)

In a meta-analysis of empirical studies of whether introducing or strengthening patent protection leads to greater innovation, Boldrin and Levine note (at 189–90):

> We have identified twenty-three economic studies that have examined this issue empirically. The executive summary: these studies find weak or no evidence that strengthening patent regimes increases innovation; they find evidence that strengthening the patent regime increases . . . patenting! (Ibid. at 216–17)

53. Bouchard et al. (2009), *supra* note 4.

2

Background: drug approval, drug patenting, pharmaceutical linkage, and public health policy*

Abstract. This chapter provides background information required to understand pharmaceutical linkage, including the relevant principles of patent law and food and drug law, with a particular focus on the various pathways and evidentiary requirements for new and follow-on drug approval, pharmaceutical linkage, as well as the manner in which public health policy and economic policy are said to converge in the form of linkage regulations.

Keywords: patent law, food and drug law, public health policy, economic policy

Pharmaceutical products occupy an established and growing niche in modern healthcare. Estimated global pharmaceutical sales were US$773 billion in 2008, up from $605 billion and only $298 billion in 2005 and 1998, respectively.[1] Sales growth has been strong in North America (12.6% per year from 1998 to 2005) compared to Europe (9.3%),[2] with the former accounting for the largest share of global sales (46%) compared to the latter (29.97%).[3]

---

*This chapter is based upon material in: M. Sawicka and R.A. Bouchard, 'Empirical Analysis of Canadian Drug Approval Data 2001–2008: Are Canadian Pharmaceutical Players "Doing More With Less?"' *McGill Journal of Law & Health* 3: 87–151 (2009); R.A. Bouchard, J. Sawani, C. McLelland, M. Sawicka, and R. Hawkins, 'The Pas de Deux of Pharmaceutical Regulation and Innovation: Who's Leading Whom?' *Berkeley Technology Law Journal* 24(3): 1461–522 (2009); R.A. Bouchard, R.W. Hawkins, R. Clark, R. Hagtvedt, and J. Sawani, 'Empirical Analysis of Drug Approval-Patenting Linkage for High Value Pharmaceuticals,' *Northwestern Journal of Technology & Intellectual Property* 8(2): 1–86 (2010).

Even in a relatively small market such as Canada,[4] more than 22,000 pharmaceutical products are available[5] and this number is growing rapidly.[6] Indeed, prescription drugs comprise the fastest rising component of domestic healthcare spending.[7] By 2006, drug expenditures in Canada grew to 17.4% of total health expenditures, up from 9.6% in 1985.[8] Indeed, drug expenditures grew faster than all other expenses within the Canadian healthcare system, with an average growth rate of 9.4% between 1985 and 2006 compared with 6.6% for total health spending.[9] Similarly, per capita expenditures increased on average 8.2% per annum between 1985 and 2006, faster than France, Germany, Japan, Sweden, Finland, Norway, and other European nations.[10] Between June 2004 and June 2005 alone, a total of 378 million prescriptions were filled in Canada.[11] According to Organization for Economic Cooperation and Development (OECD) data, Canada ranked third in the world in per capita drug expenditures by 2002, behind only the United States and France.[12] Drugs with patent protection lead the way in pharmaceutical expenditures. Between 1990 and 2008, patented drug product sales in Canada increased 764%, from CN$1.7 billion to CN$13 billion per annum.[13]

Given that gobal and domestic pharmaceutical markets are entrenched and growing more rapidly than other healthcare segments, the legal and regulatory mechanisms underpinning drug approval and the entry of brand-name and generic pharmaceuticals appropriately assume center stage.

2.1 Drug approval

While drug products have become an essential element of domestic and global public health systems, concerns have nevertheless been raised about the willingness of the public to underwrite the cost of drugs that are extensions of already marketed products. Indeed, there has been considerable debate over the last 25 years relating to the social benefits of 'new' drug products versus those referred to variously as 'follow-on,' 'incremental,' 'line extension,' 'me-too,' and 'supplemental' products. To this list one can add generic drugs that are bioequivalent to already marketed products. This is because all drug products that are not considered breakthrough or pioneering in nature represent by definition some form of technology appropriation, i.e. they come into being as a result of a party's ability to capture profits generated from their own or related inventions.[14]

Many commentators have derided the social value of follow-on innovations.[15] Others have claimed that follow-on drugs represent a critical component of pharmaceutical industry innovation and that dire consequences will follow should policy-makers alter the current basket of legal and regulatory incentives for innovation.[16] An example of the tension between the utility of new and existing therapies is provided by the intensity of debate over Health Technology Assessment (HTA)[17] and Cost Effectiveness Research (CER),[18] particularly as it relates to the American Recovery and Reinvestment Act of 2009.[19]

2.1.1 Drug approval process and terms

Given decades of effort towards global regulatory harmony, it is not surprising that the regulatory framework for drug approval in Canada parallels that of the US Food and Drug Administration (FDA) and European Medicines Agency (EMEA).[20] In each jurisdiction drugs submitted through 'new' or 'supplementary' pathways, can be classified as 'first-in-class,' 'me-too,' or 'line extensions,' under appropriate circumstances undergo some form of 'expedited review,' and can contain a 'new chemical entity' (NCE) or 'new active substance' (NAS). Typically, a sponsor files a New Drug Submission (NDS)[21] containing sufficient data on drug safety, efficacy, and quality to warrant approval (referred to as Notices of Compliance or NOCs).[22] A Supplemental New Drug Submission (SNDS) may be filed for changes to a drug already marketed by that sponsor.[23] These include amendments to dosage, strength, formulation, manufacture, labeling, route of administration, or indication.[24] Products associated with an SNDS are typically referred to as line extensions, referring to the fact that they are extensions of already marketed products.[25] Generic manufacturers submit an Abbreviated New Drug Submission (ANDS) to obtain an NOC requiring that generic drugs be pharmaceutically equivalent to the reference brand-name product.[26] Generic sponsors may also submit Supplemental Abbreviated New Drug Submissions (SANDS) when changes are made to a drug already on the market. Consequently, both brand-name and generic firms can make 'new' and 'supplemental,' or 'follow-on,' submissions.

NOCs can be granted in an expedited fashion under domestic food and drug law in two ways.[27] One is through Priority Review, which refers to the fast-tracking of eligible drug candidates 'intended for the treatment, prevention or diagnosis of serious, life-threatening or severely debilitating diseases or conditions' with an 'unmet medical need or for which a substantial improvement in the benefit/risk profile is demonstrated.'[28] Evidentiary requirements for safety, efficacy, and quality parallel those for non-priority submissions; the main difference is an accelerated review time.[29] In the second path, sponsors may be granted an 'NOC with conditions' (NOC/c)[30] for eligible NDS or SNDS submissions directed to serious, life-threatening, or severely debilitating diseases, or conditions for which there is promising evidence of clinical effectiveness based on available data.[31] In addition to less onerous evidentiary requirements, the targeted review time for NOC/c approval is significantly accelerated compared to that for standard NDS review.[32] The main difference with Priority Review is that NOC/c licensure is granted on the condition that the sponsor will perform additional post-market studies to confirm the alleged benefits and risks. Unless otherwise stated, both NOC/c and Priority Review pathways for approval will be grouped together under the single heading of Expedited Review (ER). A summary of these drug approval pathways is provided in Table 2.1.

While the definitions of new and supplementary (NDS and SNDS) brand-name submissions, standard and supplementary generic submissions (ANDS and SANDS), and pathways for expedited review (Priority Review and NOC/c) are relatively simple and straightforward, the definitions of first-in-class and me-too drugs are much less so.[33] In Canada, first-in-class drugs are those that consist of either (1) a new family of active ingredient(s), also known as a new active substance (NAS),[34] or (2) old active ingredient(s) used for the treatment of a new indication. A drug is first-in-class if there is no other drug on the market that belongs to the same compound family that is used for the same indication.[35] Conversely, me-too drugs are those that offer 'important therapeutic options,' but that may have little or no change to the benefit-risk profile.[36] Essentially, me-too drugs are comparable to other drugs in terms of compound and indication.[37] Previously referred to as a 'new chemical entity,' or NCE,[38] the definition of an NAS encompasses a wide range of chemically active substances, including (1) a chemical or biological substance that has not been previously approved for sale as a drug, (2) an isomer, derivative, or salt of a chemical substance that is already approved for sale as a drug but differs in safety and efficacy

Table 2.1 Summary of drug approval pathways

Firm type	New drug	Follow-on drugs
A. Brand	NDS NDS NAS NDS PR NDS NOC/c	SNDS SNDS PR SNDS NOC/c –
B. Generic	– –	ANDS SANDS

properties, or (3) a biological substance previously approved for sale as a drug that differs in molecular structure, the nature of the source material, or the manufacturing process.[39]

Drugs approved through NDS and SNDS routes can be classified as either first-in-class or me-too. For the NDS route, first-in-class drugs are those that contain either an NAS or are directed to a new use (or indication), whereas NDS me-too drugs neither contain a new ingredient nor are directed to a new use, but instead have an improved benefit-risk profile. For the traditional 'line extension' SNDS route, relatively small changes to existing chemical structures such as salts or isomers may still yield first-in-class or me-too designations. The difference is that while both SNDS first-in-class and me-too drugs can cover new chemical forms,[40] only drugs directed to a new use may be deemed first-in-class SNDSs.[41] Those that do not are deemed me-too.[42] Because even a follow-on first-in-class drug must be directed to a new use as opposed to just a new chemical form with altered benefit-risk, a higher level of innovation is typically ascribed to SNDS and SANDS first-in-class drugs as opposed to me-too drugs.[43] It is not surprising that drugs containing an NAS can be approved via the SNDS route given the broad overlap between SNDS (change in dosage, strength, formulation, manufacture, labeling, route of administration, or indication) and NAS (isomers, derivatives, or salts of existing drugs with differing safety and efficacy profiles and/or source material and manufacturing process) requirements.[44] The characteristics of first-in-class and me-too drugs are summarized in Table 2.2.

The final drug class investigated reflects the most innovative (MI) drugs developed by brand pharmaceutical firms in the new drug approval (NDS) category. The designation NDS MI is used based on the methodology described in Chapter 4. As discussed in detail there, merely containing an NAS is an insufficient basis for designating a drug as pioneering or strongly innovative because there is ample room in the definition for minor changes

Table 2.2 Classification scheme for first-in-class and me-too drugs

Route	FIC	Me too
A. NDS	New chemical form *– or –* New use/indication	Change in benefit : risk
B. SNDS	New chemical form *– and –* New use/indication	Change in chemical form *– and –* Change in benefit : risk

to previously approved medical ingredients, including salts, esters, solvates, polymorphs, and enantiomers. Similarly, FIC drugs do not, of themselves, constitute pioneering products based on the observation that these can also be follow-on versions of previously marketed products containing slightly modified medical ingredients or directed to new uses within a therapeutic class. The same conclusion applies to expedited review drugs where these need only be directed to drugs demonstrating moderate clinical improvement over existing therapies. The most reasonable definition is that truly pioneering drugs are those that are approved via the new drug approval pathway (NDS), contain an NAS or NCE, undergo some form of expedited review (ER), and are directed to FIC therapy. The resulting nomenclature employed in this book for all new and follow-on drugs is summarized in Table 2.3.

2.1.2 Lifecycle model and IPR rights

Emerging global drug policy places increasing importance on the need to adopt the principles of 'lifecycle' regulation.[45] Lifecycle regulation of pharmaceuticals involves all relevant research and development, clinical trial studies, regulatory approval, market authorization, and normative post-market prescribing and use by physicians and the general population.[46] As Canadian regulators recognize, the unique aspect of lifecycle regulation is the recognition that valuable knowledge about a product is continuously accumulated over its lifecycle, especially with respect to data regarding benefit-risk analysis.[47] This progression has obvious ramifications for safety problems that arise after market penetration. The assumption is that as a drug's benefit-risk profile changes with time, so too should its approval

Table 2.3 Classification scheme for new and follow-on drugs

Firm type	New drugs	Follow-on drugs
A. Brand	NDS NDS Me Too NDS NAS NDS FIC NDS ER	SNDS SNDS Me Too SNDS FIC NDS ER –
B. Generic	– –	ANDS SANDS

status,[48] thus allowing an opportunity for regulators to adapt to changing conditions over time.[49]

Canada is currently in the process of integrating the lifecycle approach into its regulatory regime.[50] Under the terms of the progressive licensing framework, plans regarding post-market studies, monitoring, safety surveillance, and risk management will be required when a sponsor files its submission.[51] The standard for initial market authorization is a positive or favorable benefit-risk profile, with maintenance of market authorization requiring a continuing favorable benefit-risk profile throughout the product's lifespan.[52] Canada is not alone in its efforts to legislate lifecycle approaches. Indeed, the FDA,[53] US Institute of Medicine (IOM),[54] and European Medicines Agency (EMEA)[55] recognized early that drug safety was well served by lifecycle models, including articulating the need for regulating therapeutic products in light of 'real-world' drug use.

Intellectual property and regulatory (IPR) rights remain a pivotal element of lifecycle models of drug regulation. In accordance with the terms of its National Pharmaceutical Strategy[56] and Smart Regulations initiative,[57] the government of Canada sees itself as a leader in developing an innovative drug regulation platform and in providing unique regulatory incentives to the pharmaceutical industry.[58] In this capacity, Canadian regulators are acting in tandem with their American and European counterparts, all of whom claim that therapeutic product development is crucial for national prosperity and productivity in the global marketplace.[59] The specific goals of the latest round of public policy reform are to: (1) facilitate biomedical innovation; (2) create incentives for drug development when the market itself does not; (3) allow for earlier access to new drugs; (4) create an informed consumer; and (5) increase the threshold for post-market drug safety. The emphasis on providing IPR rights incentives to the industry in order to support innovation follows numerous reports from the government and its consultants over the last few years on the growing productivity gap in Canada and the commercialization of novel therapeutic products emanating from publicly funded medical research.[60]

A cornerstone of Canadian domestic lifecycle regulation is NOC/c-type approval.[61] This refers to a recalibrated balance between faster access to novel remedies (appropriately termed 'flexible departure') and enhanced post-market oversight of safety, efficacy, and benefit-risk, with the possibility of revocation of initial approval if the terms of initial approval are not met. Unlike Priority Review, continuing approval after initial regulatory approval is contingent upon whether pharmaceutical sponsors meet the terms and conditions assigned to the NOC/c.[62] At first glance, emphasis on NOC/c over Priority Review may seem inconsistent with the lifecycle approach. However, fast-tracking eligible NDSs and SNDSs via Priority Review results in faster approval without a change in the amount of scientific evidence required prior to market entry.[63] The process remains front-loaded in that it does not demand that sponsors conduct post-marketing studies as a means to maintain approval status. In comparison, the NOC/c mechanism demands that sponsors are subject to legal scrutiny beyond initial market authorization in exchange for faster approval. The process is considerably more back-loaded in this regard and thus is more consistent with the lifecycle approach. It is reasonable to conclude therefore that NOC/c approvals are an excellent proxy for lifecycle regulation compared with Priority Review or approval via conventional NDS and SNDS pathways.

While lifecycle models have several advantages over existing approval models,[64] concerns persist that releasing drugs onto the market earlier may be misguided, given evidence that pharmaceutical firms typically do not meet conditions associated with approval once in the market in the absence of legislation compelling them to do so.[65] Moreover, concerns have been expressed over the reading-in of TRIPS-based provisions incorporating strong IPR rights,[66] and specific language contemplating incorporation into policy and regulations any relevant knowledge, documents, or information produced by industry and its trade organizations.[67] While it is reasonable to speculate that the goal of these provisions is to facilitate global regulatory harmony, there is some unease that practices such as these serve the nation's economic goals more than its public health mandate.[68] This interpretation is bolstered by statements from various branches of government.[69]

2.2 Patents

One of the most strongly contested aspects of pharmaceutical policy concerns the role of intellectual property and regulatory rights in providing economic incentives to firms and in shaping the agenda for basic medical research.[70] Patents are consistently claimed to be invaluable to drug development in the pharmaceutical industry,[71] in part to compensate firms for long regulatory lag periods and the high costs of innovation.

A patent for invention is a property right granted by the government to an inventor. In most developed nations, property rights associated with a patent include the right to exclude others from making, using, or selling an invention. In Canada, this right takes effect from the date the patent is granted for a period of 20 years after the filing date.[72] In exchange for the grant of patent, inventors must provide a full description of the invention and how it is enabled so that the public can benefit from disclosure and use it to develop further innovations in that or related fields. This quid pro quo between the inventor and public is referred to as the traditional patent bargain,[73] and was institutionalized for the first time in the English Statute of Monopolies 1623.[74]

The requirements for patenting and the relation thereof to drug approval in Canada generally track those in other developed nations, particularly the US and the United Kingdom (UK).[75] Section 2 of the Canadian Patent Act defines an invention as any 'new and useful art, process, machine, manufacture or composition of matter, or any new and useful improvement in any art, process, machine, manufacture or composition of matter.'[76] An invention must meet the usual three basic requirements in order to be patentable: the subject matter[77] defined in the claim must be new, useful and non-obvious.[78] The first requirement is met where the subject matter of the patent has not yet been disclosed to the public. The second is met where the subject matter provides sufficient utility or benefit to the public and achieves the purpose for which it came into being. The third is met where the subject matter constitutes an 'inventive step' or manifests sufficient 'inventive ingenuity' over the prior art to warrant the traditional patent bargain. Where an inventive step is lacking, a patent is not granted or, if granted, can be later ruled invalid on the grounds that it is 'obvious' in light of the prior art, provided that the person skilled in the art would have been led directly and without difficulty to the solution taught by the patent.[79] When the claims at issue are deemed to be obvious or anticipated (for lack of novelty), they are struck down and can no longer be used to prohibit competitors from using the invention.

2.3 Linkage regulations

2.3.1 Overview

An element of pharmaceutical patent law that until quite recently was unique to the US and Canada is a relatively novel form of legal ordering referred to as 'linkage regulations.' So named because they tie patent protection for marketed pharmaceuticals to the drug approval process, linkage regulations enable brand-name pharmaceutical firms to list as many patents as are deemed 'relevant' to a marketed product on a patent register.[80] Blockbuster drugs coming off patent protection can in this manner have a period of market exclusivity that is significantly extended beyond that for the originating patent (e.g. on the new active substance or new chemical entity). In Canada this occurs under the aegis of the Patented Medicines (Notice of Compliance) Regulations (NOC Regulations).[81]

The Canadian linkage regulations were modeled after the US Hatch-Waxman linkage regime,[82] under which patent protection under the Patent Act[83] is legally tied to drug approval under the Food, Drug and Cosmetic Act[84] via patent listings in the Orange Book.[85] The NOC Regulations came into force in 1993, at which time they replaced provisions in the Patent Act directed to compulsory licensing.

Prior to the NOC Regulations coming into force, the Supreme Court of Canada noted that patent protection and regulatory approval of pharmaceuticals were governed by different statutes as well as different policy goals and objectives. Given the specific language employed,[86] it is reasonable to conclude that the court was referring to the previously divergent goals of public health policy and industrial/economic policy. The language employed by the court further suggests that these two policy branches have formally converged in the form of the NOC Regulations and that private IPR rights are viewed as a primary driver of this convergence. Indeed, government Regulatory Impact Analysis Statements (RIAS) have forged a clear policy objective of stimulating innovation in the pharmaceutical sector predicated on industrial IPR rights, including via linkage regulations.[87] Thus, compared to the 400-year-old patent system, the linkage regime represents a novel and emerging intellectual property paradigm for protecting pharmaceutical inventions.

Linkage regulations are critical to the maintenance of monopoly pricing by brand-name pharmaceutical firms as blockbuster drugs near the end of their conventional patent protection (patents on NCEs or NASs). This is because patents listed on the patent register effectively allow for an extended 'term' of patent protection, provided that patents are deemed relevant to the already marketed product. As such, linkage regulations represent a primary mechanism by which regulators promote drug development in exchange for private IPR rights.

2.3.2 Linkage mechanism and terms

As will be discussed in greater detail in Chapter 6, the enabling section in the Patent Act for the NOC Regulations is contained in the section on infringement.[88] This, however, should not be taken to indicate that actions under the NOC Regulations are parallel to a conventional infringement proceeding. Drug patenting, including the legal analysis of validity and infringement, is inexorably tied to the output of the drug approval exercise. As noted above, to market a drug product in Canada, drug manufacturers (brand or generic) must first obtain regulatory approval for the relevant medicinal product. The form of this approval in Canada is referred to as a Notice of Compliance (NOC), which is received from the Minister of Health pursuant to regulations promulgated under the Food and Drugs Act.[89] The Minister is obliged to issue an NOC to a drug manufacturer where the drug has met all of the required regulatory standards pertaining to the safety and efficacy of the drug in question. Brand-name drug companies submit a New Drug Submission (NDS) containing 'test data,' including clinical trial and experimental data, relevant to the demonstration of health and safety. Generic firms, on the other hand, submit an Abbreviated New Drug Submission ('ANDS') based not on original test data but rather on bioequivalence[90] to the relevant Canadian reference product.[91]

Under the NOC Regulations, a 'first person,' typically a brand-name sponsor, may list patents on the patent register in connection with drug products for which they hold regulatory approval.[92] If a 'second person,' typically a generic sponsor, files a submission that makes a comparison or reference to the first person's drug based on bioequivalence, the Minister may not issue an NOC for the generic drug until the second person has addressed all listed patents. As noted above, where a generic firm files a submission that makes a comparison or reference to the first person's drug, regulators may not issue an NOC to the generic until the second person has addressed all relevant listed patents. This means the second person must accept that it will either not obtain regulatory approval relevant to its ANDS until the expiry of all listed patents[93] or to avoid this situation it must serve an 'allegation' on the first person (Notice of Allegation) that the listed patent or patents are invalid or will not be infringed by its submission,[94] together with a detailed statement of the legal and factual basis of the allegation.[95] When served with a Notice of Allegation a brand-name sponsor may within 45 days commence a judicial review application for an order that the NOC not be issued to the generic sponsor.[96]

Where the brand-name sponsor does commence such an application, an NOC will not be issued until the earliest of 24 months, the determination of the issues in court, or patent expiry.[97] In other words, by merely commencing the proceeding, the applicant receives an automatic injunction (also referred to an 'automatic stay') under circumstances where the merits of the case are not determined by the court and indeed without having to satisfy the criteria courts would normally require before enjoining issuance of an NOC.[98] At the hearing of a judicial review application under the NOC Regulations the court must determine whether the generic manufacturer's allegation is legally 'justified.' If the court finds the allegation is not so justified, the court must issue an 'order of prohibition' preventing the Minister from issuing the NOC until patent expiry.[99] If, on the other hand, the court finds the allegation is justified, the application is dismissed,[100] and an NOC may be granted to the generic sponsor provided that regulatory review is complete and no other litigation is outstanding.

Unlike parallel litigation under the US Hatch-Waxman linkage regime, an action under the NOC Regulations is by way of judicial review. Therefore it does not constitute an action for infringement.[101] A formal decision on patent infringement or validity cannot be determined in NOC proceedings, notwithstanding the fact that judicial pronouncements on validity or infringement amount to the same thing and utilize infringement case law as precedent.[102] The Federal Court of Appeal has held that the object of litigation under the NOC Regulations is solely to decide issuance of an NOC under the Food and Drug Regulations.[103] If a party seeks a formal decision on patent infringement or invalidity, they must avail themselves of remedies under the Patent Act.[104] Indeed, recent cases have arisen where pharmaceutical patents have been deemed either invalid or not infringed under NOC Regulations and valid or infringed in a later infringement proceeding.[105]

Judicial review under the NOC Regulations is considered to be an expedited proceeding and thus summary in nature. Therefore it does not entail full exploration of evidentiary matters that would otherwise be before the court in an infringement proceeding,[106] particularly *viva voce* evidence that is otherwise central to a patent infringement proceeding. Rather, litigation consists of an out-of-court exchange of affidavit evidence and cross-examination, followed by a one- to two-day hearing. Typically, numerous motions precede the actual hearing, including multiple variations on those to receive or exclude evidence. Even though judicial review proceedings under the NOC Regulations are deemed to be summary in nature, in practice it can often take up to two years to get to a hearing, which is roughly equivalent to the time required to obtain regulatory approval.

Under the provisions of the Canadian linkage regime, each patent listed on the patent register must be demonstrated in litigation to be invalid or not infringed for generic market entry. For this reason, the patent register is thus said to be 'the linchpin of the NOC Regulations' regime.[107]

The threshold for listing is relevance to an existing drug product. Early Federal Court of Appeal jurisprudence in *Eli Lilly* v. *Canada*[108] rejected the notion of a strict relevance requirement, opting instead for a broad statutory reading to the effect that patents need only be relevant to a medicine rather than the drug form specifically approved by regulators. In other words, patents could be listed generally for a drug rather than against a specific drug submission. In 2006, the government issued a RIAS accompanying amendments to the NOC Regulations explaining that listed patents were required to contain at least one specific claim to the medical ingredient, formulation, dosage form or use for which approval was granted.[109] This was followed by the decision of the Supreme Court of Canada in *AstraZeneca* v. *Canada*,[110] which supported a specific relevance requirement and cast doubt on the reasoning employed by lower courts in defending a general listing requirement. The Federal Court of Appeal, citing *AstraZeneca*, reversed its earlier ruling that a patent containing a claim for the medicine in a drug is listed generally against the drug, rather than against the specific submission for a notice of compliance upon which the patent list is based.[111] The government issued a revised guidance document in 2009 attempting to harmonize previous jurisprudence and policy grounds supporting a specific listing requirement.[112]

The intensity of the volleying back and forth between litigants, legislators, and the courts over the issue of relevance suggests that the attempt to balance the competing policy goals of encouraging new and innovative drug development and timely generic entry through the same mechanism is fraught with difficulty. As noted by the Federal Court of Appeal in *Wyeth* v. *Ratiopharm*, a generic sponsor initially may be 'required to address every patent listed in respect of the Canadian reference product to which the proposed generic version is compared, whether or not the patent is properly listed.'[113] As with the patent bargain, the stated purpose of the linkage regulations regime is to provide monopoly rights to private firms in exchange for new and innovative drugs while at the same time facilitating the timely entry of generic drugs.[114] The strength of the legal nexus between traditional patent law and drug approval will be tested in more detail in Chapter 6.

The combination of the automatic injunction, the low relevance requirement for listing patents on the patent register, the potentially endless number of patents listed for attractive drug candidates, and the summary nature of the proceedings compared to conventional infringement actions is viewed by many to present an effective and efficient mechanism for brand-name sponsors to 'evergreen' blockbuster products coming off patent.[115] The ability of the linkage regulations regime to provide a broad scope of intellectual property protection to follow-on drugs in particular is enhanced in light of the wide definition of a new active substance (NAS), the wide range of chemical modifications to existing drugs allowed under the follow-on, or supplemental new drug submission (SNDS), the approval pathway, and the wide berth given for drugs to undergo expedited review.

Given the legal requirement that patent protection under the NOC Regulations is specific to a particular submission, the wide berth for approval of new (NAS) and follow-on (SNDS) drugs raises the possibility of a 'paradoxical drug approval-drug patenting linkage.' For example, in both policy documents and case law, it is invariably assumed that there is a positive correlation between the scope of intellectual property protection afforded by the linkage regime, the degree of innovation, and the accompanying social benefit associated with a particular drug product. A positive correlation would be consistent with the intent of the federal government to balance patent enforcement over new and innovative drugs with the timely market entry of generic drugs. However, the fact that pharmaceutical companies are focusing more on evergreening older products and on incremental drug development rather than breakthrough drug development suggests that firms may be leveraging legal loopholes favoring enhanced patent protection for drugs with low innovative value. This may undermine the intent of government to use the 'special enforcement provisions' of the linkage regime to protect only those patents associated with new and innovative drugs. To the extent that patent protection is extended for already marketed drugs, it might also contravene the second pillar of the government's policy to facilitate the timely market entry of lower priced generic products. The paradoxical drug approval-drug patenting nexus is discussed in detail in Chapters 5 and 7.

The specific platform of legal rights associated with pharmaceutical products has critical public health ramifications, not only because firms and policy-makers view it as a major economic driver for innovation in the life sciences,[116] but also because the rate and direction of innovation in the pharmaceutical industry may be shaped *antecedently* by IPR rights incentives.

2.4 IPR rights and innovation policy

IPR rights and public policy promoting innovation have strong historical associations. Public policy in most developed nations still tends to assume basically a linear model of innovation, i.e. a product 'pipeline' that begins in basic research, moves on through private research and development activities, and then proceeds to commercialization in the form of products and services.[117] This model implies a strong imperative to legally protect knowledge that has been reduced to practice as it flows through the system in the form of limited-term monopolies. For pharmaceutical innovation, the process is complicated by regulatory requirements to gain market authorization for new drugs, which is perceived as the terminus for the innovation pipeline. Accordingly, there is a considerable body of established science policy that identifies IPR rights as the major economic driver of innovation, national productivity, and translational research in the medical sciences.[118]

Despite its entrenched nature, however, the theoretical and empirical case for linear models of innovation contingent on strong IPR rights is weak. Since the 1960s, much scholarly work on innovation has indicated a highly complex, iterative process of individual and organizational learning that typically involves an array of public and private sector inputs with many feedbacks.[119] This body of work suggests that innovation is a dynamic combinatory process in which the probability of innovation is linked closely to the capacity to create new combinations of knowledge, resources, and skills.[120] Other empirical studies have failed to demonstrate a conclusive link between strong IPR rights policies and generally increased levels of innovation.[121] These studies suggest that the dynamics of innovation can embrace IPR rights in some circumstances, but that these rights need not comprise an essential element for innovation to occur or to increase. The implications of this scenario are especially important for innovative product development in the medical sciences, given the vast array of public health and cost considerations involved in new drug development and regulation.[122]

The combination of the rapid spread of the pharmaceutical linkage model worldwide and publicly available data pertaining to drug approval, drug patenting, patent listing and related litigation provides a unique opportunity to develop a domestically based yet globally relevant methodology and database for the study of policies intended to encourage pharmaceutical innovation while also facilitating the timely entry of generic drugs and thus enhancing access to essential medications.

In light of the increasing disparity between the claim that an effective and efficient public health system is contingent upon IPR rights[123] and the evidence disputing the legitimacy of this model,[124] therapeutic product development therefore represents an excellent target for empirical studies of the relationship between legal incentives for innovation and product development. As noted by Pavitt, Jaffe, Mazzoleni and Nelson, and others, robust conclusions regarding the consequences for technological innovation of changes in patent policy are few and far between, in large part owing to a fundamental lack of empirical data.[125]

Notes

1. Intercontinental Marketing Services Health Inc., *Global Pharmaceutical Sales, 2001–2008* (2008); Intercontinental Marketing Services Health Inc., *Global Pharmaceutical Sales, 1998–2005* (2005). As noted by IMS, the 'value of the global pharmaceutical market in 2010 is expected to grow 4–6 percent on a constant-dollar basis, exceeding $825 billion, driven by stronger near-term growth in the U.S. market' and 'is expected to expand to $975+ billion by 2013.' Gary Gatyas and Clive Savage, *IMS Forecasts Global Pharmaceutical Market Growth of 4–6% in 2010; Predicts 4–7% Expansion Through 2013*, Intercontinental Marketing Services Health Canada, October 7, 2009.
2. Office of Fair Trading, Annex D, *Global Overview of the Pharmaceutical Industry* (2007).
3. Medicines Australia, *Global Pharmaceutical Industry Facts and Figures* 1 (2007).
4. See Patented Medicine Prices Review Board, *Annual Report 2008*, at 37 (2009), online: <http://www.pmprb-cepmb.gc.ca/cmfiles/PMPRB-AR08-E.pdf> [Patented Medicine Review Board (2009)]. Canada's share of drug sales in major markets increased from 2.4% in 2001 to 3.8% in 2008. More significantly, domestic growth in pharmaceutical sales was 7% from 2007 to 2008 compared with 2.7% in all major markets and 1% in the United States over the same time frame (ibid.).
5. Health Canada, *Access to Therapeutic Products: The Regulatory Process in Canada* 3 (2006), online: <http://www.hc-sc.gc.ca/ahc-asc/alt_formats/hpfb-dgpsa/pdf/pubs/access-therapeutic_acces-therapeutique-eng.pdf> [Health Canada, *Access to Therapeutic Products* (2006)].
6. Can. Inst. for Health Info., *Drug Expenditure in Canada 1985 to 2008*, at 6 (2009) [Can. Inst. for Health Info. (2009)].
7. Trudo Lemmens and Ron A. Bouchard, 'Regulation of Pharmaceuticals in Canada,' in *Canadian Health Law and Policy* 311, 312 (Jocelyn Downie et al. eds, 3rd edn 2007) [Lemmens and Bouchard (2007)].
8. Can. Inst. for Health Info. (2009), *supra* note 6, at 3. Total drug expenditures were CN $4 billion, $10 billion, and $18 billion in 1985, 1995, and 2002, increasing to $25.5 billion in 2006. Similarly, per capita expenditures were CN $150, $350 and $600 for the same fiscal years, increasing to $776 in 2006 (ibid., at 6–8).
9. Ibid., at 60–3.
10. Ibid., at 31.
11. Intercontinental Marketing Services Health Inc., *Compuscript Report 2004*, at 1 (2004).
12. Org. for Econ. Cooperation and Dev., *OECD Health Data 2004* (2004).
13. Patented Medicine Review Board (2009), *supra* note 4, at 23.
14. See, generally, David J. Teece, 'Profiting from Technological Innovation: Implications for Integration, Collaboration, Licensing and Public Policy,' 15 *Res. Pol'y* 285 (1986).

15. See, for example, James Love, *Consumer Project on Technology, Evidence Regarding Research and Development Investments in Innovative and Non-Innovative Medicines* 20 (2003); Joel Lexchin, 'Intellectual Property Rights and the Canadian Pharmaceutical Marketplace: Where Do We Go from Here?' 35 *Int'l J. Health Serv.* 237, 243 (2005) [Lexchin (2005)]; 'Drugs in 2001: A Number of Ruses Unveiled,' 11 *Prescrire Int'l* 58, 58 (2002).
16. See, for example, Joshua Cohen and Kenneth Kaitin, 'Follow-On Drugs and Indications: The Importance of Incremental Innovation to Medical Practice,' 15 *Am. J. Therapeutics* 89, 91 (2008).
17. See, generally, Egon Jonsson, 'Development of Health Technology Assessment in Europe,' 18 *Int'l J. Tech. Assessment Health Care* 171 (2002).
18. Comm. on Comparative Effectiveness Res. Prioritization, Inst. of Med. of the Nat'l Acads, *Initial National Priorities for Comparative Effectiveness Research* (2009); Fed. Coordinating Council for Comparative Effectiveness Res., US Dept of Health and Human Servs, *Report to the President and the Congress* (2009), online: <http://www.hhs.gov/recovery/programs/cer/cerannualrpt.pdf>; G. Caleb Alexander and Randall S. Stafford, 'Does Comparative Effectiveness Have a Comparative Edge?' 301 *J. Am. Med. Ass'n* 2488 (2009); Jerry Avorn, 'Debate about Funding Comparative-Effectiveness Research,' 360 *New Eng. J. Med.* 1927 (2009); John K. Iglehart, 'Prioritizing Comparative-Effectiveness Research – IOM Recommendations,' 361 *New Eng. J. Med.* 325 (2009); Peter Singer, 'Why We Must Ration Health Care,' *NY Times Mag.*, July 15, 2009, at MM38; Hans-Georg Eichler et al., 'Use of Cost-Effectiveness Analysis in Health-Care Resource Allocation Decision-Making: How Are Cost-Effectiveness Thresholds Expected to Emerge?' 7 *Value in Health* 518 (2004).
19. American Recovery and Reinvestment Act of 2009, Pub. L. No. 111-5, 123 Stat. 115 (2009).
20. See Lemmens and Bouchard (2007), *supra* note 7, at 321; see, generally, Patricia I. Carter, 'Federal Regulation of Pharmaceuticals in the United States and Canada,' 21 *Loy. L.A. Int'l & Comp. L. Rev.* 215 (1999). For a corresponding review of EU law, see, generally, Valerie Junod, 'Drug Marketing Exclusivity Under United States and European Union Law,' 59 *Food & Drug L.J.* 479 (2004).
21. Lemmens and Bouchard (2007), *supra* note 7, at 325; see also Food and Drug Regulations, CRC, ch. 870 [Food and Drug Regulations], at § C.08.002(1)(a) (2009). The Food and Drug Regulations are propagated under the general authority of the Food and Drugs Act, RSC, ch. F-27 (1985).
22. Food and Drug Regulations, *supra* note 21, at § C.08.002(2); Lemmens and Bouchard (2007), *supra* note 7, at 325; see also Health Can., Therapeutic Products Programme Guideline: Preparation of Human New Drug Submissions (1991), online: <http://www.hc-sc.gc.ca/dhp-mps/alt_formats/hpfb-dgpsa/pdf/prodpharma/prephum-eng.pdf>.
23. Food and Drug Regulations, *supra* note 21, at § C.08.003.
24. Ibid., at § C.08.003(2); see also Lemmens and Bouchard (2007), *supra* note 7, at 326.

25. Lexchin (2005), *supra* note 15, at 243; see, generally, Song Hee Hong et al., 'Product-Line Extensions and Pricing Strategies of Brand Name Drugs Facing Patent Expiration,' 11 *J. of Managed Care Pharmacy* 746 (2005).
26. The term 'bioequivalence' refers to the requirement that the generic product must be equivalent to the already marketed 'reference product' with regard to chemistry, manufacturing, route of administration, use, and therapeutic and adverse systemic effects. See also Food and Drug Regulations, *supra* note 21, at §§ C.08.001.1, C.08.002.1(1).
27. See, generally, Ron A. Bouchard and Monika Sawicka, 'The Mud and the Blood and the Beer: Canada's New Progressive Licensing Framework for Drug Approval,' 3 *McGill J.L. & Health* 49, 58–9 (2009) [Bouchard and Sawicka (2009)].
28. Health Can., Guidance for Industry: Priority Review of Drug Submissions 1–2, 4 (2009), online: <http://www.hc-sc.gc.ca/dhp-mps/alt_formats/hpfb-dgpsa/pdf/prodpharma/priordr-eng.pdf>.
29. Lemmens and Bouchard (2007), *supra* note 7, at 328.
30. NOC/c approvals are granted pursuant to § C.08.004(1), in compliance with the conditions of use stipulated in §§ C.08.002(1)(g), C.08.002(1)(h), C.08.006(2)(b), and C.05.006(2)(a) of the Food and Drug Regulations, *supra* note 21.
31. Health Prods. & Food Branch, Health Can., *Guidance Document: Notice of Compliance with conditions (NOC/c)* (2007), online: <http://www.hc-sc.gc.ca/dhp-mps/alt_formats/hpfb-dgpsa/pdf/prodpharma/noccg_accd-eng.pdf>.
32. Health Canada, *Access to Therapeutic Products* (2006), *supra* note 5, at 10–11.
33. See Monika Sawicka and Ron A. Bouchard, 'Empirical Analysis of Canadian Drug Approval Data 2001–2008: Are Pharmaceutical Players "Doing More With Less"?' 3 *McGill J.L. & Health* 85, 97–114 (2009) [Sawicka and Bouchard (2009)].
34. Drugs Directorate, Health Can., *Policy Issues – New Active Substance* (1991), online: <http://www.hc-sc.gc.ca/dhp-mps/alt_formats/hpfb-dgpsa/pdf/-prodpharma/nas_nsa_pol-eng.pdf> [Drugs Directorate (1991)].
35. Letters between author, David K. Lee, Dir., Office of Legislative and Regulatory Modernization, Health Can., Dr Maurica Maher, Senior Scientific Advisor, Progressive Licensing Project, Health Can., and Lesley Brumell, Supervisor, Submission and Info. Policy Div., Health Can. (April–July 2008) (on file with author) [Health Canada, personal communication].
36. Ibid.
37. Ibid.
38. Ibid.
39. Drugs Directorate (1991), *supra* note 34; Health Can., Drugs and Health Products – NOC Database Terminology, online: <http://www.hc-sc.gc.ca/dhp-mps/prodpharma/notices-avis/noc-acc/term_noc_acc-eng.php>.
40. Health Canada, personal communication, *supra* note 35.
41. Ibid.

42. Ibid.
43. For a comparison of Canadian and WHO first-in-class and me-too classification schemes, see Sawicka and Bouchard (2009), *supra* note 33, at 108 (comparing Tables 2 and 5).
44. See Bouchard and Sawicka (2009), *supra* note 27, for discussion of the difference between me-too and first-in-class drugs.
45. See Hans-Georg Eichler et al., 'Balancing Early Market Access to New Drugs with the Need for Benefit/Risk Data: A Mounting Dilemma,' 7 *Nature Revs. Drug Discovery* 818, 823–4 (2008) [Eichler et al. (2008)].
46. Health Canada, *Blueprint for Renewal: Transforming Canada's Approach to Regulating Health Products and Food* (2006), online: <http://www.hc-sc.gc.ca/ahc-asc/alt_formats/hpfb-dgpsa/pdf/hpfb-dgpsa/blueprint-plan-eng.pdf [Health Canada, *Blueprint* (2006)], at 3.
47. Ibid., at 16.
48. Ibid., at 17.
49. See ibid., at 12.
50. See Bouchard and Sawicka (2009), *supra* note 27, at 72–7.
51. Health Canada, *The Progressive Licensing Framework Concept Paper for Discussion* (2006), online: <http://www.hc-sc.gc.ca/dhp-mps/alt_formats/hpfbdgpsa/pdf/prodpharma/proglic_homprog_concept-eng.pdf> [Health Canada, *PLF Concept Paper* (2006)], at 5.
52. Ibid., at 17, 20.
53. Center for Drug Evaluation and Research, US Food and Drug Admin., *Concept Paper: Premarketing Risk Assessment* (March 3, 2003) (draft, on file with the author); Center for Drug Evaluation and Research, US Food and Drug Admin., *Concept Paper: Risk Management Programs* (March 3, 2003) (draft, on file with the author); Center for Drug Evaluation and Research, US Food and Drug Admin., *Concept Paper: Risk Assessment of Observational Data: Good Pharmacovigilance Practices and Pharmacoepidemiologic Assessment* (March 3, 2003) (draft, on file with the author); Food and Drug Admin., US Dept Health and Human Servs, *Innovation Stagnation: Challenge and Opportunity on the Critical Path to New Medical Products* (2004); Jeffery L. Fox, 'FDA Embraces Risk-Management Approach,' 21 *Nature Biotech.* 1120 (2003); see also Guidance on Drug Safety Information, 72 Fed. Reg. 10224 (March 7, 2007).
54. Committee on Data Standards for Patient Safety, Board on Heath Care Services, Philip Aspden et al. (eds), *Patient Safety: Achieving a New Standard of Care* (National Academies Press 2004). For example:

    > Reviewers in the Center for Drug Evaluation and Research (CDER) at the Food and Drug Administration (FDA) must weigh the information available about a drug's risk and benefit, make decisions in the context of scientific uncertainty, and integrate emerging information bearing on a drug's risk-benefit profile throughout the lifecycle of a drug, from drug discovery to the end of its useful life. (Ibid., at S-2)

For a discussion of a comprehensive rather than silo-based response to errors in patient care, see also Committee on Quality of Health Care in America, Institute of Medicine of the National Academies, Linda T. Kohn et al., *To Err is Human: Building a Safer Health System* (National Academy Press 2000).

55. Comm. for Medicinal Prods. for Human Use, European Meds Agency, *Report of the CHMP Working Group on Benefit-Risk Assessment Models and Methods*, EMEA/CHMP/15404/2007 (2007), online: <http://www.emea.europa.eu-/pdfs/human/brmethods/1540407en.pdf>. The EMEA states:

> The current report describes the technical and scientific highlights of all these consultations, incorporates reflections and draws recommendations from the think-tank group. Areas for improvement in the operations of the EMEA and its scientific Committees include strengthening of both the informal and formal dialogue already in place, in order to ensure a continual exchange throughout the life-cycle of the products. (Ibid., at 6)

For general discussion of 'continuing and contextual' pre-market and post-market analysis of benefit-risk approach, see, generally, Comm. for Medicinal Prods for Human Use, European Meds Agency, *Guideline on the Scientific Application and the Practical Arrangements Necessary to Implement Commission Regulation (EC) No. 507/2006 on the Conditional Marketing Authorisation for Medicinal Products for Human Use Falling Within the Scope of Regulation (EC) No. 726/2004*, EMEA/509951/2006 (2006); Comm. for Medicinal Prods. for Human Use, European Meds Agency, *Reflection Paper on Benefit-Risk Assessment Methods in the Context of the Evaluation of Marketing Authorisation Applications of Medicinal Products for Human Use*, EMEA/CHMP/15404/2007 (2008), online: <http://www.emea.europa.eu/pdfs/human/brmethods/1540407 enfin.pdf>.

56. Fed./Provincial/Territorial Ministerial Task Force on the Nat'l Pharm. Strategy, National Pharmaceutical Strategy: *Progress Report* (2006), online: http://www.hc-sc.gc.ca/hcs-sss/alt_formats/hpb-dgps/pdf/pubs/2006-nps-snpp/2006-nps-snpp-eng.pdf [National Pharmaceutical Strategy (2006)]. Intellectual property rights and pharmaceutical innovation comprise three of the five 'pillars' of the nation's pharmaceutical policy. According to the Government of Canada, the five 'pillars' of federal pharmaceutical policy are the following: (1) intellectual property; (2) pharmaceutical research and development; (3) international trade policy; (4) healthcare; and (5) consumer protection. Barbara Oullet, *Pharmaceutical Management and Price Control in Canada* 7 (March 31, 2006) (presentation to the North American Pharmaceutical Summit, on file with the Berkeley Technology Law Journal). The National Pharmaceutical Strategy states that 'Governments recognize the crucial role the innovative pharmaceutical industry plays in the development of breakthrough drugs and that intellectual property protection is key to encouraging and supporting innovation': National Pharmaceutical Strategy (2006), *supra*, at 39.

57. External Advisory Comm. on Smart Regulation, *Smart Regulation: A Regulatory Strategy for Canada* (2004), online: <http://dsp-psd.pwgsc.gc.ca/Collection/CP22-78-2004E.pdf>.
58. See Robert Peterson, Dir. General, Therapeutic Products Directorate, Lecture to the Ottowa Regional Conference, *Innovation in Drug Regulation: Canada as a Leader* (February 11, 2005) [Peterson (2005)].
59. See Ron A. Bouchard, 'Balancing Public and Private Interests in the Commercialization of Publicly Funded Medical Research: Is There a Role for Compulsory Government Royalty Fees?' 13 *B.U. J. Sci. & Tech. L.* 120, 158–64 (2007) [Bouchard, 'Balancing' (2007)].
60. See, for example, Expert Panel on Commercialization, *People and Excellence: The Heart of Successful Commercialization* 6 (2006) [Expert Panel on Commercialization (2006)]; Brian Guthrie and Trefor Munn-Venn, Conference Bd. of Can., *Six Quick Hits for Canadian Commercialization: Leaders' Roundtable on Commercialization* 1 (2005) [Guthrie and Munn-Venn (2005)]. For an analogous discussion of the importance of industrial intellectual property incentives in national productivity and prosperity in the United States, see generally Council on Competitiveness, Innovate America: National Innovation Initiative Summit and Report (2005) [Council on Competitiveness (2005)].
61. See Health Canada, *PLF Concept Paper* (2006), *supra* note 51, at 20. Health Canada states:

    > In keeping with the proposed life-cycle approach, maintenance of market authorisation could require a continuing favorable benefit-risk profile for the authorized conditions of use throughout the product's lifespan. The favorable benefit-risk profile would be based on the same elements required for initial market authorization with some possible additions, i.e., substantial evidence of efficacy, safety, and quality; substantial evidence for a favorable overall benefit-risk profile regarding the product and evidence of other important benefit-risk considerations relating to the impact of market authorization on external decision-makers. (Ibid.)

    Health Canada then clarifies the balance between the uncertainties of drug development and the importance of bringing new drugs to market as fast as reasonably possible.

    > When a manufacturer is considering departing from the baseline requirement for substantial evidence of efficacy and safety for initial market authorization, a more flexible approach regarding the underlying efficacy and safety evidence is envisaged when there is a compelling reason. While the regulatory requirement for a favorable benefit-risk profile for the drug's use under the proposed conditions would remain, initial requirements for substantial evidence of efficacy and safety may be counterbalanced against other, important evidence concerning contextual

> benefit-risk considerations. For example, the potential benefits of bringing the drug to market are deemed to outweigh the relatively increased uncertainty regarding the safety and efficacy. (Ibid., at 20–1)

62. Ibid.
63. Health Canada, personal communication, *supra* note 35.
64. See, generally, Eichler et al. (2008), *supra* note 45.
65. Union of Concerned Scientists, Voices of Scientists at FDA, *Protecting Public Health Depends on Independent Science* 1 (2006), online: <http://www.ucsusa.org/assets/documents/scientific_integrity/Voices_of_Federal_Scientists.pdf>. The Union of Concerned Scientists stated:

> From 2005 to 2007, the Union of Concerned Scientists (UCS) conducted five surveys of federal scientists to evaluate how U.S. agencies use – and misuse – science to make policy decisions . . . The results reveal extensive political interference in federal science, with serious and wide-ranging consequences for our health, safety, and environment. This interference has weakened the federal scientific enterprise and impaired the ability of U.S. agencies to serve the public interest, with the potential for long-lasting harm to the federal scientific work force. (Ibid.).

See also Daniel Carpenter et al., 'Drug-Review Deadlines and Safety Problems,' 358 *New Eng. J. Med.* 1354 (2008); David B. Ross, 'The FDA and the Case of Ketek,' 356 *New Eng. J. Med.* 1601 (2007); Gardiner Harris, 'FDA Scientists Accuse Agency Officials of Misconduct,' *New York Times*, November 18, 2008, at A15; Susan Okie, 'What Ails the FDA?' 352 *New Eng. J. Med.* 1063, 1065–6 (2005).

66. Bill C-51, 2nd Sess. 39th Parl., cl. 11 § 30(3) (Can. 2008). This bill states:

> Without limiting or restricting the authority conferred by any other provisions of this Act for carrying into effect the purposes and provisions of this Act, the Governor in Council may make the regulations that the Governor in Council considers necessary for the purpose of implementing, in relation to drugs, Article 1711 of the North American Free Trade Agreement or paragraph 3 of Article 39 of the Agreement on Trade-related Aspects of Intellectual Property Rights set out in Annex 1C to the WTO Agreement. (Ibid.)

67. Ibid., at cl. 11 § 30(7)(b).
68. Janice Graham, 'Smart Regulation: Will the Government's Strategy Work?' 173 *Can. Med. Ass'n J.* 1469, 1469 (2005).
69. See, for example, Health Prods. and Food Branch, *Health Can., Clinical Trials Regulatory Review – Stakeholder Workshop* 6 (2007), online: <http://www.hc-sc.gc.ca/dhp-mps/alt_formats/hpfb-dgpsa/pdf/prodpharma/ctrf_o_eccr_a_2007-03-26-eng.pdf> [Health Canada, *Stakeholder Workshop* (2007)]; Health Canada, *Blueprint* (2006), *supra* note 46, at 8–9; Health Canada, *PLF Concept Paper* (2006), *supra* note 51, at 21; Reg Alcock, President, Treasury Bd., Speech Accompanying the Launch of the Government of Canada's

Implementation Plan for Smart Regulation (March 24, 2005) (transcript online: <http://www.tbs-sct.gc.ca/media/ps-dp/2005/0324_e.asp>; Peterson (2005), *supra* note 58; see also Lemmens and Bouchard (2007), *supra* note 7.

70. David H. Guston, 'Innovation Policy: Not Just a Jumbo Shrimp,' 454 *Nature* 940 (2008).
71. See, generally, Michele Boldrin and David Levine, *Against Intellectual Monopoly*, chs 8, 9 (Cambridge University Press, 2008) ('Does Intellectual Property Increase Innovation?' and 'The Pharmaceutical Industry'); Stuart Macdonald, 'When Means Become Ends: Considering the Impact of Patent Strategy on Innovation,' 16 *Info. Econ. & Pol'y* 135 (2004), online: <http://www.stuartmacdonald.org.uk/pdfs/Macdonald.pdf>.
72. Patent Act, RSC ch. P 4 [Patent Act], §§ 42, 44 (1985).
73. See *Free World Trust* v. *Électro Santé Inc.*, [2000] 2 SCR 1024, 2000 SCC 66, at para. 13 (Can.) [*Free World*]; *Whirlpool Corp.* v. *Camco Inc.*, [2000] 2 SCR 1067, 2000 SCC 67, at para. 37 (Can.); *Hotchkiss* v. *Greenwood*, 52 US 248 (1850); *Graham* v. *John Deere Co.*, 383 US 1, at paras 5–9 (1965).
74. Statute of Monopolies, 1623, 21 Jac. 1, c. 23 (Eng.). The Supreme Court has noted that even prior to the Statute of Monopolies the Crown rewarded an inventor with a limited monopoly in exchange for public disclosure of 'a new invention and a new trade within the kingdom ... or if a man hath made a new discovery of any thing' (*Free World*, *supra* note 73).
75. The requirements for patenting in the United States are set out in the US Patent Act, 35 USC §§ 1–376 (2006).
76. Patent Act, *supra* note 72, § 2.
77. Section 27(4) of the Canadian Patent Act stipulates that the subject matter of the patent must be defined distinctly and explicitly in the claims section of the patent.
78. Patent Act, *supra* note 72, § 28.2(1) (subject matter defined in the claims must not have been disclosed more than one year before the filing date); ibid., at § 28.3 (subject matter must not 'have been obvious on the claim date to a person skilled in the art or science to which it pertains'). See also *Henriksen* v. *Tallon Ltd*, [1965] RPC 434 (Can.); *Burton Parsons* v. *Hewlett Packard (Canada) Ltd* [1976] SCR 555 (Can.).
79. See *Beecham Canada Ltd* v. *Procter & Gamble Co.*, [1982] 61 CPR (2d) 7 (Can.).
80. See, generally, Edward Hore, 'A Comparison of US and Canadian Laws as They Affect Generic Pharmaceutical Drug Entry,' 55 *Food & Drug L.J.* 373 (1992); Ron A. Bouchard, 'Should Scientific Research in the Lead-up to Invention Vitiate Obviousness Under the Patented Medicines (Notice of Compliance) Regulations: To Test or Not to Test?' 6 *Can. J. L. & Tech.* 1 (2007) [Bouchard, 'Scientific Research' (2007)]; Ron A. Bouchard, 'Living Separate and Apart is Never Easy: Inventive Capacity of the PHOSITA as the Tie That Binds Obviousness and Inventiveness,' 4 *U. Ottawa L. & Tech. J.* 1 (2007) [Bouchard, 'PHOSITA' (2007)].

81. Patented Medicines (Notice of Compliance) Regulations SOR/1993-133 (Can.) [Patented Medicines Notice of Compliance Regulations].
82. Drug Price Competition and Patent Term Restoration Act of 1984, 21 USC § 355 (2006).
83. 35 USC §§ 1–376 (2006).
84. Federal Food, Drug, and Cosmetic Act, 21 USC §§ 301–97 (2006).
85. Drugs approved by the FDA are listed in its 'Approved Drug Products with Therapeutic Equivalence' publication, commonly known as the 'Orange Book.' 21 USC § 355(j)(7)(A) (2006). For a description of the Orange Book in the context of patent litigation and drug development, see Andrew A. Caffrey and Jonathan M. Rotter, 'Consumer Protection, Patents and Procedure: Generic Drug Market Entry and the Need to Reform the Hatch-Waxman Act,' 9 *Va. J.L. & Tech.* 1, 4–7 (2004) [Caffrey and Rotter (2004)] and Rebecca S. Eisenberg, 'Patents, Product Exclusivity, and Information Dissemination: How Law Directs Biopharmaceutical Research and Development,' 72 *Fordham L. Rev.* 477 (2003).
86. *AstraZeneca Can. Inc.* v. *Canada*, [2006] 2 SCR 560, at para. 12 (Can.) [*AstraZeneca*]. The court noted that:

    The *NOC Regulations* lie at the intersection of two regulatory systems *with sometimes conflicting objectives*. First, is the law governing approval of new drugs, which seeks to ensure the safety and efficacy of new medications before they can be put on the market. The governing rules are set out in the Food and Drugs Act, RSC 1985, c. F-27 (FDA) and the Food and Drug Regulations, CRC [*supra* note 21]. The FDA process culminates (if successful) in the issuance of a NOC to an applicant manufacturer by the Minister of Health on the advice of his officials in the Therapeutic Products Directorate. The FDA objective is to encourage bringing safe and effective medicines to market to advance the nation's health. The achievement of this objective is tempered by a second and to some extent overlapping regulatory system created by the Patent Act [*supra* note 72]. Under that system, in exchange for disclosure to the public of an invention, including the invention of a medication, the innovator is given the exclusive right to its exploitation for a period of 20 years. *Until 1993, the two regulatory systems were largely kept distinct and separate.* (Ibid., emphasis added)

87. Evidence of legislative intent regarding balancing patent enforcement and generic entry can be found in early RIAS documents. See, generally, *C. Gaz.* Vol. 132, No. 7, March 12, 1998; Vol. 133, No. 21, October 1, 1999. Evidence of legislative intent regarding the 'original policy intent' of encouraging the development of new and innovative drugs can be found in both RIAS and related Guidance Documents: *C. Gaz.* Vol. 138, No. 50, December 11, 2004; Vol. 140, No. 24, June 17, 2006; Vol. 142, No. 13, June 25, 2008; Health Canada Guidance Document, *Patented Medicines (Notice of Compliance) Regulations*, April 3, 2009. An articulation of the government's

pharmaceutical policy as it relates to the NOC Regulations can be found in the 2006 RIAS, which (at 1510) states:

> The Government's pharmaceutical patent policy seeks to balance effective patent enforcement over new and innovative drugs with the timely market entry of their lower priced generic competitors. The current manner in which that balance is realized was established in 1993, with the enactment of Bill C-91, the Patent Act Amendment Act, 1992, S.C. 1993, c. 2.

88. The relevant provisions state that:

> It is not an infringement of a patent for any person to make, construct, use or sell the patented invention solely for uses reasonably related to the development and submission of information required under any law of Canada, a province or a country other than Canada that regulates the manufacture, construction, use or sale of any product. (Patent Act, *supra* note 72, at § 55.2(1))

Also:

> The Governor in Council may make such regulations as the Governor in Council considers necessary for preventing the infringement of a patent by any person who makes, constructs, uses or sells a patented invention in accordance with subsection (1), including, without limiting the generality of the foregoing, regulations: (a) respecting the conditions that must be fulfilled before a notice, certificate, permit or other document concerning any product to which a patent may relate may be issued to a patentee or other person under any Act of Parliament that regulates the manufacture, construction, use or sale of that product, in addition to any conditions provided for by or under that Act . . . (Ibid., at § 55.2(4))

89. Food and Drug Regulations, *supra* note 21.
90. The term 'bioequivalence' refers to the scientific basis on which generic and brand-name drugs are compared. To be considered bioequivalent, the bioavailability of two products must not differ significantly when the two products are given in studies at the same dosage under similar conditions. A product may still, however, be considered bioequivalent to a second product with different pharmacological or pharmaceutical characteristics if the difference is noted in the labeling and doesn't affect the drug's safety or effectiveness or change the drug's effects in any medically significant way. In its Guidance Document, the FDA defines bioequivalence as:

> [T]he rate and extent to which the active ingredient or active moiety is absorbed from a drug product and becomes available at the site of action. For drug products that are not intended to be absorbed into the bloodstream, bioavailability may be assessed by measurements intended to reflect the rate and extent to which the active ingredient or active moiety becomes available at the site of action.

Food and Drug Admin., US Dept of Health and Human Servs, *Guidance for Industry: Bioavailability and Bioequivalence Studies for Orally Administered Drug Products – General Considerations* (2003), online: <http://www.fda.gov/downloads/Drugs/GuidanceComplianceRegulatoryInformation/Guidances/ucm070124.pdf>.

91. Food and Drug Regulations, *supra* note 21, at § C.08.002.1.
92. Patented Medicines Notice of Compliance Regulations, *supra* note 81, at §§ 3, 4.
93. Ibid., at § 5(1)(a).
94. Ibid., at § 5(1)(b).
95. Ibid., at § 5(3)(a).
96. Ibid., at § 6(1).
97. Ibid., at § 7. If litigation was commenced prior to March 12, 1998, however, the automatic stay was 30 months as under US Hatch-Waxman legislation.
98. See *Bayer A.G.* v. *Canada*, [1993], 51 CPR (3d) 329, 337 (Can.); *Merck Frosst Canada Inc.* v. *Apotex*, [1998] 80 CPR (3d) 368, at para. 33 (Can.).
99. Patented Medicines Notice of Compliance Regulations, *supra* note 81, at § 6(1).
100. See *Pharmacia Inc.* v. *Canada*, [1994] 58 CPR (3d) 209, 217 (Can.) [*Pharmacia Inc.*]; *Pfizer Canada Inc.* v. *Nu-Pharm Inc.*, [1998] 83 CPR (3d) 1, 4 (Can.); *Apotex Inc.* v. *Canada*, [1997] 76 CPR (3d) 1, 11–12 (Can.).
101. See *Eli Lilly & Co.* v. *Apotex Inc.*, [1997] 76 CPR (3d) 1, 5–6 (Can.).
102. Bouchard, 'Scientific Research' (2007), *supra* note 80; Bouchard, 'PHOSITA' (2007), *supra* note 80.
103. *Merck Frosst Canada Inc.* v. *Canada* [1994] 55 CPR (3d) 302, 319 (Can.) [*Merck Frosst*].
104. See *Pharmacia Inc.*, *supra* note 100, at 217; *Merck Frosst*, *supra* note 103, at 320.
105. Bouchard, 'PHOSITA' (2007), *supra* note 80.
106. *Merck Frosst*, *supra* note 103, at 320.
107. *Wyeth Canada* v. *Ratiopharm Inc.*, [2007] 60 C.P.R. (4th) 375, at 22 (Can.) [*Wyeth Canada*]. In *Wyeth Canada*, the court elaborated:

> Pursuant to subsection 4(1) of the *NOC Regulations*, the right to have a patent listed on the patent register in respect of a certain drug may be exercised only by a drug manufacturer that has filed a NDS for that drug. That provision is enforced through subsection 4(5), which provides that a patent list must identify the NDS to which it relates and the date on which the NDS was filed. In addition, subsection 3(3) of the *NOC Regulations* provides that a patent cannot be listed until the NDS that is the basis for the listing application is approved by the Minister and a NOC is issued for the drug in response to that NDS. Thus, every patent listing is permanently tied to a specific NOC filed by the innovator and its originating NDS, as well as to the drug in respect of which the patent is listed. For that reason, a particular patent listing may be identified as a listing 'against' a certain NOC.

108. *Eli Lilly Canada* v. *Canada*, [2003] 3 FC 140 (Can.).
109. The Regulatory Impact Analysis Statement accompanying SOR/2006-242 contains an in-depth discussion of that policy, as well as the role played by the Patented Medicine (NOC) Regulations. The history of the relevance requirement is reviewed in a later Regulatory Impact Analysis Statement relating to the Patented Medicines (Notice of Compliance) Regulations issued April 3, 2009.
110. *AstraZeneca*, *supra* note 86.
111. *Wyeth Canada*, *supra* note 107, at 29.
112. Guidance Document: Patented Medicines (Notice of Compliance) Regulations, http://www.hc-sc.gc.ca/dhp-mps/prodpharma/applic-demande/guide-ld/patmedbrev/pmreg3_mbreg3-eng.php (April 3, 2008).
113. *Wyeth Canada*, *supra* note 107, at 34.
114. The 'original policy intent' of Parliament in enacting the NOC Regulations – to balance patent enforcement over new and innovative drugs with the timely market entry of generic drugs – is set out in numerous government Regulatory Impact Analysis Statements (RIASs), which the Supreme Court of Canada ruled are proper evidence of legislative intent. See *Biolyse Pharma Corp.* v. *Bristol-Myers Squibb Co.*, [2005] 1 SCR 533, 2005 SCC 26, at 47, 156–157 (Can.). Evidence of legislative intent regarding balancing patent enforcement and generic entry can be found in early RIAS documents. For example, see: *C. Gaz.* Vol. 132, No. 7, March 12, 1998; *C. Gaz.* Vol. 133, No. 21, October 1, 1999. Evidence of legislative intent regarding both balancing patent enforcement and generic entry in the context of the 'original policy intent' of encouraging the development of new and innovative drugs can be found in later RIAS and Guidance Documents. For example, see: *C. Gaz.* Vol. 138, No. 50, December 11, 2004; *C. Gaz.* Vol. 140, No. 24, June 17, 2006; *C. Gaz.* Vol. 142, No. 13, June 25, 2008. An example of the latter language is found in the June 17, 2006 RIAS (at 1510), which states:

    > The Government's pharmaceutical patent policy seeks to balance *effective patent enforcement over new and innovative drugs* with the timely market entry of their lower priced generic competitors. The current manner in which that balance is realized was established in 1993, with the enactment of Bill C-91, the *Patent Act Amendment Act*, 1992, S.C. 1993, c. 2. (Emphasis added)

    For commentary relating to US linkage regulations, see Caffrey and Rotter (2004), *supra* note 85.

115. 'Evergreening' refers to undue extension of the statutory monopoly attached to a drug product by means of listing on the patent register multiple patents with obvious or uninventive modifications. Under such circumstances, the patentee prolongs its monopoly beyond what the public has agreed to pay. See *Whirlpool Corp.* v. *Camco Inc.*, [2000] 2 SCR 1067, 2000 SCC 67, at 37 (Can.); *Bristol-Myers Squibb Co.* v. *Canada (Attorney General)*, [2005]

1 SCR 533, 2005 SCC 26, at 66; *AstraZeneca*, *supra* note 86, at 39. According to the highly regarded 'Romanow Report':

> A particular concern with current pharmaceutical industry practice is the process of 'evergreening,' where manufacturers of brand name drugs make variations to existing drugs in order to extend their patent coverage. This delays the ability of generic manufacturers to develop cheaper products for the marketplace and it is a questionable outcome of Canada's patent law. (Comm'n on the Future of Health Care in Canada, Building on Values: The Future of Health Care in Canada 208 (2002), online: <http://www.cbc.ca/healthcare/final_report.pdf>)

In the US, undue use of linkage regulations to prolong the patent monopoly has been referred to as 'abuse of the automatic stay provision.' See Caffrey and Rotter (2004), *supra* note 85.

116. See Canada's Research-based Pharmaceutical Companies (Rx&D), Information Guide 2002, Section 2: Industry Issues (2002), online: <http://www.canadapharma.org/Industry_Publications/Information_Guide/section2_e.html>; see also AstraZeneca Can., *The Patent Act & Linkage Regulations: Essential Tools for the Advancement of Medical Science in Canada* (2009), online: <http://www.astrazeneca.ca/documents/en/aboutus/PatentActLinkageRegulations.pdf>.
117. See Ron A. Bouchard and Trudo Lemmens, 'Privatizing Biomedical Research – A Third Way,' 26 *Nature Biotechnology* 31 (2008), at 35; see generally Vannevar Bush, *Science: The Endless Frontier* (US Government Printing Office, 1945); Donald Stokes, *Pasteur's Quadrant* (Brookings Institution Press, 1997); Benoît Godin, 'The Linear Model of Innovation: The Historical Construction of an Analytical Framework,' 31 *Sci. Tech. Hum. Values* 639 (2006).
118. In its 'Roadmap for Medical Research,' the US National Institutes of Health (NIH) defines 'translational research' as research that successfully makes the translation from the laboratory bench to the patient bedside: 'To improve human health, scientific discoveries must be translated into practical applications. Such discoveries typically begin at "the bench" with basic research – in which scientists study disease at a molecular or cellular level – then progress to the clinical level, or the patient's "bedside."' NIH Roadmap for Medical Research, online: <http://nihroadmap.nih.gov/clinicalresearch/overview-translational.asp> (last visited November 6, 2009). Similarly, the Canadian Institutes for Health Research (CIHR) has embedded the concept of 'knowledge translation' into its statutory mandate:

> The objective of the CIHR is to excel, according to internationally accepted standards of scientific excellence, in the creation of new knowledge and its translation into improved health for Canadians, more effective health services and products and a strengthened Canadian health care system. Canadian Institutes of Health Research Act § A, 2000 SC, ch. 6 (Can.)

For discussion of research in the specific context of commercialization of publically funded medical research, see, generally, Bouchard, 'Balancing' (2007), *supra* note 59; Sheldon Krimsky, *Science in the Private Interest* (Rowman & Littlefield, 2003) [Krimsky (2003)]; Expert Panel on Commercialization (2006), *supra* note 60; Guthrie and Munn-Venn (2005), *supra* note 60; Council on Competitiveness (2005), *supra* note 60.

119. See, for example, Henry Chesbrough, *Open Innovation: The New Imperative for Creating and Profiting from Technology* (Harvard Business School Press, 2003); Dominique Foray, *The Economics of Knowledge* (MIT Press, 2004); Richard Nelson and Sydney Winter, *An Evolutionary Theory of Economic Change* (Harvard University Press, 1982), 27–9, 277; W. Brian Arthur, 'Competing Technologies, Increasing Returns, and Lock-in by Historical Events,' 99 *Econ. J.* 116 (1989); Wesley M. Cohen and Daniel A. Levinthal, 'Absorptive Capacity: A New Perspective on Learning and Innovation, 35 *Admin. Sci. Q.* 128 (1990) [Cohen and Levinthal (1990)]; Giovanni Dosi, 'Technological Paradigms and Technological Trajectories: A Suggested Interpretation of the Determinants and Directions of Technical Change,' 11 *Res. Pol'y* 147, 157–8 (1982); Henry Etzkowitz and Loet Leydesdorff, 'The Dynamics of Innovation: From National Systems and "Mode 2" to a Triple Helix of University–Industry–Government Relations,' 29 *Res. Pol'y* 109 (2000); Paul Nightingale, 'A Cognitive Model of Innovation,' 27 *Res. Pol'y* 689 (1998).

120. Cohen and Levinthal (1990), *supra* note 119, at 19; W. Brian Arthur, 'The Structure of Invention,' 36 *Res. Pol'y* 274 (2007); Eric Von Hippel, *Democratizing Innovation* (MIT Press, 2005); C. Freeman, 'Technological Infrastructure and International Competitiveness,' 13 *Indus. & Corp. Change* 541 (2004).

121. David C. Mowery et al., 'The Growth of Patenting and Licensing by U.S. Universities: An Assessment of the Effects of the Bayh-Dole Act of 1980,' 30 *Res. Pol'y* 99 (2001); Mariko Sakakibara and Lee Branstetter, 'Do Stronger Patents Induce More Innovation? Evidence from the 1988 Japanese Patent Law Reforms,' 32 *Rand J. Econ.* 77 (2001); Adam B. Jaffe, 'The U.S. Patent System in Transition: Policy Innovation and the Innovation Process, 29 *Res. Pol'y* 531 (2000) [Jaffe (2000)]; Roberto Mazzoleni and Richard R. Nelson, 'The Benefits and Costs of Strong Patent Protection: A Contribution to the Current Debate,' 27 *Res. Pol'y* 273 (1998) [Mazzoleni and Nelson (1998)]. For a recent review of empirical studies, see James Bessen and Michael J. Meurer, *Patent Failure* (Princeton University Press, 2008).

122. See *Comm'n of Patents* v. *Fabwerka Hoechst*, [1964] SCR 49, 56 (Can.). In emphasizing that courts must scrutinize pharmaceutical patents carefully in order to determine if they properly merit the grant of a monopoly privilege in light of the significant public interest at stake, the court noted that:

> In the particular class of case with which we are here concerned dealing with drugs and medicines, there is considerable public interest at stake,

> and the Commissioner should most carefully scrutinize the application to see if it merits the grant of monopoly privileges, and to determine the scope of the monopoly available. (Ibid.)

See, generally, Catherine De Angelis et al., 'Clinical Trial Registration: A Statement from the International Committee of Medical Journal Editors,' 351 *New Eng. J. Med.* 1250 (2004).

123. See, for example, Bouchard and Sawicka (2009), *supra* note 27, at 65 n. 168; Eichler et al. (2008), *supra* note 45.
124. See, for example, Jaffe, *supra* note 121; Mazzoleni and Nelson (1998), *supra* note 121; Keith Pavitt, 'National Policies for Technical Change: Where Are the Increasing Returns to Economic Research?' 93 *Proc. Nat'l Acad. Sci. U.S.A.* 126 (1996) [Pavitt (1996)]; see, generally, Michele Boldrin and David K. Levine, *Against Intellectual Monopoly* (2008) [Boldrin and Levine (2008)]; Krimsky (2003), *supra* note 118.
125. Jaffe, *supra* note 121, at 544 and 588. See also: Mazzoleni and Nelson (1998), *supra* note 121; Boldrin and Levine (2008), *supra* note 124, at 216–17; Pavitt (1996), *supra* note 124, at 126.

3

Empirical analysis of drug approval*

Abstract. Canada's proposed new drug regime, termed the 'Progressive Licensing Framework' (PLF), has received considerable attention over the last number of years. PFL is an example of 'real-world' or 'lifecycle'-based models of drug development. On the one hand, its critics claim that 'flexible departure,' or expedited approval prior to completion of traditional Phase 3 clinical trials, may lead to a lower standard for drug approval and an increase in unsafe products on the market. Supporters, on the other hand, claim that more emphasis on post-market safety will effectively recalibrate the risks, benefits, and uncertainties of therapeutic product development. Here we develop a novel empirical method to analyze Canadian drug approval data during the term 2001–2008. Our objectives were to determine the types of candidates that might qualify for flexible departure under PLF and assess the rate and direction of innovative activity by the Canadian pharmaceutical system. We quantified a number of types of new and follow-on approvals, including new drug submissions, generic submissions, line extension drugs, first-in-class and me-too drugs, drugs which contained new active substances and drugs that were approved via one of two available pathways for expedited review. Our findings show that concerns expressed over PLF pushing Canada in a new direction with regard to the workings and output of its drug regulatory regime may be overstated in that the existing approval regime has already been anticipating the lifecycle approach for several years. The data also show that the rate and direction of innovative activity by pharmaceutical firms has shifted significantly over time, implying that the global pharmaceutical industry, as a whole, is 'doing more with less' with existing technologies.

Keywords: progressive licensing framework, lifecycle model of drug development, empirical analysis, new drug, follow-on drug, line extension drug, expedited review, drug withdrawal

*This chapter is based upon material in M. Sawicka and R.A. Bouchard, 'Empirical Analysis of Canadian Drug Approval Data 2001–2008: Are Canadian Pharmaceutical Players "Doing More With Less"?' *McGill Journal of Law & Health* 3: 87–151 (2009).

3.1 Introduction

As discussed in detail elsewhere,[1] the Government of Canada (GOC) announced on February 8, 2008 that it would substantially amend the existing Food and Drugs Act[2] and Food and Drug Regulations[3] to make room for its new 'Progressive Licensing Framework' (PLF) for drug approval in the form of Bill C-51.[4] Notwithstanding the nation's state of political upheaval during the time Bill C-51 was tabled, provisions such as those encompassed by this bill are almost certain to come into force at some point in the near future. This follows the development of a critical mass favoring regulatory reform in Canada, the United States (US), and the European Union (EU), spurred in large part by well described post-marketing drug safety controversies. Indeed, Health Canada has invested considerable resources in its lifecycle-based PLF platform over the last several years, which it views as demonstrating global leadership in innovative drug regulation and as a platform for providing strong incentives to pharmaceutical firms to produce innovative products under conditions where the market does not.[5]

A range of concerns have been expressed over newer regulatory models such as PLF that seek to reallocate the risks and benefits of drug development. A primary concern is that lifecycle models of this nature will in fact yield a lower threshold for initial market authorization, resulting in potentially dangerous drugs slipping through regulatory cracks.[6] Scholars, politicians, public interest groups, and media have argued that recasting drug regulation in this manner will turn the public into 'guinea pigs' for drugs that have not been adequately tested,[7] particularly under conditions where post-market studies recommended by regulators are not conducted by sponsors once approval has been given.[8] Fears of this nature are well grounded in light of over two decades of poor decisions by pharmaceutical firms to design, cover-up, or otherwise report clinical trial data selectively.[9] A second consideration relating to PLF and other lifecycle approaches is the linking of flexible approval procedures to a benefit-risk profile that is 'favorable' to the drug rather than to the more conservative, and some say more evidence-based, precautionary principle.[10] Canada is not alone in this stance, as parallel criticisms have been voiced over provisions for accelerated[11] and conditional[12] approval in the US and EU.

The twin arguments by drug agencies in support of the lifecycle approach is that it will help to (1) recalibrate the balance of pre-market and post-market safety and efficacy considerations and (2) stimulate innovation in the pharmaceutical industry, with a concomitant increase in new therapeutic products for the consuming public. In this light, it would be important to have data pertaining to historical trends in drug approval by Health Canada as it leads up to its lifecycle approach, particularly data comparing the number of approvals in the standard and expedited review streams (Priority Review and Notice of Compliance with conditions, or NOC/c) as well as expedited approvals that do (NOC/c) and do not (Priority Review) require further evidence of safety to be submitted following initial market authorization. In addition, data demonstrating trends in the types of drug approvals issued in the lead-up to PLF would be invaluable in predicting the types of products to which the public is likely to gain access in a post-PLF context. Particularly useful would be data relating to the number and percent of total approvals that were 'first-in-class,' 'me-too' (both defined below), and 'line extensions,'[13] as well as those granted to brand-name and generic pharmaceutical firms. Data of this nature would help clarify the influence of drug regulation on the rate and direction of innovative activity by the domestic pharmaceutical industry.

Considerations such as those expressed above led to this study. One of our goals was to develop an independent empirical methodology and synthetic model to investigate what types of drug candidates might qualify for flexible departure under Bill C-51 or related PLF legislation and assess the post-market fate of these candidates. A second and related goal was to use this model to identify patterns in the rate (how much) and direction (what kind) of innovative activity by Canadian brand-name and generic pharmaceutical firms and analyze this data in relation to the GOC's proposed policy goals respecting pharmaceutical regulation. We empirically analyzed 2,122 substantive Notices of Compliance (NOCs) granted by the GOC during the period 2001–2008 to assess meta-trends in the pattern of drug approvals, particularly with regard to submissions for 'new' drugs and how these compared with data on 'supplemental' me-too and line extension submissions using classifications provided by Health Canada. We found that the GOC is already approving drugs with PLF in mind, that there is a significant and potentially growing proportion of drugs entering the market with evidence of safety still required to be met through post-marketing studies, and that very few of the drugs approved during the period of analysis, including those via the two expedited streams, have been withdrawn to date. The data also speak to the strength of the functional relationship between two supposedly independent 'silos' in a regulated Therapeutic Product Lifecycle (rTPL) innovation ecology,[14] e.g. drug regulation and the national science and technology (S&T) polices designed to enhance domestic competitiveness via intellectual property and regulatory

(IPR) rights. We conclude that PLF has already been incorporated into the nation's drug regulation framework to a significant degree and that the domestic pharmaceutical industry, as a whole, is focused more on leveraging and extending the value of existing technologies and IPR rights rather than on the production of novel first-of-kind 'breakthrough' technologies.

3.2 Analysis

3.2.1 General

On its website, Health Canada posts a listing[15] of all drugs that have received an NOC since 1991. The listing is divided by year and according to the following headings: biologic products for human use; non-prescription products for human use; products for veterinary use; and prescription products for human use.

Biologics[16] are defined as 'drug products derived from biological sources that are listed on Schedule D of the Food and Drugs Act. The list includes blood products, cells and tissues, gene therapies, vaccines, radiopharmaceuticals, and therapeutic products derived through biotechnology.'[17] Schedule D also includes: allergenic substances used for the treatment or diagnosis of allergic or immunological diseases; drugs obtained by recombinant DNA procedures; drugs other than antibiotics prepared from micro-organisms; monoclonal antibodies, their conjugates, and derivatives; snake venom; and other products.[18] Non-prescription products include over-the-counter medications[19] and natural health products such as vitamins, minerals, and herbal remedies.[20] Products for veterinary use, as the name suggests, are those therapeutic products intended for use in animals. Prescription products for human use include those products that contain as medicinal ingredients any of the compounds listed in Parts I and II of Schedule F of the Food and Drug Regulations. The remainder of the paper will be directed at pharmaceutical products for human use.

NOCs can be granted in an 'expedited' fashion domestically in one of two ways.[21] One is through Priority Review,[22] which refers to the fast-tracking of eligible NDS and SNDS intended for the treatment, prevention, or diagnosis of serious, life-threatening or severely debilitating diseases or conditions wherein there exists an unmet medical need or for which a substantial improvement in the benefit-risk profile of the therapy is demonstrated.[23] Evidentiary requirements for safety, efficacy, and quality parallel those for non-priority submissions, the main difference being an accelerated review time.[24] Sponsors may also be granted an NOC with conditions (NOC/c)[25] for eligible new or follow-on submissions directed to serious, life-threatening, or severely debilitating diseases or conditions for which there is promising evidence of clinical effectiveness based on available data.[26] In addition to less onerous evidentiary requirements, the review process for NOC/c approval is significantly accelerated.[27] The most significant difference compared to Priority Review is that licensure is granted on the 'condition' that the sponsor perform additional studies to confirm the drug's alleged therapeutic benefit. Even so, the GOC has nominal jurisdiction to ensure a manufacturer's compliance through post-market surveillance.[28] Table 3.1 shows examples of NOC/c approvals recently granted by the GOC as they are presented in the Health Canada database.

A statistical analysis of NOCs issued in Canada from January 1, 2001 to December 31, 2008 inclusive was conducted. For each year, Health Canada's 'Prescription Products for Human Use' NOC listing was analyzed. A listing for a given year encompasses NOCs issued from January 1 of that year to December 31. With respect to each NOC issued, the listing provides the following information: (1) the brand name of the prescription product that received the NOC; (2) the source of the prescription product (i.e. manufacturer or company name); (3) the active ingredient of the

Table 3.1 Examples of recently issued NOC/c approvals

NOC/c	Active ingredient	Date	Indication	Significance	Priority	NAS
Isentress®	Raltegravir Potassium	2007-11-27	HIV integrase strand transfer inhibitor	HIV/AIDS	Yes	Yes
Duodopa®	Levodopa Carbidopa monohydrate	2007-03-01	Parkinson's	Parkinson's disease	No	No
Lyrica®	Pregabalin	2007-11-09	Analgesic	Neuropathic pain	No	No
Atriance®	Nelarabine	2007-09-22	Anti-neoplastic	Adult & child T-cell acute lymphoblastic leukemia/T-cell lymphoblastic lymphoma	No	Yes

prescription product; (4) the date the NOC was granted; (5) the drug identification number (DIN) assigned to the prescription product upon the granting of the NOC; (6) the therapeutic class of that product (i.e. the specific indication or condition for which that prescription product is intended to be used); and (7) any additional comments such as the dosage requirement, route of administration, and whether the NOC was granted due to the manufacturer and/or product's name change among other things. The listing explicitly states whether an NOC was issued under the NOC/c policy. Figure 3.1 illustrates how an NOC is presented in the listing.

Health Canada's NOC listing has some notable limitations. First, although it is organized alphabetically, listed drugs are not numbered. Therefore calculating the total number of NOCs issued in a particular year must be done manually. Second, the listing does not specify certain relevant information such as: (1) whether an NOC for a given prescription product was issued under New Drug Submission (NDS), Supplementary New Drug Submission (SNDS), Abbreviated New Drug Submission (ANDS), or Supplementary Abbreviated New Drug Submission (SANDS) application stream(s); (2) whether an NOC was granted under the Priority Review policy; and (3) whether a given prescription product contains a New Active Substance (NAS). Previously known as a 'New Chemical Entity' (NCE), an NAS may be directed to the following: a chemical or biological substance

Brand Name:	Cialis
Source:	Eli Lilly Canada Inc.
Active Ingredient:	Tadalafil
Comments:	Manufacturer name change; TAB (2.5mg, 5mg, 10mg, 20 mg) ORL
Date:	2007-09-11
DIN:	0229688, 02296896, 02248088, 02248089
Therapeutic Class:	cGMP-Specific Phosphodiesterase Type 5 Inhibitor/Treatment of Erectile Dysfunction
Brand Name:	Isentress ISSUED UNDER THE NOC/C POLICY
Source:	Merck Frosst Canada Ltd., Merck Frosst Canada Ltée
Active Ingredient:	Raltegravir (supplied as Raltegravir potassium)
Comments:	TAB (400mg)ORL
Date:	2007-11-27
DIN:	02301881
Therapeutic Class:	HIV integrase strand transfer inhibitor

Figure 3.1 Example of two entries as they appear in the Health Canada NOC listing.

not previously approved for sale in Canada as a drug; an isomer, derivative, or salt of a chemical substance previously approved for sale as a drug in Canada but differing in properties with regard to safety and efficacy; or a biological substance previously approved for sale in Canada as a drug, but differing in molecular structure, nature of the source material or manufacturing process.[29] Initially, we deemed drugs classified as NAS as 'first-in-class.' However, Health Canada clarified that NAS drugs are not always first in their class, although on some occasions they can be.[30] The definition of an NAS therefore determines both first-in-class and me-too compound-indication classifications (cf. Table 3.2).

Health Canada has supplemented the listings with a searchable database that includes all NOCs issued in Canada since 1994. The database can be searched by a product's brand name, drug identification number (DIN), NOC/c status, medicinal ingredient, manufacturer, submission class (NAS, Priority, Priority-NAS, or Other), therapeutic class, and type (veterinary, non-prescription, prescription, biologic, or radiopharmaceutical).

To obtain additional information for our listings for each given year, we searched the database by product type (prescription pharmaceutical) and NOC date. Because entering a full year in the date field yielded too many NOCs to hold on one page, each year was broken up into three portions. For example, 2007 was subdivided into January 1 – April 30, May 1 – August 31, and September 1 – December 31. This method generated three NOC lists for a given year, identifying drug brand name, manufacturer, NOC date, medicinal ingredient(s), and DIN. The lists are arranged by date (from most to least recent NOC) and numbered. Numbering allows for easy calculation of the total NOCs in the list. Figure 3.2 illustrates the beginning portion of the database-generated list for January 1, 2007 to April 30, 2007.

Within the database-generated list, the drug name (shown in bold capital letters) can be isolated to obtain 'Notice of Compliance Information' for a given drug. The NOC Information page provides a product's NOC date, manufacturer name, type, NOC/c status, submission type (NDS, SNDS, ANDS, or SANDS), reason for supplement if the submission is an SNDS or SANDS (i.e. change in dosage, form, or route of administration), submission class (NAS, Priority, Priority-NAS, or Other), therapeutic class, Canadian reference product if the product is a generic, company name, and country of manufacture. Furthermore, the NOC Information provides the product's DIN, medicinal ingredient(s), form, route of administration, and dosage. Figure 3.3 illustrates the Notice of Compliance Information sheet for the first drug shown in Figure 3.2, Hyoscine Butylbromide Injection Sandoz Standard.

1. HYOSCINE BUTYLBROMIDE INJECTION SANDOZ STANDARD
Manufacturer: SANDOZ CANADA INCORPORATED
NOC Date: 2007-04-27
Medicinal Ingredients: HYOSCINE BUTYLBROMIDE
DIN: 02229868

2. ATRIDOX
Manufacturer: TOLMAR INC
NOC Date: 2007-04-27
Medicinal Ingredients: DOXYCYCLINE HYCLATE
DIN: 02242473

3. PMS-TERBINAFINE
Manufacturer: PHARMASCIENCE INC.
NOC Date: 2007-04-26
Medicinal Ingredients: TERBINAFINE HCL
DIN: 02294273

4. RATIO-TAMSULOSIN
Manufacturer: RATIOPHARM INC.
NOC Date: 2007-04-26
Medicinal Ingredients: TAMSULOSIN HYDROCHLORIDE
DIN: 02294265

Figure 3.2 Example of Health Canada NOC database-generated list for January 1, 2007 to April 30, 2007. Entries shown are the first four in the database-generated list.

For each pharmaceutical in the NOC listing, we included additional data found exclusively in the NOC Information through the database-generated list. NOC Information for a given drug in the listing is also available by simply typing in a particular product's brand name and NOC date, which bypasses the database-generated list. This method, although equally effective and accurate, is painstaking as it takes a considerable amount of time to type in the drug name and NOC date and wait for the database to bring up the desired result. Therefore a database-generated list for the year, albeit broken up into three portions, was the preferred method of proceeding with the analysis.

3.2.2 Methods

Each drug within each year's (2001 to 2008) listing was classified as an NDS, SNDS, ANDS, or SANDS based on the NOC Information sheet. The total numbers of NDS, SNDS, ANDS, and SANDS were calculated for each year and then double checked by a blind party for accuracy. Unfortunately,

Notice of Compliance Information

NOC Date:	2007-04-27
Manufacturer:	SANDOZ CANADA INCORPORATED
Product Type:	PRESCRIPTION PHARMACEUTICAL
NOC with conditions:	No
Submission type:	ANDS
Submission class:	OTHER
Therapeutic class:	ANTISPASMODIC
Canadian Reference	
Product:	BUSCOPAN
Company:	BOEHRINGER INGELHEIM
Country:	CANADA

Brand 1 of 1:
HYOSCINE BUTYLBROMIDE INJECTION SANDOZ STANDARD

Product 1 of 1:
DIN: 02229868
Form: SOLUTION
Routes: INTRAMUSCULAR, SUBCUTANEUS, INTRAVENOUS

Medicinal Ingredients:

Ingredient	Strength
HYOSCINE BUTYLBROMIDE	20 MG/ML

Figure 3.3 Example of a Notice of Compliance Information sheet as it appears on the Health Canada NOC database. The sheet was obtained by selecting the first drug in the database-generated list shown in Figure 3.2.

the database is not searchable by submission class (i.e. NDS, SNDS, ANDS, and SNDS). For example, we could not search the database by SANDS and year to get a complete list of all prescription pharmaceuticals that received an NOC by virtue of a SANDS application for that year. This is a significant limitation of the Health Canada database at the time of analysis.

Initially, we counted all NOCs issued as NDSs. However, a sponsor may manufacture a drug and receive an NOC by virtue of NDS even if the drug does not differ in any respect (i.e. indication, medicinal ingredient, route of administration, or dosage) from a previous drug manufactured by that company. Health Canada mandates that where there is a change in the manufacturer and/or product name or manufacturing site, a drug manufacturer must apply for a new NOC by virtue of an NDS for any drug issued after such a change took place, even if the drug is not new in any other way.[31] These NDSs are collectively termed by Health Canada as 'administrative NDSs.'[32] Given these NDSs exist solely because of a product or manufacturer change and not because a new drug was issued an NOC, the presence of these NOCs contaminated the data. Therefore all administrative NDSs were excised prior to analysis. Administrative ANDS NOCs were excised for the same reason. In order to determine which NOCs were administrative, comments provided in the listing were reviewed. The comments clearly stated whether an NOC was granted by virtue of a simple manufacturer or product name change. Once these NOCs were identified, they were subtracted from the initial total number of NDS and ANDS NOCs to yield an accurate representation of how many substantive NDS and ANDS NOCs were issued in a given year.

The percentage of total NDSs in a given year was calculated in two ways. The first involved the inclusion of generic drugs; therefore the percentage of NDS was calculated as a fraction of the combined total for all NDS, SNDS, ANDS, and SANDS for that respective year. This is summarized by equation 3.1:

$$\% \text{ NDS} = \text{NDS} / (\text{NDS} + \text{SNDS} + \text{ANDS} + \text{SANDS}) \quad [3.1]$$

The second method involved the exclusion of generic drugs; therefore the percentage of NDS was calculated as a fraction of the combined total for all NDS and SNDS for that respective year. This is given by equation 3.2:

$$\% \text{ NDS} = \text{NDS} / (\text{NDS} + \text{SNDS}) \quad [3.2]$$

The percentage of SNDSs in a given year was calculated in the same two ways as NDSs. In the first method the percentage SNDS was calculated as a fraction of the combined total for all NDS, SNDS, ANDS, and SANDS for that respective year. This is summarized by equation 3.3:

$$\% \text{ SNDS} = \text{SNDS} / (\text{NDS} + \text{SNDS} + \text{ANDS} + \text{SANDS}) \quad [3.3]$$

In the second method, the percentage of SNDS was calculated as a fraction of the combined total for all NDS and SNDS for that respective year. This is summarized as follows:

$$\% \text{ SNDS} = \text{SNDS} / (\text{NDS} + \text{SNDS}) \quad [3.4]$$

The total number of NOCs classified as NAS was calculated for each year, 2001 to 2008 inclusive. The Health Canada database is searchable by Submission Class, which includes the following categories: NAS, Priority, Priority-NAS, and Other status. By narrowing the search to prescription pharmaceuticals, a specified year, and NAS, we obtained a numerated list of all NOCs with NAS status that were issued in each given year. Subsequently, we narrowed the search to prescription pharmaceuticals, a specified year and Priority-NAS and obtained a numerated list of all NOCs with Priority-NAS status issued in that year. To calculate the number of

NOCs classified as NAS, we added the totals of both NAS and Priority-NAS NOCs. This is summarized by equation 3.5:

Total NAS = NAS + Priority-NAS [3.5]

Prescription pharmaceuticals classified as NAS are only submitted as NDS. However, for the sake of consistency, the percentage of NAS NOCs was also calculated as a fraction of the combined total of NDS and SNDS (ANDS and SANDS were excluded). This is summarized by equation 3.6:

% NAS = NAS / (NDS + SNDS) [3.6]

The percentage of ANDS in a given year was calculated as a fraction of the combined total for all NDS, SNDS, ANDS, and SANDS for that respective year:

% ANDS = ANDS / (NDS + SNDS + ANDS + SANDS) [3.7]

The percentage of SANDS in a given year was calculated as a fraction of the combined total for all NDS, SNDS, ANDS, and SANDS for that respective year:

% SANDS = SANDS / (NDS + SNDS + ANDS + SANDS) [3.8]

The next part of the analysis involved determination of NOCs classified as first-in-class or me-too. This proved to be one of the most difficult aspects of the study, as available definitions of first-in-class and me-too by regulators are very limited. We used information obtained directly from Health Canada to define first-in-class and me-too drugs. We then designed a methodology for determining which NOCs fall under these categories. This methodology is based on the principles outlined below.

According to Health Canada, 'first-in-class' drugs are drugs that consist of either (1) a new family of active ingredient(s) or (2) old active ingredient(s) used for the treatment of a new indication (Table 3.2). Therefore a drug is deemed to be first-in-class if there is no other drug on the market that belongs to the same compound family and is used for the same indication.[33] In other words, a first-in-class drug is a drug for which there is no comparator.[34]

Conversely, 'me-too' drugs are drugs that offer important therapeutic options with little or no change to the benefit-risk profile.[35] They are drugs that are comparable to others in terms of their compound and indication.[36] Derivatives or salts of an existing compound are classified as me-too drugs.[37] As per the Health Canada definition, NAS NOCs include those directed to salts and derivatives.[38] Therefore drugs that are labeled as an 'NAS' can be either first-in-class or me-too drugs. Initially, we assumed

Table 3.2 Health Canada compound-indication classification

Year	Compound/indication	Classification
2000	Compound X (first 'X' Compound) with Indication A	First-in class
2001	Compound X with Indication B	First-in-class
2001	Compound *a*X (Compound in the family of X) with Indication A	Me-too
2001	Compound *a*X with Indication B	Me-too
2001	Compound *a*X with Indication C	First-in-class

me-too drugs could only be submitted as NDSs. The reasoning for this was that me-too drugs are neither generic drugs (ANDS or SANDS) nor line extensions (SNDS). However, as shown in Table 3.2, neither first-in-class nor me-too classifications stop at NOCs submitted as NDSs, depending on the chemical nature and use of the compound. SNDS NOCs can be classified as first-in-class or me-too; thus both can be issued as NDS and line extension (SNDS) NOCs.[39]

Based on the drug classification scheme outlined in Table 3.2, we determined which NDS and SNDS NOCs were first-in-class and me-too drugs. We analyzed all NOCs submitted as NDS for approval first. In analyzing this group, we started off with those NDSs deemed by Health Canada to have NAS status, as all first-in-class drugs would be included in this broad group. Obtaining a list of all NAS NOCs for a given year is relatively straightforward, given the ability to search the NOC database by NAS status.

We assessed each NAS for the period 2001–2008 by cross-referencing the NAS drug's active ingredient, NOC date, and indication with the Health Canada online NOC database and the World Health Organization (WHO) Collaborating Center for Drug Statistics Methodology website.[40] If the active ingredient in the NAS was the very first of its family of compounds, the drug was classified as first in class. If the active ingredient in the NAS was a member of a family of compounds in which a drug already exists but the drug was used for a new indication, the drug was also classified as a first-in-class. All NAS not deemed to be first-in class were labeled me-too NOCs. The number of first-in-class NDS NOCs was then calculated. The total number of me-too NDS NOCs for each year was calculated using equation 3.9:

$$\text{Total NDS me-too} = \text{NDS} - \text{First-in-class NDS} \qquad [3.9]$$

We then analyzed all NOCs submitted as SNDS. Because SNDS drugs are 'line extensions' of previously existing drugs, the analysis turned primarily on new indications. Essentially, if an SNDS for a particular compound was given a new indication not seen before, as determined by cross-referencing the drug's active ingredient, NOC date, and indication with the NOC database, it was deemed a first-in-class drug. The designation of first in class by virtue of a new indication was far from simple. The starting point for this process was the NAS. If Health Canada classified an NOC as being directed to an NAS, it can be assumed that the active ingredient has not been sold in Canada for that specific indication prior to issuance of the NOC. The next step was to determine whether a new indication exists for the medicinal ingredient associated with the NAS following issuance. One way to do this is via Health Canada's searchable database. We entered the medicinal ingredient described by the NAS into the appropriate database field. This yielded a list of all drugs that have the same medicinal ingredient as the NAS. Because the list is arranged by date, the NAS presents as the earliest entry in the list. The next step was to go through each drug listed above the NAS and determine whether it is an SNDS with a new indication, which is indicative of a first-in-class drug. Part of the difficulty in correctly determining first-in-class NOCs is that the NOC database includes, when describing reasons for SNDS (as opposed to NDS), NOCs directed to new indications as well as new routes of administration, dosage forms, and contra-indications.[41] Thus, within the new indication SNDS category, an NOC can be given for a new medical condition as well as for an extended treatment population, e.g. pediatric. However, only NOCs directed to new medical conditions are viewed by Health Canada as first in class.[42] Therefore, assuming that all NOCs in the extended population SNDS subclass are first in class would artificially increase the number of true first-in-class NOCs. All SNDS NOCs not deemed first-in-class were labeled me-too by default.[43]

The number of first-in-class SNDS drugs was calculated as described above. The total number of SNDS me-too drugs for each year is calculated using equation 3.10:

$$\text{Total SNDS me-too} = \text{SNDS} - \text{First-in-class SNDS} \qquad [3.10]$$

The next step was to calculate the total number of NOC/c during the period 2001–2008. By narrowing search terms on the Health Canada database to prescription pharmaceuticals, a specific year, and NOC/c, we obtained a list of all NOC/c that were issued in a given year. Because prescription pharmaceuticals provided with market authorization under the NOC/c policy are only submitted as NDS or SNDS, the percentage of NOC/c was calculated as the fraction of the total of NDS and SNDS (e.g. ANDS and SANDS were excluded). This is summarized by equation 3.11:

$$\% \text{ NOC/c} = \text{NOC/c} / (\text{NDS} + \text{SNDS}) \quad [3.11]$$

The total number of NOCs issued under Priority Review was calculated for 2001–2008 inclusive. By narrowing the database search to prescription pharmaceuticals, a specific year, and Priority Review, we obtained a numerated list of all NOCs issued under Priority Review for that given year. We then searched the database by prescription pharmaceuticals, a specific year, and Priority-NAS status and obtained a numerated list of all NOCs with NAS status that were issued under the Priority Review Policy in that given year. To calculate the total number of NOCs granted via the Priority Review stream we added the totals of both Priority and Priority-NAS NOCs as given by equation 3.12:

$$\text{Total Priority} = \text{Priority} + \text{Priority-NAS} \quad [3.12]$$

Prescription pharmaceuticals granted an NOC under the Priority Review Policy are only submitted for approval as NDS or SNDS. Thus the percentage of Priority NOCs was calculated as a fraction of the combined total of NDS and SNDS (ANDS and SANDS were excluded). This is summarized by equation 3.13:

$$\% \text{ Priority} = \text{Priority} / (\text{NDS} + \text{SNDS}) \quad [3.13]$$

The total number of non-priority NOCs was calculated for each year, 2001–2008 inclusive. We subtracted the total number of Priority Review NOCs from the combined total of NDS and SNDS for each year:

$$\text{Non-Priority} = (\text{NDS} + \text{SNDS}) - \text{Priority} \quad [3.14]$$

The percentage of non-priority NOCs was taken as a fraction of combined total NDS and SNDS for each year:

$$\% \text{ Non-Priority} = \text{Non-Priority} / (\text{NDS} + \text{SNDS}) \quad [3.15]$$

Finally, we analyzed whether NOC/c granted during the test period had their conditions met. This was done using the NOC database by following appropriate links through the 'NOC/c conditions' box, entering 'Prescription Pharmaceutical' in the Product Type field and entering January 1, 2001 to December 31, 2008 in the date field. This procedure yielded all NOC/c granted during the test period, from which we subtracted administrative NDS NOCs, as described above. The resulting list provides the drug name, drug manufacturer, NOC date, medicinal ingredient, NOC/c status, and information stating if and when the conditions were met.

Data were tabulated and analyzed using Microsoft Excel® (Microsoft Corp., Redmond, WA), GraphPad Prism® (Graphpad Software Inc., La Jolla, CA), and SigmaPlot® (Systat Software, Inc., San Jose, CA). GraphPad or SigmaPlot were used to graph data, calculate linear regressions and exponential fits, and to obtain R^2, time constants, slopes, and P values. Solid lines in Figures 3.4 to 3.10 represent linear regression fits to the data with the exceptions of Figures 3.8(c), 3.9(a), and 3.9(b), which were fit to exponential functions as described in the Results.

3.3 Results

The number of NDS NOCs for 2001–2008 inclusive (test period) was 52, 26, 46, 62, 36, 54, 37, and 25 per year, respectively. As illustrated in Figure 3.4(a), the number of NDS NOCs issued over the test period declined slightly in the presence of stochastic fluctuations. When calculated as a percentage of total brand name and generic submissions (NDS, SNDS, ANDS, and SANDS), a similar trend was seen over the test period (Figure 3.4(b)), from approximately 20% of total NOCs in 2001 to 8% in 2008. When expressed as a fraction of total brand-name submissions only (NDS and SNDS), the general trend was also toward a slight decline in NDS NOCs during the test period (Figure 4.4(c)), around an average of about 25% of total brand name submissions.

The total number of SNDS NOCs issued in the period 2001–2008 was 118, 80, 149, 138, 102, 137, 167, and 161 respectively. As illustrated by

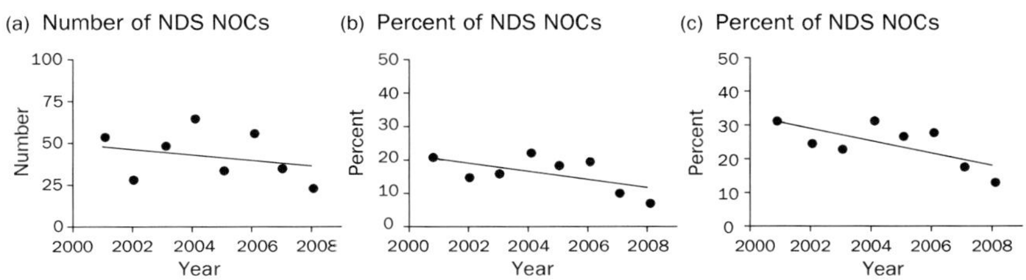

Figure 3.4 (a) Number of NDS NOCs; (b) percentage of NDS NOCs as a percentage of all NOCs (NDS, SNDS, ANDS and SANDS); (c) as a percentage of NDS and SNDS only.

Data in this and all other figures and tables are for calendar years 2001–2008 inclusive. Fits to the data are described in detail in the Methods and text. Abbreviations for this and all other figures are provided at the beginning of the text.

the data in Figure 3.5, supplementary brand name submissions generally increased over the course of the test period. The total number of SNDS NOCs increased by approximately 60% during the period 2001–2008, though there is significant scatter in the data when administrative NOCs are removed (Figure 3.5(a)). SNDS NOCs expressed as a percentage of total brand-name NOCs issued (NDS and SNDS) also increased over the test period (Figure 3.5(c)). The increase in the number and percentage SNDS NOCs can be compared with the relative lack of change in SNDS approvals when expressed as a fraction of all NOCs (Figure 3.5(b)).

Consistent with data for NDS NOCs, NOCs directed to NASs for the period 2001–2008 showed a slight decrease. The number of approvals for NASs per year was 21, 16, 16, 15, 12, 16, 20, and 14 during the test period. Figure 3.6(a) shows a declining trend, with significant scatter around an average of about 16 per year. The scatter is reduced when NAS NOCs are expressed as a percentage of total NOCs. Figure 3.6(b) demonstrates that the percentage of approvals for NAS NOCs was a small fraction of total NDS and SNDS approvals (10%) and that this fraction remained relatively constant during the test period. Along with the decline in NDS NOCs (Figure 3.4) and reciprocal increase in SNDS NOCs (Figure 3.5), the data in Figure 3.6 reveal that brand-name pharmaceutical firms are focusing less on new drug submissions and more on follow-on supplementary submissions, even when the broad scope of Health Canada's NAS definition is taken into account.

Figure 3.7 illustrates trends in market approvals issued to generic firms. The total number of NOCs in the ANDS category was 73, 57, 60, 67, 64, 75, 98, and 90 over the test period. As shown in Figure 3.7(a), the trend was toward an increase in ANDS approvals, from a low of 57 in 2002 to a

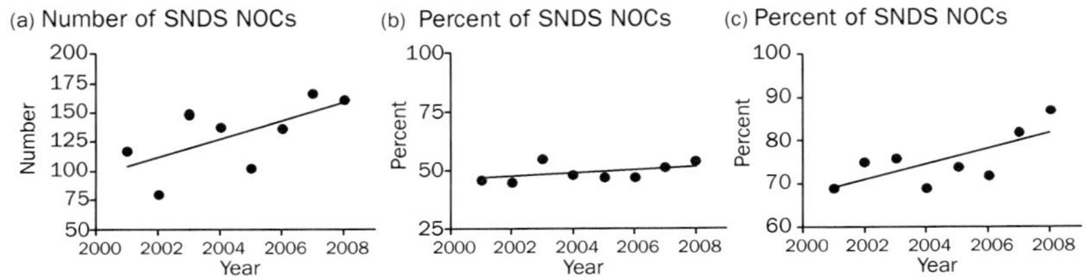

Figure 3.5 (a) Number of SNDS NOCs; (b) SNDS NOCs as a percentage of all NOCs (NDS, SNDS, ANDS, and SANDS); (c) SNDS NOCs as a percentage of NDS and SNDS only.

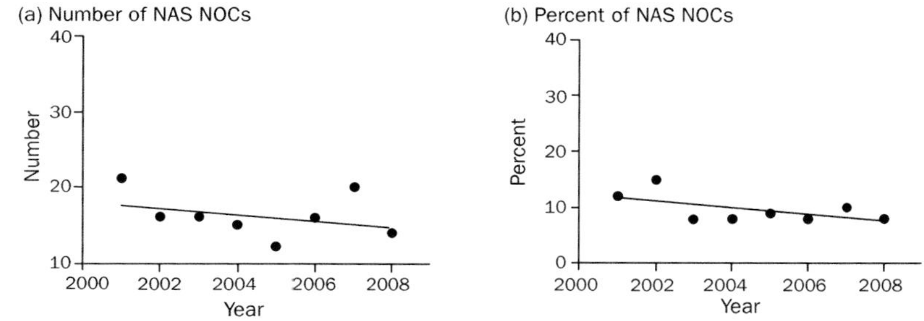

Figure 3.6 (a) Number and (b) percentage (all NDS and SNDS NOCs) of NAS NOCs.

peak of 98 in 2007. This represents an increase in ANDS NOCs of about 72% over five years. ANDS approvals represented a fairly constant fraction of total NOCs issued over the test period, accounting for about a quarter of all NOCs issued by the GOC (Figure 3.7(b)). The total number of generic supplemental NOCs also increased over the test period (11, 16, 16,

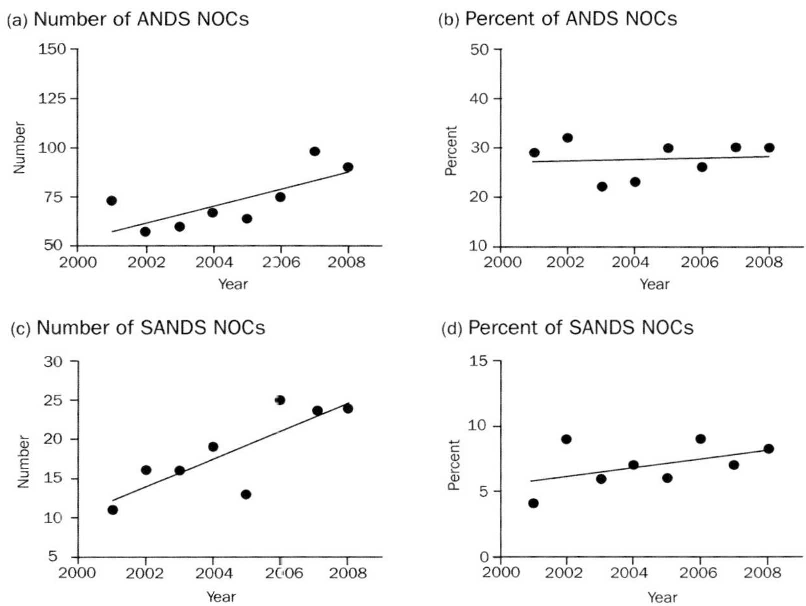

Figure 3.7 Number of and percentage of all NOCs (NDS, SNDS, ANDS, and SANDS) of ANDS ((a) and (b)) and SANDS ((c) and (d)).

19, 13, 25, 24, and 24). As illustrated in Figure 3.7(c), the number of SANDS NOCs more than doubled over this time frame, from a low of about 10 approvals per year in 2001 to a high of about 25 per year in 2007. This trend did not change when the data are expressed as a fraction of total NOCs (NDS, SNDS, ANDS, and SANDS) issued yearly over the test period (Figure 3.7(d)). Thus the number of supplemental submissions by both brand-name (Figure 3.5) and generic firms (Figure 3.7) is increasing significantly with time.

Results obtained using the method outlined in section 3.2.2 for determining the number of first-in-class and me-too NOCs are given in Figure 3.8. The number of first-in-class NOCs within the NDS category was 12, 7, 5, 7, 9, 8, 9, and 8 during the test period. Figure 3.8(a) shows that the number of these approvals was relatively constant over the period 2001–2008, within a range of 5–12 per year. As illustrated in Figure 3.8(b), the number of me-too NDS NOCs decreased slightly over the test period, with a significant amount of scatter in the data around an average of about 34 approvals per year. The number of calculated me-too NDS NOCs during the period 2001–2008 was 40, 19, 41, 55, 27, 46, 28, and 17.

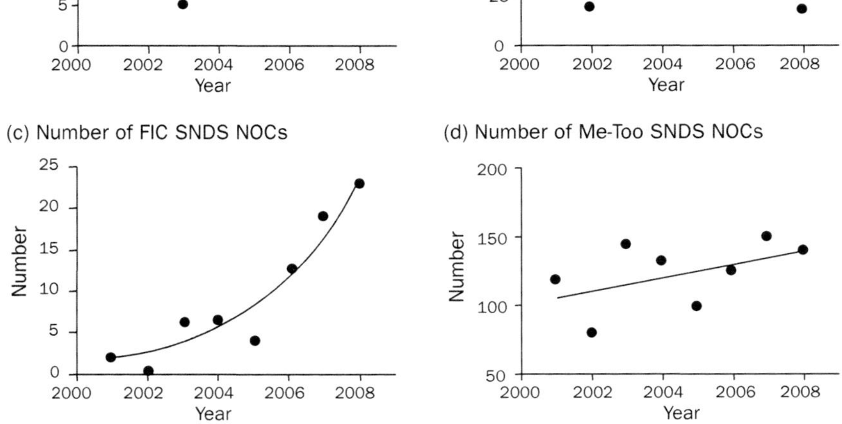

Figure 3.8 Number of (a) first-in-class NDS NOCs; (b) me-too NDS NOCs; (c) first-in-class SNDS NOCs; (d) me-too SNDS NOCs.

A substantially different situation was observed with the calculated first-in-class and me-too SNDS data. As illustrated in Figure 3.8(c), the number of first-in-class SNDS NOCs increased substantially over the test period, from a low of 1 in 2001 to a high of 22 in 2008 (1, 1, 6, 7, 4, 13, 19, and 22). We used two methods to calculate the time-dependence, slope, and potential non-linearities in the data set. For simplicity's sake, we present these in reverse order of statistical conservatism. For the first method, the data were fit to a single exponential function of the form $y = a \cdot exp^{(t/b)}$, where a is amplitude and b is the time constant. Both a and b were treated as free variables, and the fit was only to the time period 2001–2008. R^2 (squared correlation coefficient), representative of the 'goodness of fit' of the function to the data (0–1), was 0.92. This suggests significant acceleration of the increase in follow-on first-in-class approvals over time. The second method entailed the use of a linear model. We found that 86% of the variation in Figure 3.8(c) could be described linearly ($P = 0.000938$) as opposed to non-linearly.

Given the results of the exponential fit, however, we also tested for a quadratic non-linearity using an ordinary least squares regression. While this increased the coefficient of determination to 92%, the squared term was not statistically significant at $P \leq 0.05$ ($p = 0.102153$). However, given that there are only eight observations, it is possible we are faced with the cliché that 'an absence of evidence is not the same as evidence of absence.' While it was not possible to provide evidence for a non-linear term using both statistical methods, there clearly is enough of a trend to warrant further investigation as more data become available.

The number of me-too SNDS NOCs issued during the test period also increased significantly (Figure 3.8(d)), though not as dramatically as first-in-class SNDS NOCs. There was an approximate doubling of me-too SNDS NOCs over the period analyzed, from a low of 79 in 2002 to a high of 148 in 2007. Along with the data in Figures 3.4–3.6, these results demonstrate a significant trend for domestic brand-name pharmaceutical firms to concentrate their efforts on supplementary line extension-type submissions rather than on new NDS, NDS NAS, or even NDS me-too-type submissions.

Figure 3.9 shows the time-dependence of drug approval via the two expedited approval streams (NOC/c and Priority Review) over the test period. The total number of NOCs issued under the NOC/c policy was 2, 3, 4, 3, 6, 13, 10, and 10 per year during the period 2001–2008. The data illustrate that the increase in NOC/c approvals occurred in a strongly time-dependent manner, independent of whether the data were expressed in absolute terms (Figure 3.9(a)) or as a fraction of total brand-name submissions

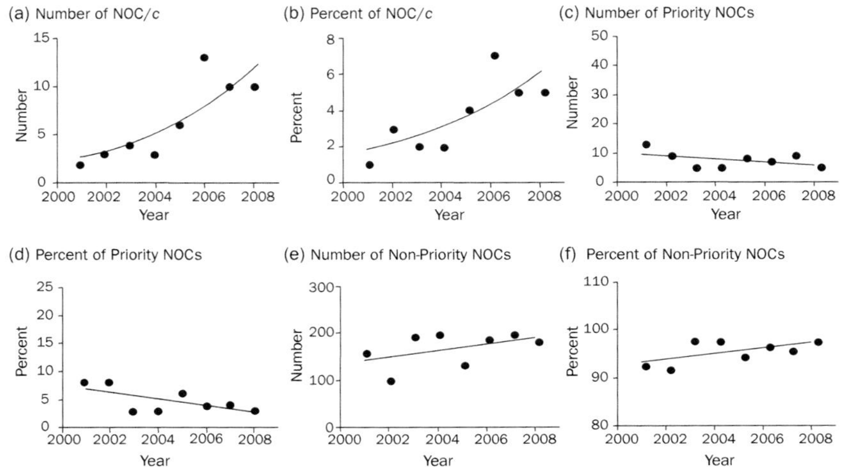

Figure 3.9 Number and percentage (percentage of all NDS and SNDS NOCs) of NOC/c ((a) and (b)); priority NOCs ((c) and (d)); non-priority NOCs ((e) and (f)).

(Figure 3.9(b)). Using the first method described for analyzing data in Figure 3.8(c), the data could be fit to a single exponential function with R^2 values of 0.7 and 0.6 for Figures 3.9(a) and 3.9(b), respectively. The linear model on the other hand did not provide a strong suggestion for a non-linear term. The coefficient of determination for the simple ordinary least squares fit was 74% and 65% for Figures 3.9(a) and 3.9(b), respectively. However, the squared terms were not statistically significant (p = 0.976373587 and 0.712446789, respectively). Even so, the data clearly demonstrate a substantial increase in the grant of NOC/c approvals over the test period, with an increase from a low of 3 in 2001 to a high of 13 in 2006 (650%, stabilizing at 500% in 2007 and 2008).

The fraction of total NOCs represented by NOC/c approvals increased from a nominal value of about 1% in 2001 to a peak of 7% of all NOCs issued by Health Canada to brand-name firms in 2006 (stabilizing at 5% in 2007 and 2008). As such, there is good evidence favoring a positive time-dependent increase in NOC/c approvals over the test period using both statistical methods. There is some evidence from the exponential fits supporting acceleration of this trend (R^2 = 0.7 Figure 3.9(a); 0.6 Figure 3.9(b)), but the trends are not as strong as that reported for Figure 3.8(c) (R^2 = 0.92) and differ from the results of the ordinary least squares analysis.

The data in Figures 3.9(a) and 3.9(b) contrast significantly with the Priority Review data set, where both the absolute number (Figure 3.9(c)) and fraction of total (Figure 3.9(d)) NOCs that were issued under the Priority Review stream decreased over the period 2001–2008 (13, 9, 5, 5,

8, 7, 9, and 5 per year). In comparison, non-Priority Review NOCs increased slightly over the test period, expressed either in absolute terms (Figure 3.9(e)) or as a fraction of total NOCs issued (Figure 3.9(f)). Indeed, comparison of data in Figures 3.9(a)–(d) demonstrate that while the number and percentage of Priority Review NOCs exceeded those for NOC/c approvals in 2001 by twofold, both trends were completely reversed by 2008. Given the relative lack of change in the fraction of total NOCs that were subject to Priority Review (Figure 3.9(f)), the data in Figure 3.9 demonstrate that brand-name firms have been highly successful in facilitating early access via the NOC/c limb of the expedited stream.

Data relating to whether or not the conditions associated with NOC/c approval were actually met during the test period are given in Figure 3.10 and Table 3.3. Figure 3.10(a) depicts the number of NOC/c approvals issued per year that *eventually* had their conditions met: the filled portion of each bar represents the number of NOC/c approvals issued in a given year that had their conditions met, while the unfilled portion represents the number of NOC/c approvals granted in a given year that have not yet had their conditions met to date (i.e. filled and unfilled portions represent the fraction of total NOC/c with conditions met and unmet, respectively). For example, in 2001 two NOC/c approvals were granted: one had its conditions met in 2004 and one has not yet had its conditions met. Therefore the bar is half filled. In 2002, three NOC/c approvals were granted, and all three have not yet had their conditions met. The data in Figure 3.10(a) suggest a significant positive trend toward NOC/c approvals

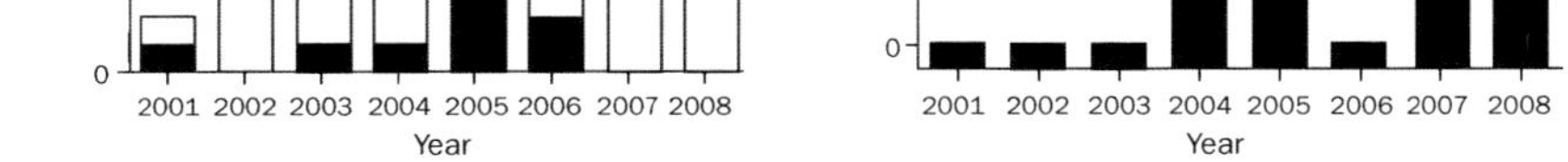

Figure 3.10 Number of NOC/c granted by the GOC during the 2001–2008 test period that had their conditions met.

(a) Filled bar portions represent the number of NOC/c issued in that calendar year that eventually had their conditions met. Unfilled bars represent NOC/c issued in that year which have not yet had their conditions met to date. (b) Year in which conditions attached to NOC/c were met independent of the year NOCs were granted.

Table 3.3 Date of NOC/c grant and date conditions associated with NOC/c were met during the period 2001–2008

Year	NOC/c (date of grant)	Conditions met NO	Conditions met YES
2001	2001-03-01	–	2004-07-5 (n = 1)
	2001-09-20	NOT met to date (n = 1)	–
2002	2002-05-28; 2002-08-07; 2002-11-25	NOT met to date (n = 3)	–
2003	2003-03-18	–	2005-07-20 (n = 1)
	2003-07-07; 2003-10-08; 2003-12-17	NOT met to date (n = 3)	–
2004	2004-06-30	–	2008-12-02 (n = 1)
	2004-06-02; 2004-12-08	NOT met to date (n = 2)	–
2005	2005-01-27; 2005-11-01; 2005-12-07	–	2007-09-11; 2008-12-02; 2008-10-23 (n = 3)
	2005-04-01; 2005-04-15; 2005-12-29	NOT met to date (n = 3)	–
2006	2006-04-24; 2006-05-12	–	2007-09-11; 2008-06-06 (n = 2)
	2006-05-03; 2006-06-16; 2006-06-26; 2006-07-18; 2006-07-28; 2006-07-28; 2006-08-17; 2006-10-06; 2006-10-18; 2006-11-07; 2006-12-14	NOT met to date (n = 11)	–
2007	2007-03-01; 2007-03-26; 2007-05-24; 2007-08-01; 2007-09-12; 2007-09-22; 2007-11-09; 2007-11-27; 2007-11-30; 2007-12-20	NOT met to date (n = 10)	–
2008	2008-01-17; 2008-03-03; 2008-05-02; 2008-06-18; 2008-07-23; 2008-09-09; 2008-09-30; 2008-10-15; 2008-12-09; 2008-12-19	NOT met to date (n = 10)	–
Total	**N = 51**	**N = 43**	**N = 8**
Percent	**100%**	**84.3%**	**15.7%**

not having their conditions met during the test period, at least in the short period of time since issuance.

Figure 3.10(b) shows the same data expressed as the year in which conditions for NOC/c approvals were met *independent of the year* NOCs were granted. Whereas Figure 3.10(a) is focused on the year NOC/c approvals were issued, Figure 3.10(b) is focused on the year conditions were met. Note that the y-axis is set slightly (–0.25) below zero. This was done in order to ensure years where no conditions were met were still represented by an observable bar. For example, in 2001, 2002, 2003, and 2006 no NOC/c licences that were issued within the test period had their conditions met. This can be contrasted with data from 2004, 2005, 2007, and 2008, where 1, 1, 2, and 4 NOC/c approvals ultimately had their conditions met. Unlike data in Figure 3.10(a), which appear to indicate a trend toward increasing non-compliance, the data in Figure 3.10(b) demonstrate a smaller yet parallel trend toward an increased likelihood that conditions attached to an NOC/c were met over the test period.

Finally, we analyzed the number of NOCs approved during the period 2001–2008 that were withdrawn for safety reasons.[44] As illustrated in Table 3.4, a very small percentage of NOCs issued during the test period have been withdrawn in Canada to date.

Withdrawal data can be parsed in two ways: first, as withdrawn NOCs (n = 10) expressed as a fraction of total NOCs (n = 2,122) granted over the test period; and second, as withdrawn products (n = 4) expressed as a fraction of total products (n = 608) associated with the larger number of NOCs. For the first procedure, 2,122 NOCs were issued over the test period, 10 of which were withdrawn within the same time frame. This amounts to 0.47% issued NOCs that were withdrawn. However, this value is somewhat misleading because consumers do not purchase NOCs. Rather they purchase and consume, and drug agencies typically regulate, drug products. Of 608 products receiving NOCs during the course of the test period, only four were withdrawn (Gatifloxacin, June 29, 2006; Lumaricoxib, October 3, 2007; Tegaserod, March 30, 2007; Valdecoxib,

Table 3.4 Drug withdrawals for expedited and standard review streams for NOCs approved 2001–2008 in Canada and comparator jurisdictions

Submission class	NOC issued	Withdrawals (country)		
	Canada	Canada	US	France
	2001–8	2001–8[45]	2001–7[46]	2001–8[47]
A. Expedited				
NOC/c	51	0	0	0
Priority Review	61	0	0	0
B. Standard				
NDS	338	4	1	0
SNDS	1,052	0	0	0
ANDS	584	0	0	0
SANDS	148	0	0	0
TOTAL	2,122	4	1	0

April 7, 2005). As noted above, this his amounts to a small percentage (0.66%) of marketed products issued in the test period that were subsequently withdrawn for safety reasons within the same time frame.

Withdrawals in Canada were slightly higher than withdrawals for the same drug pool in at least two comparator jurisdictions (0.2%, US; 0%, France). However, of the total number of products or NOCs withdrawn in Canada for safety reasons during the test period (n = 4), none were withdrawn in the two expedited streams (NOC/c, Priority Review). Data were drawn from published studies in Canada,[45] the US,[46] and France.[47]

3.4 Discussion

Data from the qualitative and quantitative analyses undertaken here suggest that concerns expressed over PLF pushing Canada in a new direction concerning the workings and output of its drug regulatory regime may be somewhat overstated. The data demonstrate that the approval mechanism enshrined in the existing Food and Drugs Act and Food and Drug Regulations already anticipates the lifecycle approach, at least as it is described in the *Blueprint*,[48] PLF Concept Paper,[49] and Bill C-51.[50] Analysis of eight years of GOC approval statistics shows that new drug submissions have been on the decline for at least this long, while supplementary submissions from both brand-name and generic firms during this time have conversely increased. Moreover, Priority Reviews, which have the same or similar evidentiary requirements as standard review submissions, declined slightly over the period analyzed. By contrast, NOC/c submissions, which have reduced front-end evidentiary requirements compared to standard submissions, increased substantially. Thus, despite little or no change in the unmet medical needs of the Canadian population, a relatively small but significant percentage of drugs have entered our national market increasingly earlier in their product development lifecycle.

The data further imply that the Canadian pharmaceutical industry as a whole may be 'doing more with less.' This conclusion applies to both the rate and direction of innovative activity undertaken by brand name and generic firms. New or standard drug submissions are flat while supplementary and generic submissions have increased substantially. Even approvals for new me-too drugs remained relatively constant or slightly elevated when compared to line extensions and new uses. The data reveal a trend away from development of novel 'breakthrough' pharmaceuticals over the course of the test period. Results of this nature may provide an example of policy resistance,[51] whereby government policy inhibits or prevents the very thing it seeks to facilitate through the unintended consequences of its action(s).[52]

3.5 Interpretation of data

Our analysis of NOCs issued in Canada in the period 2001–2008 yields a number of major observations. First, the data demonstrate that the current drug regulatory regime already anticipates the lifecycle approach. Second, it provides insight into the types of drug submissions that are likely candidates to receive expedited drug approval under the terms of flexible departure. Third, the data speak to the issue of innovation patterns in the area of pharmaceutical development. Together, the data have important implications for the manner in which PLF is likely to be rolled out, the types of drugs that the public are likely to see on the market in the near future, and those drugs with which they are likely to be provided in the long term, absent significant changes in IPR rights associated with drug approval and marketing.

Data generated in this study show that the existing regulatory system in Canada is already moving in a direction consistent with what is proposed under the PLF system: that is, toward earlier access to drugs that occupy the 'extraordinary need' niche with emphasis on post-market surveillance. This is most clearly exemplified by the NOC/c data set, expressed either as the number of NOC/c or as a fraction of total NOCs (Figures 3.9(a) and 3.9(b)). As described in the Results, while the absolute number of NOC/c approvals is relatively small (peaking at 13 in 2006), the number when expressed as a function of total brand-name NOCs granted by the GOC is not insignificant (7%). Moreover, it is evident that the fractional number of NOC/c approvals is increasing significantly over time (from 1% in 2001 to 7% in 2006) and that this increase is occurring in a strongly time-dependent manner (Figures 3.9(a) and 3.9(b)). The trend toward increasing NOC/c approvals is occurring despite a slight downward trend in new drug submissions expressed either in absolute terms (Figure 3.4(a) or as a function of total brand-name submissions (Figure 3.4(c)). Even more dramatically, the escalation in NOC/c approvals has been accompanied by a reverse trend in Priority Review NOCs (compare Figures 3.9(a) and 3.9(c)). Since the NOC/c policy issues NOCs faster and under the condition that additional post-market authorization safety and/or efficacy studies are undertaken, there is an overall increase in drugs that are being authorized in a manner similar to that contemplated by Health Canada in the *Blueprint* and PLF Concept Paper policies and in Bill C-51.

The data also suggest that the trend toward flexible departure is being accompanied by a small but significant trend for sponsors to meet conditions associated with NOC/c approval (Figure 3.10(b)). This conclusion is tempered by the large number of outstanding NOC/c approvals where the conditions have not yet been met (Figure 3.10(a); Table 3.4). A second caveat is the fact that there is not a great deal of data in this regard given the gap between issuance and conditions met in later years which does not apply to analysis of approvals per se. The observation that an increasing number of drugs are being made available to the public under the circumstance that they meet certain conditions in order to maintain market authorization demonstrates that Health Canada is already approving drugs with PLF in mind. Positively, none of these drugs has been recalled for safety reasons to date (Table 3.4).

Of interest, the data show that the number and fraction of total NOCs issued under the Priority Review policy have steadily declined over the test period (Figure 3.9(c)). The number has hovered fairly constantly around 7 or 8 per year (Figure 3.9(c)) compared with increases in the number and fraction of non-priority NOCs (Figures 3.9(e) and 3.9(f)). At first glance, this might seem inconsistent with the notion that the GOC is anticipating PLF. For example, given that progressive licensing is partially geared toward enhanced access, it only seems logical that NOCs issued under Priority Review should also be increasing. On more careful examination, however, it is evident that a decreasing number of Priority Reviews is anticipatory of PLF. The policy for fast-tracking eligible NDS and SNDS is intended to provide enhanced availability of products for the treatment, prevention, or diagnosis of serious, life-threatening, or severely debilitating diseases or conditions where there is an unmet medical need or for which a substantial improvement in the benefit-risk profile of the therapy is demonstrated.[53] Unlike the NOC/c policy, Priority Review is aimed at getting drugs approved faster *without* a change in the amount of scientific evidence required for approval prior to market entry. According to leadership at Health Canada, this ensures that drug manufacturers jump ahead of others in the approval queue.[54] Moreover, Priority Review policy, unlike the NOC/c policy, does not demand that sponsors conduct post-marketing studies as a means to continue or maintain the NOC. Priority Review is essentially a fast-tracking mechanism without any further evidentiary obligations imposed on industry. This might be seen to accord less with PLF policy than the NOC/c mechanism. While both streams promote faster drug approval, only the latter is centered on the lifecycle approach, which demands that in return for faster drug approval, a drug's safety and efficacy must be subject to legal scrutiny beyond initial market authorization. Thus it is reasonable to speculate that in anticipation of the PLF regime, Health Canada might shift somewhat away from the Priority Review stream as the primary means of enhancing access toward the NOC/c stream.

Anticipation of PLF and consequently faster drug approval is also evident by other trends in the data set. For instance, the percentage of NDS

NOCs decreased over the test period (Figure 3.4(b)) whereas the number (Figure 3.5(a)) and fraction (Figure 3.5(b)) of supplemental submissions increased. SNDSs are also known as 'line extensions' of previously existing products, usually involving changes to a pre-existing drug such as a change in the route of administration (e.g. oral to intravenous), dosage form (e.g. tablet to capsule), salt form (e.g. besylate to mesylate), or indication (e.g. antidepressant to anxiolytic). For the most part, getting a line extension or SNDS onto the market is a faster process compared to drugs approved via the new drug submission stream. This is true even where approval times for SNDS and NDS are roughly equal, as production and marketing of line extension products takes less time than producing and marketing truly new drugs, owing to manufacturing experience and related competencies. Thus an increasing number of yearly SNDS NOCs is indicative of a general focus on faster access, if not faster approval. This conclusion is supported by the observation that the number of New Active Substances (NAS) is decreasing over time (expressed either in absolute terms (Figure 3.6(a)) or as a fraction of total brand-name NOCs (Figure 3.6(b)) issued), particularly given the broad NAS definition employed by the GOC.

The present data also have important implications for the rate and direction of innovation by domestic pharmaceutical firms. For example, approvals relating to both types of NDSs (Figure 3.4) declined over the test period. By comparison, the number of supplemental submissions increased when expressed either in absolute terms (Figure 3.5(a)) or as a fraction of total brand-name submissions (Figure 3.5(c)). Together, the data indicate that pharmaceutical companies are increasingly doing more with less, implying that firms are expending fewer and fewer resources on developing breakthrough drugs and more on extending the utility of already existing products. This trend is also demonstrated by the decreasing number of NAS NOCs with time (Figure 3.6), because drugs in this group include those that differ minimally from pre-existing drugs such as salts, enantiomers, and other derivatives of already marketed compounds. Furthermore, the number of SNDS deemed to be first in class by virtue of new indications escalated in a strongly time-dependent and potentially non-linear ($R^2 = 0.92$, Figure 3.8(c)) manner. Brand-name pharmaceutical firms are therefore strongly concentrating their efforts on getting as much value as possible from their existing drug development activities rather than focusing on the development of first-in-kind products. The data are in line with results from Health Canada indicating that there has been a 225% increase in the number of clinical trial applications since 2001, compared with only a 19% increase in firm R&D spending over a similar time period.[55] A parallel conclusion arises from the analysis of generic NOC data. For example, we found that the number of ANDS and SANDS yielding NOCs during the test period increased substantially. This was true independently of whether the data were expressed in absolute terms (Figures 3.7(a) and 3.7(c)) or as a percentage of total NOCs (Figures 3.7(b) and 3.7(d)). The increase in the number of ANDS (75%, Figure 3.7(a)) and SANDS (100%, Figure 3.7(c)) NOCs was greater than the corresponding increase in NDS (no change, Figure 3.4(a)) and SNDS (15%, Figure 3.5(a)) NOCs. Absolute values for ANDS and SANDS are expected to reflect the increasing release of generic drugs into the market as the number of drugs that come off patent protection under the NOC Regulations increases. This trend is reflected in the data expressed as a fraction of total NOCs (Figures 3.7(b) and 3.7(d)) as well.

One of the most intriguing findings of the study is that the number of new me-too (Figure 3.8(b)) and first-in-class (Figure 3.8(a)) NDS NOCs decreased slightly over the test period. By contrast, the number of follow-on me-too SNDS (Figure 3.8(d)) and first-in-class SNDS (Figure 3.8(c)) NOCs increased significantly. Me-too SNDS NOCs in particular doubled over the test period. Moreover, first-in-class SNDS NOCs increased in a strongly time-dependent manner, from 1 to 22. The slope of this increase well exceeds even that for generic supplemental submissions (Figure 3.7(c)). These data provide support for the conclusion that the Canadian domestic pharmaceutical industry is 'doing more with less.' Brand-name firms in particular appear to be expanding the market exclusivity duration of existing products, though firms obviously need to get on the market with at least one new compound in a given chemical class prior to expansion via SNDS. Together with data showing a decline in all types of new or standard submissions by brand-name firms (Figures 3.4(c), 3.6(a), 3.8(a), and 3.8)) and an increase in other types of supplementary submissions assessed (Figures 3.5(c), 3.8(c), and 3.8(d)), the results suggest that (1) the Canadian pharmaceutical industry, as a whole, is expending fewer of its resources on developing novel 'first-of-kind' technologies and more on leveraging existing technologies and (2) that technology appropriation is alive and well in Canada.[56]

3.6 Study limitations

3.6.1 Empirical considerations

The study is limited by the restrictions typical of empirical studies. First, data analyzed were only those for the test period. The year 2001 was chosen as our starting point, as this was the date when substantial amendments to Canadian drug regulation were made that affected both the mechanisms and speed of approval.[57] Second, there is significant scatter of the data from one year to the next which impeded a more strongly powered analysis. For example, we not only obtained yearly means as reported in Figures 3.1–3.10, but also calculated quarterly bins for each year in order to improve the statistical power in linear and non-linear analyses. However, we could not use this data owing to a small trend towards quarterly differences in the data set, e.g. there was a trend towards more approvals granted in the third and fourth quarters of each year. However, this trend did not reach statistical significance, necessitating the use of yearly averages. As a consequence, both sample sizes and statistical power were reduced. Finally, while we developed a novel method by which to obtain and analyze approval data independently rather than using GOC or PMPRB Annual Reports, we were nevertheless limited to the results publicly disclosed by Health Canada.[58] Equally important, our analysis was dependent on Health Canada's method of determining the definition of an NAS, which in turn substantially influenced the methods used to calculate the number of first-in-class and me-too drugs. This is discussed in more detail below.

3.6.2 Me-too and first-in-class criteria

The compound-indication method summarized in Table 3.2 yields a fraction of me-too and first-in-class drugs that may differ from methods used by other agencies. For example, the WHO Collaborating Center for Drugs Statistics Methodology[59] produces a different result as to what NOCs would have been classified as first-in-class or me-too, yielding more me-too than first-in-class NOCs. The reason for this discrepancy is that under the WHO methodology, compounds that are in the same chemical family as the original first-in-class drug are all deemed to be me-too drugs irrespective of whether they are directed to new indications. Table 3.5 illustrates this concept.

However, the methods used to obtain the data in Table 3.5 differ from those used by Health Canada to classify NOCs, particularly in the SNDS category. The Health Canada methodology focuses not on chemical class but rather on both chemical class and indications. Nevertheless, assuming for the moment that the WHO classification is the right one for the purposes of this discussion, using it to analyze our data would have the effect of converting a certain number of supplemental first-in-class SNDS NOCs to new me-too NDS NOCs. While this might appear on the surface

Table 3.5 WHO compound-indication classification

Year	Compound/indication	Classification
2000	Compound X (first 'X' Compound) with Indication A	First-in-class
2001	Compound X with Indication B	Me-too
2001	Compound *a*X (Compound in the family of X) with Indication A	Me-too
2001	Compound *a*X with Indication B	Me-too
2001	Compound *a*X with Indication C	Me-too

to shift the emphasis from 'supplemental' to 'new' submission approvals, both me-too NDS and first-in-class SNDS NOCs are directed to products that are extensions of existing technologies, largely via new use indications, as opposed to first-of-kind technologies. Therefore using the WHO framework would not alter our major observations and conclusions, including (1) that the pharmaceutical industry as a whole is doing more with less and (2) that an increasing number of drugs are being approved with significant post-marketing obligations over the test period, while NOCs in other expedited streams (e.g. Priority Review) have remained relatively constant or decreased slightly over the same time frame.

3.6.3 Innovative value of me-too and line extensions

We did not undertake a study of, nor are we offering a model for, innovation in the domestic Canadian pharmaceutical marketplace. Therefore we provide definitions for neither 'innovation' nor what constitutes an 'innovative' therapeutic product. Rather, the point of the present study was to independently analyze several years of drug *approval* data, and to analyze the data from the perspective of the policies underpinning the emerging PLF regime. These include policies pertaining to safety and efficacy, expedited review (NOC/c and Priority Review), IPR rights, user fees, precautionary principle, etc.[60] Our concern, within the four corners of the present study, was whether NOCs were directed to (1) 'new' active substances, 'new' drug submissions, 'first-in-class' drugs, 'priority' review drugs, and drugs approved via the NOC/c stream or to (2) 'me-too' drugs, 'line extension' drugs, 'abbreviated' generic submissions, and other 'supplemental' submissions. We are mindful of the controversial nature of the debate surrounding the economic and therapeutic value of me-too and line extension drug products in Canada,[61] France,[62] the US,[63] the EU,[64] and the UK,[65] as well as recent reports on the need to facilitate innovation[66] and generic competition[67] in the context of shifting drug approval and associated IPR rights regimes. We are also mindful of the tendency of certain technological and regulatory systems to experience 'lock-in'[68] as a result of increasing returns,[69] and that the data described in this study may be a potential example of one or both of these processes. The relevance of the data to the issue of innovation in the pharmaceutical sector is the subject of data described in Chapter 4 on the empirical relationship between patterns of drug approval, patenting, and litigation. Finally, given that Canada and the US are the first two jurisdictions with established linkage regulations tying drug approval and drug patenting,[70] we have narrowed the interpretation of our empirical data and the associated literature review[71] to primarily the North American context governed by emerging lifecycle regulation models with additional comments regarding global regulation where necessary.

3.7 Assessing the lifecycle approach: the long view

In an earlier work by our group,[72] a number of concerns are reviewed that, when combined, have provided the impetus for substantial law reform in the area of drug regulation. These include considerations relating to the speed and mechanism of approval, the relation of the former to fee-for-service user fees, the relation of the latter to a shift from the precautionary principle to risk management principles, and an increase in the public-private partnership characteristic of the approval process, including government vetting of increasing IPR rights associated with pharmaceutical products. The possibility exists that these issues have combined to result in more drug withdrawals, black box warnings, and dosage form discontinuations for safety reasons, and a significant expansion and acceleration of mortality and morbidity associated with high-profile drug withdrawals. The lifecycle approach has been criticized as only worsening many of these problems. This is particularly true of the focus on access at the cost of post-market safety and prolonged market monopolies on line extension and me-too drugs. The results in this chapter do little to ameliorate many of these concerns, as the data indicate the GOC is already anticipating PLF in its current regulatory efforts and that pharmaceutical firms are increasing their focus on extending the lifecycle of existing products and technologies rather than inventing new breakthrough products.

We have referred to the rTPL innovation ecology here and elsewhere as an example of a dynamic, emergent, complex adaptive system. What makes a system complex as opposed to merely complicated is the strong nature of the interrelationships and interdependencies of the actors and institutions making up a system or network. In the manner of a spider web, tweaking one strand affects all other strands in the web. As noted by Gell-Mann,[73] complex systems are characterized by broad rules that have increasing applicability and universality as the symmetry and elegance of the rules increase. We believe this applies to innovation ecologies regulated by law,[74] particularly where large-scale public and private rights must be balanced. In order to assess the legitimacy of PLF as a regulatory tool in the service of a highly complex and adaptive pharmaceutical, clinical, economic, and political system, one must therefore look to both sides of the access-safety equation to see what value PLF has for so-called adaptive[75] or robust[76] policy-making. Too narrow a focus on access or post-licensing obligations can only lead to a viewpoint that will miss critical information that arises outside of its bandwidth. PLF is expressly intended to replace static, linear, one-sided, front-loaded, and time-locked models of drug development and regulation. Its legitimacy should be assessed that way, hence the need for the 'long view.'

On one side of a shifted evidentiary balance, a lower threshold for initial market authorization will almost certainly equate to faster access to new drugs. The obvious danger of this is that potentially dangerous drugs may slip through the regulatory cracks, compromising patient safety.[77] Scholars, politicians, public interest groups, and media have argued that recasting the decision-making matrix for safety and efficacy in this manner will turn the public into guinea pigs for drugs that have not been adequately tested.[78] This position has been taken by Wright,[79] who claims that 'regardless of the safeguards that are put in place, reducing the safety evidence required before new drugs are approved will make it very difficult to monitor and catch problems before it's too late.' Indeed, there is significant evidence to suggest that post-market studies that have been recommended by regulators thus far are not usually conducted by sponsors once approval has been given.[80] If this scenario were to continue, it is not difficult to envision how the lifecycle approach would create an 'evidence-free zone' for drug approval.[81] In the absence of reciprocal balancing by post-market surveillance, criticisms of this nature are well grounded in light of poor decisions by pharmaceutical firms to design, cover up, or otherwise report clinical trial data selectively.[82]

Another significant question relating to PLF is the issue of flexible departure, concerns over which go well beyond the issue of faster approval times. These concerns flow from the fact that, under the terms of the proposed PLF regime, evidence of safety and efficacy in the context of flexible departure would be limited to reports of the most commonly occurring adverse drug reactions,[83] presumably overlaid by the broader requirement for an 'evidence-based' benefit-risk profile numerically favorable to the drug.[84] Particular attention has been directed to the possibility that the standard for flexible departure under Bill C-51 (≥51% evidence of benefit-risk)[85] will lead to an industry-focused benefit-risk assessment framework.[86] Indeed, the issue of a shifted evidentiary framework has attracted consistent attention from commentators since the GOC held its stakeholder workshops in 2006–2007, crystallizing with the announcement of Bill C-51 on April 8, 2008. Similar concerns have been expressed over provisions for accelerated[87] and conditional[88] approval in the US and EU.[89] Despite these criticisms, however, it is reasonable to speculate, based on policy documents published by Health Canada, the US Institute of Medicine (IOM), the European Medicines Agency (EMEA), and the FDA that the precautionary principle will not be replaced at the locus of the decision-making process in emerging lifecycle models. The 'semi-quantitative' decision-making matrix elaborated by the EMEA[90] in particular suggests that both objective and subjective metrics will be used as part of the benefit-risk analysis. This implies that a moderate articulation of the precautionary principle will be subsumed within benefit-risk calculations.[91]

Having said this, it remains true that an explicit ≥51% benefit-risk standard differs significantly from a soft or normative evidentiary standard of 85%, 75%, or even 65%. Indeed, one of the major implications of emphasizing faster access to innovative drugs is that enhanced access necessarily brings with it risks beyond those already present under the constraints of the existing clinical trial platform.[92] This is particularly true for drugs subject to early release to the public via flexible departure. Nevertheless, while drug agencies in Canada,[93] the US,[94] and the EU[95] have said that the risks of drug development must be shouldered by those that demand new and untested drugs, public opinion polls have clearly demonstrated that post-market safety should *not* be sacrificed for quick access to drugs. For example, in 2002, about the time that several high-profile safety withdrawals were coming to light and well before the GOC's major policy articulations supporting PLF,[96] an exemplary study showed that two-thirds of the respondents indicated a preference to wait for 'thorough safety testing' of new drugs, with two-fifths of the public stating that getting drugs approved 'as fast as possible' is the 'least important principle of the drug approval process ...'[97] Regulators moving to embrace emerging lifecycle models would thus do well to heed the growing body of empirical studies on complex public health systems. Results from these investigations imply that in the absence of recognition of the dynamic nature of positive and negative feedback loops within the regulatory process, drug regulation has the potential to tilt precariously: first into subtle forms of policy resistance,[98] then into more obvious forms of policy failure,[99] and, potentially, into system collapse.[100] Given the persistence of serious, high-profile post-marketing safety controversies in the last decade, it could be speculated that the latter of these mechanisms presents the strongest stimulus for regulatory reform.

While the existing drug approval regime has raised many concerns over real or perceived conflicts of interest, it cannot be overlooked that the GOC's PLF lifecycle initiative, as well as parallel initiatives by the FDA and EMEA, is specifically intended to rectify some of these ills. Public perception of the intent behind these initiatives has not been helped by the previous 'black box' nature of drug approval,[101] which is one of the dragons these agencies claim they want to slay with the lifecycle approach.[102] As already noted, in various discussion and policy guidance documents, the GOC, the FDA, and the EMEA all appear to be explicitly grappling with the inherent uncertainties, risks, and complexities of drug development. It is an obvious truism that this is not an easy path to walk and, as recognized by the major drug agencies in the US[103] and Canada,[104] it will take active cooperation from the full range of public and private actors responsible for drug development, regulation, and consumption to make it work. As such, it is becoming increasingly accepted that the complexity, uncertainty, and risks of an rTPL innovation ecology in the medical sciences go hand in hand. They must be understood that way if we are to take the lessons learned from centuries of 'linear' mental models and apply them to our growing understanding of complex 'systems' models[105] such as PLF which attempt to account for risk and uncertainty while also providing regulatory order. There will be those who resist this evolution, but their numbers will eventually be whittled away as empirical data challenge the simplistic assumptions underpinning the majority of linear models.[106]

In addition to offering a more realistic understanding of the risks and uncertainties involved in an rTPL ecology, there are other factors that render the lifecycle approach more advantageous than the existing regime. First, data on the correlation between user fee implementation and safety withdrawals are equivocal, even though data relating to the speed of review are not.[107] While some studies show a positive correlation, several detailed and statistically powered studies demonstrate a convincing lack of change in the pattern of withdrawals before and after user fees were implemented. Despite these differences, there appears to be significant acceleration in the incidence of serious adverse effects associated with withdrawals when they do happen, potentially due to the speed and breadth of market penetration and physician prescribing practices. Therefore, it would be desirable to have more studies on this issue in order to design a truly effective and efficacious lifecycle-based regulatory scheme. Moreover, as suggested by Carpenter et al.[108] and Olson,[109] even where it has been empirically demonstrated, an increase in post-user fee withdrawal rates may be due to the effects of reviewers working toward mandated deadlines rather than shorter review times per se. As noted by the authors, this situation could be rectified, at least in part, by devoting more resources toward staffing, including funds appropriated from parent public health agencies rather than via industry user fees.[110] Others have suggested curtailing direct-to-consumer advertising as a reasonable means to reduce accelerated market penetration and thus acceleration of the rate of adverse effects incidence.[111] As increasingly recognized by stakeholders in public debates and government-sponsored stakeholder workshops, it will be critical to educate the public as to the realities of information asymmetry and the principles of informed consent when requests are made for experimental therapies.

There is also the role of the physician-patient nexus to consider. Indeed, complexity theory posits that each actor is just as important as the next in producing positive, negative, and unintended outcomes in a complex system.[112] Even after the severity of recent drug-withdrawal and conflict-of-interest controversies, society continues to be recalcitrant to lay blame on physicians. Along these lines, individual members of the public can no longer claim to be passive receptacles of drugs they assume are safe and efficacious. Each actor in the rTPL ecology must accept accountability for their role in the failure of the linear model of drug innovation. The necessity of distributing accountability to include not just obvious targets such as drug companies and government, but also physicians and the public, was recognized by the IOM in its influential report on drug regulation.[113] Narrowing clinical trial populations to hit desired safety or efficacy signals for market authorization differs from the scope of drug-prescribing practices by physicians. Both types of practices have different sets of motivations and incentives.[114] Physicians, if they are to play a positive rather than a negative role in moving PLF forward, must be more cognizant and prudent in their prescribing habits regardless of demands on their time. One prospective outcome of the principle of unintended consequences is that even one physician prescribing a drug off-label,[115] no matter what his motives (selfish or altruistic), can contribute to a non-linear avalanche of similar prescribing practices.[116] Positive feedback loops such as those initiated by pharmaceutical advertising or patient advocacy groups may serve to speed this process exponentially. Support for this assumption comes from the apparent acceleration of mortality and morbidity associated with recent high-profile drug withdrawals as well as the speed of drug agency withdrawals in response to this trend.[117] The FDA's rebuke[118] to 'think it through' when managing benefits and risks applies equally well to patients and physicians. The relevance of this approach is underscored by the multiple layers of unknowns in the so-called 'real-world' use of drugs,[119] which, once understood, should countenance caution rather than innovation in prescribing and consuming practices.

It will of course be left to government as elected representatives to balance the range of competing public and private interests in the commercialization and regulation of publicly funded medical research. Purposive legal-regulatory balancing is new neither to legal nor political communities, as is evident in the rich interplay between IPR rights and competition law as well as rights balancing in human rights and administrative and constitutional law.[120] This body of jurisprudence suggests that the goals of society and those of individuals can be appropriately prioritized and balanced and that it is the role of law to do so. Interestingly, there is some evidence to suggest that the withdrawal rate due to post-marketing safety considerations is declining along with reductions in approvals involving new active substances, even though the breadth of this submission classification in terms of chemical structure and indication is very wide. If borne out by further empirical research, these data suggest that as pharmaceutical firms increase their benefit-risk ratio and reduce the costs of developing therapeutic products, the benefit-risk profile and social costs of public drug consumption will change correspondingly.

3.8 Government as representative public agent

The most important actor in the rTPL innovation ecology is the government as the elected agent of the public. Balancing layer upon layer of public and private interests in the GOC's proposed lifecycle model therefore requires strong, if not aggressive, government leadership in punishing breaches of post-market licence terms and conditions. Drug agencies, however, are not neutral actors. Rather, they are political actors that demonstrate their preferences through relevant networks of laws and regulations.[121] Of concern in this regard is the fact that the PLF framework enshrined in Bill C-51 contains a highly flexible multi-stage, multi-threshold process for the suspension and revocation of clinical trial and market authorizations.[122] Such flexibility, combined with wide discretionary powers,[123] provides the legal grounds for the GOC to take either a strong or lax approach to industry post-market compliance, notwithstanding new provisions directed to enforcement.[124] As discussed previously,[125] the question is an open one as to which position the GOC will take.

It is not surprising that pharmaceutical firms, being self-interested actors, have complied poorly or not at all with their post-market obligations.[126] Despite claims that much of this has to do with a lack of jurisdiction by relevant drug agencies,[127] there is no question that these same agencies and pharmaceutical firms have pushed hard to locate common ground in their respective innovation and drug approval mandates. It is imperative, however, that governments maintain an arm's length relationship with industry if they are to embrace the regulatory norms of increased transparency and post-market safety[128] and to avoid charges of bias and unfairness in the discharge of their public health mandates. This will be hampered to the extent that (1) there is tension in the function of these agencies to stimulate the economy and protect the public, and (2) when public health agencies do focus on the latter they are pushed by other governmental agencies and departments to focus on the former. Indeed, as noted by us[129] and others,[130] it is not just the Therapeutic Products Directorate (TPD) or the Health Products and Food Branch (HPFB) or even Health Canada that is fully responsible for drug regulation and approval. Since the repeal of compulsory licensing in favor of the current linkage regulation regime in 1993,[131] the public health mandate of the GOC relating to drug regulation has become increasingly bifurcated. For example, while Health Canada administers the Food and Drugs Act and Regulations, Industry Canada is responsible for administering both the Patent Act[132] and the NOC Regulations,[133] which link drug approval to drug patenting.[134] Further, the Privy Council is responsible for setting the tone for domestic regulation/deregulation and the increasing scope of regulatory harmony with food and drug agencies in other jurisdictions. A parallel situation exists in the US with the Hatch-Waxman[135] linkage regime tying patent protection under the US Patent Act[136] to drug approval under the Food, Drug, and Cosmetic Act[137] via patent listings in the Orange Book.[138]

One need not even focus on interagency conflict, as this tension is very much alive and well within drug agencies themselves. As noted by Psaty[139] and Weiss Smith,[140] the basic criterion for drug approval is that its benefits outweigh its risks, yet the FDA apparently views its 'dilemma' (even after the IOM Report was issued) as weighing the trade-off between access and safety.[141] A similar situation exists in the EU[142] and Canada.[143] How this trade-off is parsed is now recognized to permeate all aspects of the regulatory decision-making process,[144] with particular consequences for the assessment of both the benefits and risks of new drugs[145] under circumstances where vital information is provided only by pharmaceutical sponsors. This tension has produced a clear push-pull dynamic concerning the traditional gatekeeping role of elected government in public health and its now established responsibility to enhance national productivity and prosperity via innovative medical research.[146] Governments fulfill this obligation in part through policies favoring strong IPR rights for marketed products, despite ample evidence that stacking IPR rights is not the path to greater therapeutic product development.[147]

Here and elsewhere we have provided theoretical[148] and empirical qualitative[149] and quantitative[150] evidence to suggest that too much of a focus on closed IPR rights may stifle innovation in an open rTPL ecology. Emphasis on private IPR rights in a public health context leads naturally to questions relating to the efficiency and effectiveness of innovation from a truly societal perspective,[151] owing not least to the possibility that consumers are paying monopoly prices for drugs that may offer little or no improvement over existing therapeutic products.[152] Related to this concern is the possibility that core public values underpinning public healthcare, IPR rights seen to drive national innovation, and public lobbying efforts in support of enhanced access to novel drugs may be quietly, but importantly, evolving over time away from communitarian interests. The result is that traditional conflict of interest models may now be in the direct firing line of sophisticated corporate strategists and lobbying groups. A shift in societal values of this nature may be related to the apparently growing emphasis in developed nations on legal rights protecting personal autonomy and individual choice over those rights emphasizing government fiduciary obligations and other collective rights, a trend that may have co-evolved with the importance of the individual over the collective in everyday life more generally.[153]

A shift in public values of this nature may be reflected in the apparently **autopoietic** standardization of government-industry partnerships over time.[154] Geographic differences in the norms of these partnerships in the context of drug regulation have been described.[155] Under this view, Canada is claimed to be a 'middle-way' jurisdiction, between the US and France, where substantial partnerships and co-dependencies exist side by side with some arm's length adversarialism between the GOC and industry. Canadian policy development relating to drug development and drug regulation has been described as a form of clientele pluralism,[156] where a narrow economic interest (e.g. multinational pharmaceutical) strongly informs governmental policy-making in order to 'preserve and protect the structural basis of that interest.' There is little doubt that, based on a review of the *Blueprint*,[157] Concept Paper,[158] and Bill C-51,[159] and related disclosures by the GOC,[160] clientele pluralism has strongly informed both the policy and legislation underpinning the nation's lifecycle approach to drug regulation. Enhanced regulatory partnering predictably raises the spectre of regulatory (or mission) creep.[161] Indeed, this scenario has been consistently acknowledged by drug agencies themselves[162] and is viewed by many to tilt the balance of power toward corporations and away from the public interest.[163] Global harmonization efforts favoring standardization of drug approval may thus trigger a further downward spiral in standard-setting.[164] This trend may, ironically, be enhanced rather than mitigated by a novel and untested regulatory mechanism.[165]

Gaps between regulatory science and the science of regulation represent a vital issue for emerging lifecycle models of drug regulation. This is particularly true of the Canadian PLF regime, given the scope of concerns expressed over flexible departure and the substantial degree of discretionary power retained by the GOC in relation to the suspension and revocation of clinical trials and marketing authorizations. Consequently, and for the purposes of maintaining a robust distributive balance of public and private interests in therapeutic drug development and regulation, drug agency leadership will somehow need to retain the political and normative power to 'step away' from their industrial partners in order to enforce fundamental legal powers relating to post-market safety. These powers include revoking expedited or otherwise probationary market authorizations where it is in the public's best interests rather than the best interests of relevant government-industry partnerships.

3.9 Summary and conclusions

The data in this chapter suggest that concerns to the effect that lifecycle-based regulation represents a new direction with regard to Canada's drug regulatory regime may be somewhat overstated. Indeed, our empirical analysis shows that the nation's existing approval mechanism may already be anticipating the lifecycle approach and that this anticipation is occurring in an accelerated fashion. For this reason, we propose that flexible departure does not represent a new direction in Canadian drug regulation. Patients are already gaining more rapid access to experimental drugs that have a critical need for significant evidence of safety (and potentially efficacy) after the drug has entered the marketplace. Indeed, between 2006 and 2008, 5–7% of all NOCs issued by Health Canada to brand-name pharmaceutical firms met this requirement. Remarkably, the trend for Priority Review and NOC/c approvals has completely reversed in the last seven years, with

NOC/c approvals now almost double that of Priority Review. To date, none of the drugs approved via these streams has been withdrawn for post-market safety reasons. Given that the available evidence suggests that very few of the post-marketing obligations recommended by regulators are actually met by pharmaceutical firms in other jurisdictions, it would appear that one side of the access-safety balance may be receiving more attention than the other from regulators. It is hoped that this gap, and the attendant ability of drug agencies to enforce post-market terms and conditions, will be remedied by the provisions of Bill C-51 (or future related legislation). In this regard, it is imperative that the GOC demonstrates strong and sustained leadership in suspending or revoking clinical trial and market authorizations where firms do not meet their obligations. This would be particularly relevant under conditions where drugs gain early market access via flexible departure. If not, it is plausible that a leftward shift in the access-safety balance will lead to more rather than less post-market safety issues. Strong leadership will also be vital where the incidence of serious adverse effects escalates in a non-linear or otherwise strongly time-dependent manner.

The data further suggest that the Canadian system of pharmaceutical innovation may be 'doing more with less.' This conclusion applies equally to the rate and direction of innovative activity undertaken by brand-name and generic firms. New or standard drug submissions have been flat while supplementary and generic submissions have increased substantially. Even NOCs for NAS and me-too drugs declined when compared to NOCs directed to line extensions and new indications. Data presented in Figures 3.1–3.10 imply that the Canadian pharmaceutical industry, as a whole, is focusing on prolonging market share and leveraging the utility of existing technologies rather than on the development of first-in-kind breakthrough products. As such, the data support the conclusion that technology appropriation is alive and well in Canada. An incremental approach to drug development of this nature is supported by innovation theory, which suggests that firms will only innovate in an area to the extent they capture all or most of the surplus from incentives they generate.[166] Even so, too much of a focus on incremental innovation propped up by entrenched IPR rights has the potential to downplay or minimize important discourse(s) relating to the social returns from innovation.[167]

Firms are obtaining increasingly more supplementary NOCs, more IPR rights per marketed product, and more control over pre-approval and post-approval processes with fewer pre-market evidentiary requirements, and thus lower costs of drug development; however, it is not only the pharmaceutical industry that may be doing more with less. The public is clearly gaining more rapid access to experimental drugs aimed at addressing presumed unmet medical needs. In balancing this benefit the public is also being asked to shoulder more risk with less evidence of pre-market safety and efficacy in the context of flexible departure. Moreover, individuals are being exposed to fewer truly breakthrough drugs while paying more for those whose market value is being propped up by strong IPR rights, although this is offset somewhat by the concomitant increase in the availability of generic products. Whether the public will have more post-market protection on the other side of the balance is an open question, as it cannot be predicted what style of leadership the GOC will bring to bear on the issue.

Finally, regulators are experiencing perhaps the greatest challenges to both limbs of the access-safety balance. Indeed, owing to uncertainties regarding post-market compliance and enforcement, it is not clear at this point whether governments will gain more clarity from less focus on the pre-market approval process and more on the post-marketing stage. Certainly, the speed of the approval process has increased owing to user fee implementation, enhanced regulatory harmony with other jurisdictions, and increased cooperation with firms. Unclear, however, is whether or not drug regulators will ultimately have a better overall drug safety record as they attempt to recalibrate tolerance of risk and uncertainty at pre-market and post-market approval stages. It is hoped that when implementing the lifecycle approach, public health agencies fully embrace the complexity and systems nature of the rTPL innovation ecology in which drug regulation is embedded.

Taking an adaptive, learning-based approach to drug regulation has a number of advantages over historical linear models of drug development and regulation. First, it allows regulators to accept that there is no such thing as an 'optimal' front-loaded policy. Second, it will help broaden agency capacity bandwidth, in turn allowing regulators to adopt a paternalistic, partnership, or adversarial stance in its bargaining scenarios as necessary and sufficient. This should allow a regulatory culture to grow organically in response to complex environmental signals and therefore to help avoid the pitfalls of the existing front-loaded regime. Finally, taking an approach that is both adaptive and distributive in nature may afford government an excellent opportunity to react swiftly in response to dynamically changing post-marketing safety signals in a manner that is in the best interests of the public rather than those of government-industry partnerships.

Notes

1. Ron A. Bouchard and Monika Sawicka, 'The Mud and the Blood and the Beer: Canada's New Progressive Licensing Framework for Drug Approval,' 3 *McGill J. of L. & Health* (2009) [Bouchard and Sawicka (2009)].
2. Food and Drugs Act, RSC 1985, c. F-27 [Food and Drugs Act].
3. Food and Drug Regulations, CRC, c. 870 [Food and Drug Regulations].
4. Bill C-51, An Act to amend the Food and Drugs Act and to make consequential amendments to other Acts, 2nd Sess., 39th Parl., 2008 [Bill C-51].
5. Robert Peterson, *Innovation in Drug Regulation: Canada as a Leader* (Lecture delivered at the Ottawa Regional Conference: 'Building Excellence in Clinical Research and Clinical Trials,' February 11, 2005) [Peterson, *Innovation* (2005)].
6. Paul C. Hébert, 'Progressive Licensing Needs Progressive Open Debate,' 176 *Canadian Medical Association Journal* 1801 [Hébert (2007)]; James M. Wright, 'Progressive Drug Licensing: An Opportunity to Achieve Transparency and Accountability?' 176 *Canadian Medical Association Journal* 1848 (2007). See also Hans-Georg Eichler et al., 'Balancing Early Market Access to New Drugs with the Need for Benefit/Risk Data: A Mounting Dilemma,' 7 *Nature Reviews Drug Discovery* 818 (2008) [Eichler et al. (2008)], citing Sir David Cooksey, *A Review of UK Health Research Funding* (HMSO, 2006); Ismail Kola and John Landis, 'Can the Pharmaceutical Industry Reduce Attrition Rates?' 3 *Nature Reviews Drug Discovery* 711 (2004).
7. Carly Weeks, 'New Drug Rules Pose Grave Risks: Critics,' *Globe and Mail* (February 8, 2008) [Weeks, 'Critics' (2008)], at L6.
8. See, generally, US Institute of Medicine: Committee on the Assessment of the US Drug Safety System, *The Future of Drug Safety: Promoting and Protecting the Health of the Public* (National Academies Press, 2007), online: Institute of Medicine of the National Academies <http://www.iom.edu/CMS/3793/26341/37329.aspx> [IOM Report (2007)]. See also US Government Accountability Office, *Drug Safety: Improvement Needed in FDA's Postmarket Decision-making and Oversight Process* (Government Accountability Office, 2006); Jerry Avorn, 'Paying for Drug Approvals – Who's Using Whom?' 356 *New Eng. J. Med.* 1697 (2007); Bruce M. Psaty and Sheila P. Burke, 'Protecting the Health of the Public – Institute of Medicine Recommendations on Drug Safety,' 355 *New Eng. J. Med.* 1753 (2006) [Psaty and Burke (2006)], at 1754; Bruce M. Psaty and R. Alta Charo, 'FDA Responds to Institute of Medicine Drug Safety Recommendations – In Part,' 297 *Journal of the American Medical Association* 1917 (2007) [Psaty and Charo (2007)], at 1917; Tufts Center for the Study of Drug Development, *FDA Requested Postmarketing Studies in 73% of Recent New Drug Approvals* 6:4 Impact Report 1 (2004); US Food and Drug Administration, Report on the Performance of Drug and Biologics Firms in Conducting Postmarketing Commitment Studies,' 70 *Federal Register* 8379 (2005); US Food and Drug Administration, 'Report on the Performance of Drug and

Biologics Firms in Conducting Postmarketing Commitment Studies,' 71 *Federal Register* 10978 (2006); US Food and Drug Administration, 'Report on the Performance of Drug and Biologics Firms in Conducting Postmarketing Commitment Studies,' 72 *Federal Register* 5069 (2007).

9. Craig J. Whittington et al., 'Selective Serotonin Reuptake Inhibitors in Childhood Depression: Systematic Review of Published versus Unpublished Data,' 363 *Lancet* 1341 (2004); Jeffrey R. Lisse et al., 'Gastrointestinal Tolerability and Effectiveness of Rofecoxib versus Naproxen in the Treatment of Osteoarthritis: A Randomized, Controlled Trial,' 139 *Annals of Internal Medicine* 539 (2003); Gregory D. Curfman, Stephen Morrissey, and Jeffrey M. Drazen, 'Expression of Concern: Bombardier et al., "Comparison of Upper Gastrointestinal Toxicity of Rofecoxib and Naproxen in Patients with Rheumatoid Arthritis,"' 343 *New Eng. J. Med.* 1520 (2005); Gregory D. Curfman, Stephen Morrissey, and Jeffrey M. Drazen, 'Expression of Concern Reaffirmed,' 354 *New Eng. J. Med.* 1193 (2006); Bruce M. Psaty et al., 'Potential for Conflict of Interest in the Evaluation of Suspected Adverse Drug Reactions: Use of Cerivastatin and Risk of Rhabdomyolysis,' 292 *Journal of the American Medical Association* 2622 (2004); Bruce M. Psaty and Curt D. Furberg, 'COX-2 Inhibitors: Lessons in Drug Safety,' 352 *New Eng. J. Med.* 1133 (2005); Bruce M. Psaty and Noel S. Weiss, 'NSAID Trials and the Choice of Comparators: Questions of Public Health Importance,' 356 *New Eng. J. Med.* 328 (2007); Bruce M. Psaty, Noel S. Weiss, and Curt D. Furberg, 'Recent Trials in Hypertension: Compelling Science or Commercial Speech?' 295 *Journal of the American Medical Association* 1704 (2006).

10. Sheila Weiss Smith, 'Reply to Galson,' 357 *New Eng. J. Med.* 2521 (2007) [Weiss Smith, 'Reply to Galson' (2007)]. (Weiss elaborates on this approach (at 2521), stating that drug-approval decisions are based on a relatively narrow 'evidence-based' interpretation of benefit-risk:

> Benefits are defined according to the intended effect and intended population, as proposed by the sponsor. These factors are measured in efficacy studies performed in a modest number of carefully selected patients, who may or may not reflect the characteristics of the broader population likely to receive the drug. Furthermore, benefits may be extrapolated from surrogate markers ... [and] [t]he approval question becomes 'are there persons for whom the potential benefits could outweigh the known risks?' This standard is reasonable in limited circumstances, particularly for drugs for imminently fatal conditions ... otherwise, such a narrow interpretation of risks and benefits, which tends to favor industry over public health, has resulted in many of the FDA's most prominent failures.

See also Sheila Weiss Smith, 'Sidelining Safety – The FDA's Inadequate Response to the IOM,' 357 *New Eng. J. Med.* 960 (2007) [Weiss Smith, 'Sidelining' (2007)]; Steven K. Galson, 'The FDA and the IOM Report, Note to Editor,' 357 *New Eng. J. Med.* 2520 (2007).

11. US Food and Drug Administration, *Fast Track, Accelerated Approval and Priority Review: Accelerating Availability of New Drugs for Patients with Serious Diseases* (May 2006), online: US Department of Health and Human Services <http://www.fda.gov/ForConsumers/ByAudience/ForPatientAdvocates/SpeedingAccesstoImportantNewTherapies/ucm128291.htm> [FDA, *Fast Track*].
12. European Medicines Agency (EMEA): Committee for Medicinal Products for Human Use (CHMP), *Guideline on the Scientific Application and the Practical Arrangements Necessary to Implement Commission Regulation (EC) No. 507/2006 on the Conditional Marketing Authorisation for Medicinal Products for Human Use Falling Within the Scope of Regulation (EC) No. 726/2004* (EMEA, 2006) online: EMEA <http://www.emea.europa.eu/pdfs/human/regaffair/50995106en.pdf> [EMEA CHMP, *Guideline*].
13. Working definitions are provided in Section I.B for 'first-in-class,' 'me-too,' 'line extension,' and 'new active substance.'
14. For discussion of innovation ecology in the basic and medical sciences, see William A. Wulf, 'Changes in Innovation Ecology,' 316 *Science* 1253 (2007) [Wulf (2007)]; Ron A. Bouchard, '*KSR* v. *Teleflex* Part 2: Impact of U.S. Supreme Court Patent Law on Canadian and Global Systems-Based Innovation Ecologies,' 15 *Health L.J.* 247 (2008) [Bouchard, 'Systems' (2008)]; Ron A. Bouchard, 'Reflections on the Value of Systems Models for Regulation of Medical Research and Product Development,' 17 *Health L. Rev.* 28 (2008) [Bouchard, 'Reflections' (2008)].
15. Health Canada, *Drugs and Health Products – Notice of Compliance Listings*, online: Health Canada <http://www.hc-sc.gc.ca/dhp-mps/prodpharma/notices-avis/list/index-eng.php>.
16. Health Canada, *Biologics, Radiopharmaceuticals and Genetic Therapies*, online: Health Canada <http://www.hc-sc.gc.ca/dhp-mps/brgtherap/index-eng.php>.
17. Eileen McMahon and Teresa A. Reguly, 'Canada: Follow-on Biologics in Canada,' 3 *Update* 43 (2008) at 43, online: Mondaq: Pharmaceutical, Healthcare & Life Sciences <http://www.mondaq.com/article.asp?articleid=61359>.
18. Food and Drugs Act, *supra* note 2, at Sch. D.
19. For a listing of non-prescription pharmaceuticals given a Notice of Compliance from 1991 to the present date see Health Canada, *Drugs and Health Products – Notice of Compliance Listings*, online: Health Canada <http://www.hc-sc.gc.ca/dhp-mps/prodpharma/notices-avis/list/index-eng.php#2008>.
20. For a comprehensive description of natural health products see Health Canada, *Drugs and Health Products – Natural Health Products*, online: <http://www.hc-sc.gc.ca/dhp-mps/prodnatur/index-eng.php>.
21. For a detailed discussion of expedited review pathways in Canada, see Bouchard and Sawicka (2009), *supra* note 1, at Section I.B.

22. Health Canada, *Guidance for Industry: Priority Review of Drug Submissions*, online: Health Canada <http://www.hc-sc.gc.ca/dhp-mps/alt_formats/hpfb-dgpsa/pdf/prodpharma/priordr-eng.pdf> [Health Canada Priority Review Guidance Document].
23. Ibid., at 1–2.
24. Trudo Lemmens and Ron A. Bouchard, 'Regulation of Pharmaceuticals in Canada,' in Jocelyn Downie, Timothy Caulfield, and Colleen Flood (eds), *Canadian Health Law and Policy*, 3rd edn (LexisNexis, 2007) 311 [Lemmens and Bouchard (2007)], at 328; Health Canada Priority Review Guidance Document, *supra* note 22.
25. NOC/c is granted pursuant to s. C.08.004(1), in compliance with the conditions of use stipulated in s. C.08.002(1)(g), C.08.002(1)(h), C.08.006(2)(b), and C.05.006(2)(a).
26. Health Canada, *Guidance for Industry: Notice of Compliance with conditions* (Public Works and Government Services Canada, 2007), online: Health Canada <http://www.hc-sc.gc.ca/dhp-mps/alt_formats/hpfb-dgpsa/pdf/prodpharma/noccg_accd-eng.pdf>. A candidate for NOC/c must have the potential to provide an effective treatment, prevention, or diagnosis of a disease or condition for which no drug is presently marketed in Canada or a significant increase in efficacy and/or significant decrease in risk such that the overall benefit/risk profile is improved over existing therapies, preventative or diagnostic agents for a disease, or condition that is not adequately managed by a drug marketed in Canada.
27. Health Canada, *Access to Therapeutic Products: The Regulatory Process in Canada – Target Review Times*, online: Health Canada <http://www.hc-sc.gc.ca/ahc-asc/pubs/hpfb-dgpsa/access-therapeutic_acces-therapeutique-eng.php#6.2>.
28. Lemmens and Bouchard (2007), *supra* note 24, at 329.
29. Health Canada, *Drugs and Health Products – New Active Substance* (June 4, 1991), online: Health Canada <http://www.hc-sc.gc.ca/dhp-mps/prodpharma/applic-demande/pol/nas_nsa_pol-eng.php> [Health Canada NAS]; Health Canada, *Drugs and Health Products – NOC Database Terminology* (October 1, 2004), online: Health Canada <http://www.hc-sc.gc.ca/dhp-mps/prodpharma/notices-avis/noc-acc/term_noc_acc-eng.php>.
30. Personal communications with David K. Lee (Director, Progressive Licensing Project, TPD, Health Canada), Dr Maurica Maher (Senior Scientific Advisor, Progressive Licensing Project, TPD, Health Canada), and Ms Lesley Brumell (Supervisor, Submissions Processing, Submission and Information Policy Division (SIPD), Health Canada) (April–July 2008) [Health Canada personal communication]. One of us (Bouchard) also participated in Health Canada's PLF stakeholder workshops in November 2006, May 2007, and June 2007.
31. Health Canada personal communication, *supra* note 30.
32. Ibid.
33. Ibid.

34. Ibid.
35. Ibid.
36. Ibid.
37. Ibid.
38. Health Canada NAS, *supra* note 29.
39. Health Canada personal communication, *supra* note 30.
40. Online: World Health Organization Collaborating Center for Drug Statistics Methodology <http://www.whocc.no/atcddd/> [WHO website].
41. Food and Drug Regulations, *supra* note 3 at s. C.08.003(2).
42. Health Canada personal communication, *supra* note 30.
43. Ibid.
44. A drug withdrawal or recall has the effect of removing a health product, such as a prescription or non-prescription pharmaceutical, from the marketplace. On its website, Health Canada addresses the issue of safety and drug withdrawals and states: 'Health Canada posts safety alerts, public health advisories, warnings, recalls, press releases, and other notices from industry on marketed health products, including Natural Health Products and medical devices.' Health Canada, *Drugs and Health Products – Advisories, Warnings and Recalls*, online: Health Canada <http://www.hc-sc.gc.ca/dhp-mps/medeff/advisories-avis/index-eng.php> [Health Canada, *Recalls*].

    The website elaborates by saying:

    > This service to health professionals, consumers, and other interested parties informs and educates Canadians about new health risks associated with the use of certain marketed health products. Recalls are initiated by importers and manufacturers after recognizing that there may be a safety concern related to a specific health product. Health Canada works with the health product industry to ensure hazardous products are removed from the marketplace in an effective and efficient manner.

45. Joel Lexchin, 'Drug Withdrawals from the Canadian Market for Safety Reasons, 1963–2004,' 172 *Canadian Medical Association Journal* 765 (2005) [Lexchin, 'Withdrawals' (2005)]. Updated via personal communication with Joel Lexchin, September 23, 2008 and March 4, 2009; Health Canada, *Recalls*, *supra* note 44.
46. Amalia M. Issa et al., 'Drug Withdrawals in the United States: A Systematic Review of the Evidence and Analysis of Trends,' 2 *Current Drug Safety* 177 (2007). Updated March 4, 2009 using information from US Food and Drug Administration, *Index to Drug-Specific Information*, online: FDA <http://www.fda.gov/cder/drug/DrugSafety/DrugIndex.htm>.
47. Pascale Olivier and Jean-Louis Montastruc, 'The Nature of Scientific Evidence Leading to Drug Withdrawals for Pharmacovigilance Reasons in France,' 15 *Pharmacoepidemiology and Drug Safety* 808 (2006) (updated via personal communication with Pascale Olivier, September 28, 2008 and March 4, 2009).

48. Health Canada, *Blueprint for Renewal: Transforming Canada's Approach to Regulating Health Products and Food* (October 2006), online: Health Canada <http://www.hc-sc.gc.ca/ahc-asc/alt_formats/hpfb-dgpsa/pdf/hpfb-dgpsa/blueprint-plan-eng.pdf> [Health Canada, *Blueprint*].
49. Health Canada, *The Progressive Licensing Framework Concept Paper for Discussion*, online: Health Canada <http://hc-sc.gc.ca/dhp-mps/homologation-licensing/develop/proglic_homprog_concept-eng.php> [Health Canada Concept Paper].
50. Bill C-51, *supra* note 4.
51. John D. Sterman, 'All Models Are Wrong: Reflections on Becoming a Systems Scientist,' 18 *Systems Dynamics Review* 501 (2002) [Sterman, 'Reflections' (2002)].
52. In *AstraZeneca Canada Inc.* v. *Canada (Minister of Health)*, 2006 SCC 49, [2006] 2 SCR 560 at para. 39, Justice Binnie stated that it is 'entirely understandable' that brand-name pharmaceutical firms avail themselves of loopholes in the NOC Regulations that permit evergreening of older products by 'adding bells and whistles' to them after the original patent has expired. See also Ron A. Bouchard, 'Should Scientific Research in the Lead-Up to Invention Vitiate Obviousness Under the Patented Medicines (Notice of Compliance) Regulations: To Test or Not to Test?' 6 *CJLT* 1 (2007) [Bouchard, 'Test' (2007)]; Ron A. Bouchard, 'Living Separate and Apart Is Never Easy: Inventive Capacity of the PHOSITA as the Tie That Binds Obviousness and Inventiveness,' 4 *U. Ottawa L. & Tech. J.* 1 (2007) [Bouchard, 'PHOSITA' (2007)]; See also Ron A. Bouchard, 'Balancing Public and Private Interests in the Commercialization of Publicly Funded Medical Research: Is There a Role for Compulsory Government Royalty Fees?' 13 *B.U.J. of Sci. & Tech. L.* 120 (2007) [Bouchard, 'Balancing' (2007)].
53. Health Canada Priority Review Guidance Document, *supra* note 22.
54. Health Canada personal communication, *supra* note 30.
55. Health Canada: Health Products and Food Branch, *Clinical Trials Regulatory Review – Stakeholder Workshop* (March 26, 2007), online: Health Canada <http://www.hc-sc.gc.ca/dhpmps/alt_formats/hpfb-dgpsa/pdf/prodpharma/ctrf_o_eccr_a_2007-03-26-eng.pdf> [Health Canada Stakeholder Workshop].
56. As used here, the term 'appropriation' refers to a party's ability to capture profits generated from their own inventions or related inventions.
57. Health Canada Stakeholder Workshop, *supra* note 55. According to Health Canada at 6, the objectives of the 2001 regulations were to 'shorten application review times without endangering health and safety; improve safety mechanisms for research subjects; regulator to be more involved in clinical trial monitoring and follow-up; remove obstacles to additional R&D; improve access to innovative therapies and advice from Canadian physicians with research experience.'
58. For an example of differences in the empirical analysis of a 'partially' reported database versus governmental analysis of a 'full' data set, see Daniel

Carpenter, Evan James Zucker, and Jerry Avorn, 'Drug-Review Deadlines and Safety Problems,' 358 *New Eng. J. Med.* 1354 (2008) [Carpenter et al. (2008)], at 1360, the subsequent Letter to the Editor from FDA Officials and Correction by the authors: Clark Nardinelli, Michael Lanthier, and Robert Temple, 'Letter to the Editor,' 359 *New Eng. J. Med.* 95 (2008); Daniel Carpenter, 'Reply to Letter to the Editor,' 359 *New Eng. J. Med.* 96 (2008) [Carpenter, 'Reply' (2008)].

59. WHO website, *supra* note 40.

60. Bouchard and Sawicka (2009), *supra* note 1.

61. Joel Lexchin, 'Intellectual Property Rights and the Canadian Pharmaceutical Marketplace: Where Do We Go from Here?' 35 *International Journal of Health Services* 237 (2005), at 243 [Lexchin, 'IP Rights' (2005)]. See also Patented Medicine Prices Review Board, Government of Canada, *Annual Report 2000*, online: Patented Medicine Prices Review Board <http://www.pmprb-cepmb. gc.ca/english/View.asp?x=113&mp=91> [Patented Medicine Prices Review Board Annual Report].

62. 'Drugs in 2001: A Number of Ruses Unveiled,' 11 *Prescrire International* 58 (2002) ['Drugs in 2001' (2002)].

63. James Love, *Evidence Regarding Research and Development Investments in Innovative and Non-Innovative Medicines* (Consumer Project on Technology, 2003), online: Consumer Project on Technology <http://www.cptech.org/ip/health/rnd/evidenceregardingrnd.pdf>; Song Hee Hong et al., 'Product-Line Extensions and Pricing Strategies of Brand Name Drugs Facing Patent Expiration,' 11 *Journal of Managed Care and Pharmacy* 746 (2005) [Hong et al. (2005)]. See also Joseph A. DiMasi and Cherie Paquette, 'The Economics of Follow-on Drug Research and Development,' 22: Suppl. 2 *Pharmacoenomics* 1 (2004).

64. Juan-José Ganuza, Gerard Llobet, and Beatriz Dominguez, 'R&D in the Pharmaceutical Industry: A World of Small Innovations,' 55 *Management Science* 539 (2009) [Ganuza et al. (2009)].

65. John Abraham and Courtney Davis, 'A Comparative Analysis of Drug Safety Withdrawals in the UK and the US (1971–1992): Implications for Current Regulatory Thinking and Policy,' 61 *Social Science & Medicine* 881 (2005); see also John Abraham and Courtney Davis, 'Deficits, Expectations, and Paradigms in British and American Drug Safety Assessments: Prising Open the Black Box of Regulatory Science,' 32 *Science, Technology & Human Values* 399 (2007); John Abraham, 'Sociology of Pharmaceuticals Development and Regulation: A Realist Empirical Research Programme,' 30 *Sociology of Health and Illness* 869 (2008).

66. US Government Accountability Office, *New Drug Development: Science, Business, Regulatory and Intellectual Property Issues Cited as Hampering Drug Development Efforts* (United States Government Accountability Office, 2006), online: US GAO <http://www.gao.gov/new.items/d0749.pdf>; EC, DG Competition Staff, Pharmaceutical Sector Inquiry: Preliminary Report

(28 November 2008); International Expert Group on Biotechnology, Innovation and Intellectual Property, *Toward a New Era of Intellectual Property: From Confrontation to Negotiation: A Report from the International Expert Group on Biotechnology, Innovation and Intellectual Property* (Montreal, 2008), online: Innovation Partnership <http://www.theinnovationpartnership.org/data/ieg/documents/report/TIP_Report_E.pdf>.

67. Competition Bureau, *Benefiting from Generic Drug Competition in Canada: The Way Forward* (Public Works and Government Services Canada, 2008). See also Roy J. Romanow Commission on the Future of Health Care in Canada, *Building on Values: The Future of Health Care in Canada* (Public Works and Government Services Canada, 2002) [Romanow (2002)].
68. Timothy J. Foxton, 'Technological Lock-in and the Role of Innovation,' in G. Atkinson, S. Dietz, and E. Neumayer (eds), *Handbook of Sustainable Development* (Edward Elgar, 2006).
69. W. Brian Arthur, 'Increasing Returns and the Two Worlds of Business,' *Harvard Business Review* 100 (1996).
70. Gunars K. Gaikis, 'Pharmaceutical Patents in Canada: An Update on Compulsory Licensing,' 42 *Patent World* 19 (1992); Edward Hore, 'A Comparison of US and Canadian Laws as They Affect Generic Pharmaceutical Drug Entry,' 55 *Food & Drug L.J.* 373 (2000) [Hore (2000)]; Andrew A. Caffrey and Jonathan M. Rotter, 'Consumer Protection, Patents and Procedure: Generic Drug Market Entry and the Need to Reform the Hatch-Waxman Act,' 9 *Va. J.L. & Tech.* 1 (2004) [Caffrey and Rotter (2004)], at 4–7. See also Rebecca S. Eisenberg, 'Patents, Product Exclusivity, and Information Dissemination: How Law Directs Biopharmaceutical Research and Development,' 72 *Fordham L. Rev.* 477 (2003); Bouchard, 'PHOSITA', *supra* note 52.
71. Bouchard and Sawicka, *supra* note 1.
72. Ibid.
73. See, generally, Murray Gell-Mann, *The Quark and the Jaguar: Adventures in the Simple and the Complex* (W.H. Freeman, 1994). The practical implications of elegance and symmetry in physics and mathematics are explored elegantly by Gell-Mann in the videocast, *Beauty and Truth in Physics*, TED TV VideoCast (March 2007), online: TED Blog <http://blog.ted.com/2007/12/murray_gellmann.php>. But see Bruce Edmonds and Scott Moss, 'From KISS to KIDS: An "Anti-Simplistic" Modeling Approach,' in P. Davidsson, P. Logan, and K Takadama (eds), *Multi-Agent and Multi-Based Simulation*, vol. 3415 (Springer Berlin/Heidelberg, 2004), at 130.
74. Bouchard, 'Systems' (2008) and Bouchard, 'Reflections' (2008), *supra* note 14. See also Wulf (2007), *supra* note 14; David H. Guston, 'Innovation Policy: Not Just Jumbo Shrimp,' 454 *Nature* 940 (2008) [Guston (2008)]; Fred Gault and Sasanne Huttner, 'A Cat's Cradle for Policy,' 455 *Nature* 462 (2008).
75. For a detailed review of adaptive policy in a legal context, see J.B. Ruhl, 'Regulation by Adaptive Management: Is It Possible?' 7 *Minnesota Journal of*

Law Science & Technology 21 (2005) and references therein. See also Guston (2008), *supra* note 74.

76. For a detailed review of robust policy-making in a political and international relations context, see: Robert Jervis, *System Effects: Complexity in Political and Social Life* (Princeton University Press, 1997); Neil E. Harrison (ed.), *Complexity in World Politics: Concepts and Methods of a New Paradigm* (SUNY Press, 2006).
77. *Supra* note 6.
78. Weeks, 'Critics' (2008), *supra* note 7.
79. Ibid. See also Carly Weeks, 'Experts Sound Alarm on Drug-Approval Plan: Under Sweeping New Changes, Drug Companies Only Have to Prove that Benefit of Product Outweighs the Harm,' *Globe and Mail* (April 9, 2008), at A7.
80. *Supra* note 8.
81. Edwin A.M. Gale, 'Lessons from the Glitazones: A Story of Drug Development,' 357 *Lancet* 1870 (2001).
82. *Supra* note 9. See also Trudo Lemmens, 'Leopards in the Temple: Restoring Scientific Integrity to the Commercialized Research Scene,' 32 *J.L. Med. & Ethics* 641 (2004); Trudo Lemmens, '*Piercing* the *Veil* of Corporate Secrecy about Clinical Trials,' 34 (5) *Hastings Center Report* 14 (2004).
83. Health Canada Concept Paper, *supra* note 49, at 19. For a more detailed discussion of the proposed evidentiary threshold under PLF, see Bouchard and Sawicka (2009), *supra* note 1, at Section I.F(a) and Section II.
84. Weiss Smith, 'Reply to Galson' (2007), *supra* note 10, at 2521.
85. Bill C-51, *supra* note 4, at cl. 8 ss. 18–19.
86. Hébert (2007), *supra* note 6; Wayne Kondro, 'Health Canada Proposes New Regulatory Regime for Drugs,' 176 *Canadian Medical Association Journal* 1261 (2007).
87. FDA, *Fast Track*, *supra* note 11.
88. EMEA CHMP, *Guideline*, *supra* note 12.
89. For review, see Eichler et al. (2008), *supra* note 6, at 823.
90. European Medicines Agency (EMEA): Committee for Medicinal Products for Human Use (CHMP), *Report of the CHMP Working Group on Benefit-Risk Assessment Models and Methods* (EMEA, 2007), online: EMEA <http://www.emea.europa.eu/pdfs/human/brmethods/1540407en.pdf> [EMEA CHMP (2007)]; European Medicines Agency (EMEA): Committee for Medicinal Products for Human Use (CHMP), *Reflection Paper on Benefit-Risk Assessment Methods in the Context of the Evaluation of Marketing Authorization Applications of Medicinal Products for Human Use* (EMEA, 2008), online: EMEA <http://www.emea.europa.eu/pdfs/human/brmethods/1540407enfin.pdf> [EMEA CHMP (2008)].
91. For a discussion of the potential role of the precautionary principle in the PLF regime, see Bouchard and Sawicka (2009), *supra* note 1, at Section I.C.
92. Eichler et al. (2008), *supra* note 6.

93. Peterson, *Innovation* (2005), *supra* note 5; Health Canada, *Blueprint*, *supra* note 48.
94. IOM Report, *supra* note 8.
95. EMEA CHMP (2007) and EMEA CHMP (2008), *supra* note 90; European Medicines Agency (EMEA): Evaluation of Medicines for Human Use, *Innovative Drug Development Approaches: Final Report from the EMEA/CHMP-Think-Tank Group on Innovative Drug Development* (EMEA, 2007).
96. Peterson, *Innovation* (2005), *supra* note 5; Health Canada, *Blueprint*, *supra* note 48.
97. Commission on the Future of Health Care in Canada, *Public Input on the Future of Health Care: Results from the Issue/Survey Papers* (Pollara, 2002), online: Pollara <http://www.pollara.ca/Library/Reports/3461_pollara_english.pdf> (prepared by Pollara for the Commission). See also Romanow (2002), *supra* note 67.
98. Bouchard, 'Balancing' (2007), *supra* note 52; Lemmens and Bouchard (2007), *supra* note 24. See also Sterman, 'Reflections' (2002), *supra* note 51.
99. See, generally, Barry Bozeman, 'Public Value Failure: When Efficient Markets May Not Do,' 62 *Public Administration Review* 145 (2002) [Bozeman (2002)]; Barry Bozeman and Daniel Sarewitz, 'Public Values and Public Failure in US Science Policy,' 32 *Science and Public Policy* 119 (2005) [Bozeman and Sarewitz (2005)].
100. See, generally, Robert M. May, Simon A. Levin, and George Sugihara, 'Ecology for Bankers,' 451 *Nature* 893 (2008). See also Per Bak and Maya Paczuski, 'Complexity, Contingency, and Criticality,' 92 *Proceedings of the National Academy of Sciences* 6689 (1995) [Bak and Paczuski (1995)].
101. Ann Silversides, *Transparency and the Drug Approval Process at Health Canada* (2005), online: Woman and Health Protection <http://www.whp-apsf.ca/pdf/transparency.pdf> (citing (at 3) Abby Hoffman, head of Health Canada's Therapeutics Access Strategy, who made this comment in an address to the June 10, 2004 Health Canada public consultation).
102. Health Canada, *Blueprint*, *supra* note 48; Health Canada Concept Paper, *supra* note 49; Bill C-51, *supra* note 4; Neil Yeates, David K. Lee, and Maurica Maher, 'Health Canada's Progressive Licensing Framework,' 176 *Canadian Medical Association Journal* 1846 (2007) [Yeates et al. (2007)].
103. IOM Report (2007), *supra* note 8.
104. Peterson, *Innovation* (2005), *supra* note 5.
105. John H. Miller and Scott E. Page, *Complex Adaptive Systems: An Introduction to Computational Models of Social Life* (Princeton University Press, 2007) [Miller and Page (2007)].
106. Sterman, 'Reflections' (2002), *supra* note 51; Benoît Godin, 'The Linear Model of Innovation: The Historical Construction of an Analytical Framework,' 31 *Science, Technology & Human Values* 639 (2006). (It should be said, however, that Godin himself (at p. 35) referred to systems models of innovation as a 'plate of spaghetti and meatballs.')

107. Bouchard and Sawicka (2009), *supra* note 1, at Section I.B and Section I.E.
108. Carpenter et al. (2008), *supra* note 58.
109. Mary K. Olson, 'The Risk We Bear: The Effects of Review Speed and Industry User Fees on New Drug Safety,' 27 *Journal of Health Economics* 175 (2008).
110. Daniel Carpenter et al., 'Approval Times for New Drugs: Does the Source of Funding for FDA Staff Matter?' *W3 Health Affairs* 618 (2003), at 623.
111. For review, see Lemmens and Bouchard (2007), *supra* note 24.
112. Miller and Page (2007), *supra* note 105; Sterman, 'Reflections' (2002), *supra* note 51; John D. Sterman, *Business Dynamics: Systems Thinking and Modeling for a Complex World* (Irwin/McGraw-Hill, 2000); James Gleick, *Chaos: Making a New Science* (Penguin, 1988); M. Mitchell Waldrop, *Complexity: The Emerging Science at the Edge of Order and Chaos* (Simon & Schuster, 1992); John L. Casti, *Complexification: Explaining a Paradoxical World Through the Science of Surprise* (HarperCollins, 1994); Albert-Laszlo Barabasi, *Linked* (Penguin Group, 2002).
113. IOM Report (2007), *supra* note 8. Specifically, the IOM called on the FDA, industry, prescribing physicians, the healthcare delivery system, academic researchers, patients, and the general public to contribute to enhanced accountability of the drug regulatory system, underscoring (at S-4) that the 'FDA's credibility is intertwined with that of the industry, and a more credible drug safety system is in everyone's best interest.'
114. Lexchin, 'Withdrawals' (2005), *supra* note 45, at 765.
115. Lemmens and Bouchard (2007), *supra* note 24, at 335–7.
116. For a description of how small events can give rise to large system-wide effects, see Bak and Paczuski (1995), *supra* note 100.
117. Carpenter et al. (2008), *supra* note 58, at 1355.
118. US Center for Drug Evaluation and Research (FDA), *Think It Through: A Guide to Managing the Benefits and Risks of Medicines*, online: FDA <http://www.fda.gov/Drugs/ResourcesForYou/ucm079492.htm>. See also Sharon Smith Holston, *The Value of Patient's Perspective in FDA's Decision Process* (Presentation at 10th IMS International Symposium, Brussels, November 3, 1997), online: FDA <http://www.fda.gov/ForConsumers/ByAudience/ForPatientAdvocates/PatientInvolvement/ucm123864.htm>.
119. Health Canada, *Blueprint*, *supra* note 48; Health Canada Concept Paper, *supra* note 49; EMEA CHMP (2007) and EMEA CHMP (2008), *supra* note 90; IOM Report, *supra* note 8. For a review of uncertainties in the context of balancing access and safety, see Eichler, *supra* note 6.
120. Ron A. Bouchard, '*KSR* v. *Teleflex* Part 1: Impact of U.S Supreme Court Patent Law on Canadian Intellectual Property and Regulatory Rights Landscape,' 15 *Health L.J.* 221 (2007) [Bouchard, 'Landscape' (2007)].
121. Christopher J. Bosso, *Pesticides and Politics: The Life Cycle of a Public Issue* (University of Pittsburgh Press, 1987).

122. Bill C-51, *supra* note 4, at cl. 8 ss. 18–19.
123. Ibid., at cl. 8 ss. 15.1, 18.1–18.9, 19.1–19.9, 20.1–20.9, 21, 21.1–21.2, cl. 10 ss. 23.1–23.9, 24.1, and cl. 11 s. 30.
124. Ibid., at cl. 10 ss. 23 and 24.
125. Lemmens and Bouchard (2007), *supra* note 24, at 365.
126. Union of Concerned Scientists, *Voices of Scientists at FDA: Protecting Public Health Depends on Independent Science* (Union of Concerned Scientists, 2006), online: Union of Concerned Scientists <http://www.ucsusa.org/assets/documents/scientific_integrity/fda-survey-brochure.pdf> [Union (2006)]; David B. Ross, 'The FDA and the Case of Ketek,' 356 *New Eng. J. Med.* 1601 (2007) [Ross (2007)]. See also Susan Okie, 'What Ails the FDA?' 352 *New Eng. J. Med.* 1063 (2005) [Okie (2005)]; Gardiner Harris, 'FDA Scientists Accuse Agency Officials of Misconduct,' *New York Times* (November 18, 2008) [Harris (2008)], at A15; Carpenter et al. (2008), *supra* note 58.
127. Health Canada, *Blueprint*, *supra* note 48; Health Canada Concept Paper, *supra* note 49; Yeates et al. (2007), *supra* note 102; IOM Report, *supra* note 8; US Food and Drug Administration: Department of Health and Human Services, *The Future of Drug Safety – Promoting and Protecting the Health of the Public: FDA's Response to the Institute of Medicine's 2006 Report* (January 2007), online: FDA <http://www.fda.gov/NewsEvents/Newsroom/PressAnnouncements/2007/ucm108833.htm>. See also Psaty and Charo (2007), *supra* note 8.
128. For a general discussion of the need for transparency in pre-market and post-market stages in the US, Canada, and the EU, see IOM Report (2007), *supra* note 8; Weiss Smith, 'Sidelining' (2007), *supra* note 10; Psaty and Burke (2006) and Psaty and Charo (2007), *supra* note 8; Health Canada, *Blueprint*, *supra* note 48; Health Canada Concept Paper, *supra* note 49; Yeates et al. (2007), *supra* note 102; EMEA CHMP, *Guideline*, *supra* note 12; EMEA CHMP (2008), *supra* note 90.
129. Bouchard, 'Balancing' (2007), *supra* note 52; Ron A. Bouchard and Trudo Lemmens, 'Privatizing Biomedical Research – A "Third Way,"' 26 *Nature Biotechnology* 31 (2008) [Bouchard and Lemmens (2008)].
130. Weiss Smith, 'Sidelining' (2007), *supra* note 10, at 961; Janice Graham, 'Smart Regulation: Will the Government's Strategy Work?' 73 *Canadian Medical Association Journal* 1469 (2005) [Graham (2005)]; Psaty and Burke (2006), *supra* note 8.
131. Bouchard, 'Test' (2007) and Bouchard, 'PHOSITA' (2007), *supra* note 52; Bouchard, 'Landscape' (2007), *supra* note 120. See also Hore (2000), *supra* note 70.
132. RSC 1985, c. P-4.
133. Patented Medicines (Notice of Compliance) Regulations, SOR/93-133 [NOC Regulations].
134. Bouchard, 'Test' (2007), *supra* note 52.

135. Drug Price Competition and Patent Restoration Act 1984, Pub. L. No. 98-417, 98 Stat. 1585 (codified as amended at 21 USC § 355 (2000), commonly known as the Hatch-Waxman Act).
136. 35 USC §§ 1–376 (2000).
137. 21 USC §§ 301–399a (2004). See also Food and Drugs, 21 CFR §§ 1–1499 (2003)
138. 21 USC §§ 355(j)(7)(A) (2004). For a detailed description, see Caffrey and Rotter (2004), *supra* note 70.
139. Psaty and Charo (2007), *supra* note 8, at 1919.
140. Weiss Smith, 'Sidelining' (2007), *supra* note 10, at 961.
141. But see Galson (2007), *supra* note 10.
142. Eichler et al. (2008), *supra* note 6.
143. Graham (2005), *supra* note 130; Bouchard 'Balancing' (2007), *supra* note 52.
144. Marcia Angell, *The Truth About the Drug Companies: How They Deceive Us and What To Do About It* (Random House, 2004); Jerome P. Kassirer, *On the Take: How Medicine's Complicity with Big Business Can Endanger Your Health* (Oxford University Press, 2005); John Abramson, *Overdo$ed America: The Broken Promise of American Medicine* (HarperCollins, 2004); Jay S. Cohen, *Overdose: The Case Against the Drug Companies* (Penguin, 2001); Philip J. Hilts, *Protecting America's Health: The FDA, Business, and One Hundred Years of Regulation* (Alfred A. Knopf, 2003); Ray Moynihan and Alan Cassels, *Selling Sickness: How the World's Biggest Pharmaceutical Companies Are Turning Us All Into Patients* (GreyStone Books, 2005).
145. Weiss Smith, 'Sidelining' (2007), *supra* note 10.
146. Gordon Schiff, '*Contested Ground: Public Purpose and Private Interest in the Regulation of Prescription Drugs* by Peter Davis,' 19 *Journal of Public Health Policy* 240 (1998); Derek Bok, *Universities in the Marketplace: The Commercialization of Higher Education* (Princeton University Press, 2003); Sheldon Krimsky, *Science in the Private Interest: Has the Lure of Profits Corrupted Biomedical Research?* (Rowman & Littlefield, 2003); Janet Atkinson-Grosjean, *Public Science, Private Interests: Culture and Commerce in Canada's Networks of Centres of Excellence* (University of Toronto Press, 2006).
147. Anita Varma and David Abraham, 'DNA is Different: Legal Obviousness and the Balance Between Biotech Inventors and the Market,' 9 *Harvard J.L. & Tech.* 53 (1996); Glynn S. Lunney Jr, 'E-Obviousness,' 7 *Mich. Telecomm. & Tech. L. Rev.* 363 (2001); Bouchard, 'Test' (2007) and Bouchard, 'PHOSITA' (2007), *supra* note 52.
148. Bouchard, 'Systems' (2008) and Bouchard, 'Reflections' (2008), *supra* note 14.
149. Bouchard, 'Balancing' 2007), *supra* note 53; Bouchard, 'Test' (2007) and Bouchard, 'PHOSITA' (2007), *supra* note 52.
150. Bouchard and Sawicka (2009), *supra* note 1.

151. For a discussion of the public policy implications of the terms 'efficiency' and 'effectiveness', see Janice Gross Stein, *The Cult of Efficiency*, rev. 2nd edn (House of Anansi Press, 2001) [Stein (2001)].
152. Lexchin, 'IP Rights' (2005), *supra* note 61; 'Drugs in 2001' (2002), *supra* note 62; Patented Medicine Prices Review Board Annual Report, *supra* note 61; Tim Hubbard and James Love, 'A New Trade Framework for Global Healthcare R&D,' 2(2) *PLoS Biology* 147 (2004); Hong et al. (2005), *supra* note 63.
153. Stein (2001), *supra* note 151; Joseph Heath, *The Efficient Society: Why Canada Is as Close to Utopia as It Gets* (Penguin, 2001); Amartya Sen, *Equality of What?* (Tanner Lecture on Human Values delivered at Stanford University, May 22, 1979), online: Tanner Lectures on Human Values <http://www.tannerlectures.utah.edu/lectures/documents/sen80.pdf>.
154. Autopoiesis refers to the process of self-creation and/or self-organization (Gr. auto (αυτό) for 'self' and poiesis (ποίησις) for 'creation' or 'production'). The term underscores a fundamental interrelationship between the structure and function of a system, typical examples being living systems and biological cells. For a general discussion of the importance of the interrelationships of actors in social and technological networks, see Bruno Latour, *Science in Action: How to Follow Scientists and Engineers through Society* (Harvard University Press, 1987); Bruno Latour, *We Have Never Been Modern* (Harvard University Press, 2007).
155. Mary E. Wiktorowicz, 'Emergent Patterns in the Regulation of Pharmaceuticals: Institutions and Interests in the United States, Canada, Britain and France,' 28 *J. Health Pol.* 615 (2003) [Wiktorowicz (2003)].
156. Ibid., citing (at 43) M.M. Atkinson and W.D. Coleman, 'Corporatism and Liberal Policy,' in A. Carson (ed.), *Organized Interests and the State* (Sage, 1985).
157. Health Canada, *Blueprint*, *supra* note 48.
158. Health Canada Concept Paper, *supra* note 49.
159. Bill C-51, *supra* note 4.
160. Health Canada Stakeholder Workshop, *supra* note 55; Peterson, *Innovation* (2005), *supra* note 5.
161. Michael M.E. Johns, Mark Barnes, and Patrick S. Florencio, 'Restoring Balance to Industry-Academia Relationships in an Era of Institutional Financial Conflicts of Interest,' 289 *Journal of the American Medical Association* 741 (2003); Michele Boldrin and David K. Levine, 'The Economics of Ideas and Intellectual Property,' 102 *Proceedings of the National Academy of Sciences of the United States of America* 1252 (2005); Daniel P. Carpenter, 'The Political Economy of FDA Drug Review: Processing, Politics, and Lessons for Policy,' 23(1) *Health Affairs* 52 (2004); Stuart Macdonald, 'When Means Become Ends: Considering the Impact of Patent Strategy on Innovation,' 16 *Information Economics and Policy* 135 (2004);

Wayne A. Ray and C. Michael Stein, 'Reform of Drug Regulation – Beyond an Independent Drug-Safety Board,' 354 *New Eng. J. Med.* 194 (2006).

162. Union (2006), Okie (2005), Ross (2007), and Harris (2008), *supra* note 126; Carpenter et al. (2008), *supra* note 58; John Abraham, 'The Pharmaceutical Industry as a Political Player,' 360 *Lancet* 1498 (2002).
163. See, generally, both Bozeman (2002) and Bozeman and Sarewitz (2005), *supra* note 99.
164. P. Lurie and L.D. Sasich, 'Safety of FDA-Approved Drugs,' 282 *Journal of the American Medical Association* 2297 (1999); John Abraham and Tim Reed, 'Trading Risks for Markets: The International Harmonization of Pharmaceuticals Regulation,' 3 *Health Risk & Society* 113 (2001); Wiktorowicz (2003), *supra* note 155.
165. M.H. Hoeflich and Karen Norheden Hoeflich, 'Accelerating Science: A Problem for the Legal System,' 60 *University of Missouri-Kansas City Law Review* 717 (1992).
166. Ganuza et al. (2009), *supra* note 65, citing (at 2) W.D. Nordhaus, *Invention, Growth, and Welfare: A Theoretical Treatment of Technological Change* (MIT Press, 1969).
167. E. Richard Gold, 'The Reach of Patent Law and Institutional Competence,' 1 *U. Ottawa L. & Tech. J.* 263 (2004); Bouchard and Lemmens (2008), *supra* note 129.

4

Empirical analysis of pharmaceutical innovation and drug approval-drug patenting linkage*

Abstract: Global drug development is undergoing a redefinition of the responsibilities of those who develop, regulate, and consume therapeutic products. This shift has been accompanied by growing debate over the validity of the claim that an efficiently functioning public health system requires acceptance of lifecycle models of drug regulation that promote early access to innovative therapeutic products in exchange for strong intellectual property and regulatory (IPR) rights. Indeed, IPR rights are assumed necessary for all stages of the therapeutic product lifecycle, including publicly funded medical research, university technology transfer, private research and development activities, regulatory submissions, and now even the post-market stage. Advocates claim that without such rights pioneering drug development would not occur and that the public would be left without breakthrough remedies. The goal of the research discussed in this chapter is to investigate this claim empirically and to assess how IPR rights might be used more effectively to encourage innovation in the medical sciences. We empirically extend our analysis of drug approvals in the previous chapter to encompass an analysis of the level of innovation associated with drug products approved by domestic regulators. We further extend this analysis to include an empirical assessment of the manner in which the linkage regulations are employed by pharmaceutical firms to extend patent monopolies on blockbuster products. The chapter concludes with a discussion of whether linkage has been a successful vehicle for encouraging the development of both new and generic drugs as well as whether it is advisable to collapse public health policy into economic policy, such as occurs with linkage regulations.

*This chapter is based upon material in R.A. Bouchard, J. Sawani, C. McLelland, M. Sawicka, and R. Hawkins, 'The Pas de Deux of Pharmaceutical Regulation and Innovation: Who's Leading Whom?' *Berkeley Technology Law Journal* 24(3): 1461–522 (2009).

Keywords: pharmaceutical linkage regulations, patent law, innovation, empirical analysis, new drugs, follow-on drugs, drug patenting, patent listing, patent litigation, market exclusivity

4.1 Introduction

Continuing with the framework developed in Chapter 3 the goal of this chapter is to develop an independent empirical methodology to identify patterns in the rate and direction of innovative activity by pharmaceutical firms and to analyze these data in relation to well defined regulatory incentives for pharmaceutical innovation via the provision of strong intellectual property and regulatory (IPR) rights. The work is designed to probe the functional and structural link between drug approval, drug patenting, drug litigation, and pharmaceutical innovation. In this chapter, data are presented on the relationship between drug approval, drug regulation, and drug innovation in the domestic Canadian market. We extended our analysis of drug approvals in Chapter 3, with a particular focus on the level of innovation associated with the types of drugs being approved and how approvals were consistent with emerging lifecycle models of drug regulation.[1] The second major aspect of the work is a pilot study on the legal nexus between drug approval, drug patenting, and litigation, which we propose reflects trends in the broader influence of government regulation on innovation in the global pharmaceutical industry. Specifically, we argue that the global pharmaceutical industry is leaning away from the development of new drugs and towards incremental changes in existing drugs as a result of firms locking in to discrete IPR rights targets provided for by law.

The study is split into three sections. The first is an empirical investigation into the type of drugs approved by domestic regulators as regulatory incentives intended to stimulate innovation came into force. The primary goal here is to quantitatively analyze various types of 'new' and 'follow-on' drugs. A related, though smaller, component is to investigate trends for these drug types in the context of Canada's emerging lifecycle regulatory regime for drug approval, referred to as the 'Progressive Licensing Framework.'[2] Given its emphasis on promoting early access, enhanced post-market scrutiny, and strong IPR rights, progressive licensing offers an excellent opportunity to probe the relationship between drug approval, drug patenting, and innovation in an emerging drug regulation model.

The second is an empirical study of patents and patent litigation associated with the various types of drug approvals identified in the first section. The primary goal of this project is to show how government regulation shapes the domestic market for brand-name and generic products. Particular attention is given to changes in patenting and litigation patterns before and after the establishment of the Canadian 'linkage regulations' regime in 1993, referred to as the Patented Medicines (Notice of Compliance) Regulations (NOC Regulations).[3] Linkage regulations are critical to drug development, as they legally tie drug approval to drug patenting and litigation and thus represent a primary mechanism by which regulators promote drug development in exchange for IPR rights.

The third section is an analytical model of regulated pharmaceutical innovation, which focuses on the effectiveness of regulatory incentives intended to encourage innovation. Of particular interest is the synchronization of drug approval, patenting, and litigation data to the establishment of NOC Regulations and progressive licensing. As noted in Chapter 2, progressive licensing is still being formally incorporated into the nation's regulatory regime. Therefore the majority of the analysis focuses on the relationship between drug approval, patenting, and litigation under the NOC Regulations.

4.2 Methods

4.2.1 Drug approval

Statistical analysis of drug approvals issued in Canada from January 1, 2001 to December 31, 2008 was performed as described previously.[4] Absolute numbers and fractional percentages of various types of drug approvals were calculated for each year during the eight-year test period in annual, quarterly, monthly, and daily increments. Drug approvals used for calculation include NDS, SNDS, ANDS, and SANDS submissions, those directed to a NAS, first-in-class drugs, me-too drugs, and drugs approved via the two expedited review streams (Priority Review and NOC/c).

For the present purposes, 'new' drugs were those that were either approved through the New Drug Submission (NDS) stream, contained a new active substance (NAS), or directed to first-in-class (FIC) drugs. In contrast, 'follow-on' drugs were either brand-name drugs approved through the Supplementary New Drug Submission (SNDS) stream, approved via the SNDS stream directed to FIC therapies, approved via the SNDS stream containing an NAS, or generic drugs approved via either the standard Abbreviated New Drug Submissions (ANDS) stream or the follow-on Supplementary ANDS (SANDS) stream. The classification system is summarized for convenience in Table 4.1.

Table 4.1 Classification scheme for new and follow-on drugs

Firm type	New drugs	Follow-on drugs
A. Brand	NDS NDS Me Too NDS NAS NDS FIC NDS ER	SNDS SNDS Me Too SNDS FIC NDS ER –
B. Generic	– –	ANDS SANDS

4.2.2 Drug patenting

We also conducted a study on the relationship between drug approval, drug patenting, and drug litigation. This involved statistical analysis of patenting patterns associated with 16 of the most profitable drug products in Canada.[5] We chose the top 16 drugs for our initial study given that this cohort was likely to display the strongest patenting and patent listing patterns. This is because pharmaceutical companies have a vested interest to protect the market on their most profitable drugs, and the primary means of doing so is via patenting. Each of the drugs studied under the patent analysis were approved in Canada between 2001 and 2008 and were analyzed as part of the drug approval data shown in Figures 4.1–4.3. Unlike the drug approval study, the drug patenting study was not restricted to a certain time period. This was necessary because many of the patents on drug products for which approval was granted during the 2001–2008 test period were filed and issued before 2001.

A detailed patent search of the Canadian Intellectual Property Office (CIPO) database was conducted for each drug approved and analyzed in Sawicka and Bouchard.[6] The CIPO search employed broad search terms for each drug in question with an effort to cast the widest possible net so that even patents with a remote possibility of being relevant would be returned by the search engine and made available for analysis and classification. The search was designed to return all patents owned or assigned to the drug's manufacturer – including those owned by its parent company, subsidiaries, and partners – that made claims regarding the specific medicinal ingredients associated with the drug or claims regarding the general therapeutic class(es) to which the drug belongs. The patent search for each drug was comprised of two search strings: (1) a specific search string that returned patents likely to be relevant to the specific drug in question; and (2) a general search string that returned patents that were likely to be relevant to the general therapeutic class associated with the drug in question. Both are provided in Table 4.2.

The specific search string used Boolean operators to return all patents owned by the drug manufacturer or its affiliates that mention either the drug's chemical name(s), code name(s), brand name(s), chemical class(es), or chemical formula(e) and have priority dates between the date of Canada's Confederation and the start date of the study. Databases such as the CIPO, the Canadian Patent Register (CPR), the US Patent and Trademark Office (USPTO), and the Orange Book (OB) databases as well as secondary sources were used to acquire an exhaustive list of all possible chemical names, code names, brand names, and chemical classes associated with a particular drug. In determining the chemical formula, precedence was given to formulae expressed in patents found on CIPO and USPTO databases. The owners referred to within the search string refer not only to the drug's manufacturer but also to its possible parent company, subsidiary, and partner(s). This list of owners was cross-referenced using CIPO, CPR, USPTO, and OB databases as well as searches of case law and secondary sources where necessary.

The general search string used Boolean operators to return all patents owned by the drug manufacturer or its affiliates not previously found by the specific search string that mention the therapeutic class(es) to which the drug belongs or make specific reference to the drug's active site. The therapeutic class and active site of a drug are obtained by reference to the CIPO, the CPR, and their American counterparts, the USPTO and OB databases, and secondary sources such as company websites and Internet searches. These sources were used to acquire an exhaustive list of all

Table 4.2 Search strings for data collection and analysis

Search string	Boolean operators
A. Specific search string	((*chemical name*)<OR>(*code name*)<OR>(*brand name*)<OR>(*chemical class*)<OR> (*chemical formula*))<AND>(*owners*<IN> OWNER)<AND>(PAPD>=1867-07-01)<AND> (PAPD<=*study start date*)
B. General search string	((*therapeutic class*)<OR>(*active site*))<AND><NOT>(*chemical name*)<AND><NOT> (*code name*)<AND><NOT> (*brand name*)<AND><NOT>(*chemical class*)<AND><NOT> (*chemical formula*)<AND>(*owners*<IN> OWNER)<AND>(PAPD>=1867-07-01)<AND> (PAPD<=*study start date*)

possible chemical names, code names, brand names, and chemical classes associated with a particular drug.

Combined, the two search strings returned a broad list of potential patents owned or assigned to the Canadian manufacturer or its subsidiaries and partners. The legitimacy of the search terms was confirmed using Health Canada's drug approval data, as well as manufacturer, securities, and exchange websites, from which ownership histories were ascertained. Patents were individually inspected and pruned when deemed irrelevant to drugs in the study. The USPTO database, which provides a history of prior art, was also used as a means of cross-referencing patents for relevance. Relevant patents were sorted by priority date and cross-referenced with the patents registered on the CPR pursuant to linkage regulations.

4.2.3 Patent listing and litigation

We quantified patents identified using the search method that were also listed on the Canadian Patent Register (CPR) under NOC Regulations. Patents listed on the register can be litigated numerous times since they can be listed for multiple Drug Identification Numbers (DINs) under the NOC Regulations. Patent listing is a critical step to potential extension of patent monopolies for drugs coming off patent protection because generic firms must demonstrate in litigation that each patent on the list is either invalid or not infringed by the generic product to obtain market approval. For our purposes, only the date of first instance (the earliest date on which the patent was registered) for each patent was collected and analyzed.

In addition to analyzing patents listed on the patent register, we also investigated the case law pertaining to patents litigated under the NOC Regulations. We assessed the number and types of trials, the number of patents litigated in these trials, the number and types of legal decisions on listed and litigated patents (motions, trial and appellate decisions), whether listed patents were valid and infringed (brand name victory) or invalid and not infringed (generic victory), and the theoretical and actual extension of patent monopolies via the operation of linkage regulations.

4.2.4 Analytical model

The third element of the study was the synthesis of empirical data from the drug approval, patenting, and litigation studies into an analytical model. The focus of the analysis is on the impact of regulatory incentives designed to facilitate breakthrough pharmaceutical innovation via the provision to firms of strong IPR rights. Throughout the study we compare data relating to the time courses of varying types of drug approvals with concomitant drug patenting, patent listing, and litigation data. Particular attention was given to the synchronization, if any, of approval, patenting, listing, and litigation data to the times for establishment of the NOC Regulations and proposal of the Progressive Lifecycle Framework, as both were intended to facilitate enhanced access to novel therapeutic products in exchange for strong IPR rights. However, since most of the data relate to the period before the Progressive Lifecycle Framework was fully integrated into Canadian law, the majority of the analysis relates to the linkage regulations. Further elaborating the rTPL concept introduced in Chapter 3, the analysis has been cast in terms of a complex adaptive innovation ecology in the final section of the chapter.

4.2.5 Data analysis

Drug approval, patenting, patent listing, and litigation data were collected, statistically analyzed, and graphed as described previously[7] using a combination of Excel® (Microsoft Corp., Redmond, WA), GraphPad Prism® (Graphpad Software Inc., La Jolla, CA), and SigmaPlot® (Systat Software, Inc., San Jose, CA). Legal decisions relating to listed and litigated patents were obtained using Quicklaw™ (Lexis Nexis®) and Westlaw® (Thomson Reuters®). Economic data relating to prescribed pharmaceuticals were obtained with permission from IMS Health Inc. (Canada) and from published reports from the Canadian Institute for Health Information (CIHI). Patent data were obtained from the Canadian (CIPO) and US (USPTO) patent databases.

4.3 Results

4.3.1 Drug approval

To empirically investigate the relationship between drug regulation and innovative therapeutic product development, we first reviewed market authorizations for pharmaceuticals in Canada over the period 2001–2008 (test period).[8] The year 2001 was taken as the starting point for analysis, as major amendments to the nation's food and drug legislation and regulations were made at that time which affected both the goals and mechanism of national drug regulation.[9] Market authorizations in Canada are referred to as Notices of Compliance (NOC). We analyzed a total of 3,837 NOCs. Of these 45% were administrative in nature, e.g. product manufacturer or name change. This left 2,122 approvals for detailed analysis. These approvals were attached to 608 marketed drug products, amounting to an average of 3.5 approvals per product.

Using the classification scheme described in section 4.2 and summarized in Table 4.1, we found that follow-on drugs constituted the vast majority of drugs approved in the domestic market over the period 2001–2008. For example, in 2001 the total number of follow-on approvals was 2.39 times greater than that for total new drug approvals. This constituted 70.5% of all approvals in Canada over the test period and 65.33% of approvals granted to brand-name pharmaceutical firms. As shown in Figure 4.1(a), this trend intensified over the test period. By 2008, the number of follow-on approvals was 6.32 times greater than new drug approvals. This constituted 86.4% of all approvals in Canada and 86.02% of brand name approvals over the same time frame. Approvals directed to line extension drugs (SNDS, □) accounted for 34% in 2001, increasing to 47% in 2008. By comparison, the more innovative supplementary first-in-class drugs (SNDS FIC, ●) made up the smallest fraction of all follow-on approvals (5.4% in 2001). While the number of SNDS FIC approvals was small, it nevertheless increased sharply over time, from 1 in 2001 to 22 in 2008. As shown in Figure 4.1(a), follow-on approvals granted to generic firms based on bioequivalence to previously marketed products also increased significantly over the test period. Both standard (ANDS, ■) and supplementary (SANDS, O) generic approvals increased by 28.6% and 118.2%, respectively, over 2001 values. Therefore, all four categories of follow-on drugs increased over the test period.

Figure 4.1(b) demonstrates opposite trends for all new drug categories over the course of the test period, and that these changes took place from a smaller baseline. Approvals granted for all new drugs combined declined from 29.5% of total approvals in 2001 to 13.69% in 2008. Similarly, approvals granted to brand name pharmaceutical firms decreased from 34.67% of total approvals in 2001 to 13.44% 2008. These data represent a reduction of 55% and 48% in total approvals and approvals granted to brand name firms respectively over the eight-year test period. As the regression lines illustrate, the approvals for all three new drug metrics (NDS:O; NAS: ●; NDS FIC: ■) declined steadily over the course of the test period.

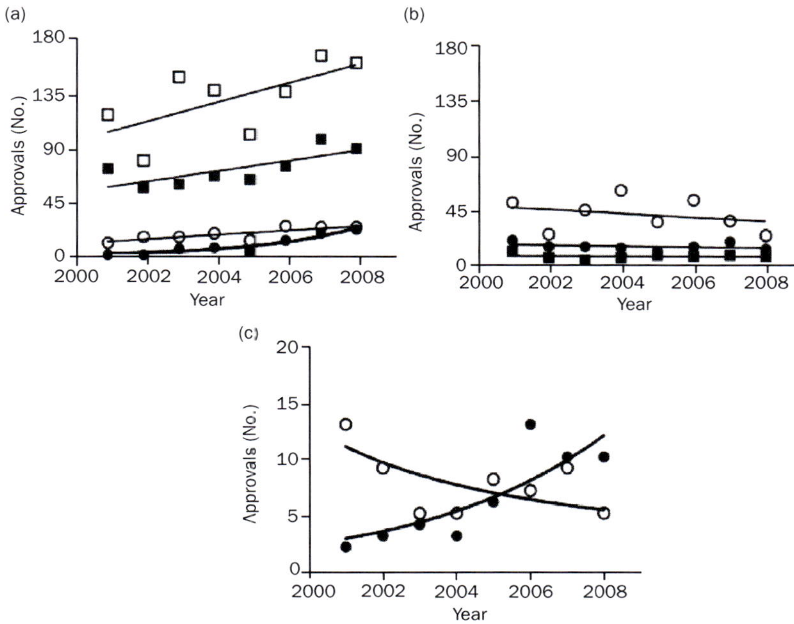

Figure 4.1 Shifting patterns of drug approval and drug regulation during the period 2001–2008.

(a) Market authorizations for several types of 'follow-on' drug increased over the 2001–2008 test period. This includes brand name Supplemental New Drug Submission (SNDS; □) and SNDS first-in-class (SNDS FIC; ●) approvals, and generic Abbreviated New Drug Submission (ANDS; ■) and follow-on Abbreviated New Drug Submission (SANDS; ○) approvals. (b) In contrast, approvals granted to brand-name firms for 'new' drug submissions declined from a smaller baseline over the same period. This included approvals from New Drug Submission (NDS; ○), New Active Substance (NAS; ●), and NDS first-in-class (NDS FIC; ■) streams. (c) Expedited review pathway for drug approval is shifting towards probationary-type approval consistent with emerging lifecycle models of regulation: expedited drug approvals with no post-market evidentiary obligations (Priority Review; ○) decreased over the 2001–2008 test period while those with significant post-market obligation conditions (NOC/c; ●) increased steeply over the same time frame.

Time series plots for new and follow-on approvals are presented in Figure 4.2. Approval data for both classes of drugs are expressed as approvals per day plotted by month and year over the test period. The data illustrate that both new (●) and follow-on (●) drug approvals were well spaced out over the course of a given year rather than aggregated in a given month or year, particularly when viewed over the course of the entire test period. Therefore there was no daily or monthly variation skewing yearly averages discussed in relation to Figures 4.1 and 4.3. Comparative data for all new and follow-on approval categories in 2001 and 2008 are provided in Table 4.3.

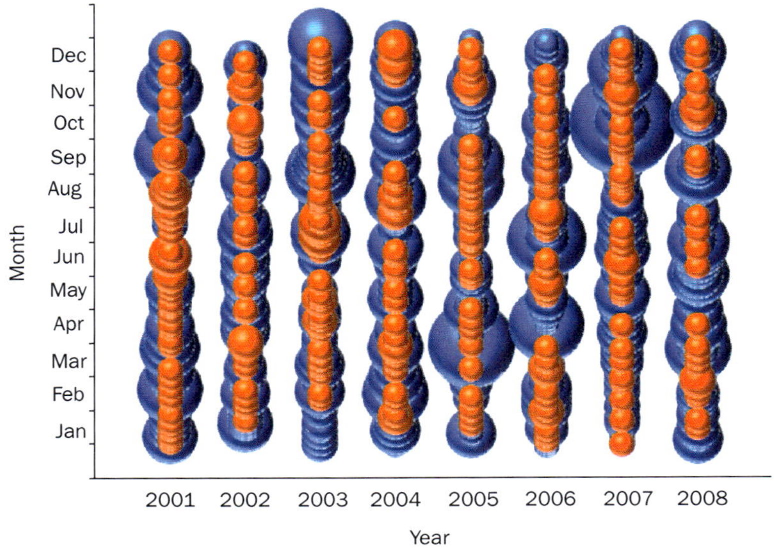

Figure 4.2 Time series distribution for new and follow-on drug approvals during the period 2001–2008.

Bubbles represent approvals granted per day for 'new' (●) and 'follow-on' (●) drugs as defined in the text accompanying Figure 4.1. Bubble diameter is a linear representation of the number of approvals granted per day distributed over the course of the test period expressed yearly and by month. The data illustrate that both new and follow-on drug approvals were well spaced out over the course of the test period rather than being aggregated in a given month or year, particularly when viewed over the course of the entire eight-year test period.

Table 4.3 Comparison of 2001 and 2008 drug approval data

Drug type	**2001**		**2008**		Δ **(%)**
	N =	% total	N =	% total	
A. New drugs	52	20.4%	25	83.3%	–51.9
NDS	52	100.0%	25	100.0%	–1.9
NDS FIC	12	23.1%	8	32.0%	–33.3
NDS NAS	21	40.4%	14	56.0%	–33.3
B. Follow-on drugs	203	79.6%	275	91.7%	35.5
SNDS	118	58.1%	161	58.5%	36.4
SNDS FIC	1	0.5%	22	8.0%	2,100.0
ANDS	73	36.0%	90	32.7%	23.3
SANDS	11	5.4%	24	8.7%	118.2

Figures 4.3(a)–(d) are area diagrams illustrating cumulative approval data for various categories of new and follow-on drug products. As shown in Figure 4.3(a), only 16% (n = 338) of the 2,122 drugs approved over the period 2001–2008 were deemed to be 'new' drugs. This refers to NDS submissions, including those directed to first-in-class therapies and those including a new active substance. By contrast, 84% (n = 1,784) of approved drugs were 'follow-on' in nature, including brand-name SNDS approvals, generic ANDS and SANDS approvals, and brand-name SNDS approvals directed to first-in-class therapies.

Figure 4.3(b) shows the results of a more nuanced analysis of follow-on drugs, this time focusing on comparison of me-too and first-in-class drugs. Of all drugs approved between 2001 and 2008, 59% (n = 1,252) were me too. Of note, the fraction of me-too drugs was substantially greater than all first-in-class drugs, irrespective of whether they were NDS or SNDS (6.5%; n = 138). The requirements for NDS and SNDS first-in-class and me-too drugs are summarized for convenience in Table 4.4.

Generic drugs were the final follow-on category to be assessed. The split between total brand name and generic drugs approved from 2001 to 2008 is shown in Figure 4.3(c). Of all drugs approved over the test period, 65.5% were directed to brand name products while the remaining 34.5% were directed to generic products.

Data for the most innovative drugs approved during the test period are given in Figure 4.3(d). Only a small fraction (6.1%) of drugs approved (n = 130) during the test period contained an NAS. Similarly, of 2,122 drugs approved, only 5.3% (n = 112) went through the two expedited approval streams (Priority Review or NOC/c), and of these only a small number (n = 26) were also directed to first-in-class therapies and contained an NAS. This amounted to 1.23% of total drug approvals over the eight-year test period and 1.87% of total brand-name approvals over the same period. These results illustrate that the typical drug approved by Canadian regulators over the period 2001–2008 was most likely to be a follow-on drug approved via the SNDS stream rather than a new drug approved via either the NDS stream or either expedited stream (Priority Review or NOC/c). The likelihood that a drug approved during the test period satisfied the most stringent requirements for a breakthrough drug was close to zero (1.23%; or 1.87% brand approvals).

As discussed above, there are two forms of expedited drug approval in Canada: 'Priority Review' and approval via the 'NOC with conditions' (NOC/c) pathway.[10] Priority Review allows appropriate candidates to be shifted forward in the approval queue without a change in the evidentiary requirements for safety and efficacy required for conventional NDS

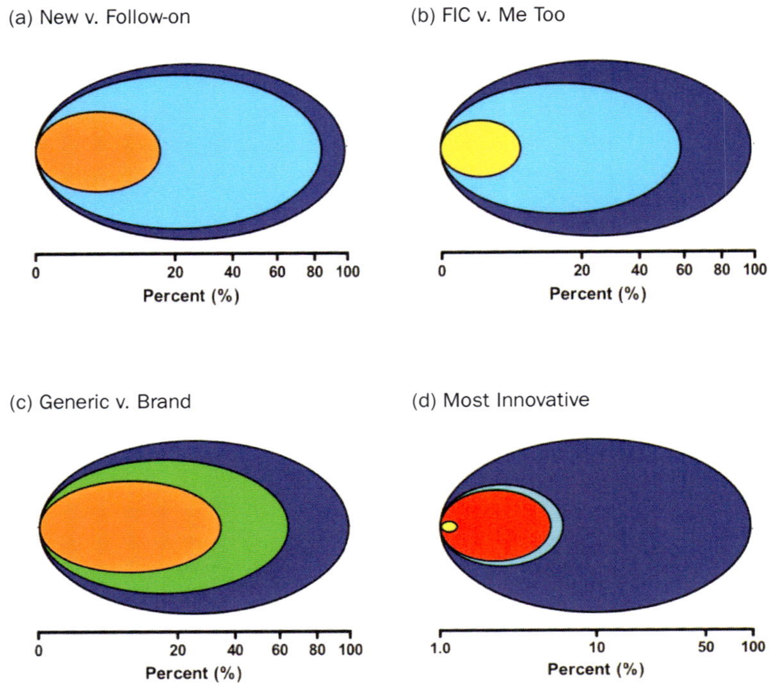

Figure 4.3 Profile of pharmaceutical innovation in Canada between 2001 and 2008.

(a) *New v. follow-on approvals*. Of total drugs approved over the test period, 15% constituted New Drug Submissions (NDS: ●) while 84% were for 'follow-on' drugs (SNDS, ANDS, and SANDS: ●). (b) *Types of follow-on approvals*. Of follow-on approvals, 6.1% were for supplementary 'first-in-class' (SNDS FIC: ●) drugs while 59% were for 'me-too' drugs (●). (c) *Brand name v. generic approvals*. Of all drugs approved during the test period, 65.5% of approvals were granted to brand-name drug companies (NDS and SNDS:) and 34.5% to generic companies (ANDS and SANDS: ●). (d) *Most innovative drugs*. While 6.5% of approvals during the test period were directed to New Active Substances (●; NAS) and 5.3% of all NDS and SNDS submissions were approved under an expedited review process (●; Priority Review and NOC/c), only 1.23% of all drugs approved over the period 2001–2008 were also directed to FIC therapies and contained an NAS (●). Areas are approximations of calculated means for the entire test period. Note that area scales are linear for panels (a)–(c) and log for panel (d).

approval. Drug candidates must be directed to the treatment of a serious, life-threatening, or severely debilitating disease with an unmet medical need or for which a substantial improvement in the benefit-risk profile is demonstrated.[11] By contrast, the NOC/c pathway allows a drug to gain market access prior to completion of traditional Phase 3 clinical trials, provided that it is directed to a serious, life-threatening, or severely

Table 4.4 Classification scheme for first-in-class and me-too drugs

Route	First in class	Me too
A. NDS	New chemical form *or* New use/indication	Change in benefit : risk
B. SNDS	New chemical form *and* New use/indication	Change in chemical form *and* Change in benefit : risk

debilitating disease for which no drug is marketed or where the candidate presents a better overall benefit-risk profile than existing therapies. Unlike the Priority Review stream, continuing approval via the NOC/c stream is contingent upon whether pharmaceutical sponsors meet the conditions assigned to the NOC/c. For this reason, NOC/c approval is a reasonable proxy for emerging lifecycle models of drug regulation.[12]

Data in Figure 4.1(c) suggest that Canadian regulators may be shifting away from Priority Review as the dominant mechanism for expedited review towards the NOC/c pathway. Priority Review approvals (O) decreased from 14 in 2001 to a low of 6 in 2008, declining 57% over the eight-year test period. By comparison, the number of NOC/c approvals (●) escalated strongly over time, from a minimum of 2 in 2001 to a maximum of 13 in 2006 (stabilizing at 10 in 2007–2008). Compared to the 57% decline in the number of Priority Review approvals, peak NOC/c approvals increased by 650%. The totals for both streams over the test period were not dissimilar: 61 and 51 for Priority Review and NOC/c, respectively. However, as illustrated by the data and fits in Figure 4.1(c), the trends for the two pathways crossed over in 2005.

Of interest, the legal basis for Priority Review and NOC/c approval is not expressly provided for under the current Food and Drugs Act[13] or regulations.[14] Rather, both are grounded in administrative instruments known as 'guidance documents' that do not have the force of law.[15] Data described in Figure 4.1(c) therefore demonstrate that Canadian regulators are already anticipating the lifecycle regulatory framework proposed in Bill C-51,[16] along with its recalibrated balance of pre-market and post-market access, safety and efficacy. Together, the data in Figures 4.1–4.3 suggest that Canadian regulators are focusing on faster approval with enhanced post-market surveillance at the same time as approval is geared more towards follow-on rather than towards breakthrough drug development.

4.3.2 Drug patenting

Figure 4.4 shows data relating to drug patenting and patent listing of drugs approved for sale in Canada during the period 2001–2008. The data are for 16 of the most profitable drugs sold in Canada for which an NOC was granted during the test period (approval subset). The list parallels the top 16 drugs sold in the United States during the same period.[17]

As illustrated in Figure 4.4(a), total patents granted on the approval subset had a bell-shaped distribution (Gaussian; $R^2 = 0.91$), peaking in 2001 (■). There were 772 patents on 16 products, corresponding to an average patent per product ratio of 48:1. The calculated inflection point, representative of the take-off point from the baseline, for total patents issued yearly occurred about 1991 (1991.35). This was just before the linkage regulations came into force in 1993. That the inflection point preceded the NOC Regulations is not surprising in light of the significant negotiations leading up to TRIPS and the coming into force of the linkage regulations regime. Cumulative patents for the subset rose over time in a manner that was well fit by a sigmoidal function (□; $R^2 = 0.99$), peaking at about 2004. The calculated inflection point (1994.70) was slightly later than that calculated for total patents (1991), occurring just after the linkage regulations came into force. Figure 4.4(b) (top) gives the same data re-plotted as a function of the year after the first patent was issued. Patents on approved drugs were granted over a relatively long term of 25 years (◇), peaking at 77 patents per year on the twelfth year after the first patent was granted. As illustrated in Figure 4.4(b) (♦), this amounted to an average of 3.34 patents per product per year.

4.3.3 Patent listing and litigation

Over the last decade, there have been increasing claims to the effect that the linkage regulation regime is used more as a sword than a shield by brand-name pharmaceutical firms.[18] Figure 4.4(a) illustrates the manner in which patents for the approval subset were listed on the patent register over the test period. The time course for cumulative listed patents (●) was well described by a sigmoid function ($R^2 = 0.99$), with a relatively steep slope, an inflection point near 2001 (2001.10), and an apparent peak in 2008. Importantly, the curves for cumulative patents (□) and the fraction of patents that were listed on the patent register (●) converged strongly over time. This result supports the conclusion that brand-name firms are listing patents they obtain on the patent register in a timely fashion in order to delay generic entry.[19]

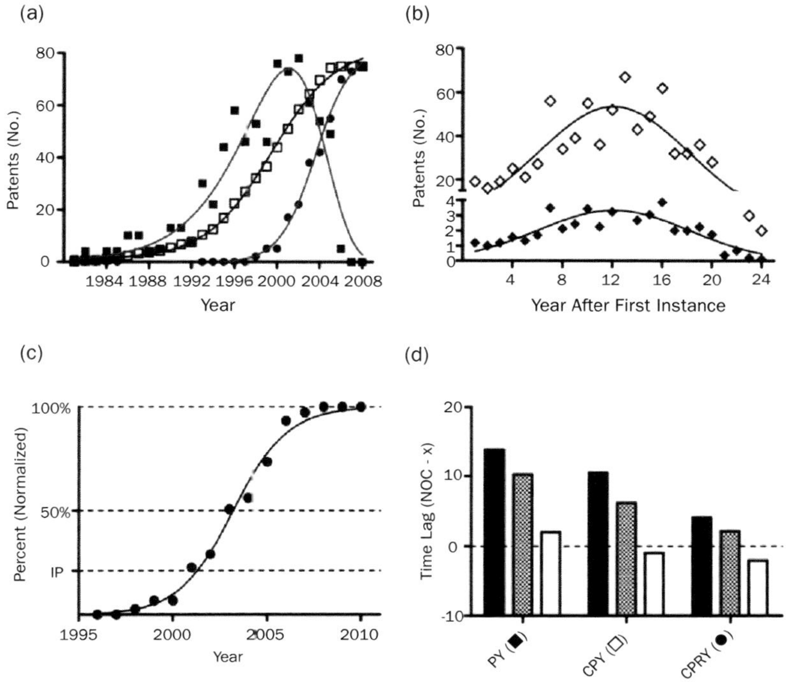

Figure 4.4 Patenting and patent listing patterns associated with drug approval.

(a) Total patents issued by year associated with a subset of 16 top selling drugs (■); cumulative number of patents associated with the sub-set (□); and cumulative number of patents listed on the patent register under linkage regulations associated with the sub-set (●). Note the strong convergence of total and listed patents over the course of the test period. (b) Total (◇) and average (◆) number of patents on approved drugs within the subset plotted as a function of the time after the priority date on which the first patent on the subset was issued. (c) Method used to calculate the temporal gap between the date of mean drug approval on the patent subset (2005) and the inflection point (IP), 50th and 100th percentile of normalized maximum drug patenting and approvals. Data are from the cumulative number of patents (●) above. (d) Graph expressing the temporal relationship between drug approval and the IP, 50th and 100th percentile of maximal normalized patents granted per year (PY), cumulative patents per year (CPY) and cumulative patents listed on the patent register per year (CPRY). Time points are calculated as the difference between the date of drug approval (NOC) and the date of the IP, 50th and 100th percentile (NOC-x). The data suggest drug patent listing may be a better proxy for drug approval than drug patenting per se.

Of 772 patents granted on the approval subset, 77 were listed on the patent register between 1998 and 2008. On average there were 4.81 listed patents per product. As indicated by the difference between the average number of patents per year (3.34) and the average number of listed patents per product (4.81), domestic linkage regulations allow patents to be listed on more than one product. Unlike drug patenting, which occurs only in an anterograde direction (i.e. patents must be new, non-obvious, and have utility over the prior art), patents may be listed on the patent register in either an anterograde or retrograde direction. For example, originating patents relating to proton pump blockers may be listed not just for the first-generation product Losec® (racemic mixture of R and S omeprazole Mg^{2+}) but also the second-generation product Nexium® (S enantiomer, esomeprazole Mg^{2+}), and vice versa.

We next investigated the temporal relationship between NOC grant, patent issue and patent listing. From each of the curves in Figure 4.4(a), we calculated three values: (1) the inflection point at which the data deviated most strongly from baseline values (closed bars) and the point at which each curve reached the (2) 50th (hatched bars) and (3) 100th percentile (open bars) of normalized maximum values. The inflection point was calculated as the zero point of the second derivative of fits to the data. Each of the three values was then plotted as a function of the average date on which the subset received marketing approval (2005). This was done to obtain a measure of the delay between drug approval and drug patenting and listing. The procedure is demonstrated for cumulative patent listing data in Figure 4.4(c) (●).

As illustrated by the bar graphs in Figure 4.4(d), there was a significant lag between the date on which NOCs were granted and the dates on which patents on the same drug product were granted. This pattern was observed independently of whether patents were expressed by year of grant (patent per year (PY)) or cumulatively (cumulative patents per year (CPY)). This is not surprising in light of the regulatory lag between drug patenting and drug approval. The data were different, however, for patent listing (cumulative patents registered per year (CPRY)). As shown in Figure 4.4(d), average data for both the inflection point and 50th percentile exceeded the null point by only 4 and 2 years, respectively. This can be compared with 10 and 8 years for corresponding data for cumulative patents (CPY). The lag between drug approval and patent listing was even greater for patenting data expressed as a function of year of grant (PY). Of interest, the calculated values for the 50th percentile and peak patent listing for CPRY were 1–2 years on either side of the null point. This result indicates there was virtually no significant lag between drug approval and patent listing as the test period progressed. While the data obtained do not provide conclusive evidence for a causal relationship between drug regulation and drug development, they suggest that patent listing is a substantially better proxy for drug approval than drug patenting.

Given the results in Figure 4.4, we further probed the nexus between drug approval, drug patenting, and patent listing, particularly as it relates to potential extension of the term of patent protection afforded to drugs that are already approved in Canada. Figure 4.5 shows a comparison of potential and actual periods of extended patent protection for the average drug product in the approval subset due to the operation of linkage regulations. Here 'potential' is used to refer to the hypothetical extension of patent protection under patent legislation and linkage regulations if all patents granted were in fact listed on the patent register. In comparison, the 'actual' term of extended patent protection refers to the extension of the duration of patent protection beyond that afforded by the originating patent alone as a result of those patents actually registered on the patent list. The sigmoid curves represent the start and end dates for the potential term of patent protection as a function of patents associated with approved drugs. The term starts with the priority date of the 'originating patent,' e.g. the first patent on the drug, typically that on the NAS/NCE (●), and ends 20 years from the filing date of the originating patent plus the cumulative terms of all 'subsequent patents' (●) associated with the marketed drug. This is illustrated by the corresponding horizontal lines and shading in Figure 4.5. Patents actually listed on the register are represented by appropriate symbols (♦) and horizontal patent term lines.

The average period of patent protection associated with originating patents was about 20 years, from 1983 to 2003. This represents an average of patent terms before (17 years from date of grant) and after (20 years from filing date) amendments made to the Patent Act pursuant to TRIPS. In comparison, the duration of potential extended patent protection associated with subsequent patents was about twofold longer, lasting from about 1987 to 2026. This yields a term of extended patent protection due to the operation of linkage regulations of about 43 years per drug on average. However, this calculation does not reflect the actual period of extended patent protection, which would only be a function of cumulative terms for patents actually listed on the register. Of the average of 48 patents per product on the approval subset, 10% (4.81 patents per product) were listed on the register.

Termination of listed patents was spaced fairly evenly along the sigmoidal curve between 2010 and 2025 rather than being clumped together at the front end of the data set. The even distribution of listing resulted in the extension of the term of patent protection from the end of the NAS patent in 2003 to termination of the latest listed patent in 2025. The extension of the average patent term owing to linkage regulations amounts to an increase of 22 years, representing a doubling of the duration of patent protection beyond that associated with the originating patent. As illustrated by the appropriate symbols (♦) and shading in the figure, there was little difference between potential and actual terms of patent extension for the approval subset. This was due to the strategic timing of patent listing by brand-name drug firms, e.g. firms stagger the registration of their strongest patents to obtain the longest period of protection. Of note, comparison of data in Figures 4.3 and 4.5 demonstrate that while the average drug approved in Canada over the test period has an arguably low innovative value, the average period of patent protection afforded to products in the approval subset is in fact quite substantial.

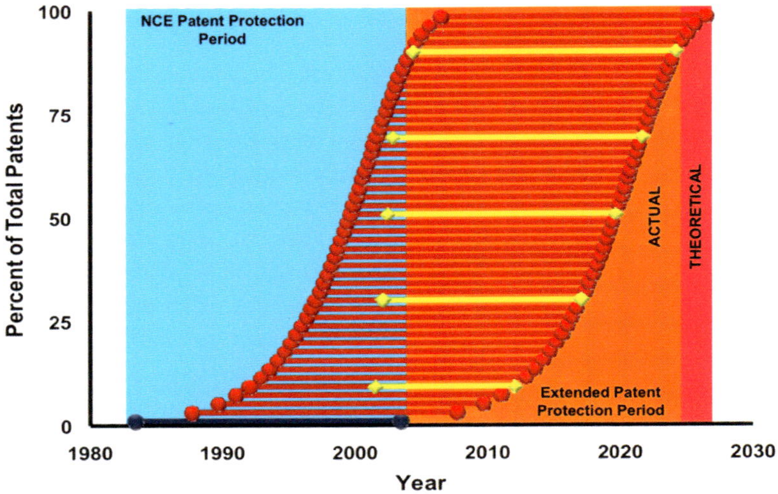

Figure 4.5 Extension of patent monopoly for marketed drugs via operation of linkage regulations.

Period of extended patent protection for averaged drugs in the subset (n = 16). Left and right sigmoid curves represent cumulative patent protection start and end dates. The term of patent protection was deemed to begin on the priority date. Terms are shown for the 'originating patent' on the New Active Substance/New Chemical Entity (●; n = 1) and all 'subsequent patents' (●; n = 21). The date on which patents were listed on the register is also shown (◆; n = 5). The duration of theoretical and actual patent protection under linkage regulations associated with originating and subsequent patents are illustrated by representative horizontal lines and shading along the time axis. Note the period of patent protection associated with originating patents lasted about twenty years (■), from 1983 to 2003. In comparison, the duration of extended patent protection associated with all 'subsequent patents' was much longer (~twofold; ■), lasting from about 1987 to 2028. Of the 48 patents granted per drug, an average of 5 were listed on the patent register. The term of protection associated with these patents ran from 1993 to 2025 (■). This yielded an actual extended period of patent protection of 22 years beyond that afforded by the originating patent. Note that due to strategic listing of patents on the patent register (◆), there was little difference between theoretical and actual patent protection under linkage regulations.

The importance of the timing of shifts in innovation profiles, expedited drug approval, drug patenting, and patent listing is underscored by the data in Figure 4.6. In this analysis, drug patenting and listing represent patent incentives for innovation whereas expedited drug approval is taken as a measure of lifecycle-based regulatory incentives for innovation. The data for 'new' and 'follow-on' innovations represent the fits to NDS data and SNDS, ANDS, and SANDS data from Figures 4.1(a) and 4.1(b). Data for lifecycle regulation were taken as the fit to NOC/c data from Figure 4.1(c). Drug patenting and patent listing curves are those from Figure 4.4(a).

A comparison of fitted curves in Figure 4.6 indicates that neither the steep time-dependent changes in patent grant and patent listing preceding (Figure 4.6(a)) nor the NOC/c approval in the midst of relatively linear trends for new and follow-on drugs (Figure 4.6(b)) appear to provide a measurable correlate for pioneering drug development, at least as reflected by the data and fits to new and follow-on drugs. Each of these three metrics had a relatively non-linear trend upwards either before or during the test period while by comparison the trend for new drug approvals was linear and in the downward direction (with a corresponding increase in follow-on approvals). That these trends (1) occurred before and during the comparatively linear changes in new and follow-on drug approval by regulators (Figures 4.1 and 4.6) and (2) were observed independent of the temporal association of drug approval, drug patenting, and patent listing (Figure 4.4(d)) suggests that the current basket of IPR rights targets does not provide a strong incentive for pioneering drug development.

Finally, there has been sharp criticism of the practice of 'evergreening' drug products via linkage regulations in the United States and Canada.[20] Evergreening refers to extending the market monopoly on a drug facing originating patent expiration through listing of further relevant patents on the patent register for minor modifications to the marketed drug. An example of this phenomenon from our data set is presented in Figure 4.7.

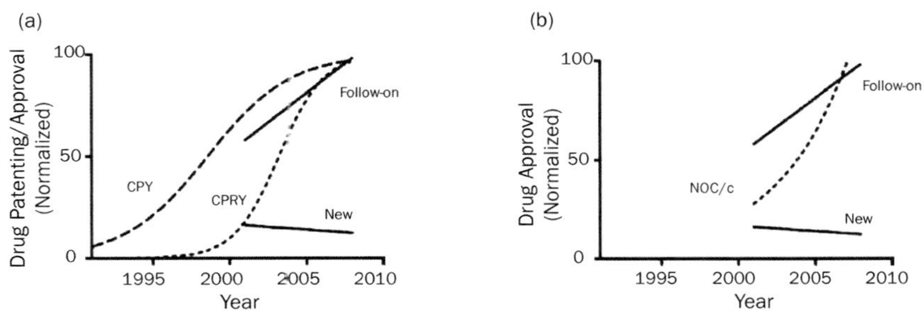

Figure 4.6 Comparison of the timing of trends for drug innovation, lifecycle regulation, patent grant, and patent listing.

(a) Overlay of time courses of fits to normalized cumulative patents per year (CPY; long dash), cumulative listed patents per year (CPRY; short dash), new drug approvals (new; downward linear) and follow-on drug approvals (follow-on; upward linear). Data for 'new' and 'follow-on' innovations were calculated from NDS and SNDS/ANDS/SANDS curves in Figures 4.1(a) and 4.1(b). Drug patenting and listing data are from Figure 4.4(a). (b) Overlay of new drug approvals and follow-on drug approvals from panel (a) and lifecycle-based NOC/c approvals (NOC/c; short dash). Data for expedited review were taken from Figure 4.1(c). Comparison of these curves suggests that steep time-dependent changes in patent grant, patent listing, or NOC/c approval as a proxy for lifecycle regulation appear to be unrelated to the accompanying linear trends for new and follow-on drug approval data.

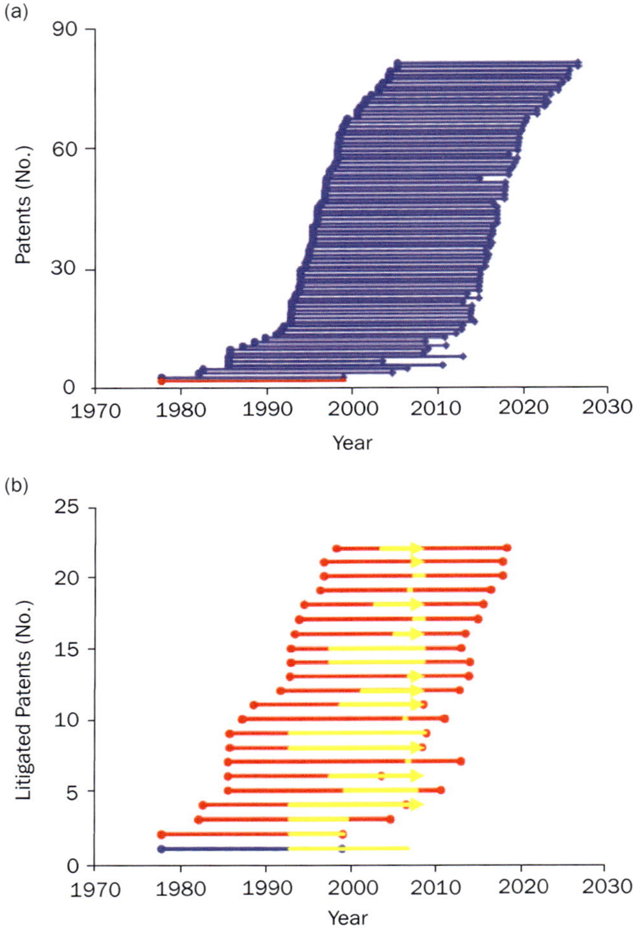

Figure 4.7 Example of extension of patent monopoly for omeprazole.

(a) Relative to the forms of drugs marketed between 2001 and 2008, 82 patents were granted in relation to Losec® and Nexium®. As observed for averaged data on the subset of 16 drugs, the timing of grant and duration of cumulative patents followed a sigmoidal course, with patent protection beginning in 1978 and extending to about 2025. The first regulatory approval for omeprazole was in 1989. Data for the first New Chemical Entity (●) and all subsequent patents (●) are provided. (b) Of the 82 patents granted on the two drugs, 22 were listed on the patent register and litigated under linkage regulations. Priority dates and patent terms are represented by appropriate symbols (●) and lines. Initiation, duration and termination of litigation on individual patents are represented by orange lines. Completely solid orange lines represent completed litigation. Right-facing arrows (→) represent litigation which is still ongoing, e.g. where it has not yet been determined that the listed patent was valid and infringed (brand-name victory) or invalid and not infringed (generic victory). For details of individual trials, see text.

Omeprazole, marketed in Canada as Losec® (Prilosec® in the United States) and the second-generation product Nexium® are widely considered to be two of the most profitable drugs developed over the last several decades on a global basis. Not surprisingly, they have also been the subject of prolonged and highly contentious litigation in both the United States and Canada. The chemistry and mechanism of action of both drugs is highly similar. Indeed, as illustrated in Table 4.5, their chemical names and formulae are almost identical. The difference between the compounds, as alleged in litigation in both jurisdictions,[21] is that the magnesium salt form of omeprazole (Losec®) undergoes a chemical shift following ingestion that converts a portion of the racemic mixture that is potentially inactive to the fully active chemical form (Nexium®).[22] This chiral shift has been claimed to double the effective drug concentration.[23]

Setting aside the scientific veracity of this claim for the moment, the question arises of how pharmaceutical firms are able to strategically employ minor but potentially significant changes to already patented and marketed compounds in order to maintain market share through either 'blocking patents' (inactive patents that nevertheless serve as a barrier to market entry) or via patents that are listed on the patent register specifically in order to deter or initiate litigation.

We identified 82 patents associated with the two drugs that were granted over a period of twenty years. Together, the patents had a cumulative term of patent protection of close to fifty years. As shown in Figure 4.7(a), the time course and duration of patent protection were sigmoidal, similar to the averaged data in Figure 4.5(a). Data are given for the first NCE patent (●) and all subsequent patents (●) identified using the methodology described above. The priority dates for the first and final patent were 1978 and 2005, respectively. Therefore the period of hypothetical patent protection on the omeprazole group ran from 1975 to about 2025. In comparison, the first NOC for omeprazole (Losec®) was granted on June 13, 1989, yielding a regulatory gap of close to ten years.

Table 4.5 Comparison of omeprazole (Losec®) and esomeprazole (Nexium®)

Brand name	Formula	Chemical name
Losec®	$C_{17}H_{19}N_3O_3S$	6-methoxy-2-((4-methoxy-3,5-dimethylpyridin-2-yl) methylsulfinyl)-1*H*-benzo[*d*]imidazole
Nexium®	$C_{17}H_{19}N_3O_3S$	(*S*)-5-methoxy-2-[(4-methoxy-3,5-dimethylpyridin-2-yl) methylsulfinyl]-*H*-benzoimidazole

Of 82 patents that were deemed relevant to omeprazole, 22, or 27% of all relevant patents, were listed on the patent register. This value is substantially greater than the 10% listed patents observed with the cohort of 16 drugs in Figure 4.5 and the 5% of listed patents on the much larger cohort of 95 high-value drugs in Chapter 5. In other words, fractional listing increased from 5% on a large cohort of most profitable drugs, then to 10% as the cohort was narrowed to the top 16 drugs, and, finally, to 25% of all patents identified on two of the top selling blockbuster drugs. Relevant to the analysis of whether the linkage regulations are working as intended in Chapter 6, the data indicate a positive and strong correlation between the percentage of patents granted that are listed on the patent register and profitability. If not listed on the register at some future point in time, the remaining patents were deemed to function as so-called blocking patents. As noted above, patents could be listed on more than one drug product provided they are legally relevant to the marketed product. This is reflected in the fact that the 22 patents were the subject of 75 individual legal determinations.

All 22 listed patents have or continue to be disputed at trial in some form or another. This is shown in Figure 4.7(b), which illustrates listed and litigated patents (●) and the timing and duration of ongoing (→) and final (—) litigation. Litigation over 15 of the 22 patents lasted in excess of two years, with 14 final trial decisions to date (for some patents, multiple times, as indicated below). Final decisions were at the Federal Court of Canada, Federal Court of Appeal, or Supreme Court of Canada. As might be expected with so many patents being litigated multiple times, decisions on the merits were not harmonious from one decision to the next.[24] Indeed, there were numerous instances (n = 11) where a court at one level decided that patents were invalid or not infringed with one set of litigants while a different court at the same level decided that the same patents were valid and infringed with differing litigants. In addition to litigation under the NOC Regulations, there were also three related patent infringement actions involving listed patents, one of which is ongoing (data not shown).

Figure 4.7 does not include data relating to individual trials. While this would have provided a better sense of just how extensive the litigation was over these two drugs, it would have complicated the figure unnecessarily. For example, over the period 1993–2009, there were 61 separate trials on 22 listed patents, including 310 motions (mean = 5.08 per trial) and 25 final trial decisions. Of final decisions, 14 went on to appeal at the Federal Court of Appeal and 8 went on to the Supreme Court of Canada. Litigation occurred over a term of 16 years, essentially from the time the linkage regulations came into force in 1993 until the present. Four trials on 12 patents are currently ongoing.

Given that the NDS patent expired in 1999, extended patent protection on omeprazole has been ongoing for at least ten years. But this does not necessarily equate to a decade of guaranteed legal protection under the linkage regulations, owing to the requirement that generics must first obtain approval for market entry themselves and demonstrate in litigation all relevant patents are invalid or not infringed by their product.[25] Of 25 final decisions levied by the courts, there were 13 cases where patents listed on the register were judged to be invalid or not infringed. The average date of the first automatic injunction for all litigants was February 2001. This represented the date on which drug approvals granted, or to be granted, to generic firms were 'put on hold.' The average date on which the group of 13 trials ended, and thus the date of 'reactivation' of average generic approval, was December 2003. Therefore litigation over patents relating to Losec® and Nexium® resulted in a delay of market entry of close to three (2.83) years for the group. According to IMS Health,[26] sales of the two drugs in drugstores and hospitals over the same time frame were CN $1.4 billion. In comparison, total spending on prescription pharmaceuticals rose from CN $11.7 billion in 2001 to CN $17.97 billion in 2004,[27] representing an increase of 92%. This includes an increase in out-of-pocket consumer spending from CN $2.56 billion to CN $3.36 billion. It is reasonable, however, to speculate that 'but for' the existence of the linkage regime that generic entry may have occurred closer to expiry of the NCE patent, with an accordingly shorter period of delayed entry. Either way, the linkage regulations regime has proved to be a highly effective mechanism for extending market monopolies on profitable pharmaceuticals.

4.3.4 Limitations

Conclusions from our pilot study may be tempered by two limiting factors. The first is that the time frame for the drug approval study is smaller (2001–2008) than that for the patenting (1978–2008) and patent listing (1993–2008) studies. This owes to the fact our initial work on drug approval was done prior to undertaking the patent study. The year 2001 was chosen as our starting point in the drug approval study because substantial amendments to Canadian drug regulation were made at this time that affected both the mechanisms and speed of approval.[28] It will therefore be important for future work to include approval data from before the domestic linkage regulations came into force in 1993.

The second, and related, limitation is that the approval data set was for 608 drugs while our pilot study on drug patenting and linkage regulations was for only 16 drugs. For reasons given in the Methods section, this made good sense for the pilot study. We attempted to extrapolate the approval data back in time. However, given the yearly scatter in the data set and resulting confidence levels, this was not feasible. We obtain some assurance from the consistent nature of the daily and monthly scatter of approval data described in Figure 4.2. More importantly, as described in Chapter 5 we have now increased our data set to 95 of 608 approved drugs between 2001 and 2008 in a follow-up study. The results (data not shown) indicate that all major patterns for drug patenting and patent listing shown in Figures 4.4–4.7 are repeated not just for the entire 'most profitable' data set, but for three different sub-groups (most profitable, n = 33; NOC/c, n = 22; Priority Review, n = 46). In particular, there was no substantial difference in the patenting data in Figures 4.4(a)–4.4(d) (n = 16) and the twofold larger data set of most profitable drugs in the expanded study (n = 33). Even so, future research must complete the patenting data for not only the 608 drugs approved during the period 2001–2008, but also for the broader drug approval data as it grows to encompass and backdate the coming into force of the linkage regulations in 1993 and beyond.

4.4 Discussion

4.4.1 Trends in global drug development

Data in Figure 4.1 demonstrate that the number of 'new' drug approvals is decreasing significantly over time while the number of follow-on approvals is increasing. Cumulative data in Figure 4.3 show that the number of truly innovative drug products is vanishingly small (1.23% of total and 1.87% of brand-name approvals) over the eight-year test period. In general, our qualitative findings relating to pharmaceutical innovation parallel those observed in other jurisdictions.[29] That is, the multinational pharmaceutical industry is leaning away from breakthrough drug development towards less innovative products referred to variously as follow-on, incremental, supplemental, line extension, me-too and bioequivalent drugs.

While our data do not speak directly to claims that diminished innovation is due to the loss of 'low-hanging fruit'[30] or to the spiraling costs of drug development,[31] the data reported on the nexus between drug approval and patenting provide a third plausible explanation for the diminution of breakthrough product development. The results shown in Figures 4.1–4.7 suggest that innovation policy and drug regulation contingent on IPR rights can profoundly shape the rate and direction of innovative activity by multinational pharmaceutical firms *antecedently*, towards incentives provided for by law and away from truly breakthrough products under conditions where the two do not necessarily coincide.

Depending on the source and degree of industry affiliation, published definitions of what constitutes an innovative drug range considerably, from as low a threshold as simply containing an NAS,[32] to the slightly more stringent requirements of either being directed to first-in-class therapies[33] (irrespective of whether approval is directed to a new or follow-on drug) or to follow-on drugs that nevertheless undergo Priority Review.[34] However, merely containing an NAS is an insufficient basis for designating a drug as pioneering or strongly innovative because there is ample room in the definition for minor changes to previously approved medical ingredients, including salts, esters, solvates, polymorphs and enantiomers. A similar conclusion applies to drugs that are only directed to first-in-class therapies, as these can also be follow-on versions of previously marketed products containing slightly modified medical ingredients or directed to new uses within a therapeutic class. Moreover, where Priority Review need only be directed to drugs demonstrating moderate clinical improvement over existing therapies, it is also an insufficient proxy for strong innovation. A more reasonable definition is that truly pioneering drugs are those that are approved via the new drug approval pathway (NDS), contain an NAS or NCE, undergo some form of Priority Review, and are directed to a first-in-class therapy.[35] Only in combination do these requirements approach a reasonable definition for a truly breakthrough technology.

Regulatory agencies in North America have previously attempted to derive innovation indices for pharmaceuticals. For example, in 2000, the Canadian Patented Medicines Prices Review Board (PMPRB)[36] released data to the effect that of drugs approved between 1996 and 2000, 44.8% were line extensions and 49.6% were new versions of marketed drugs with moderate, little, or no improvement. Only 5.5% of all drugs approved represented a substantial therapeutic advance. These results parallel data from a large-scale study of innovation in the French prescription drug market demonstrating that of drugs approved over the term 1981–2001, the most innovative drugs represented only 3% of total approvals, while drugs with some important therapeutic gain and those with little to no therapeutic gain represented 8% and 89% of total approvals, respectively.[37]

For the United States, Kaitin et al. reported data from an analysis of drugs approved by the FDA between 1978 and 1989 that were rated by the agency as having an important therapeutic gain, a modest gain, and little to no gain.[38] Only NCEs which excluded salts, esters, and other dosage forms of previously approved drugs were studied. The authors found that only 14.7% of approvals had the strongest innovation rating, whereas 34.5% and 49.5% were deemed modestly or weakly innovative. A more recent study by the NIHCM[39] demonstrated that of all drugs approved by the FDA during 1989–2000, 15%, 28%, and 57% were deemed to be the 'most innovative' (NCE plus Priority Review), 'moderately innovative' (follow-on plus Priority Review) and 'modestly innovative' (follow-on), respectively.

As in Figures 4.1(a)–4.1(b), in the NIHCM and French studies, approvals for standard follow-on drugs increased steeply over the test periods, while data for the most innovative drugs remained flat over time. The fact that the values of 14.7% and 15% from the Kaitin and NIHCM studies represent NCEs with important therapeutic gain or drugs approved via the NDS stream, rather than drugs also undergoing Priority Review and directed to first-in-class therapies, suggests that the number of truly breakthrough drugs in these studies was more in line with data in Figures 4.1–4.3. With the exception of the French study, each of these indices were reported shortly after policy initiatives impacting drug development came into force, such as linkage regulations in the United States and Canada, the consolidation of US patent appeals courts, and legislation facilitating technology transfer and commercialization via strong IPR rights.[40]

4.4.2 Role of drug patenting and linkage regulations

Despite potential weaknesses in the empirical underpinnings of the innovation indices noted above, it is of interest that there has never developed a parallel empirical literature relating to the social benefits of public health and/or innovation policy that is strongly contingent on IPR rights.[41] The social benefits of innovation are raised under the linkage regulations regime through the terms of the traditional patent bargain. This refers to the grant of a limited monopoly in exchange for public disclosure of socially valuable knowledge.[42] In a public health context where drug approval and drug patenting are linked, the essence of the patent bargain may be viewed as the exchange of extended patent protection for a socially beneficial level of pharmaceutical innovation. Thus the public expects, and should expect, something of substantial social value in exchange for extended patent protection and monopoly pricing. In other words, there should be a strong legal and functional nexus between public health policy and patent policy supported by empirical or other data.

Undue extension of patent protection for poorly innovative drugs via linkage regulations is similar in manner to so-called 'weak' patents. Weak patents are those that provide poor levels of innovation over relevant prior art.[43] Leading courts have consistently held that patents of this nature stifle innovation,[44] chill competition,[45] encroach on the legal mandate of promoting the progress of science and useful arts,[46] and encourage inefficient transfers of wealth.[47] Relevant to the pharmaceutical market, weak patents hijack the IPR rights landscape[48] and allow patentees to extract unwarranted monopoly rents when they would otherwise receive nothing for non-inventive disclosures.[49] Policies underpinning patent protection must be sufficiently worthwhile to the public to warrant the restrictive effect of the patent monopoly,[50] and weak pharmaceutical patents in particular have been held to offend the public interest.[51]

The applicability of jurisprudence relating to weak patents may be particularly relevant to linkage regulations owing to two considerations that do not apply to other industries. The first is the weak relevance standard for listing, which as discussed above provides a very broad target for patentees when aiming for the automatic injunction under both US and Canadian linkage regulations.[52] This injunction, an earlier form of which has been referred to as 'Draconian,'[53] prevents generic firms from market entry until all patents on the register are proved in litigation to be invalid or not infringed.[54] The second is the empirical observation in both jurisdictions that litigation on the merits of contested patents under linkage regulations results in decisions where up to 50–75% of listed patents are deemed by the courts to be either invalid or not infringed by generic products.[55] It is reasonable to speculate that the administrative costs of prolonged litigation under linkage regulations are passed on to consumers in the form of extended monopoly pricing and other rent-seeking behaviors.[56]

A linkage regulation regime that provides patent protection on poorly innovative drugs that extends well beyond the term of originating patents not only has the potential to debilitate the patent system in the short term,[57] but also to weaken pharmaceutical innovation in the long run. Innovation is weakened due to the fact that the combination of a weak relevance requirement and automatic injunctions takes patent protection to a point near its logical extreme. The data reported here suggest that if linkage regimes provide fertile grounds for firms to compete at a lower level of innovation, they also discourage firms from innovating at a level of competition that would provide the greatest benefit to society.

This dilemma can be illustrated by a comparison of data in Figures 4.3 and 4.5. On the one hand, Figure 4.3 demonstrates that a very small fraction of drugs approved by regulators over the eight-year test period could be considered truly breakthrough in nature. This includes drugs approved via the NDS stream (16%), those containing an NAS (6.1%), total NDS and SNDS drugs directed to first-in-class therapies (6.5%), those that underwent one of two pathways for expedited review (5.3%), and those that met the most stringent requirements for breakthrough products (1.23%). On the other hand, Figure 4.5 illustrates that patent protection under linkage regulations does not discriminate between poorly or strongly innovative drugs. It offers broad and long-lasting IPR rights to pharmaceutical firms regardless of the types of products being introduced into the marketplace. This is particularly relevant for follow-on drug products, which are recognized to entail lower risks and costs to pharmaceutical firms.[58] As suggested by data in Figures 4.1(c) and 4.6(b) and elsewhere,[59] the evolution toward a lifecycle-based regulatory approach to drug approval will likely do little to affect the rate and direction of innovative activity by firms absent shifts in legal incentives for breakthrough and follow-on drug development.

The data in Figures 4.4–4.7 further supports discordance between the basket of IPR rights incentives for innovation and resulting product development. For example, the close temporal relationship between drug approval and patent listing in Figure 4.4(d) and the strong convergence in Figure 4.4(a) of patent grant and patent listing following linkage regulations coming into force provide evidence for the conclusion that patent listing evolved into a more effective target, and thus a better proxy, for drug approval than drug patenting per se once the linkage regime came into effect. Other evidence for this conclusion comes from data in Figure 4.6, which demonstrate that steep time-dependent changes in drug patenting, patent listing, and the evolution toward lifecycle regulation appeared to have occurred independently of concomitant trends for new and follow-on drug approvals. The outcome of this dynamic, supported by averaged data for 16 drugs (Figure 4.5) and the single example of omeprazole (Figure 4.7), is that when given the opportunity pharmaceutical firms will leverage government policy and regulation in order to maintain market share for drugs coming off patent rather than developing new blockbuster drugs. The results are not dissimilar to studies of complex political systems, where 'yardsticks' designed to measure progress reorient behavior narrowly towards the fulfillment of yardstick metrics.[60] The implication of this scenario is that firms are aiming ex ante at legal targets which provide the most return on investment rather than the most benefit to the public.

4.4.3 Convergence of economic and public health policy

The data reported here challenge two key assumptions that have underpinned public health policy and economic/industrial policy in industrialized nations for at least the past half century. The first is that strong IPR rights protection is essential to motivate and increase the amount of innovation that occurs in the economy. The second is that public health goals can best be met by encouraging innovation in private industry, essentially by merging public health goals with industrial development goals, buttressed by the IPR rights regime. Importantly, our findings do not indicate abnormal behavior by pharmaceutical companies, but rather the failure of government policy and regulations to produce a specifically desired effect, namely the increased production of truly innovative drugs. It is entirely understandable that pharmaceutical firms avail themselves of regulatory incentives allowing product evergreening after the original patent has expired where it maximizes the benefit and minimizes the risk to shareholders.[61]

Our findings suggest that the blending of industrial and health policy goals may be ineffective and possibly counterproductive in terms of public health outcomes. They also suggest that although new lifecycle regulatory regimes have great potential to increase the efficiency of public health provision by placing new remedies in clinical environments sooner, the efficacy of this approach can be weakened through inadequate monitoring and supervision, such that pharmaceutical firms perceive a higher incentive to exploit existing patented technologies in new ways rather than increasing the flow of new technologies. At a more general level, the data lend empirical substance to an emerging consensus that, in many circumstances, IPR rights may be an inhibitor of innovation.

Although our study was based on domestic Canadian data, we argue that the results are significant within the global context of drug regulatory reform and innovation policy. First, efforts have been underway for some time to harmonize the goals and mechanisms of drug regulation globally. Second, in most developed nations, university-based translational research, firm research and development activities, and national science and technology policy are closely integrated and likewise mirror one another. Third, qualitative trends in approval of new and follow-on drugs track one another fairly closely in most major jurisdictions, and the drug patents that we analyzed represent the most profitable drugs not only in Canada, but also in US and EU markets. Fourth, as discussed in Chapter 7, while the 'product cluster,' or patent portfolio-based, model of drug development has been observed increasingly worldwide, it is likely that nations with pharmaceutical linkage regimes present multinational pharmaceutical firms with the 'path of least resistance' to multi-generational product-patent clusters. Given that a small number of multinational pharmaceutical corporations are responsible for drug innovation globally[62] and are doing so increasingly in partnership with drug regulators,[63] it is reasonable to speculate that drug development and regulation in OECD economies is steadily converging upon a risk management philosophy whereby critical benefit-risk calculations are made not only for drug approval, but also drug development.

We conclude that policy and legislative incentives designed to stimulate innovation in the pharmaceutical industry have had the opposite effect, and that shifting to a lifecycle regulatory model is unlikely to alter this scenario absent effort to balance legal and regulatory incentives for breakthrough and follow-on drug development.

4.4.4 Analytical model: pharmaceuticals and the ecology of innovation

What is the role of private IPR rights, if any, in the decline of pharmaceutical innovation observed here and elsewhere? What are the social benefits of a regulatory system that appears to offer preferential incentives for follow-on drugs rather than truly breakthrough remedies? How does the convergence of public health and industrial/economic policies impact public health, and by what mechanisms? These are important questions as pharmaceutical linkage spreads globally and as nations head into their own latest round of reforms pertaining to drug regulation and the commercialization of publicly funded medical research.

In this book, we describe qualitatively and quantitatively various elements of the legal landscape governing biomedical innovation in such a way as to indicate that it functions as a strongly networked *innovation ecology*. We refer to this ecology as a regulated Therapeutic Product Lifecycle, or rTPL.[64] A highly simplified rTPL diagram is provided in Figure 4.8, which represents the lifecycle of therapeutic product development and regulation as a system ecology where the 'whole is greater than the sum of its parts.' Here, innovation is not depicted as a linear 'pipeline,' or process, moving from basic medical research in universities to applied research in firms and then on to commercialized products.[65] Rather, the grouping of network nodes in the figure (arbitrarily but functionally connected) are interconnected and interdependent in an iterative manner over time. The functioning of the system cannot be understood from analysis of the properties of individual nodes.[66] Important for the present

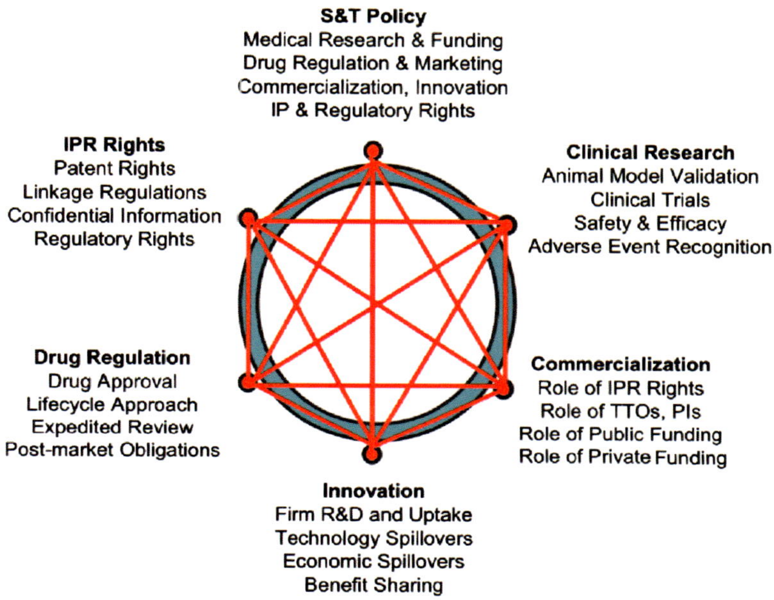

Figure 4.8 Systems model of a regulated Therapeutic Product Lifecycle (rTPL) innovation ecology.

Innovation is represented as an iterative process over time involving several functional groupings, including national science and technology (S&T) policy, clinical research, university and firm commercialization, innovation by private firms, drug regulation by national governments, and intellectual property and regulatory (IPR) rights covering both drug submissions and marketed products. Large red nodes represent functional groupings and include sub-functions enumerated in the figure. Red lines are multi-directional between nodes and sub-functions and are independent of time (acknowledging that the process generally moves clockwise).

study, strongly altering the function of one element in the system, in this case the basket of IPR rights intended to stimulate innovation, has the potential to alter the behavior of the entire system.[67]

It occurs to us that feedback between the various nodes in this innovation ecology is indicative of phenomena associated with complex adaptive systems, in which positive and negative feedback governs system learning, growth, and self-regulation.[68] In both biological and social systems, it has been demonstrated that strong positive feedback has the potential to move a system away from fitness or operational efficiency, even to the point of inducing the system to collapse.[69] In a complex system, 'order' can help the functioning of the system, but hinder it in other ways. For example, it has been observed in a range of natural and biological systems that imposition of too much order can yield a system that is inflexible.[70] Moreover, this inflexibility has the potential to move the system away from a state of fitness, in this case the production of breakthrough drugs. Once major patterns and institutions have been fully explored in a highly regulated system, the system may transition into what Kaufmann refers to as 'detail mode'[71] where its further evolution is limited to modest improvements on increasingly optimized designs. Indeed, some evidence suggests that the more complicated the system, the more autonomous agents in the system become, thus reducing the levels of control that it is possible to wield over them without stifling fitness or efficiency.[72]

Based on the reasoning above, it would seem to be a reasonable conjecture that a complex adaptive innovation ecology, such as we have depicted as an rTPL, may then be one with a large degree of potential creativity and productivity balanced by an equal degree of uncertainty and instability and effected through positive and negative feedback loops, including those initiated by law. This discussion has potentially significant implications for the interpretation of existing pharmaceutical policy, regulation, and literature, including the data reported here. In our previous work on pharmaceutical innovation and litigation,[73] we suggested that regulatory preferences that do not respect the complex nature of the system they seek to regulate (including over-regulation masquerading as under-regulation) have the potential to harm the innovative outputs of the system. This result can be affected by either allowing undue capture of resources or benefits into the hands of discrete actors or through loss of innovative capacity relative to practical considerations of use, including those incentivized through regulatory preferences.

The model in Figure 4.8 envisions all steps in the innovation process as interdependent, particularly over the longer horizon.[74] At the 'beginning' of the process, national science and technology policies are negotiated and initiated to drive national innovation priorities.[75] These policies set the balance between economic and public health goals and expenditures.[76] The next point is represented by publicly funded medical research,[77] which is now desired by policy-makers to be strongly 'translational' in nature and therefore underpinned by strong IPR rights.[78] The mid-point of the process is where clinical trial results become increasingly available, at which point firms identify attractive technologies and begin to layer more substantial IPR rights over them, particularly patent rights. These patent rights, and the various spin-out firms they can create (e.g. from technology transfer), then become metrics, which in turn are used to determine what constitutes effective and efficient national science and technology policies and practices.[79] Finally, we move towards the perceived terminus of the process, where products are at or near the regulatory approval point and firms have identified targets for either novel breakthrough products or incremental innovations with strong evergreening potential.[80] At this point, and especially at later points in the rTPL,[81] linkage regulations and regulatory rights become dominant forms of IPR rights protection.[82]

However, as noted earlier, the mid-point and end-point of the pharmaceutical innovation system are increasingly merging, as regulators move towards lifecycle regulatory models which allow for early or flexible departure of drugs prior to the completion of traditional Phase 3 trials, with greater post-market surveillance. Moreover, both pharmaceutical, and more recently biotechnology, firms operating under the linkage regime can now layer IPR rights on products at all stages of development, including those about to come off patent, those in regulatory review, and those in development. For example, data examined in Chapter 4 indicate that the linkage regime operating in conjunction with established patent law and the drug approval regime allows firms to produce a substantial number and array of patent classifications. These patents can, in turn, be used to list on the patent register in order to prohibit generic entry on older drugs and to support follow-on drug development submissions, thus further collapsing the drug development cycle. Together, the data presented in Chapters 3–5 support the need to extend and broaden the innovation analysis to include the entire landscape of interconnections between drug approval, patenting, and litigation, as well as the nexus between broader national science and technology policies and the effects thereof on the rate and direction of firm innovation.[83]

Schumpeter noted that innovations of different magnitudes tended to appear in cycles of varying lengths, geared largely to the rate at which advantages from innovations declined over time through increasing use and imitation.[84] For policies and regulations aimed at stimulating innovation, the risk is always that they may catch one of these cycles at the wrong moment, thus contributing more to the declining phase of an existing cycle than to the development phase of a new one. They may do this by damaging the incentives that drive new entrants or by preserving practices that have become inefficient.[85] Clearly this applies to inefficient or ineffective regulatory policies that lead to increasingly poor performance as judged by the goals and objectives of policy-makers, in this case an increased supply of truly innovative remedies.

Based on data here and elsewhere,[86] we propose that the current lifecycle of pharmaceutical development *and* regulation may be nearing a point of exhaustion such as Schumpeter would have recognized. Evidence for this includes: a strongly increasing trend towards ever smaller incremental innovation in the last decade (Figure 4.1); an increase in the low level of innovation being supported by a combination of weak patents and linkage regulations (Figures 4.4–4.7); a decreasing number of truly breakthrough drugs as well as drugs containing NCEs and NASs (Figures 4.1 and 4.3); a substantial number of patents per drug (Figure 4.4); the fact that many patents under linkage regulations are either invalid or infringed when tested on the merits;[87] and the growth in both the scope and depth of IPR rights associated with poorly innovative drug products over the last twenty years.

As noted by many commentators, the basket of IPR rights afforded to pharmaceuticals has grown to encompass an astounding array of mechanisms, which may be interpreted as micro levels of order or details as per the discussion above. These include increased patent terms, decreased standards for obviousness, utility and subject matter requirements for patenting, allowance for listing of weak patents via linkage regulations, the automatic stay provision barring generic entry, loss of compulsory licensing provisions, and the ever growing basket of regulatory rights associated with drug submissions.[88] It is not just a coincidence that the basket of IPR rights attached to pharmaceutical products is growing in both scope and depth at a time when innovation is widely considered to be faltering.

Even if the current rTPL is not near the point of exhaustion, data such as those reported here should provide useful information for jurisdictions contemplating some form of linkage regulations or other types of linkages between public health and economic policies. Moreover, in jurisdictions that maintain IPR rights are integral to innovation, the results may offer an opportunity to correct or fine-tune existing policies underpinning innovation, including adjusting economic incentives in accordance with the degree of objective evidence in relation to innovation[89] and accompanying social benefits.[90]

Notes

1. For a discussion of lifecycle drugs, see, generally, Hans-Georg Eichler et al., 'Balancing Early Market Access to New Drugs with the Need for Benefit/Risk Data: A Mounting Dilemma,' 7 *Nature Revs. Drug Discovery* 818, 823–4 (2008) [Eichler et al. (2008)]; Neil Yeates, David K. Lee, and Maurica Maher, 'Health Canada's Progressive Licensing Framework,' 176 *Canadian Medical Association Journal* 1845 (2007) [Yeates et al. (2007)].
2. See, generally, *Products and Food* (2006) online: <http://www.hc-sc.gc.ca/ahc-asc/alt_formats/hpfb-dgpsa/pdf/hpfb-dgpsa/blueprint-plan-eng.pdf

[Health Canada, *Blueprint*]; Health Canada, *The Progressive Licensing Framework Concept Paper for Discussion* (2006), online: <http://www.hc-sc.gc.ca/dhp-mps/alt_formats/hpfbdgpsa/pdf/prodpharma/proglic_homprog_concept-eng.pdf> [Health Canada, *PLF Concept Paper*]; Yeates et al. (2007), *supra* note 1.

3. Patented Medicines (Notice of Compliance) Regulations SOR/1993-133 (Can.).
4. See Monika Sawicka and Ron A. Bouchard, 'Empirical Analysis of Canadian Drug Approval Data 2001–2008: Are Pharmaceutical Players "Doing More With Less"?' 3 *McGill J.L. & Health* 85, 97–114 (2009) [Sawicka and Bouchard (2009)], at 92.
5. Andrew Humphreys, 'MedAdNews 200 – World's Best-Selling Medicines,' *MedAdNews*, July 2007 [Humphreys (2007)]. The drugs analyzed were: Lipitor™, Advair™, Plavix™, Nexium™, Norvasc™, Zyprexa™, Diovan™, Risperdal™, Effexor™, Pantoloc™, Singulair™, Seroquel™, Prevacid™, Crestor™, Prilosec™, and Altace™. Note that the list does not correspond literally to that in the United States. Rather, we chose for initial study working backwards from number one, a group of 16 drugs that were on the US list and which also had approval dates between 2001 and 2008 as identified in Sawicka and Bouchard (2009), *supra* note 4.
6. See ibid.
7. See ibid.
8. See also Ron A. Bouchard and Monika Sawicka, 'The Mud and the Blood and the Beer: Canada's New Progressive Licensing Framework for Drug Approval,' 3 *McGill J.L. & Health* 49, 58–9 (2009) [Bouchard and Sawicka (2009)]; Sawicka and Bouchard (2009), *supra* note 4.
9. Ibid., *supra* note 4, at 107.
10. Ibid., at 87.
11. Health Canada, *Guidance for Industry: Priority Review of Drug Submissions* (2006), online: <http://www.hc-sc.gc.ca/dhp-mps/alt_formats/hpfb-dgpsa/pdf/prodpharma/priordr-eng.pdf> [Health Canada, *Priority Review*], at 1–2.
12. For a discussion of this issue see Bouchard and Sawicka (2009), *supra* note 8, at 105–6.
13. See Food and Drugs Act, RSC, ch. F 27 (1985).
14. See Food and Drug Regulations, CRC, ch. 870 (2009).
15. See Bouchard and Sawicka (2009), *supra* note 8, at 52.
16. Sawicka and Bouchard (2009), *supra* note 4, at 117.
17. Humphreys (2007), *supra* note 5. See also note 5, *supra*, for the list of drugs analyzed. Risperdal™, Effexor™, Pantoloc™, Singulair™, Seroquel™, Prevacid™, Crestor™, Prilosec™, and Altace™.
18. See, generally, Ron A. Bouchard, 'Living Separate and Apart is Never Easy: Inventive Capacity of the PHOSITA as the Tie That Binds Obviousness and Inventiveness,' 4 *U. Ottawa L. & Tech. J.* 1 (2007) [Bouchard 'PHOSITA' (2007)], at 46–52; Ron A. Bouchard, 'Should Scientific Research in the Lead-up

to Invention Vitiate Obviousness Under the Patented Medicines (Notice of Compliance) Regulations: To Test or Not to Test?' 6 *Can. J. L. & Tech.* 1 (2007) [Bouchard, 'Scientific Research' (2007)]; Andrew A. Caffrey and Jonathan M. Rotter, 'Consumer Protection, Patents and Procedure: Generic Drug Market Entry and the Need to Reform the Hatch-Waxman Act,' 9 *Va. J.L. & Tech.* 1, 4–7 (2004) [Caffrey and Rotter (2004)]; Roy J. Romanow, *Commission on the Future of Health Care in Canada, Building on Values: The Future of Health Care in Canada: Final Report* (2002), 208–10, online: <http://dsp-psd.pwgsc.gc.ca/Collection/CP32-85-2002E.pdf>; Edward Hore, 'A Comparison of US and Canadian Laws as They Affect Generic Pharmaceutical Drug Entry,' 55 *Food & Drug L.J.* 373 (1992) [Hore (1992)], at 8–10; Adam B. Jaffe, 'The U.S. Patent System in Transition: Policy Innovation and the Innovation Process,' 29 *Res. Pol'y* 531 (2000) [Jaffe (2000)].

19. *AstraZeneca Canada Inc.* v. *Canada (Minister of Health)*, [2006] 2 SCR 560, at para. 29; see, generally, Bouchard, 'PHOSITA' (2007), *supra* note 18, at 50.
20. *Pfizer, Inc.* v. *Apotex, Inc.*, 480 F.3d 1348 (Fed. Cir. 2007); *Bristol-Myers Squibb Co.* v. *Canada*, [2005] 1 SCR 533 (Can.) [*Bristol Myers*]; *Apotex Inc.* v. *Merck Frosst Canada Inc.*, [1998] 2 SCR 193 (Can.) [*Apotex*], at para. 33; see also Caffrey and Rotter (2004), *supra* note 18.
21. No final trial or appeal decisions relating to omeprazole enantiomers have been released to date. For a notation of the seven ongoing applications under the NOC Regulation pertaining to esomeprazole (Nexium®) see *AstraZeneca Canada Inc.* v. *Apotex Inc.*, [2008] FC 537 (Can.). There are a number of Canadian and US appeal decisions regarding enantiomers under the NOC Regulations. See, for example, *AstraZeneca AB* v. *Ranbaxy Pharms., Inc.*, 2008 US Dist. LEXIS 102097 (DNJ December 15, 2008); *Dr. Reddy's Labs, Ltd.* v. *AstraZeneca, AB*, No. 08-2496, 2008 US Dist. LEXIS 66176 (DNJ August 28, 2008); *Ivax Pharms., Inc.* v. *AstraZeneca*, AB, No. 08-2165, 2008 US Dist. LEXIS 66177 (DNJ August 28, 2008); *AstraZeneca* v. *Ranbaxy Pharms., Inc.*, No. 05-5553, 2008 US Dist. LEXIS 6337 (DNJ January 25, 2008); *Pfizer Canada Inc.* v. *Minister of Health and Ranbaxy Laboratories Ltd.* [2008] FCA 108; *Janssen-Ortho Inc.* v. *Novopharm Ltd.*, [2007] FC 809 (Can.); *Apotex Inc.* v. *Sanofi-Synthelabo Can. Inc.*, [2006] FCJ 1945 (Can.). For additional judicial consideration of the anti-competitive and/or fraudulent nature of such patenting and marketing strategies see: *Walgreen Co.* v. *AstraZeneca Pharm.* LP, 534 F. Supp. 2d 146 (DDC 2008); *Pa. Employees Benefit Trust Fund* v. *Zeneca Inc.*, 499 F.3d 239 (3d Cir. 2007).
22. T. Lind et al., 'Esomeprazole Provides Improved Acid Control vs. Omeprazole in Patients With Symptoms of Gastro-oesophageal Reflux Disease,' 14 *Alimentary Pharmacology & Therapeutics* 861 (2000). For a review of chirality in sulphur compounds, see Ronald Bentley, 'Role of Sulfur Chirality in the Chemical Processes of Biology,' 34 *Chem. Soc. Rev.* 609 (2005) [Bentley (2005)].
23. Bentley (2005), *supra* note 22.

24. Bouchard, 'PHOSITA' (2007), *supra* note 18.
25. *Merck Frosst Canada Ltd.* v. *Apotex Inc.*, [2009] FCA 187 (Can.); *Apotex*, *supra* note 20.
26. Intercontinental Marketing Services Health Inc., *2003 Annual Report to Shareholders* (2003), online: <http://www.imshealth.com/portal/site/imshealth>; Intercontinental Marketing Services Health Inc., *2002 Annual Report to Shareholders* (2002), online: <http://media.corporate-ir.net/media_files/NYS/RX/reports/ar2002.pdf>; Intercontinental Marketing Services Health Inc., *2001 Annual Report to Shareholders* (2001), online: <http://www.imshealth.com/portal/site/imshealth>. See also Intercontinental Marketing Services Health Inc., *Canadian Pharmaceutical Industry Review 2001*; Intercontinental Marketing Services Health Inc., *Canadian Pharmaceutical Industry Review 2002*; Intercontinental Marketing Services Health Inc., *Canadian Pharmaceutical Industry Review 2003* (on file with author).
27. Canadian Institute for Health Information, *Drug Expenditure in Canada, 1985 to 2008*, online: <http://secure.cihi.ca/cihiweb/dispPage.jsp?cw_page=PG_1990_E&cw_topic=1990&cw_rel=AR_80_E> [CIHI (2008)]. Note that the 2008 value was forecasted by the report and is not an actual value.
28. Health Canada, Health Products and Food Branch, *Clinical Trials Regulatory Review – Stakeholder Workshop* (March 26, 2007), at 6, online: <http://www.hc-sc.gc.ca/dhp-mps/alt_formats/hpfb-dgpsa/pdf/prodpharma/ctrf_o_eccr_a_2007-03-26-eng.pdf> [Health Canada Stakeholder Workshop] (explaining that the objectives of the 2001 regulations were to: '[s]horten application review times without endangering health and safety; [i]mprove safety mechanisms for research subjects; [r]egulator to be more involved in clinical trial monitoring and follow-up; [r]emove obstacles to additional R&D; [i]mprove access to innovative therapies and advice from Canadian physicians with research experience').
29. See, for example, 'New Medicines in 2007: Regulatory Agencies and Policy Makers Leave Public Health in the Hands of the Pharmaceutical Industry,' 17 *Prescrire Int'l* 78 (2008) ['New Medicines in 2007']; Domenico Motola et al., 'An Update on the First Decade of the European Centralized Procedure: How Many Innovative Drugs,' 62 *Brit. J. of Clinical Pharmacology* 610 (2006); Editorial, 'European and French Pharmaceutical Market Assessed by Prescrire in 2005: Mainly Bogus Innovation,' 30 *Farmacia Hospitalaria* 68 (2006); John Abraham and Courtney Davis, 'A Comparative Analysis of Drug Safety Withdrawals in the UK and the US (1971–1992): Implications for Current Regulatory Thinking and Policy,' 61 *Soc. Sci. & Med.* 881 (2005); National Institute for Health Care Management, *Changing Patterns of Pharmaceutical Innovation* 7 (2002) [National Institute for Health Care Management (2002)]; 'Drugs in 2001: A Number of Ruses Unveiled,' 11 *Prescrire Int'l* 58 (2002) ['Drugs in 2001']; Kenneth I. Kaitin et al., 'Therapeutic Ratings and End-of-Phase II Conferences: Initiatives to Accelerate the Availability of Important New Drugs,' 31 *J. Clinical Pharmacology* 17 (1991) [Kaitin et al. (1991)].

30. Fredric J. Cohen, 'Macro Trends in Pharmaceutical Innovation,' 4 *Nature Revs Drug Discovery* 78, 82 (2005) [Cohen (2005)].
31. See, generally, Joseph A. DiMasi et al., 'The Price of Innovation: New Estimates of Drug Development Costs,' 22 *J. Health Econ.* 151 (2003).
32. J.D. Kleinke, 'Commentary: Much Ado About a Good Thing,' 325 *BMJ* 1168 (2002).
33. Cohen (2005), *supra* note 30. Committee on Knowledge Assessment, National Research Council, *Prospectus for National Knowledge Assessment* (1996).
34. National Institute for Health Care Management (2002), *supra* note 29.
35. Ibid.
36. Patented Medicine Prices Review Board, *Annual Report 2000* (2001), online: <http://www.pmprb-cepmb.gc.ca/English/View.asp?x=113&mp=91>.
37. 'Drugs in 2001,' *supra* note 29, at 59; see also 'New Medicines in 2007,' *supra* note 29, at 78–82. Note that the 2001 French study included new drugs and also new indications for existing drugs already on the market. Moreover, generic drugs were rated as no improvement over existing drugs. For discussion of the 2000 Canadian and 2001 French studies in the context of the Canadian pharmaceutical marketplace see, generally, Joel Lexchin, 'Intellectual Property Rights and the Canadian Pharmaceutical Marketplace: Where Do We Go From Here?' 35 *Int'l J. Health Serv.* 237, 243 (2005).
38. Kaitin et al. (1991), *supra* 29, at 17–24.
39. National Institute for Health Care Management (2002), *supra* note 29, at 8.
40. Jaffe (2000), *supra* note 18; Bhaven N. Sampat, 'Patenting and US Academic Research in the 20th Century: The World Before and After Bayh-Dole,' 35 *Res. Pol'y* 772 (2006); see Ron A. Bouchard, 'Balancing Public and Private Interests in the Commercialization of Publicly Funded Medical Research: Is There a Role for Compulsory Government Royalty Fees?' 13 *B.U. J. Sci. & Tech. L.* 120, 158–64 (2007).
41. Roberto Mazzoleni and Richard R. Nelson, 'The Benefits and Costs of Strong Patent Protection: A Contribution to the Current Debate,' 27 *Res. Pol'y* 273 (1998) [Mazzoleni and Nelson (1998)]; Keith Pavitt, 'National Policies for Technical Change: Where Are the Increasing Returns to Economic Research?' 93 *Proc. Nat'l Acad. Sci. U.S.A.* 126 (1996) [Pavitt (1996)].
42. See, for example, *KSR Int'l* v. *Teleflex, Inc.*, 550 US 398, 419 (2007) [*KSR Int'l*]; *Whirlpool Corp.* v. *Camco Inc.*, [2000] 2 SCR 1067, at 37 (Can.) [*Whirlpool*]; *Graham* v. *John Deere Co. of Kan. City*, 383 US 1, 17–18 (1966) [*Graham*]; see also Ron A. Bouchard, '*KSR* v. *Teleflex* Part 1: Impact of U.S Supreme Court Patent Law on Canadian Intellectual Property and Regulatory Rights Landscape,' 15 *Health L.J.* 221 (2007) [Bouchard, 'Landscape' (2007)].
43. *KSR Int'l*, *supra* note 42.
44. *Hotchkiss* v. *Greenwood*, 52 US 248 (1851).

45. *Whirlpool*, *supra* note 42, 2 SCR 1067; *Free World Trust* v. *Electro Sante Inc.*, [2000] 2 SCR 1024 (Can.); *Royal Typewriter Co.* v. *Remington Rand, Inc.*, 168 F.2d 691 (2d Cir. 1948).
46. *KSR Int'l*, *supra* note 42.
47. Anita Varma and David Abraham, 'DNA is Different: Legal Obviousness and the Balance Between Biotech Inventors and the Market,' 9 *Harv. J.L. & Tech.* 53, 55 (1996). For a general discussion of the relevance of weak patents to innovation, see also Glynn S. Lunney, Jr, 'E-Obviousness,' 7 *Mich. Telecomm. & Tech. L.R.* 363 (2001) [Lunney (2001)] and Bouchard, 'PHOSITA' (2007), *supra* note 18.
48. See *Royal Typewriter Co.* 168 F.2d, at 693–4.
49. See Lunney (2001), *supra* note 47, at 384.
50. *Graham*, *supra* note 42.
51. See, for example, *R.* v. *Nova Scotia Pharm. Soc'y*, [1992] 2 SCR 606 (Can.); *Comm'n of Patents v. Farbwerke Hoechst Aktiengesellschaft*, [1964] SCR 49, 56 (Can.).
52. Caffrey and Rotter (2004), *supra* note 18; Hore (1992), *supra* note 18. For a detailed discussion of the standard for relevance, see the Regulatory Impact Analysis Statement ('RIAS') accompanying the Regulations Amending the Food and Drug Regulations (Data Protection): Regulatory Impact Analysis Statement, *C. Gaz.* Part II, Vol. 140, October 18, 2006 [RIAS].
53. *Merck Frosst Can. Inc.* v. *Canada*, [1998] 2 SCR 193 at 33 (Can.). This passage has been cited by the court in later decisions. See, for example, *AstraZeneca Can., Inc.* v. *Canada*, [2006] SCR 560, 2006 SCC 52, at 17 (Can.) [*AstraZeneca*]; *Bristol Myers*, *supra* note 20.
54. *Bristol Myers*, *supra* note 20.
55. Federal Trade Commission, 'Generic Drug Entry Prior to Patent Expiration: An FTC Study' (2002), online: <http://www.ftc.gov/os/2002/07/genericdrugstudy.pdf> [FTC (2002)]; see Caffrey and Rotter (2004), *supra* note 18, at 13–14; Ed Hore, 'Patently Absurd: Evergreening of Pharmaceutical Patent Protection under the Patented Medicines (Notice of Compliance) Regulations of Canada's Patent Act 5,' 11 (2004), online: <http://www.canadiangenerics.ca/en/news/docs/patently_absurd_04.pdf>.
56. See Michele Boldrin and David K. Levine, 'Against Intellectual Monopoly' (2008) [Boldrin and Levine (2008)], at 260–5.
57. *Whirlpool*, *supra* note 42, at 37; *Graham*, *supra* note 42.
58. Cohen (2005), *supra* note 30, at 79.
59. Sawicka and Bouchard (2009), *supra* note 4.
60. See, generally, Robert Jervis, 'System Effects: Complexity in Political and Social Life' (1997) [Jervis (1997)].
61. *AstraZeneca*, *supra* note 53, at 39 (Can.). Discussing the 'general' relevance requirement articulated by the Federal Court of Appeal in *Eli Lilly Canada Inc.* v. *Canada* 2003 FCA 24, Justice Binnie stated:

Given the evident (and entirely understandable) commercial strategy of the innovative drug companies to evergreen their products by adding bells and whistles to a pioneering product even after the original patent for that pioneering product has expired, the decision of the Federal Court of Appeal would reward evergreening even if the generic manufacturer (and thus the public) does not thereby derive any benefit from the subsequently listed patents.

62. Boldrin and Levine (2008), *supra* note 56, at 241–2.
63. See, generally, Mary E. Wiktorowicz, 'Emergent Patterns in the Regulation of Pharmaceuticals: Institutions and Interests in the United States, Canada, Britain, and France,' 28 *J. Health Pol., Pol'y & L.* 615 (2003).
64. Ron A. Bouchard, 'Reflections on the Value of Systems Models for Regulation of Medical Research and Product Development,' 17 *Health L. Rev.* 28 (2008) [Bouchard, 'Reflections' (2008)]; Sawicka and Bouchard (2009), *supra* note 4.
65. Benoît Godin, 'The Linear Model of Innovation: The Historical Construction of an Analytical Framework,' 31 *Science, Technology & Human Values* 639 (2006) [Godin (2006)]; Donald Stokes, *Pasteur's Quadrant* (Brookings Institute Press, 1997) [Stokes (1997)].
66. Dean Rickles et al., 'A Simple Guide to Chaos and Complexity,' 61 *J. Epidemiology & Community* 933 (2007).
67. John H. Miller and Scott E. Page, *Complex Adaptive Systems: An Introduction to Computational Models of Social Life* (Princeton University Press, 2007), at 9.
68. Feedback interactions in complex systems have received increased attention in recent years. See, generally, Albert-Laszlo Barabási, *Linked: How Everything Is Connected to Everything Else and What It Means for Business, Science, and Everyday Life* (Plume, 2003); Steven Johnson, *Emergence: The Connected Lives of Ants, Brains, Cities and Software* (Scribner, 2002) [Johnson (2002)]; John H. Holland, *Hidden Order: How Adaptation Builds Complexity* (Addison-Wesley, 1995); Stuart Kauffman, *At Home in the Universe: The Search for the Laws of Self-Organization and Complexity* (Viking, 1995) [Kauffman (1995)]; John H. Holland, *Adaptation in Natural and Artificial Systems* (MIT Press, 1992); M. Mitchell Waldrop, *Complexity: The Emerging Science at the Edge of Order and Chaos* (Simon & Schuster, 1992); Brian W. Arthur, 'Positive Feedbacks in the Economy,' 262 *Sci. Am.* 92, 92–9 (1990) [Arthur (1990)]; Grégoire Nicolis and Ilya Prigogine, *Exploring Complexity: An Introduction* (W.H. Freeman 1989); James Gleick, *Chaos: Making a New Science* (Viking, 1988).
69. See, for example, Robert M. May et al., 'Complex Systems: Ecology for Bankers,' 451 *Nature* 893 (2008). For a look at the role of feedback in policy failure, see, generally, Barry Bozeman and Daniel Sarewitz, 'Public Values and Public Failure in US Science Policy,' 32 *Sci. and Pub. Pol'y* 119 (2005); Barry Bozeman, 'Public Value Failure: When Efficient Markets May Not Do,' 62 *Pub. Admin. Rev.* 145 (2002); John D. Sterman, 'All Models Are

Wrong: Reflections on Becoming a Systems Scientist,' 18 *Sys. Dynamics Rev.* 501 (2002). For a review of feedback in complex international political systems, see, generally, Jervis (1992), *supra* note 60; Neil E. Harrison (ed.), *Complexity in World Politics: Concepts and Methods of a New Paradigm* (SUNY Press, 1997).

70. Kauffman (1995), *supra* note 68, at 26.
71. Ibid., at 14.
72. Johnson (2002) *supra* note 68, at 186.
73. For a general discussion of the problems inherent in linear legislative and jurisprudential models of pharmaceutical innovation and how they may be mitigated by systems models of innovation, see, generally, Ron A. Bouchard, '*KSR v. Teleflex* Part 2: Impact of U.S. Supreme Court Patent Law on Canadian and Global Systems-Based Innovation Ecologies,' 15 *Health L.J.* 247 (2007) [Bouchard, 'Systems' (2007)]; Bouchard, 'Reflections' (2008), *supra* note 64; Bouchard, 'PHOSITA' (2007), *supra* note 18.
74. Arthur (1990), *supra* note 69.
75. Bouchard, 'Landscape' (2008), *supra* note 42; Bouchard, 'Systems' (2007), *supra* note 73; Ron A. Bouchard, 'Reflections on the Value of Systems Models for Regulation of Medical Research and Product Development,' 17 *Health L. Rev.* 28 (2008) [Bouchard, 'Reflections' (2008)]; Bouchard and Sawicka (2009), *supra* note 8, at 57–8.
76. Ron A. Bouchard and Trudo Lemmens, 'Privatizing Biomedical Research – A Third Way,' 26 *Nature Biotechnology* 31 (2008).
77. See ibid.; Ron A. Bouchard, 'Balancing Public and Private Interests in the Commercialization of Publicly Funded Medical Research: Is There a Role for Compulsory Government Royalty Fees?' 13 *B.U. J. Sci. & Tech. L.* 120 (2007).
78. See ibid., at 2–3.
79. For discussion of the failure of linear models of 'basic' and 'applied' research and development to account for the innovation process, see, generally, Godin (2006), *supra* note 65; Stokes (1997), *supra* note 65.
80. Bouchard, 'Scientific Research' (2007), *supra* note 18, at 13; Bouchard, 'PHOSITA' (2007), *supra* note 18, at 22–3.
81. For discussion of linkage and regulatory rights, how they relate to traditional food and drug law, and the points in the drug development cycle at which they come into play, see, generally, Caffrey and Rotter (2004), *supra* note 18; Rebecca S. Eisenberg, 'Patents, Product Exclusivity, and Information Dissemination: How Law Directs Biopharmaceutical Research and Development,' 72 *Fordham L. Rev.* 477, 483 (2003); Hore (1992), *supra* note 18.
82. Bouchard, 'PHOSITA' (2007), *supra* note 18, at 48; Bouchard and Sawicka (2009), *supra* note 8, at 63–4.
83. Bouchard, 'Systems' (2007), *supra* note 73, at 258–62; Bouchard, 'Reflections' (2008), *supra* note 75, at 38–9.

84. Joseph A. Schumpeter, *Business Cycles: A Theoretical, Historical and Statistical Analysis of the Capitalist Process* (McGraw-Hill, 1939); see also Gert-Jan Hospers, 'Joseph Schumpeter and His Legacy in Innovation Studies,' 18 *Knowledge Tech. & Pol'y* 20 (2005) (reviewing the relevance of Schumpeter's work for current innovation theory and practice).
85. Ibid., at 32.
86. For a review of cumulative empirical studies of pharmaceutical innovation and patenting, see Boldrin and Levine (2008), *supra* note 56, particularly Chapter 8 ('Does Intellectual Property Increase Innovation?') and Chapter 9 ('The Pharmaceutical Industry'); James Bessen and Michael J. Meurer, *Patent Failure* (Princeton University Press, 2008).
87. See, for example, FTC (2002), *supra* note 55; Caffrey and Rotter (2004), *supra* note 18; Valerie Junod, 'Drug Marketing Exclusivity Under United States and European Union Law,' 59 *Food & Drug L.J.* 479 (2004); Hore (1992), *supra* note 18.
88. RIAS, *supra* note 52. While regulatory rights spread globally via provisions to this effect in TRIPS and other US-based trade agreements, they have been the subject of increasing scrutiny recently, including within the United States. For example, Senator Bernie Sanders (I-VT) recently put forward an amendment to the healthcare reform bill that would eliminate data exclusivity where duplicating clinical trials involving human subjects violates Article 20 of the Declaration of Helsinki on Ethical Principles for Medical Research Involving Human Subjects pertaining to clinical trial ethics. James Love, 'Senator Sanders' Amendment 2858 Would Replace Data Exclusivity With Cost Sharing, If New Trials Violate Medical Ethics,' December 9, 2009, online: <http://keionline.org/node/707>.
89. An alternative to patent-specific prizes and rewards may be to modify already existing price control methodologies employed by governments (e.g. Patented Medical Prices Review Board of Canada) or insurers and other institutional payers to incorporate an 'innovation index' factor such as that described in Figure 4.3(d) in their pricing algorithms. Prices could be increased or decreased in accordance with empirical assessment of whether approved drugs are highly innovative (NDS + NAS + ER + FIC or NDS + NAS + FIC), moderately innovative (NDS + ER + NAS or NDS + NAS), less innovative (SNDS + ER + FIC or SNDS + FIC), poorly innovative (SNDS), or not innovative at all (ANDS, SANDS).
90. Joseph Stiglitz, 'Scrooge and Intellectual Property Rights: A Medical Prize Fund Could Improve the Financing of Drug Innovations,' 333 *BMJ* 1279 (2006); Michael Abramowicz, 'Perfecting Patent Prizes,' 56 *Vand. L. Rev.* 115 (2003); Aidan Hollis, 'Optional Rewards for New Drugs for Developing Countries' (April 5, 2005) (unpublished manuscript, on file with the World Health Organization), online: <http://www.who.int/entity/intellectualproperty/submissions/Submissions.AidanHollis.pdf>; Aidan Hollis, 'An Efficient

Reward System for Pharmaceutical Innovation' (January 17, 2005) (unpublished manuscript, on file with the University of Calgary), online: <http://econ.ucalgary.ca/fac-files/ah/drugprizes.pdf>; Paul Grootendorst, *Patents, Public-Private Partnerships or Prizes: How Should We Support Pharmaceutical Innovation?*, Social and Economic Dimensions of an Aging Population, Research Paper No. 250, online: <http://socserv2.socsci.mcmaster.ca/~sedap/p/sedap250.pdf>.

5

Empirical analysis of drug patenting in multiple high-value cohorts*

Abstract: This study was designed to empirically investigate two related phenomena within the context of the emerging linkage regulation model of intellectual property protection. The first was to probe the legal nexus between drug approval, drug patenting, and patent listing under the linkage regime for high-value pharmaceuticals as vetted by regulators and the market. While the patent regime has been claimed by both pharmaceutical firms and regulators to be integral for innovative drug development, the role of drug approval-drug patenting linkage in pharmaceutical innovation is far less clear. Evidence relating to drug approval-drug patenting linkage, especially for high-value pharmaceuticals, would therefore be valuable at a time when other jurisdictions might be contemplating similar provisions. The second was to address how certain characteristics of the existing drug approval framework, such as relatively low thresholds for drugs to accrue a new active substance designation (equivalent to new chemical entity), to be approved as a follow-on drug as opposed to a new drug, and to go through an expedited rather than conventional approval process, might be linked to patenting and patent listing patterns. Given the requirement under linkage law for intellectual property protection to be linked to a specific drug submission, we were particularly interested in exploring data relating to what we refer to as a 'paradoxical drug approval-drug patenting linkage,' that is a legal linkage whereby the largest scope of intellectual property protection accrues to drugs with the least innovative character.

Keywords: pharmaceutical linkage regulations, patent law, empirical analysis, drug patenting, patent listing, most profitable drugs, expedited review, intellectual property rights layering

*This chapter is based upon material in R.A. Bouchard, R.W. Hawkins, R. Clark, R. Hagtvedt, and J. Sawani, 'Empirical Analysis of Drug Approval-Patenting Linkage for High Value Pharmaceuticals,' *Northwestern Journal of Technology & Intellectual Property* 8(2): 1–86 (2010).

5.1 Introduction

As noted in Chapter 4 patent and regulatory rights are increasingly assumed to be essential for all stages of the therapeutic product lifecycle. This includes publicly funded medical research, university technology transfer, private research and development activities, the regulatory submission cycle, and the post-market stage. Indeed, patent rights are seen to be so important to the drug development exercise that drug patenting and drug approval are now legally linked through a novel form of legal ordering referred to as 'linkage regulations,' the subject of this study. Linkage regulations allow firms to list patents deemed relevant to an already marketed product in order to extend market exclusivity. Generic firms must successfully litigate each patent on the patent register prior to gaining market entry. Patenting and litigation under linkage regulations are critical to brand-name and generic markets, as they represent a primary mechanism by which regulators promote drug development in exchange for intellectual property rights. As we have seen throughout this book, the linkage regime in Canada has reached a stage of some maturity since coming into force in 1993. This provides an excellent opportunity to empirically investigate how patents and linkage regulations are intertwined and are employed by multinational pharmaceutical firms in order to protect high-value innovations.

The study in this chapter was designed to empirically investigate two related phenomena within the context of the emerging linkage regulation model of intellectual property protection. The first was to probe the legal nexus between drug approval, drug patenting, and patent listing under the linkage regime for high-value pharmaceuticals as vetted by regulators and the market. While the patent regime has been claimed by both pharmaceutical firms and regulators to be integral for innovative drug development, the role of drug approval-drug patenting linkage in pharmaceutical innovation is far less clear. Evidence relating to drug approval-drug patenting linkage, especially for high-value pharmaceuticals, would therefore be valuable at a time when other jurisdictions might be contemplating similar provisions. The second was to address how certain characteristics of the existing drug approval framework, such as relatively low thresholds for drugs to accrue a new active substance designation (equivalent to new chemical entity), to be approved as a follow-on drug as opposed to a new drug, and to go through an expedited rather than conventional approval process, might be linked to patenting and patent listing patterns. Given the requirement under linkage law for intellectual property protection to be linked to a specific drug submission, we were particularly interested in exploring data relating to what we refer to as a 'paradoxical drug approval-drug patenting linkage.' That is, a legal linkage whereby the largest scope of intellectual property protection accrues to drugs with the least innovative character.

The goal of the study described in this chapter is to empirically probe the legal and functional link between drug approval, drug patenting, and drug litigation for high-value pharmaceutical innovations. As already noted, patenting and litigation under linkage regulations are critical to both brand-name and generic markets, as they represent the primary mechanism by which regulators promote drug development in exchange for intellectual property rights. We were also interested in gathering data pertaining to the manner in which certain characteristics of drug approval-drug patenting linkage, such as the threshold requirements for a new and follow-on drug approval and expedited review, might direct firm patenting and linkage regulations activities.

The remaining analysis is split into four parts. First we provide an overview of the methodology employed in our empirical study. We then describe the data relating to patenting and patent listing under the NOC Regulations. A number of different groups were analyzed: the entire cohort of drugs, most profitable drugs by sales, drugs approved via an expedited approval process without significant post-market conditions, drugs approved via expedited approval with significant post-market conditions, and drugs approved via a combination of the latter two pathways. Approved drugs and patents were also analyzed in relation to their patent type classification (chemical, process, combination, use, etc.) and World Health Organization therapeutic class designation (cardiovascular, antibiotic, antineoplastic, etc.). Following this, we interpret the data and provide a brief synthesis of the results in relation to existing intellectual property and food and drug policy. The final part is a summary and conclusions section.

5.2 Methods

5.2.1 General

The term 'drug approval-drug patent linkage' is used throughout this chapter to refer to the specific legal nexus between drug approval under food and drug law and drug patenting under patent legislation via the linkage regulations regime, in this case the Patented Medicine (Notice of Compliance) Regulations, or NOC Regulations. Drugs were analyzed in this study in two ways. First, the characteristics of the entire cohort of 95 drugs were evaluated. Patenting per calendar year, patenting expressed as a function of the time after the priority date on which the first patent on the subset was issued, patent listing per year, cumulative patenting and patent listing, and the temporal lag between the average date of drug approval, the average date of patent issue, and the average date of patent listing were also explored. Finally, patent type classifications and therapeutic class for drugs and patents for the cohort were investigated. Secondly, drugs were subdivided into four further groups: Most Profitable drugs (n = 33); Priority Review (n = 40); drugs receiving an NOC with conditions (NOC/c; n = 16); and drugs receiving NOC/c approvals that were also approved via Priority Review (PR-NOC/c; n = 6). All drugs had at least one approval in between 2001 and 2008, as described in Sawicka and Bouchard.[1] Drugs were thus split into categories representing products already vetted by the market to be blockbuster in nature and those that were granted expedited review status by regulators in the hope they would be.

As indicated by the designations just described, expedited approvals were divided into three categories. The reason for this approach is that NOCs can be granted in an expedited fashion under Canadian food and drug law in two primary ways which can be combined to create a third category.[2] The first is through Priority Review,[3] which refers to the fast-tracking of eligible drug candidates intended for the treatment, prevention, or diagnosis of serious, life-threatening or severely debilitating diseases or conditions wherein there exists an unmet medical need or for which a substantial improvement in the benefit-risk profile is demonstrated.[4] Evidentiary requirements for safety, efficacy, and quality parallel those for non-priority submissions, the main difference being an accelerated review time.[5] The second is the 'NOC with conditions' (NOC/c) pathway.[6] NOC/c approval is granted for eligible NDS or SNDS submissions directed to serious, life-threatening or severely debilitating diseases or conditions for which there is promising evidence of clinical effectiveness based on available data.[7] In addition to less onerous evidentiary requirements, the review process for NOC/c approval is significantly accelerated.[8] The main difference with Priority Review is that NOC/c licensure is granted on the condition that the sponsor perform additional studies to confirm alleged benefits. The third category, PR-NOC/c approvals, are drugs that represent the highest potential value for pharmaceutical firms. This is because of the combination of expedited review with lower pre-approval evidentiary requirements that would be seen by regulators to be aimed at target populations with the highest degree of unmet medical needs and/or benefit : risk.

The Canadian Intellectual Property Office (CIPO) website provides public access to its comprehensive electronic database housing all patents issued or pending issuance in Canada. The database contains patent documents from 1869 to the present. The electronically available patent information consists of patent document images which include the patent cover page, abstract, claims, description, drawings, and bibliographic and text data which provide a patent summary, patent details, and the patent claims excised of all drawings.[9] The online portal allows for searches to be performed against the bibliographic and text data fields only. Images are not searchable but can be viewed for any particular patent that has been returned in a given search.

Presently, the database permits searching for patent documents by number, by words in the inventor, inventor country, owner, owner country, title, abstract, and claims fields, or by International Patent Classification (IPC), Canadian Patent Classification (CPC), Patent Cooperation Treaty (PCT) applications, availability of license, and language of filing. These searches can be combined or modified by Boolean operators and restricted to selected date ranges on any date field. The search results screen lists all patents captured by a particular search string by their patent number and truncated title. Details of patents can be viewed by clicking on the patent number.

Patents within the CIPO database are not classified according to claimed uses for which the inventions have acquired patent protection or by the products and technologies that apply or make use of the protected invention. This makes it difficult to link patented inventions to the commercial products for which they provide exclusivity. In the case of medicinal drugs, this shortcoming makes it difficult to link drug patents to the brand-name drug products for which they provide brand-name pharmaceutical companies with commercial exclusivity. Canadian brand-name pharmaceutical companies can voluntarily list patents relevant to drug products approved for use and sale in Canada by registering these patents with the Canadian Patent Register (CPR) pursuant to NOC Regulations. As noted above, patent listing under the CPR is analogous to the listing of patents in the Orange Book under the US Hatch-Waxman linkage regime. As registering patents is voluntary and at the discretion of the individual pharmaceutical companies, the patent list cannot be considered comprehensive or even representative of all patents associated with a specific drug product. Specific searches of the CIPO and other data bases were thus undertaken.

5.2.2 Drug patenting

In order to identify the full breadth of patent protection associated with a specific Canadian drug product, every patent within the CIPO database must be considered as a possible candidate, which may then be pruned for lack of relevance. The first level of pruning is achieved by employing carefully tailored searches of the online CIPO database. These searches can be formulated so as to return only those patents owned or assigned to the drug's manufacturer (including those owned by its parent company/subsidiaries and partners) that make claims regarding the specific medicinal ingredients associated with the drug or claims regarding the general therapeutic class(es) to which the drug belongs. Each drug therefore has two search strings: (1) a general search string that returned patents that were likely to be relevant to the general therapeutic class associated with the drug in question; and (2) a specific search string that returned patents likely to be relevant to the specific drug in question. Both are discussed in detail in Chapter 4. In all, the two search strings returned over 20,000 patents for analysis. Patents were reviewed and pruned for relevance according to the methodology described. In addition, a significant number of patents were pruned for administrative reasons, similar to the manner in which administrative regulatory approvals were excised in Chapter 3. The resulting database contained 3,850 patents deemed relevant to the cohort of 95 drugs. Patent trees were constructed whereby the number, type, and timing of patents granted in relation to a specific drug or follow-on drugs could be assessed and visualized. An example of such an analysis is provided in Figure 5.1.

5.2.3 Patent listing

Patents may be listed on the Canadian Patent register (CPR) provided they are legally relevant to the already marketed Canadian drug product against which they are listed. A patent's presence on the CPR thus signals that the listing pharmaceutical company acknowledges the patent to be an effective mechanism for enforcing its commercial exclusivity on the drug product to which the patent has been linked. Registered patents are typically the subject of much litigation and constitute valuable data regarding how many

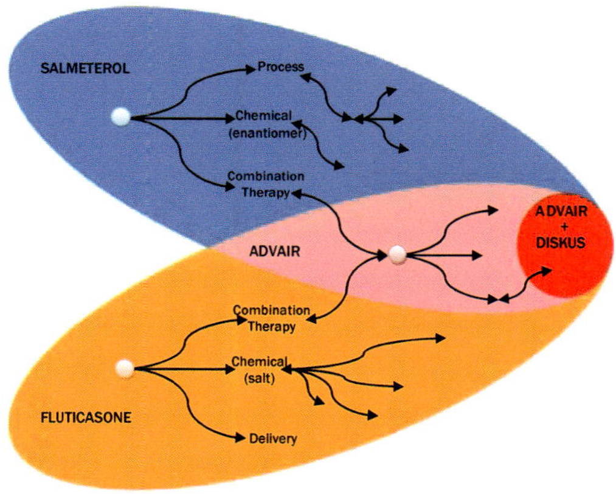

Figure 5.1 Example of patent tree analysis for Advair Diskus®.

Patents were identified using the specific and general search strings described in section 5.2 on methods. In addition to quantifying patents per drug, the patent tree method allows assessment of how specific drugs evolve into related drug forms or (in this case) drug products representing combinations of known drugs. In addition, the patent tree analysis allows for identification of relevant patent types based on the classification nomenclature described in section 5.2 on methods. Finally, the patent tree analysis provides data not only relating to drug development, but also on the type of patents selected by pharmaceutical companies for listing on the patent register in order to prevent generic entry.

patents granted for a specific drug product are listed on the CPR and thus deemed valuable by pharmaceutical companies in regard to protecting blockbuster drugs coming off patent.[10] The CPR website provides access to all patents currently registered to brand-name firms in relation to Canadian drug products and also provides the data for all patents removed from the register due to expiration or invalidity since 2002. Upon request, the CPR was able to provide additional information regarding patents that were removed from the database prior to 2002 for the purposes of this study. The comprehensive database obtained provides an exhaustive list of all patents that effectively contribute to the commercial exclusivity of Canadian drug products investigated in this study. We quantified patents identified that were listed on the CPR under the NOC Regulations. Patents listed on the register can be litigated numerous times owing to the fact that they can be listed for multiple drug identification numbers (DINs) under the NOC Regulations. For our purposes, only the date of first instance (the earliest date on which the patent was registered) for each patent was collected and analyzed.

5.2.4 Patent class

The growing divergence between breakthrough drugs and me-too and line extension drugs is becoming of increasing concern to policy-makers and public and institutional payers in light of the growing basket of intellectual property and regulatory rights attached to these products regardless of whether they are new or follow-on in nature. The primary regulatory mechanisms underpinning patent and linkage incentives for developing follow-on drugs are: the broad range of substances falling within the definition of a new active substance (NAS) and the range of substances and uses meeting the requirements for a supplemental new drug submission (SNDS) supporting line extension and other follow-on drugs.

Previously referred to as a 'new chemical entity' (NCE),[11] the definition of an NAS encompasses a wide range of chemically active substances, including: (1) a chemical or biological substance not previously approved for sale as a drug; (2) an isomer, derivative, or salt of a chemical substance that is already approved for sale as a drug but differing in properties with regard to safety and efficacy; or (3) a biological substance previously approved for sale as a drug, but differing in molecular structure, nature of the source material or even manufacturing process.[12] The scope of regulatory approval based on an NAS is therefore very broad, and forms the basis for a wide berth of new (NDS) and supplementary (SNDS) drug submissions, including whether drugs are classified as first-in-class or me-too drugs.[13] An SNDS in particular may be filed for changes to a drug that is already marketed by a sponsor,[14] including minor changes to dosage, strength, formulation, manufacture, labelling, route of administration, or indication.[15] Thus small changes in chemical properties, route of administration, or use may result in approval within NDS or SNDS approval streams. Importantly, patents may be listed on the patent register in respect of both NDS and SNDS drugs.[16]

In order to gain a better understanding of the patenting patterns associated with high-value drugs, a novel patent classification system was created for this study. Each patent deemed relevant to the cohort of 95 drugs was classified in one or more of the following classes relevant to NDS and SNDS approvals: chemical derivative, chemical salt, chemical enantiomer, chemical crystal, process intermediate, process preparation, delivery, administration, combination therapy, and use/indication. Patents were classified as such based on specific information contained in the claims and description of each patent analyzed. The detailed patent classification system used to analyze the data is summarized in Table 5.1.

Table 5.1 Patent classification system

Classification	**Code**	**Description**
Administration	A	Patent makes a claim(s) regarding the route of administration (e.g. oral, suppository, intravenous) or dosage forms of the medicinal ingredient.
Chemical (crystal)	C_C	Patent makes a claim(s) regarding the crystalline structure of the medicinal ingredient.
Chemical (derivative)	C_D	Patent makes a claim(s) regarding a chemical derivative(s) of the medicinal ingredient obtained via a simple reaction or the substitution of a functional group.
Chemical (enantiomer)	C_E	Patent makes a claim(s) regarding a specific enantiomer of the medicinal ingredient.
Chemical (salt)	C_S	Patent makes claim(s) regarding a specific salt form of the medicinal ingredient.
Combination therapy	C_T	Patent makes claim(s) regarding the therapeutic combination of the medicinal ingredient with one or more different drug products.
Delivery	D	Patent makes claim(s) regarding the in vivo delivery and bio-availability of the medicinal ingredient.
Packaging	P	Patent makes claim(s) regarding the function and aesthetics of the commercial and non-commercial packaging of the medicinal ingredient.
Process (intermediate)	P_I	Patent makes claim(s) regarding the chemical intermediates required in the manufacturing process of the medicinal ingredient.
Process (preparation)	P_P	Patent makes claim(s) regarding the process and methods of manufacture of the medicinal ingredient.
Use	U	Patent makes claim(s) regarding the medical indication for which the medicinal ingredient provides cure or alleviation of symptoms.

5.2.5 Therapeutic class

In addition to classifying patent types, each of the 95 drugs studied was also classified in relation to its therapeutic class. The therapeutic class was assessed using the World Health Organization's Anatomical Therapeutic Classification (ATC) System. As described on the WHO website,[17] the ATC classification divides drugs into groups according to the organ or system on which they act and their chemical, pharmacological and therapeutic properties. The broadest level of classification is the 'First Level,' which represents the 14 primary anatomical sites of drug action. The WHO ATC System used to analyze therapeutic class is summarized in Table 5.2.

5.2.6 Data analysis

Drug approval, drug patenting, and patent listing data were identified, collected and analyzed as described previously.[18] Similar methods were used for the analysis of patent and drug classification results. All data were statistically analyzed and graphed using a combination of Excel, Access (Microsoft Corp.), and GraphPad Prism (Graphpad Software Inc.).

Table 5.2 First-level WHO Anatomical Therapeutic Classification System

Centre	Classification
A	Alimentary Tract and Metabolism
B	Blood and Blood Forming Organs
C	Cardiovascular
D	Dermatological
G	Genito-Urinary and Sex Hormones
H	Systemic Hormonal (excluding Sex and Insulin)
J	Systemic Antiinfectives
L	Antineoplastic and Immunomodulatory
M	Musculo-Skeletal
N	Nervous System
P	Antiparasitic, Insecticides, Repellents
R	Respiratory
S	Sensory
V	Various

General patenting and patent listing data were fit using a number of parametric functions, including: a Gumbel-Min function of the form $f(x) = A \cdot [(1/\sigma) \cdot \exp(((x - \mu)/\sigma) - \exp((x - \mu)/\sigma))]$; a Gompterz sigmoid function of the form $f(x) = A \cdot [\exp(b \cdot \exp(c \cdot \exp(d(x - e))]$; a normal Gaussian function of the form $f(x) = A \cdot [(1/2\pi\sigma)\text{^}(1/2) \cdot \exp(-1/2 \cdot \exp((x - \mu)/\sigma)\text{^}2)]$; and a Log Pearson III fit of the form $f(x) = A \cdot [(1/x|\beta|\Gamma(\alpha) \cdot ((\ln(x) - \gamma)/\beta)\text{^}(\alpha - 1) \cdot \exp((\ln(x) - \gamma)/\beta)]$ where $\Gamma(\alpha)$ is the gamma function. Goodness of fit to the data was assessed using the Kolmogorov-Smirnov goodness-of-fit test.

Patenting data were further explored in Figure 5.4 using linear regression and exponential analyses. Total patenting data were fit to a four-parameter single exponential function of the form: $A \cdot \exp(b \cdot (Y - d)) + B$, where A is amplitude, B is the rate constant of the exponential function and Y is calendar year. All parameters were allowed to 'float.' We also tested a two-parameter single exponential equation of the form: $A \cdot \exp(b \cdot (Y - V)$, where V was fixed at 1977 (the beginning of the data set) or 1993 (the coming-into-force date of the linkage regulations regime). We further probed whether the coming into force of the linkage regulations regime resulted in a different exponential function using a linear regression analysis. Data were fit by an exponential functional of the form: $Y = \alpha \cdot \exp[(\beta_0 + \beta_1 I)t + \varepsilon]$, where Y is total patents, ε is a noise term with zero mean and constant variance, t is the year, and I is an indicator variable taking on the value 1 for year 1993 and later, and zero otherwise. A log transform was used to test the null hypothesis that $\beta_1 = 0$ using linear regression.

5.3 Results

5.3.1 Full cohort of 95 high-value drugs

5.3.1.1 Drug patenting and patent listing

Patenting and patent listing data for the full cohort of 95 drugs are shown in Figure 5.2. A total of 3,850 patents were granted in relation to the cohort (●). This amounted to an average of 40 patents per drug (40.5 : 1.0). Patenting occurred over a relatively long period of almost 35 years, from 1977 to the final year analyzed (2008). A significant take-off point of patenting from baseline levels occurred about 1983, with peak patenting in 2003. The distribution of patenting data over time followed a general bell-shaped pattern that was strongly skewed to the left. The fit to the total patent data in Figure 5.2(a) is a Gumbel-Min distribution, with an $R^2 = 0.9582$. For reasons discussed in relation to Figure 5.3, this function was selected over others as providing the best overall visual fit to the data. Cumulative patents for the cohort rose over time in a manner that was well fit by a sigmoidal function (■; R^2 = 0.9962). The most rapid phase of patenting occurred between 1994 and 2004, with peak patenting activity taking place by about 2006.

Figure 5.2(b) (top) gives the same patent data re-plotted as a function of the year after the first patent on the cohort was issued. The distribution of patenting activity expressed as the year after first instance rose and fell in a general bell-shaped pattern (◇), with patenting activity peaking over a prolonged period of 8 to 16 years after the priority date for first patent on

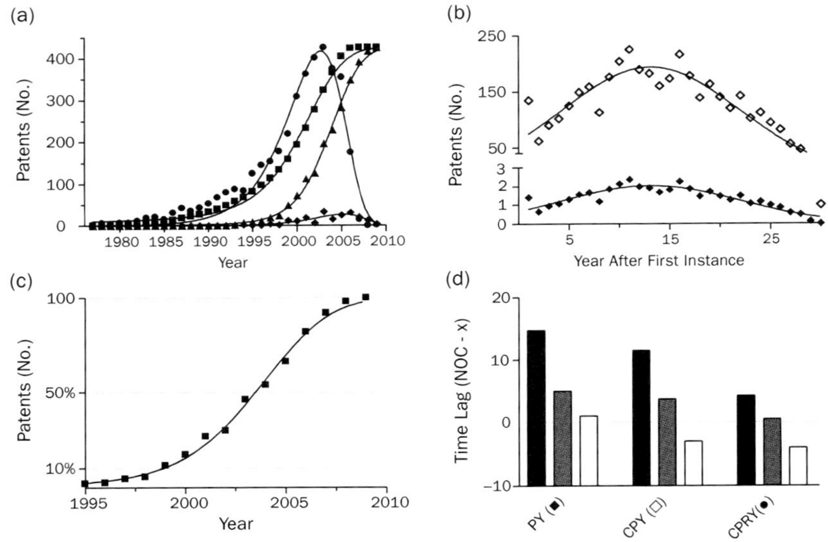

Figure 5.2 Patenting and patent listing patterns associated with cohort.

(a) Total patents issued by year (●), cumulative number of patents (■), total patents listed on the patent register by year (◆), and cumulative number of patents listed on the patent register (▲). Data are for the cohort of 95 drugs and are the sum of data for all sub-groups analyzed (Most Profitable; Priority Review; NOC/c; PR-NOC/c). Note the convergence of cumulative issued and cumulative listed patents over the test period. (b) Total (◇) and average (◆) number of patents on approved drugs plotted as a function of the time after the priority date on which the first patent on the subset was issued. (c) Method used to calculate the temporal gap between the average date of drug approval on the cohort (2004) and the 10th (M_{10}), 50th (M_{50}), and 100th (M_{100}) percentile of maximal drug patenting and patent listing data. Data are those from the cumulative number of patents (■) above. (d) Graph expressing the temporal relationship between drug approval, drug patenting and patent listing. Bars indicate M_{10}, M_{50}, and M_{100} values for patents per year (PY), cumulative patents per year (CPY), and cumulative patents registered on the patent register per year (CPRY). Time points are calculated as the difference between the date of average drug approval (NOC) and x (NOC-x), where x = the date of the 10th, 50th, and 100th percentile of patenting, cumulative patenting, and patent listing, respectively.

the group. The fit to the data is a conventional Gaussian distribution, with $R^2 = 0.8779$. The peak of the Gaussian fit was 14 years after the priority date on first patent. As illustrated in the lower data set in Figure 5.2(b) (◆), average patenting activity peaked at about 2.5 patents per product per year. Patenting activity remained at this level between the eighth and sixteenth year after the first patent on the cohort was granted.

Figure 5.2(a) also shows the manner in which patents for the cohort were listed on the patent register. Of the 3,850 patents associated with the cohort, 196 were listed on the patent register between 1993 and 2008 (◆). Thus about 5% of all patents granted to brand-name pharmaceutical firms were listed on the patent register under the linkage regulations in order to block generic entry. The distribution of patenting listing expressed per calendar year for the entire cohort peaked at about 25 patents per year around 2005. The time course for cumulative listed patents (▲) was well described by a sigmoid function ($R^2 = 0.9976$). The slope of patent listing was greatest between 2000 and 2005 with an apparent peak in 2008. The curves for cumulative patents (■) and the fraction of these patents that were listed on the patent register (▲) converged over time, supporting the conclusion that brand-name firms are listing most if not all patents they obtain on the patent register in a timely and efficient fashion in order to delay generic entry.[19]

The data in Figures 5.2(a) and 5.2(b) indicate that drugs in the cohort were subject to strong patent protection and that a significant number of these patents were listed on the patent register in order to prohibit generic entry. Given the close relation between drug patenting and patent listing, we were interested in further probing the timing between drug approval, drug patenting, and patent listing. From each of the curves in Figure 5.2(a) we calculated three values: the 10th (M_{10}; filled bars), 50th (M_{50}; hatched bars) and (c) 100th (M_{100}; open bars) percentile of normalized maximum values. Each of the three values was then plotted as a function of the average date on which the cohort received marketing approval (2004). This was done to obtain a measure of the delay between drug approval, drug patenting, and patent listing. The procedure is demonstrated for cumulative patent listing data in Figure 5.2(c) (■).

The procedure described above differs slightly from that used in the pilot study of drug patenting and patent listing described in Chapter 4.[20] There, we calculated the inflection point at which the data deviated most strongly from baseline values, as well as the point at which each curve reached the 50th and 95th percentile of maximum values. The inflection point was calculated as the zero point of the second derivative of fits to the data. The reason for using a different method in the present work is that total patenting activity in our pilot study was well fit using a Gaussian distribution. By contrast, the skewed relationship observed with a much larger data set (n = 95 drugs; Figure 5.2(a)) resulted in a slow rather than sharp rise in patenting activity, necessitating the use of simpler M_{10}, M_{50}, and M_{100} values.

As illustrated in Figure 5.2(d), there was a significant lag between the date on which drug approval was granted and the dates on which patents on the same drug product were granted. This gap was observed independent of whether patents were expressed by year of grant (patent per year (PY)) or cumulatively (cumulative patents per year (CPY)), and likely reflects the regulatory lag between drug patenting and drug approval. As patenting activity shifted from 10% to 50% and eventually 100% maximal values, the gap between M_{10}, M_{50}, and M_{100} values and date of average drug approval (NOC-x) progressively declined. Even so, M_{10} and M_{50} remained 4–15 years earlier than the date of average approval for patenting expressed per year and cumulative patenting.

The data were different for patent listing. As demonstrated in Figure 5.2(d), average M_{10} and M_{50} data for cumulative patents listed on the register per year (cumulative patents registered per year (CPRY)) exceeded the null point by only 4 and 0.5 years compared to 12 and 5 years for CPY. Therefore both the take-off point (M_{10}) and the point of half maximal (M_{50}) patent listing occurred much closer to the date of average drug approval for the cohort compared to patenting activity expressed per year or cumulative patenting. In fact, data points for 50% and 100% CPRY were 0.5 and 4.0 years on either side of the null point.

The data in Figure 5.2(d) show that the lag between the average date of drug approval and the average date of cumulative patent listing decreased progressively over the course of the test period. For example, the differential between M_{10} and M_{100} values decreased from 15.75 years for PY, to 8.5 years for CPY, and 0.25 years for CPRY. Ironically, the average date of approval for the cohort drugs was actually four years *later* than the average date of cumulative patent listing (NOC-x = –4.0). The likely reason for this result is the relative speed and flexibility of the process for patent listing compared to that for drug approval. Patent listing occurs in the order of days. This is a much shorter time frame than that for even supplemental (SNDS) drug approval, which occurs over a shorter time span than conventional new (NDS) drug approval. Combined, the data suggest that patent listing under linkage regulations may be a better proxy for drug approval (and thus potentially a better surrogate for drug development incentives) than drug patenting per se.

As demonstrated in Figure 5.2(a) the distribution of patenting data over time was far from symmetrical and not Gaussian in nature. The distribution skewed strongly to the left. There was a slow lead up of patenting activity for the years leading up to the coming into force of linkage regulations in 1993. From that point onwards, the data were more in line with a conventional bell-shaped distribution. This raises the question of whether there is more than one underlying process contributing to total patenting activity and, if so, what its characteristics might be. In order to determine which statistical distribution best fits the patenting data for the cohort, we tested a wide array of statistical distributions (n = 61)[21] for goodness of fit using the Kolmogorov-Smirnov goodness-of-fit test. The best scoring distribution across the data set was the Gumbel-Min distribution (0.1037 K-S Score), followed by the Log-Pearson III distribution (0.1073 K-S Score). For comparison purposes, the normal Gaussian distribution is also shown, which had a K-S score of 0.1699. Data and fits for the three distributions are provided in Figures 5.3(a)–(c). The Pearson function fit the low rising component and peak component well, but not the second more rapid component. The single Gaussian missed both the slow and rapid rising phases and only fit the peak portion of the bell-shaped data set. By contrast, the Gumbel-Min function fit the rapidly-rising, peak and descending portions of the data set, leaving the slowly rising lower amplitude portion poorly fit. As the Gumbel-Min had the best K-S score and visually fit the data sets the most accurately of the fits tested, it was used for visual comparative purposes from this point forward.

The fits in Figures 5.3(a)–(b) suggest that there may be two components to the rising phase of the patenting curve. We attempted to further characterize this possibility in a number ways. The first step was to determine if the data represented the sum of two bell-shaped distributions. We fit the data to two Gaussian functions, one from 1977 to 1993 and the other from 1993 to 2009. The break point of 1993 was selected as this is where the slower component of patenting appeared to evolve into a faster component on visual inspection. As shown in Figure 5.3(d), the data were not well fit using this procedure. In particular, data points between 1991 and 1996, encompassing the potential transition point from a slow to fast component, were very poorly fit. Also, the declining phase of patenting activity between 2005 and 2009 was poorly fit. Thus the data did not represent a sum of two Gaussian functions.

We next assessed whether the data might represent the sum of two exponential components. Data were again split into two epochs. The first was from 1977 to 1993 and the second from 1993 to 2001, the point of

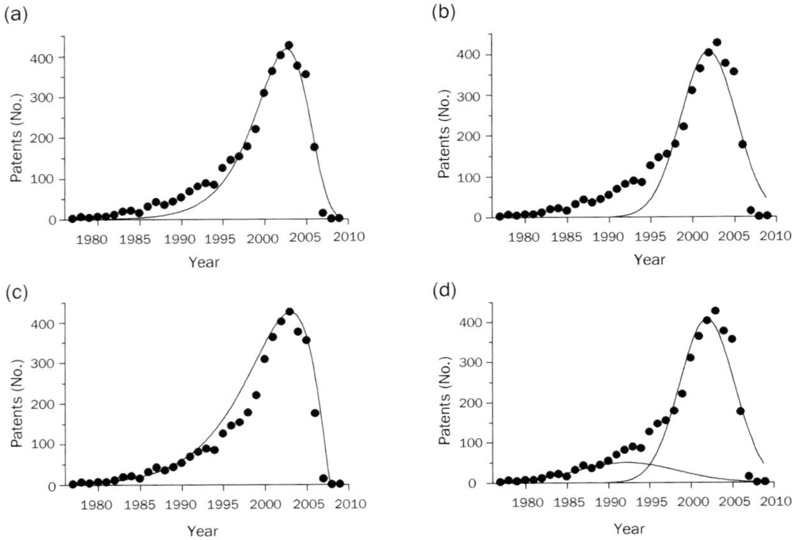

Figure 5.3 Goodness of fit for patent distribution expressed per calendar year.

Total patents plotted by calendar year (●) fit to (a) Gumbel-Min, (b) conventional Gaussian, and (c) Log-Pearson functions. The Kolmogorov-Smirnov (K-S) test was used as a goodness-of-fit test for the relationship of data points to the functions chosen. K-S statistics for Gumbel-Min, Gaussian, and Pearson functions were 0.1037, 0.1073, and 0.1699, respectively. Data were also poorly fit to the sum of two normal Gaussian distributions (d). The Pearson function fit the low rising component and peak component well, but did not fit well the second more rapid component. The single Gaussian missed both the slow and rapid rising phases and only fitted the peak portion of the bell-shaped data set. By contrast, the Gumbel-Min function fit the rapidly rising, peak, and descending portions of the data set, leaving the slowly rising lower amplitude portion poorly fit. As the Gumbel-Min had the best K-S score and visually fit the data sets the most accurately of the fits tested, it was used for comparative purposes from this point forward.

maximal rate of increase in patenting activity. As illustrated in Figure 5.4(a), the data could be well fit to a sum of two single exponentials of the form: $A \cdot \exp(b \cdot (Y - d)) + B$, where A is amplitude, B is the rate constant of the exponential function, and Y is calendar year. All four parameters were allowed to float (i.e. were not fixed). A_1 and A_2 were 12.60 and 30.24 for the 1977–1993 and 1993–2001 epochs, respectively, suggesting the presence of two components of patenting in the data set. The time constants, representing the rate of change of patenting functions, were 0.1467 and 0.2875 for τ_1 and τ_2, respectively. Thus the growth rate was much faster for the second larger amplitude phase of patenting (1/0.2875 = 3.48 years) compared to the smaller and slower first phase of patenting (a/0.1467 = 6.82 years). In other words, the amount of patenting was 2.5x greater and 2.0x faster between

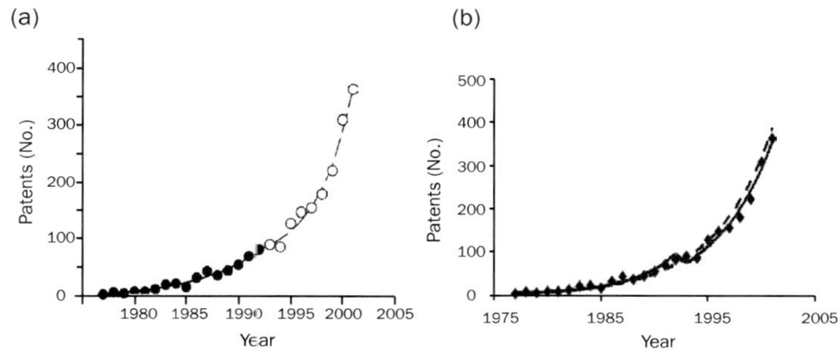

Figure 5.4 Fit of 1977 to 2003 patenting data to exponential functions.

Data were fit to two single exponential functions using two different procedures. In panel (a), data were split into two epochs: 1977–1993 (●) and 1993–2001 (O), the point of maximal rate of increase in patenting activity. Data were then fit to a sum of two single exponential four-parameter functions as described in the text. Solid and dashed lines are fits to epochs one and two, respectively. Amplitudes and time constants were 12.60 and 0.1467, and 30.24 and 0.2875, for the first and second epochs respectively. The fits suggest the presence of a small and slower phase of patenting followed by a larger and faster phase. In panel (b), linear regression analysis was undertaken to probe whether a year-specific change in the patent regime in 1993 resulted in a second exponential function. We assumed a data-generating process with the functional form: $Y = \alpha \cdot \exp[(\beta 0 + \beta 1\ I)t + \varepsilon]$, where Y is total patents, ε is a noise term with zero mean and constant variance, t is the year, and I is an indicator variable taking on the value 1 for year 1993 and later, and zero otherwise. A log transform allowed testing of the null hypothesis ($\beta 1 = 0$) using linear regression. The result ($p = 0.006955$) suggests there is a shift in the exponential growth of patenting in 1993. Raw data (◆) are the same as those in (a).

1993 and 2001 than between 1977 and 1993. A similar result was obtained when a two-parameter equation was used: $A \cdot \exp(b \cdot (Y - V)$, where V is a fixed parameter (1977 or 1993). A_1, A_2, τ_1, and τ_2, were 5.4058, 73.5989, 0.1772, and 0.1971, respectively. Thus, for both two- and four-parameter exponentials, there was a large, fast, and later phase of patenting superimposed on a relatively small, slower, and earlier phase.[22]

A linear regression analysis was undertaken to probe whether a year-specific change in the patent regime in 1993 resulted in a second exponential function (Figure 5.4(b)). We assumed a data generating process with the functional form: $Y = \alpha \cdot \exp[(\beta_0 + \beta_1 I)t + \varepsilon]$, where Y is total patents, ε is a noise term with zero mean and constant variance, t is the year, and I is an indicator variable taking on the value 1 for year 1993 and later, and zero otherwise. A log transform allowed testing of the null hypothesis ($\beta_1 = 0$) using simple linear regression. The associated p-value of 0.006955 supports the conclusion that there is a shift in the exponential growth of patenting in 1993. However, the negative sign on the coefficient suggests that the growth in total patenting follows a slightly slower growth exponential after 1993 than before.

Both approaches in Figure 5.4 assume underlying exponential functions. The first allows more parameters to shift, but does not test whether the change in 1993 is statistically significant. The second allows only one parameter to change, but includes a hypothesis test to demonstrate that the change is statistically significant, and therefore we may conclude that the regime change had a measurable effect. This shows up in a slight bump in 1993. Since the change in legal framework would suggest a shift at this time, and because the hypothesis test confirms that a change took place, we conclude that the growth in total patenting was affected when the linkage regime came into force in 1993. In other words, the linkage regime *itself* altered patenting behavior by firms.

We next investigated changes in global patterns of peak patenting per drug for the cohort. Figure 5.5 shows the results of an analysis of changes in the average time it took for peak patenting per drug over the course of the period 1977 to 2000 for the 95 drugs in the cohort. Data are expressed as the time after the year of first issuance of a patent for a given drug. This was done to probe the patenting strategy of pharmaceutical firms over the test period. Drugs were included in the analysis only if their patenting activity clearly peaked prior to 2008. As indicated by the numbers on top of relevant symbols (■) the number of drugs per calendar year was

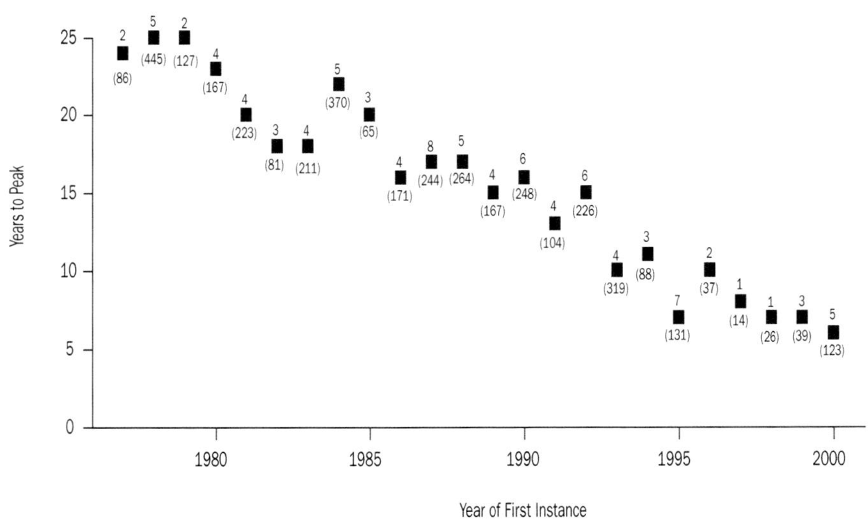

Figure 5.5 Analysis of average year to peak patenting per drug for cohort.

The number of drugs with patents peaking in a given year is provided on top of each symbol (■), which represents the average number of drugs with peak patenting activity in a given year. Numerical values at the bottom of symbols represent the total number of patents for drugs. The data demonstrate a continuing trend towards faster peak patenting per drug over the term 1976 to 2000. The average year of first patent instance for the cohort was 1986.

dispersed fairly evenly, with slight peaks in 1978 and in between 1987 and 1990. Similarly, the numbers in brackets at the bottom of the symbols demonstrate that the number of cumulative patents per category per year was also dispersed fairly evenly over the test period.

During the first four years of the test period (1977–1980) the average year to peak patenting activity was about 25 years. For the five years between 1986 and 1991 this value declined to about 15 years, and decreased further to eight years for the five-year period between 1996 and 2000. Thus there was a reduction of the time to peak patenting from a maximum of 25 years in 1979 to a minimum of 7.5 years in 2000. This equals a 330% increase in the speed of maximal patenting per drug over the course of 20 years. While this conclusion is somewhat tentative given the lower numbers of patents towards the end of the test period, the data suggest that pharmaceutical firms have become significantly more efficient in their patenting efforts over time. This conclusion is consistent with the substantial growth in patent listing in the last decade, the convergence of patenting and patent listing data, and the decreasing time lag between drug approval and drug patenting and patent listing (Figures 5.2(a)–(d)).

5.3.1.2 Patent class

Patents associated with the cohort were further investigated according to the patent classification scheme described in section 5.2 (Methods). Both absolute numbers of patents per classification and the average number of classifications per drug were calculated. Figure 5.6(a) shows data expressed as the average number of patents per drug for each group. There were 5,859 individual patent classifications associated with the cohort of 95 drugs. This amounted to an average of about 62 (61.67) patent classifications per drug. This is a truly remarkable number of patent classes per drug. Patents for the cohort were distributed in three numerical bins: 1–5 patents per drug, 6–10 patents per drug, and greater than 10 patents per drug. The majority of classifications (7/11, or 64%) had 1–5 patents per drug that were widely dispersed throughout the classification system. Most of these patents were directed to intermediate processes and chemical forms, particularly the latter. Specific chemical forms were, in order of prevalence: chemical derivatives (C_D), chemical crystalline forms (C_C), chemical salts (C_S), and chemical enantiomers (C_E). Only three of the classifications contained drugs with 6–10 patents each. These were directed to patents on uses, routes of administration, and processes of preparation. The classification with the largest number of patents per drug was combination therapies (C_T). This class had a peak of 23 patents per drug, representing by far the largest patent classification. The rank order of patent classification for the cohort was: C_T>>AUP_P>>$C_D DP_I C_C C_E C_S I$. Raw data are provided in Table 5.4 below.

In addition to the detailed patent classification scheme described above, we also derived a simplified patent classification scheme. The rationale for undertaking this procedure was that patents are often referred to simply as 'chemical,' 'process,' 'combination,' or 'use' patents. For convenience, the Delivery and Packaging classes in the detailed scheme were folded into the Administration class. The 5,859 classifications were directed fairly broadly to combination (36.7%), route of administration (23.9%), use (15.0%), process (12.7%), and chemical (12%) patents. The rank order of general patent classifications was C_T>A>UPC. Raw data for the cohort are provided in Table 5.6. The large number of patents and patent classifications associated with the cohort (Figure 5.6; Tables 5.5 and 5.6 below) indicate there is a large 'pool' of highly diverse patents from which to draw for both NDS and SNDS submission and patent listing purposes.

5.3.1.3 Therapeutic class

The final analysis for the cohort was by WHO therapeutic class. Generally, the drugs analyzed in this study fell into 10 of the 14 WHO ATC classes. As illustrated in Figure 5.6(b), the cohort of 95 drugs could be divided into three discrete groups: 0–5, 5–15, and greater than 15 drugs per class. The largest group was Antineoplastic/Immunomodulator (n = 23). The second largest was composed of Alimentary Tract & Metabolism (n = 12), Cardiovascular System (n = 16), Systemic Antiinfectives (n = 15), and Nervous System (n = 15) classes. Together these groupings accounted for the large majority of drugs (81 of 95; 85.26%). The remaining 14 drugs were dispersed among five further classes with much smaller values: Blood & Blood Forming Organs (n = 2); Musculo-Skeletal System (n = 3); Respiratory System (n = 5); Sensory Organs (n = 2); and Various (n = 2). The rank order of WHO classifications for the cohort was L>CJNA>>RMBSV. Raw data for the cohort are provided in Table 5.7 below.

In addition to drugs per therapeutic class, we also analyzed patents per therapeutic class. Figures 5.6(c) and 5.6(d) show a comparison of total patents and patents per drug plotted against ATC class. As indicated by the data in the bar graphs, there was substantial variability in the number of patents associated with the various therapeutic classes depending on whether the data were plotted as total number of patents per class or average number of patents per drug per class. Of 3,850 patents granted on the entire cohort, 46% (n = 1,750; 45.5%) were associated with only two

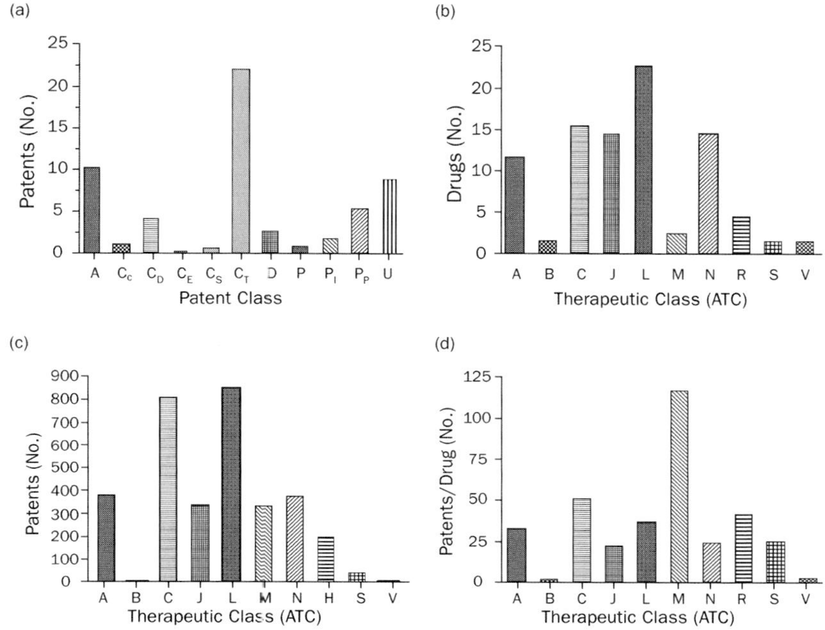

Figure 5.6 Patent classifications and WHO ATC classifications for cohort.

(a) Bar graph illustrating patent classifications for the cohort of 95 drugs. There were 5,859 individual patent classifications associated with the cohort, amounting to about 61 classifications per drug. The majority of classifications (7/11) had 1–5 patents per drug widely dispersed throughout the classification system. Most were directed to intermediate processes and chemical forms, particularly chemical derivatives, chemical crystalline forms, chemical salts, and chemical enantiomers. Two classifications contained drugs with 6–10 patents each. These were directed to patents on uses and routes of administration. Combination therapies was the largest class, with 23 patents per drug. Panels (b)–(d) are bar graphs showing data for the cohort analyzed with respect to the first-level WHO Anatomic Therapeutic Class (ATC) drug classification scheme. Data are expressed as (b) number of drugs in the cohort per ATC class, (c) number of patents in the cohort per ATC class, and (d) number of patents per drug per ATC class. Details of both classification systems are described in section 5.2 on methods.

therapeutic classes: Antineoplastic/Immunomodulator (n = 900) and Cardiovascular (n = 850). A second, and equally large, grouping (n = 1,725; 44.81%) was composed of Alimentary Tract & Metabolism (n = 400), Nervous System (n = 400), Antiinfectives (n = 350), Musculo-Skeletal (n = 350), and Hormonal (n = 225), with remaining patents (10%) split between Sensory Organs (n = 50), Blood Forming Organs (n = 5), and Various (n = 5). As such, the rank order of total patents distributed within the WHO ATC classification was LC>NMJH>>SBV.

Figure 5.6(d) shows patents analyzed per drug for the various therapeutic classes. While the cohort had on average 40 patents per drug (Figure 5.1), the average number of patents per ATC classification varied tremendously, from a low of 3.5 to a high of 116. The largest class by far was Musculo-Skeletal drugs, which had an average of 116 patents per drug. This was followed by Cardiovascular (n = 55), Respiratory (n = 45), Antineoplastic/Immunomodulator (n = 38), Alimentary Tract and Metabolism (n = 33), Sensory Organs (n = 27), Nervous System (n = 25), Antiinfectives (n = 25), Blood (n = 5), and Various (n = 3.5). The most significant deviation of patenting per ATC class from total patenting data was that while almost 50% of all patents were distributed within the Antineoplastic, Immunomodulatory, and Cardiovascular classifications (Figure 5.6(c)), peak patenting activity per drug was associated with a much more broad set of therapeutic classifications (Figure 5.6(d)). The rank order of patents per drug per ATC class was M>CRLA>SNC>BV.

5.3.2 Most Profitable, Priority Review, NOC/c, and PR-NOC/c sub-cohorts

5.3.2.1 Drug patenting and patent listing

Patenting and patent listing patterns for most profitable drugs (Most Profitable; n = 33), expedited drug approvals without significant post-market obligations (Priority Review; n = 40), expedited approvals with significant post-market obligations (NOC/c; n = 16), and drugs subject to expedited approval via the Priority Review stream that also received NOC/c approvals (PR-NOC/c; n = 6) are shown in Figure 5.7.

The patenting and patent listing patterns observed for the four groups were in general quite similar. As with patenting activity for the cohort (Figure 5.2), patenting expressed per calendar year had a bell-shaped pattern which was skewed to the left. As per Figure 5.3, all fits to the data are Gumbel-Min functions. Fits were R^2 = 0.9487 for Most Profitable (■), 0.9329 for Priority Review (▼), 0.9151 for NOC/c (◆), and 0.9606 for PR-NOC/c (●) groups, respectively. Peak patenting occurred within a small temporal window for all four groups (2003–2005). Peak patenting for the Most Profitable group (n = 179) exceeded that for the Priority Review group (n = 150) and was a little over three times (325%) greater than that observed for the NOC/c (n = 55) and PR-NOC/c (n = 56) groups. The threefold increase in patents for the Most Profitable group can be seen both

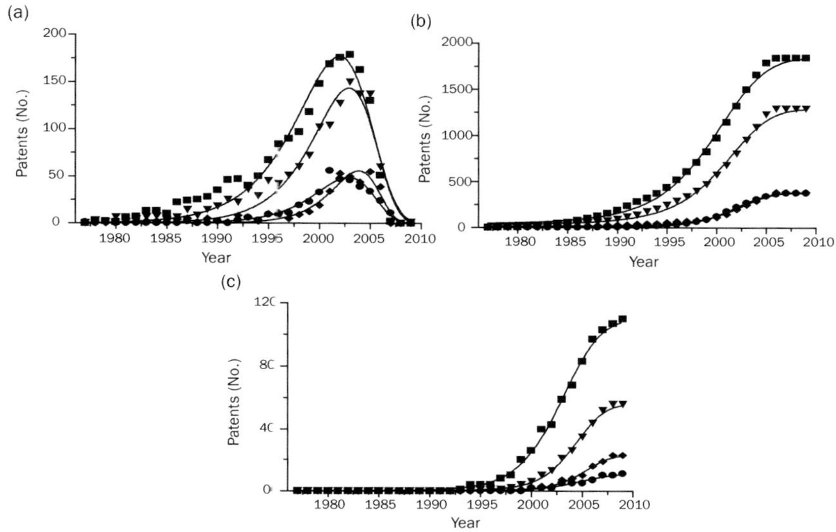

Figure 5.7 Comparison of drug patenting, cumulative patenting, and cumulative patent listing for Most Profitable, Priority Review, NOC/c, and PR-NOC/c groups.

Data are shown for (a) patents per calendar year, (b) cumulative patenting activity, and (c) cumulative patent listing for Most Profitable (■), Priority Review (▼), NOC/c (◆), and PR-NOC/c (●) groups. Fits to the data are Gumbel-Min for panel (a) and Gompertz sigmoid functions for panels (b) and (c).

in the raw (Figure 5.7(a)) and cumulative (Figure 5.7(b)) data, with a more pronounced peak in the cumulative data. The onset of patenting activity was earliest for Most Profitable drugs, followed by Priority Review, NOC/c, and PR-NOC/c drugs. While the onset appeared to be earlier for the PR-NOC/c group compared to the NOC/c group (Figure 5.7(a)), cumulative patenting activity for both groups was nearly identical (Figure 5.7(b)). All four data sets for cumulative patenting were well fit by a sigmoid function, with R^2 values of 0.9960, 0.9956, 0.9927, and 0.9997 for Most Profitable, Priority Review, NOC/c, and PR-NOC/c groups, respectively. Peak cumulative patenting followed a similar order as patenting activity expressed per calendar year: Most Profitable (n = 1,846), Priority Review (n = 1,291), NOC/c (n = 387), and PR-NOC/c (n = 379).

The data in Figures 5.7(a) and 5.7(b) indicate that the large majority of patenting activity (80%) occurred in relation to Most Profitable and Priority Review drugs, with much smaller overall patenting levels associated with the NOC/c and PR-NOC/c groups. While true in absolute terms, this conclusion is somewhat tempered when data for expedited review are parsed in a more nuanced manner. For example, the average number of patents per drug was 55.9, 31.5, 24.19, and 63.17 for Most Profitable, Priority Review, NOC/c, and PR-NOC/c, respectively. Therefore, while the number of patents per drug in the Most Profitable, Priority Review, and NOC/c groups tracked the rank order for peak patenting per drug by calendar year (Figure 5.7(a)) and cumulative patenting (Figure 5.7(b)), normalized data indicate (1) that NOC/c drugs did not differ substantially from Priority Review drugs and (2) that drugs approved with both Priority Review and NOC/c status (PR-NOC/c) had a disproportionally high number of patents per drug compared to either the Priority Review or NOC/c groups alone. A summary of patent data for all groups studied is provided in Table 5.3.

Figure 5.7(c) shows patent listing data for the Most Profitable (■), Priority Review (▼), NOC/c (◆), and PR-NOC/c (●) groups. In general, data for the listing of patents on the patent register under the linkage regulations again paralleled that for patenting. The Most Profitable drugs had the largest number of listed patents (n = 110), followed by Priority Review (n = 56), NOC/c (n = 23), and PR-NOC/c (11). Thus firms listed 5.96%, 4.34%, 5.94%, and 2.90% of patents granted in relation to Most Profitable, Priority Review, NOC/c, and PR-NOC/c drugs, respectively. This can be compared with 5.1% of patents for the entire cohort (Figure 5.2). Of interest, while the number of average patents per drug was very large for the PR-NOC/c group compared to the other groups, the fraction of these patents listed was the smallest for all of the groups studied to date.

Normalized patenting, cumulative patenting, and cumulative patent listing data within each of the four groups are provided in Figures 5.8(a)–5.8(c). As with the cohort (Figure 5.2), the general bell-shaped and

Table 5.3 Summary of drug patenting data

Patents	Total (N = 95)	MP (N = 33)	PR (N = 40)	NOC/c (N = 16)	PR-NOC/c (N = 6)
Patents	3,850	1,846	1,291	387	379
Patents per drug	40.5	55.9	32.3	24.2	63.2
Listed patents	199	110	56	23	11
Average patent date	2000	1999	2000	2001	2001

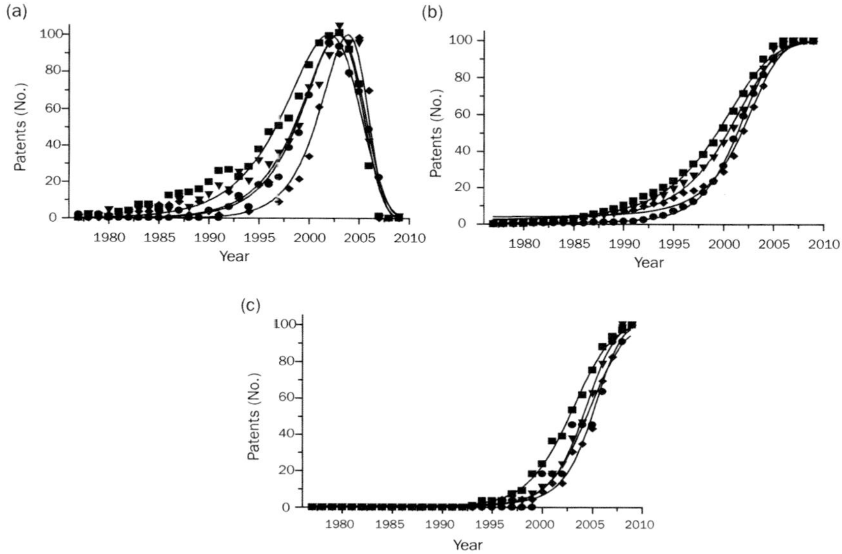

Figure 5.8 Comparison of normalized drug patenting and patent listing patterns for Most Profitable, Priority Review, NOC/c, and PR-NOC/c groups.

Data are shown for (a) normalized patents per calendar year, (b) cumulative patenting activity, and (c) cumulative patent listing for Most Profitable (■), Priority Review (▼), NOC/c (◆), and PR-NOC/c (●) groups. Fits to the data are Gumbel-Min for panel (a) and Gompertz sigmoid functions for panels (b) and (c).

sigmoidal patterns for normalized patenting and patent listing data were observed in all four groups. Patenting activity expressed per calendar year rises and falls with time, and cumulative patenting lags behind cumulative patent listing in each case. However, there was an important difference between groups in relation to the degree to which patenting activity per calendar year was skewed to the left. The rank order for leftward skewing was Most Profitable>Priority Review>>PR-NOC/c>NOC/c. The fact that the two groups with the largest patenting activities over time (Most Profitable and Priority Review) were those that skewed most strongly to the left explains this tendency in the cohort (Figure 5.2(a)). Cumulative patenting and patent listing were both well fit by a sigmoid function. R^2 values for cumulative patenting activity were 0.9960, 0.9956, 0.9927, and 0.9997 for Most Profitable, Priority Review, NOC/c, and PR-NOC/c, respectively. R^2 values for cumulative patent listing were 0.9977, 0.9979, 0.9923, 0.9775 for the same groups.

While both cumulative patenting and cumulative patent listing followed sigmoidal patterns for the four groups studied, there were significant differences between groups. In particular, the date of onset of patenting and patent listing and the rates of growth to maximal levels differed between groups. Both cumulative patenting activity and patent listing were shifted to the right for Priority Review and both NOC/c groups compared with the Most Profitable group. The apparent take-off point for patenting in the Most Profitable group was about 1988. This can be compared to the NOC/c and PR-NOC-c groups, which had apparent take-off points close to 1993, the date on which the NOC Regulations came into force. A similar pattern emerged in the patent listing data, where the apparent take-off points for the Most Profitable and PR-NOC/c groups appeared to be about 1995 and 2000, respectively. Similarly, the most rapid phase of cumulative patenting occurred between 1995 and 2000 for the Most Profitable and Priority Review groups (Figure 5.8(b)) whereas that for NOC/c and PR-NOC/c groups occurred later, between 2000 and 2004. Data for patent listing paralleled this trend (Figure 5.8(c)). Finally, visual inspection of the slopes for cumulative patenting and listing activity suggests there may be different rates of convergence of patenting and patent listing curves over time for the different groups. Differences in convergence of this nature would be important, as they may reflect strategic responses by pharmaceutical firms to safety and efficacy signals generated in both the pre-market and post-market phases of drug development.

Figure 5.9 shows a more detailed analysis of the relationship between drug approval, drug patenting and patent listing for the Most Profitable, Priority Review, NOC/c, and PR-NOC/c groups. As observed for the cohort (Figure 5.2(d)), there was a significant lag between the date on which drug approval was granted and the dates on which patents on the same drug product were granted. This delay gradually declined as patenting activity shifted from 10% to 50% and 100% maximal values. As observed with general patenting activity and patent listing (Figures 5.7 and 5.8), there were small but significant differences between groups. For example, there was a progressive decline in the lag between drug approval and the 10th, 50th, and 100th percentile of maximal patenting per year (PY) from Most Profitable, to Priority Review, NOC/c, and PR-NOC/c. The onset of significant patenting activity (M_{10}) declined from 19 years, to 16, 13, and 11 years for these groups. However, at the M_{100} level, the lag had reduced to essentially zero for all four groups. There was even less difference between CPY and CPRY data, which had M_{10}, M_{50}, and M_{100} values within 1–3 years of each other. The rank order for proximity of drug

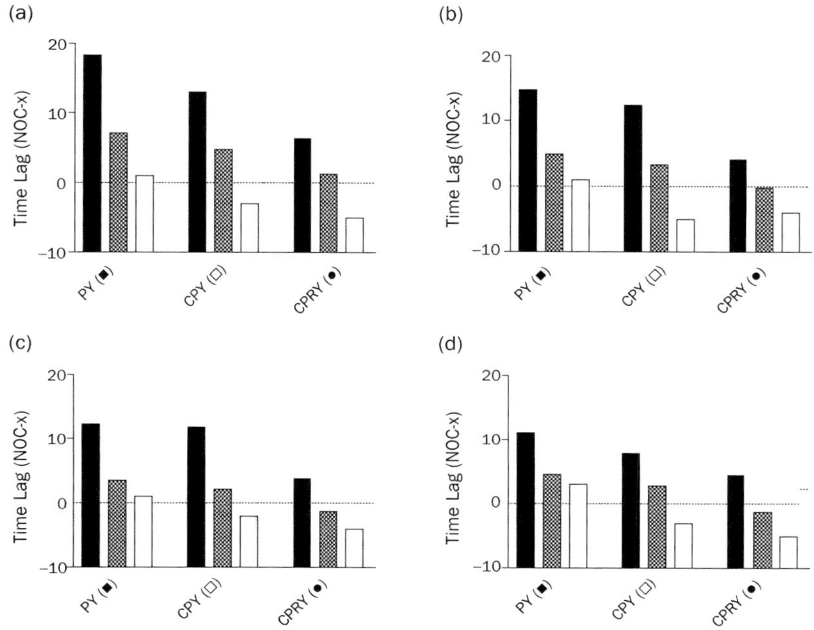

Figure 5.9 Comparison of temporal relationship between drug approval, drug patenting, and patent listing for Most Profitable, Priority Review, NOC/c, and PR-NOC/c groups.

(a)–(d) Bar graphs illustrating the temporal relationship between drug approval, drug patenting and patent listing. As in Figure 5.2(d), bars represent M_{10}, M_{50}, and M_{100} values for patents per year (PY), cumulative patents per year (CPY), and cumulative patents registered on the patent register per year (CPRY) for Most Profitable, Priority Review, NOC/c, and PR-NOC/c groups, respectively. Time points are calculated as the difference between the date of average drug approval (NOC) and x (NOC-x), where x = the date of the 10th, 50th, and 100th percentile of patenting cumulative patenting, and patent listing, respectively.

patenting and patent listing to drug approval was PR-NOC/c>NOC/c>Priority Review>Most Profitable. As such, the data demonstrate that the NOC/c regime provides a highly flexible mechanism for pharmaceutical firms to provide intellectual property protection to drugs, even under conditions where they are still in the regulatory approval phase.

Figure 5.10 shows a comparison of changes in the average time it took for peak patenting per drug over the period 1977 to 2000 for the four groups. Data are expressed as the time after the year of first issuance of a patent for a given drug. Fits are to a Gumbel-Min function and are for visual inspection purposes only. The data suggest that the general decline in peak patenting cycles per drug observed for the cohort in Figure 5.5 was

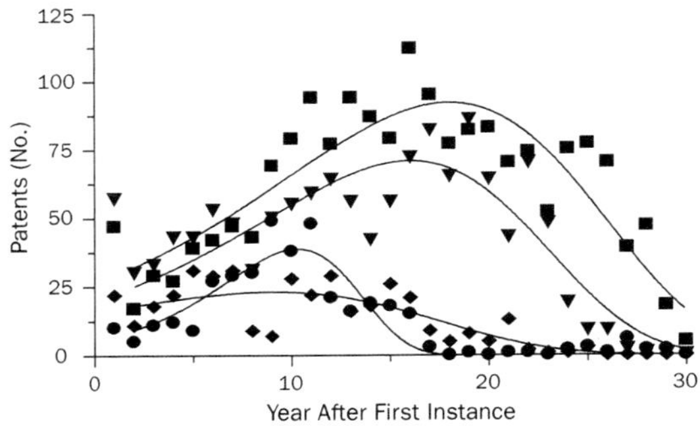

Figure 5.10 Comparison of year to peak patenting per drug for Most Profitable, Priority Review, NOC/c, and PR-NOC/c groups.

Symbols represent the average number of drugs with peak patenting activity in a given year for Most Profitable (■), Priority Review (▼), NOC/c (●), and PR-NOC/c (◆) groups, respectively.

reflective of group-specific differences in peak patenting per drug over time. For example, peak patenting per drug for the Most Profitable group (■) had a bell-shaped pattern over time, peaking between 15 and 17 years after the priority date of the first patent granted on the group. This pattern was repeated from a lower baseline for Priority Review drugs (▼).

While the pattern was bell-shaped for Priority Review, it was nevertheless shifted to the left by 3–4 years. The same was true for the NOC/c (●) and PR-NOC/c (◆) groups, which were shifted down and to the left yet again. Thus, as one moves from Most Profitable to Priority Review, to NOC/c, and eventually PR-NOC/c, peak patenting occurs at progressively fewer years after the date of the first patent on the group, and this peak generally involves fewer and fewer patents per drug. A caveat for this conclusion, as shown clearly by the fits to the raw data, is that even the Gumbel-Min function provided generally poor fits to the data. R^2 values were 0.8437, 0.8391, 0.7228, and 0.8510 for Most Profitable, Priority Review, NOC/c, and PR-NOC/c groups, respectively. Moreover, as discussed in section 5.3.3 on limitations below, the data sets for NOC/c and PR-NOC/c are less likely to be complete or nearing completion than those for the Most Profitable and Priority Review groups. Even so, the data in Figure 5.10 demonstrate a slow but steady downward and leftward shift towards fewer patents and earlier year after first instance peaks for the groups as described.

5.3.2.2 Patent class

Patents associated with Most Profitable, Priority Review, NOC/c, and PR-NOC/c drugs were assessed according to the patent classification scheme described in the section on methods. Data in Figure 5.11 represent patent classifications per drug for each group. As observed for the cohort (Figure 5.6), all four groups shared a 'W'-shaped distribution, with the Combination Therapy class providing the middle peak and Administration and Use patents providing generally ascending bookends. There were 5,732 individual patent classifications associated with the cohort of 95 drugs. Of these, 2,762, 1,886, 582, and 502 classifications were associated with Most Profitable, Priority Review, NOC/c, and PR-NOC/c groups, respectively. The results differed substantially when the data were expressed as the number of patent classifications per drug: there were 83.7, 46.0, 36.4, and 83.7 classifications per drug for the Most Profitable, Priority Review, NOC/c, and PR-NOC/c groups, respectively. Thus, while the PR-NOC/c group had the least number of patent classifications overall, it had the largest number of patent classifications per drug.

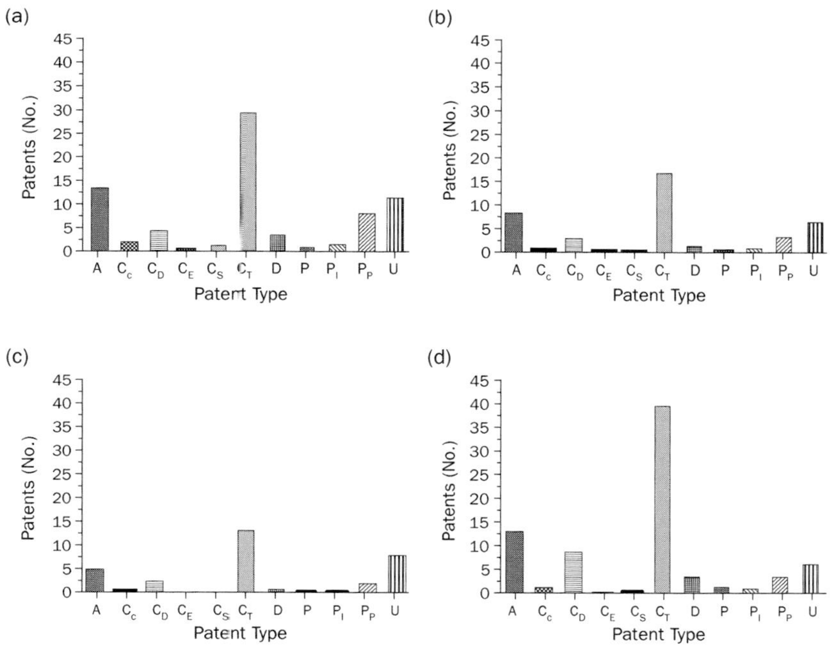

Figure 5.11 Comparison of patent classifications for Most Profitable, Priority Review, NOC/c, and PR-NOC/c groups.

(a)–(d) Bar graphs illustrating patent classifications per drug for Most Profitable, Priority Review, NOC/c, and PR-NOC/c groups, respectively.

Patents could be split into four numerical bins for each group: 0–5, 5–10, 10–15, and greater than 15 patents per drug. The ratio was very similar for each group: 7 : 1 : 2 : 1 for Most Profitable, 8 : 2 : 0: 1 for Priority Review, 8 : 2 : 1 : 0 for NOC/c, and 7 : 2 : 1 : 1 for PR-NOC/c. The most significant difference was in the number of patents per class in the 10–15 and 15+ ranges. The largest class was the 15+ category for the PR-NOC/c group (Figure 5.11(d)), which had a maximum of 40 Combination Therapy patents per drug. This can be compared to 32 (Figure 5.11(a)), 17 (Figure 5.11(b)), and 15 (Figure 5.11(c)) for Most Profitable, Priority Review, and NOC/c drugs. Administration and Use patent classes represented the two next largest classifications. PR-NOC/c, Most Profitable, Priority Review, and NOC/c drugs were associated with 14, 15, 10, and 5 Administration patents on average, while Use patents were 7, 13, 7, and 10 for the PR-NOC/c, Most Profitable, Priority Review, and NOC/c groups. Of interest, while the PR-NOC/c group had by far the lowest number of drugs (n = 6) with the lowest number of patents (n = 379), listed patents (n = 11), and patent classifications (n = 502), when averaged out for the number of drugs per group each of these metrics was the highest, or next to the highest, among groups. Raw data for the detailed classification scheme are provided in Table 5.4. Rank order classification data are given in Table 5.5.

In addition to the detailed patent classification scheme, Most Profitable, Priority Review, NOC/c, and PR-NOC/c drugs were also analyzed via the

Table 5.4 Summary of detailed patent classification data

Patent class	**Total (n = 95)**	**MP (n = 33)**	**PR (n = 40)**	**NOC/c (n = 16)**	**PR-NOC/c (n = 6)**
Administration	1,008	473	358	91	82
Chemical (Crystal)	136	93	23	4	10
Chemical (Derivative)	439	176	156	48	56
Chemical (Enantiomer)	44	26	12	0	1
Chemical (Salt)	84	72	9	0	3
Combination Therapy	2,131	1,003	686	223	242
Delivery	284	150	89	19	25
Packaging	109	54	36	9	10
Process (Intermediate)	196	83	71	12	9
Process (Preparation)	551	294	161	37	24
Use	877	410	285	139	40

Table 5.5 Summary of general patent classification data

Patent class	Total (n = 95)	MP (n = 33)	PR (n = 40)	NOC/c (n = 16)	PR-NOC/c (n = 6)
Administration	1,401	677	483	119	117
Chemical	703	367	200	52	70
Process	747	377	232	49	33
Combination	2,131	1,003	686	223	242
Use	877	410	285	139	40

simplified scheme. The 5,732 classifications were directed broadly to Combination, Route of Administration, Use, Process, and Chemical patents, the range for which depended on the group studied. One consistent observation was that the largest group was Combination patents, followed by either Use or Administration patents. The rank order of general classifications was C_T>>A>UPC for the Most Profitable drugs, C_T>A>UPC for Priority Review, C_T>UA>CP for NOC/c, and C_T>A>C>UP for PR-NOC/c. Thus the general W-shaped pattern breaks down somewhat when data are analyzed with the general scheme, with NOC/c and PR-NOC/c drugs in particular containing a relatively larger fraction of Use and Chemical patents.

In light of the large allowance for new uses and chemical derivatives allowed under the definition of new active substance (NAS) and supplemental new drug submissions (SNDS) streams, the larger number of patents making up the Use and Chemical pools observed here would be attractive to sponsors seeking to obtain patent protection for follow-on SNDS drugs. Raw data for the general classification scheme are provided in Table 5.5. A comparison of the rank orders for the general classification scheme is provided in Table 5.6.

5.3.2.3 Therapeutic class

Finally, the four groups were analyzed by WHO therapeutic class. Unlike the cohort analysis (Figure 5.6), the data shown in Figure 5.12 for Most Profitable, Priority Review, NOC/c, and PR-NOC/c groups did not fall into a broad range of therapeutic classes. Data for each group fell into one of only two numerical bins: those with 0–5 drugs per ATC class and those with 5–10 drugs per class. The ratio of drugs in each group was 2 : 3, 7 : 3, 2 : 1, and 3 : 0 for Most Profitable, Priority Review, NOC/c, and PR-NOC/c drugs, respectively.

Table 5.6 Comparison of rank orders for patent classifications

Group	Code rank order
Detailed classification	
Cohort (n = 95)	C_T>>AUP_P>>C_DD$P_I$$C_C$$C_E$$C_S$I
Most Profitable (n = 33)	C_T>>AU>P_P>C_DD$C_C$$P_I$$C_S$$C_E$P
Priority Review (n = 40)	C_T>>AU>$P_P$$C_DDP_I$$C_S$$C_EPC_C$
NOC/c (n = 16)	C_T>UA>$P_P$$C_DDP_IPC_C$$C_S$$C_E$
PR-NOC/c (n = 6)	C_T>>A>C_DU>P_PD$C_C$$P_IPC_S$$C_E$
General classification	
Cohort (n = 95)	C_T>A>UPC
Most Profitable (n = 33)	C_T>>A>UPC
Priority Review (n = 40)	C_T>A>UPC
NOC/c (n = 16)	C_T>UA>CP
PR-NOC/c (n = 6)	C_T>A>C>UP

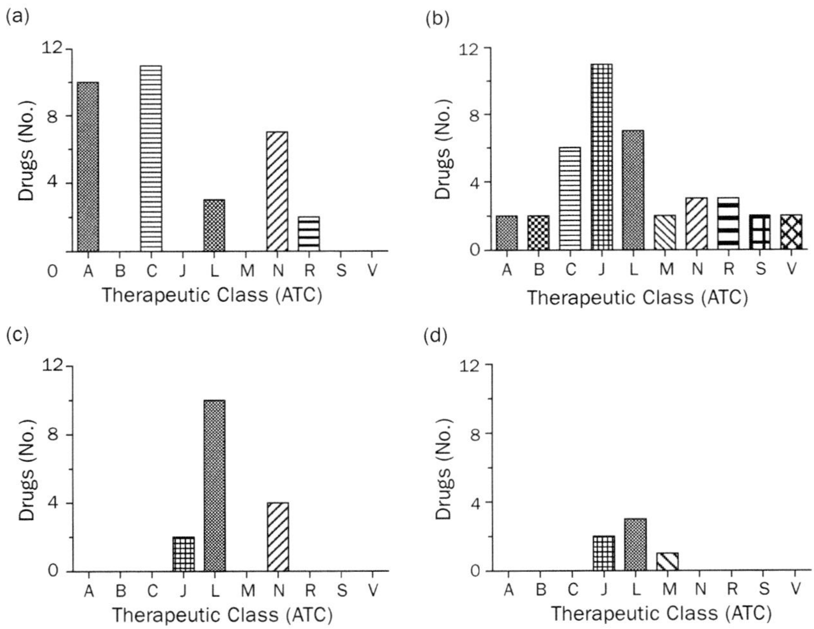

Figure 5.12 Comparison of first-level WHO ATC Drug Classifications for Most Profitable, Priority Review, NOC/c, and PR-NOC/c groups.

(a)–(d) Bar graphs illustrating drug classifications for Most Profitable, Priority Review, NOC/c, and PR-NOC/c groups. Bars represent the number of drugs in each group per ATC class, respectively.

Both NOC/c and PR-NOC/c had only three classifications each in total, while even the Most Profitable group only had five. The group with the largest number of classifications (Priority Review) was also that in which ATC classifications were distributed most broadly. While there was no repetitive pattern between groups, generally the largest ATC classes were Alimentary Tract & Metabolism (A), Cardiovascular System (C), Systemic Antiinfectives (J), and Antineoplastic/Immunomodulator (L), with an average of 10 drugs per therapeutic class in most groups studied. Raw data for the Cohort and Most Profitable, Priority Review, and NOC/c groups are provided in Table 5.7. Rank orders for the groups are given in Table 5.8.

Table 5.7 Summary of WHO Drug Classification data

Drug class	**Total (n = 95)**	**MP (n = 33)**	**PR (n = 40)**	**NOC/c (n = 16)**	**PR-NOC/c (n = 6)**
Alimentary Tract/Metabolism	12	10	2	–	–
Cardiovascular	16	11	6	–	–
Systemic Antiinfectives	15	–	11	2	2
Antineoplastic/ Immunomodulatory	23	3	7	10	3
Nervous System	15	7	3	4	–
Blood/Blood Forming Organs	2	–	2	–	–
Musculo-Skeletal	3	–	2	–	1
Respiratory	5	2	3	–	–
Sensory	2	–	2	–	–
Various	2	–	2	–	–

Table 5.8 Comparison of rank orders for WHO Drug Classifications

Group	**Code rank order**
Cohort (n = 95)	L>CJNA>>RMBSV
Most Profitable (n = 33)	CAN>LR
Priority Review (n = 40)	JLC>NRABMSV
NOC/c (n = 16)	L>NJ
PR-NOC/c (n = 6)	LJM

5.3.3 Limitations

Patenting over time for the cohort and most of the sub-groups studied followed a general bell-shaped pattern over time expressed per calendar year in absolute terms (Figure 5.2(a)), year after first patent instance (Figure 5.2(b)), or following normalization for maximal values (Figure 5.8(a)). As described in detail in Figure 5.3, the distribution was not Gaussian in nature (single or double). The distribution of patenting skewed strongly to the left, with a slow gradual phase of patenting activity from 1977 to about 1993, followed by a larger and potentially faster component of patenting. As illustrated by the two procedures shown in Figures 5.4(a) and 5.4(b), these phases were well fit to the sum of two single exponential functions with a break point around 1993, the year the NOC Regulations came into force. That two exponential processes were identified using two different methods strongly suggests that firm patenting activities have been significantly affected by the coming into force of the linkage regulations.

A significant limitation of the analysis described in the preceding paragraph is that the descending phase of the bell curve could be an artefact of analyzing an ongoing process. This would be consistent with the observation that the rate (although not the amplitude) of the second phase of patenting after 1993 was slower than the first phase under certain conditions (e.g. broadening the second epoch from 1993–2001 to 1993–2003). There are reasons, however, to speculate that a true descending phase may prevail with a longer observation period. First, patenting activity on the cohort and sub-groups may reflect a process that is ongoing, but at a reduced rate. This is consistent with the differences in the average date of patenting for drugs already deemed 'most profitable' by the marketplace (1999) compared to drugs which have been more recently approved via either the NOC/c or PR-NOC/c expedited review stream (2001). The observations that the listing of patents on the patent register declines after peaking (Figure 5.2(a)) and peak patenting per drug over time has declined considerably in the last two decades (Figures 5.5 and 5.10) may also be supportive evidence for this conclusion.

Further evidence for a legitimate declining phase is provided by amendments made to the NOC Regulations. Two sets of changes were made to the linkage regulations between 2004 and 2007 that may have hastened both existing office actions at the PTO and patent listing. As noted above, under the provisions of domestic linkage regulations, each patent listed on the patent register must be demonstrated in litigation to be invalid or not infringed for generic market entry. Prior to amendments in 2006,[23] any patent listed on the register had to be successfully overcome in litigation. Up to this time, it was possible to list a patent on the register *shortly before* an NOC was granted to a generic firm or *shortly after* a generic firm had 'won' on all contested patents to date (i.e. successfully demonstrated that all patents listed were either invalid or not infringed). However, as recognized earlier by the US Federal Trade Commission in its investigation of evergreening under Hatch-Waxman,[24] practices such as these result in abuse of the automatic stay provision. Following the 2006 amendments, generic firms are only obliged to litigate patents listed *before* its Notice of Allegation is filed. As such, only patents listed before litigation is initiated can be used by brand-name firms to trigger the automatic injunction. The second amendment was in relation to the relevance requirement. As discussed above, early appellate jurisprudence rejected a strict relevance requirement, opting instead for a reading such that patents need only be relevant to a medicine rather than the drug form specifically approved by regulators.[25] However, this was altered in 2006 when amendments were made such that listed patents were required to contain at least one specific claim to the medical ingredient, formulation, dosage form, or use for which approval was granted.[26]

The importance of these amendments to the present work is a potential escalating effect on the rate of patenting and patent listing in between at least 2004 and 2007, as firms were first consulted by government during the RIAS phase and then later involved in accelerated listing and litigation activities in anticipation of these two loopholes closing. At some point, however, patenting and patent listing would eventually decline back to a certain equilibrium as the deadline for listing would be fixed to the date of generic Notice of Allegation as well as the date on which all patents on the register were shown in litigation to be either invalid or not infringed by the generic product. At this point we would expect to see a descending portion of a bell-shaped distribution, however skewed at its earlier stages. However, it is not yet clear that this point has been reached in the present analysis.

A second limitation of the analysis was that the PR-NOC/c results described in Figures 5.7–5.12 were strongly influenced by patenting and patent listing data associated with just one drug, celecoxib.[27] Including data for this drug in the PR-NOC/c group had the effect of increasing total patenting per year and cumulative patenting to the level of the NOC/c group (Figures 5.7(a) and 5.7(b)) and shifting cumulative patenting (Figure 5.8(b)) and patent listing (Figure 5.8(c)) to the left compared to the NOC/c group. As illustrated by the raw data in Figure 5.13, when the results for celecoxib are subtracted, there is a progressive trend downward and to the right for peak, cumulative, and normalized patenting and patent listing

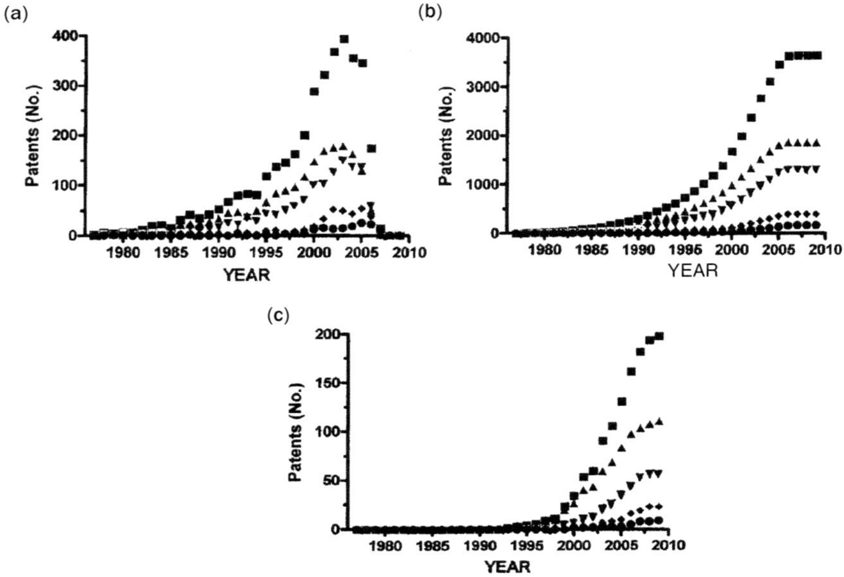

Figure 5.13 Comparison of drug patenting, cumulative patenting, and cumulative patent listing for the cohort, Most Profitable, Priority Review, NOC/c, and PR-NOC/c groups in the absence of data for celecoxib.

Raw data are shown for (a) patents per calendar year, (b) cumulative patenting activity, and (c) cumulative patent listing for the cohort (■), Most Profitable (▲), Priority Review (▼), NOC/c (◆), and PR-NOC/c (●) groups after subtracting PR-NOC/c data for the selective COX-2 inhibitor celecoxib (Celebrex™).

with a clear and distinct rank order of cohort>Most Profitable>Priority Review>NOC/c>PR-NOC/c. While this renders the visual representation and separation of the data visually cleaner, we nevertheless felt it was appropriate to include all data for the PR-NOC/c group. The rationale for this strategy was that celecoxib is an excellent example of the type of drug regulators hope to see going through expedited review and onto Most Profitable status.

5.4 Discussion

Our analysis of drug approvals, drug patenting, and patent listing under linkage regulations yields a number of important observations. First, the data demonstrate that both the patent and linkage regulation regimes are heavily used by pharmaceutical firms. Data on the cohort of 95 drugs indicate that for every drug marketed there were at least 40 patents per drug and of these about 5% were listed on the patent register in order to prevent generic entry. While 5% may seem a small fraction for listing, strategic placement of a very small number of patents on the patent register over time has been shown to effectively double the period of patent protection on blockbuster drugs, from an average term of 22 years to a term of 43 years.[28] Moreover, comparison of the data in Chapters 4 and 5 reveal that that as the profitability of drugs goes up, so too does the fraction of listed patents.

Second, the data show increasing use of linkage regulations over time. When analyzed in relation to drug approval data, the results suggest that intellectual property protection via linkage regulations may in fact be a better proxy for innovation by firms than drug patenting per se. Combined, the patent and linkage regulation regimes provide a substantial legal fence to protect high-value pharmaceuticals. Indeed, over the last three decades, firms have engaged in progressively faster drug approval, patenting, and patent listing in order to broaden the area fenced in by these mechanisms.

Third, the array of patent classifications supporting this endeavour is substantial, encompassing a broad range of chemical, use, process, combination, and delivery patents. A total of 5.859 patent classifications were observed in a total of 95 drugs, amounting to 62 patent classifications per drug. These patents can in turn be used to support both a broad array of 'new' and 'follow-on' drug approvals and for patent listing purposes in order to prevent generic entry on already approved drugs.

Fourth, patents identified in this study are directed to a broad scope of therapeutic classes, with particular concentrations in the areas of unmet medical need preferred by drug regulators.

Fifth, while patent protection under the linkage regime is specific to a particular submission, the data suggest that firms are well poised to leverage loopholes in the operation of the regulations supporting a paradoxical drug approval-drug patenting linkage.

Finally, data on PR-NOC/c and NOC/c approvals indicate that the linkage regime represents a highly flexible tool in the hands of sophisticated firms. Combined with relatively low evidentiary thresholds for certain types of new and follow-on drug approvals, the speed of patent listing and relatively low relevance requirement for listing enable pharmaceutical firms to rapidly identify attractive drug targets for legal protection, even during the regulatory approval stage.

Together, the results show that the existing drug approval system, traditional patent law, and the emerging linkage regime operate in an interdependent and iterative manner to provide a strong mechanism for pharmaceutical firms to efficiently identify attractive drug candidates for intellectual property rights protection at all stages of development, including drugs about to come off patent protection, drugs moving through the regulatory approval stage, and drugs that are currently in development.

5.4.1 Drug patenting

The data demonstrate that the patent regime is heavily utilized by pharmaceutical firms in order to legally protect attractive drug candidates. This includes drugs that already have strong market value (Most Profitable) as well as drugs that underwent some form of expedited approval in the hopes they would be so (Priority Review, NOC/c, PR-NOC/c). As illustrated in Figure 5.2(a), the average drug in the cohort was associated with a very large number of patents (3,850), corresponding to a patent per drug ratio of 40 : 1. These patents were issued over a substantial term of close to 35 years, with the most rapid patenting occurring over a comparatively short time frame (1997–2004; Figure 5.2(a)). Averaged patenting activity exhibited a significant plateau over an eight-year period after the year of first instance (Figure 5.2(b)). During this time, peak patenting was maintained at an average of about 2.5 patents per drug per year.

The data in Figures 5.3 and 5.4 strongly suggest there were multiple phases of patenting activity. Fits to the data suggest there were at least two components, a slower and smaller amplitude component up to 1993 and a faster and larger amplitude component following 1993. More specifically, the amount of patenting was approximately 2.5 times greater and 2 times faster between 1993 and 2001 than patenting patterns from 1977 to 1993. The break in patenting activity in 1993 coincides well with the coming into force of the domestic linkage regulations regime at this time. As such, the data indicate the linkage regime itself has significantly influenced patenting activity by pharmaceutical firms.

A related observation was that overall patenting activity for the cohort exhibited a steady decline in the time taken to achieve peak patenting per drug over the term 1977–2000 (Figure 5.5). Indeed, there was a threefold increase in the speed of peak patenting per drug over the test period. Together, the data in Figures 5.2–5.5 suggest that pharmaceutical firms have become increasingly efficient at using the patent regime over the last three decades.

Data in Figure 5.6 and Tables 5.4–5.6 illustrate that the cohort was associated with a substantial array of patent classifications and WHO drug classifications. There were 5,859 individual patent classifications on the cohort. This yielded an average of close to 62 classifications per marketed drug. These were distributed widely across functional patent types, with particular concentrations for Combination Therapy, Use, and Administration patents, and a second large grouping for Chemical and Process patents. As already noted, the two main regulatory mechanisms underpinning a paradoxical drug approval-drug patent linkage are the wide definition of a new active substance (NAS) and the wide scope of uses and chemical derivatives permitted under the supplementary new drug submission (SNDS) stream.

As noted earlier, an NAS may include isomers, derivatives, or salts of chemical substances already approved for sale or biological substances previously approved but differing in molecular structure, nature of the source material or even manufacturing process.[29] Similarly, an SNDS may be filed for changes to a drug that is already marketed by a sponsor, including minor changes to dosage, strength, formulation, manufacture, labeling, route of administration, or use/indication. Therefore it is noteworthy that the three largest patent classes for the cohort were combination therapies, uses, and routes of administration. Each of these patent classifications lends itself well to follow-on drug development. It may also be observed that the patent classification typically thought to underwrite breakthrough drug development, Chemical patents, represented the smallest fraction of classifications studied.

The patent classification data reported here demonstrate that the patent pool supporting submissions directed either to an NAS or the SNDS approval stream is very large indeed. Importantly, these patents can also be used to prohibit generic entry on already approved drugs via the patent listing provisions. Thus the broad patent classifications observed here can be used to (1) support follow-on drug development and (2) prevent generic entry on drugs that are already on the market and coming off patent.

Figures 5.6(b)–5.6(d) and related tables show that there was a wide range of WHO therapeutic classes represented by the cohort. Nevertheless, the majority (81 of 95) of drugs were located in the Antineoplastic/ Immunomodulator, Alimentary Tract & Metabolism, Cardiovascular, Systemic Antiinfective, and Nervous System classifications. The distribution of drugs (Figure 5.6(a)), and patents associated with them (Figure 5.6(c)), in the cohort are similar to recent data reported for domestic ethical sales by therapeutic class.[30] As illustrated by comparison data in Table 5.9, the top therapeutic classes by ethical sales were Cardiovascular,

Table 5.9 Comparison of therapeutic rankings for ethical sales and WHO Classifications

Rank	Therapeutic class (ethical purchase)	Rank	Therapeutic class (this study)
1	Cardiovascular	1	Antineoplastic
2	Anti-Lipidemic	2	Cardiovascular
3	Psychotherapeutics	3	Nervous System
4	Gastro-Intestinal	3	Ant-Infectives
5	Oncology	4	Alimentary
6	Anti-Arthritics	5	Respiratory
7	Bronchial	6	Musculo-Skeletal
8	Analgesics	7	Sensory
9	Neurological	7	Blood
10	Anti-Infectives	7	Various

Psychotherapeutics, Gastro-Intestinal, Oncology, Anti-Arthritics, Bronchial, Analgesics, Neurological and Anti-Infectives. Assuming it is reasonable to fold lipid-lowering drugs into the Cardiovascular class, psychotropics within the Neurological class, and analgesics within the Anti-Arthritic class, the top seven therapeutic classes by domestic ethical purchase strongly track the top six WHO ATC therapeutic classes observed in this study. When developing high-value drugs, pharmaceutical firms are therefore ensuring strong representation of drug candidates and associated patents in therapeutic classes that are already well established in the market.

5.4.2 Drug approval-drug patenting linkage

Data reported here show strong and increasing use of linkage regulations by pharmaceutical firms in order to restrain generic competition. Listing of patents for the cohort on the patent register was generally bell-shaped in nature and began shortly after the linkage regulations came into force in 1993 (Figure 5.2(a)). The most rapid phase of listing occurred between 2000 and 2005. The data further demonstrate a strong degree of convergence between cumulative patenting and cumulative patent listing over time. Indeed, data relating to the temporal lag between drug approval, drug patenting, and patent listing (Figure 5.2(d)) suggest that patent listing may be a better proxy for drug development and approval than drug patenting per se. As illustrated in previous work,[31] while the total fraction of patents granted on the cohort listed was relatively small (5%), strategic staggering of patent listing over time by pharmaceutical firms can more than double the effective period of patent protection for high-value drugs.

We also obtained data potentially relevant to a paradoxical drug approval-drug patenting linkage. While firms have available to them two avenues for leveraging this type of linkage (new and follow-on submissions), data reported here combined with that in our earlier work demonstrate that this pathway is being primarily utilized only for follow-on drugs. This finding is consistent with the general focus of pharmaceutical firms on incremental innovation and technology appropriation and away from breakthrough drug development.[32] That firms may be obtaining the most extensive patent protection on drugs with the least innovative value is an important observation given the original policy intent in enacting the NOC Regulations to balance patent enforcement over new and innovative drugs with the timely market entry of generic drugs.[33] A related observation is that the linkage regime was intended to operate in accordance with established principles of patent law and to further the societal imperative of encouraging the development of novel medical therapies.[34] That private firms may be obtaining extended patent protection for weakly inventive products while at the same time generic competition is chilled and the public are deprived of reasonably priced pharmaceuticals raises the possibility that the quid pro quo of the traditional patent bargain is being breached, yielding a result that would be at odds with legislative intent. The implication of the empirical data described in Chapters 3–5 for the *vires* of the NOC Regulations[35] is discussed in Chapter 6.

5.4.3 System flexibility and lifecycle-based 'rights layering'

The data in the later half of the study illustrate that, in combination, the evidentiary requirements for drug approval, drug patenting under the traditional patent system, and drug patenting and listing under the emerging linkage regime provide pharmaceutical firms with a large degree of flexibility in layering intellectual property rights on high-value drugs in a manner that is both absolute and strongly context-specific.

Generally, there was a dominant pattern that emerged when patenting and patent listing data for the Most Profitable, Priority Review, NOC/c, and PR-NOC/c groups were analyzed. Patenting activity expressed per calendar year was generally bell-shaped and skewed to the left (Figures 5.7(a) and 5.8(a)) and cumulative patenting and patent listing data were well fit by sigmoidal functions (Figures 5.7(b) and 5.7(c)). The strongest patenting activity occurred between 1998 and 2003 (Figure 5.8(b)), while the strongest listing activity occurred later, between 2000 and 2005 (Figure 5.8(c)). The time lag between drug approval and cumulative patent listing was much reduced compared to cumulative patenting or patenting activity expressed per calendar year (Figures 5.9(a)–(d)). Finally, there was a wide distribution of patent classifications for all groups, with a similar W-shaped pattern and similar classification peaks (Figure 5.11). This suggests that pharmaceutical firms are leveraging a harmonized drug development, patenting, and patent listing strategy for all groups studied.

Despite these similarities, however, there were significant differences between groups that are revealing. As illustrated in Figure 5.7, peak patenting, cumulative patenting, and cumulative listing were much greater for Most Profitable and Priority Review drugs compared to either NOC/c or PR-NOC/c drugs. Approximately 80% of all patents and listed patents were associated with the Most Profitable and Priority Review groups. Of interest, these two groups also displayed the most leftward skewing in the distribution of total patenting activity (Figure 5.8) and the earliest onset of cumulative patenting (Figure 5.8(b)) and cumulative patent listing (Figure 5.8(c)) activity. By contrast, patenting activity per year was much more symmetrical for both NOC/c and PR-NOC/c groups (Figures 5.8(a) and 5.13), and cumulative patenting and patent listing was shifted to the right in both groups (Figures 5.8(b), 5.8(c), and 5.13), with PR-NOC/c drugs being shifted farthest to the right. The general order of Most Profitable>Priority Review>NOC/c>PR-NOC/c was repeated when differences in peak patenting per drug over time were assessed. As one moved progressively through this spectrum, peak patenting occurred in progressively fewer years after the date of patent first instance and this peak was progressively lower in number (Figure 5.10). That the Most Profitable group would have the greatest patenting, patent listing, and patent classification values is not surprising given that this group of drugs has already been identified by the market as highly profitable. This is corroborated by the fact that this group had the earliest average patent priority date (Table 5.3) and cumulative patenting and patent listing activity.

Differences in the data are consistent with the observation that one group (Most Profitable) has already reached 'high-value' status, while the remaining three (Priority Review, NOC/c, PR-NOC/c) were more recently approved in the hopes they would follow suit. Thus it is not surprising that the Most Profitable group had the strongest and earliest patenting and patent listing trends (Figures 5.7 and 5.8). Of interest, there was a five-year gap between the mid-point of normalized patenting for the four sub-groups studied (Figure 5.8(a)) which declined to only two years for cumulative patent listing (Figure 5.8(b)). This corresponded to the observation that the lag between approval and patenting and patent listing was tightest for NOC/c and PR-NOC/c approvals compared to Most Profitable, with Priority Review in between (Figure 5.9). Combined, the data demonstrate a strong degree of responsiveness by both regulators and firms to regulatory signals suggesting a drug candidate may be a high-value drug.

A second major contributing factor for differences between the Priority Review, NOC/c, and PR-NOC/c groups is the issue of post-market evidentiary requirements. For instance, we observed stronger and earlier patenting and patent listing for Priority Review compared to NOC/c and PR-NOC/c groups (Figures 5.7 and 5.8). It may be recalled that Priority Review represents a pathway for expedited review with no change in pre-market evidentiary requirements whereas NOC/c and PR-NOC/c approvals entail significant post-market safety and efficacy reporting requirements. While the Priority review group had about three times the patenting activity and patent listing than either NOC/c group (Figure 5.7), it is noteworthy that the speed of patenting and, particularly, patent listing were very similar in the three groups (Figure 5.8), indicating that firms can make up lost ground when regulatory signals favoring drug approval arise.

Considerations such as these also likely inform data pertaining to differences in peak patenting per drug when expressed as year after first instance (Figure 5.10). The largest peak (~100 patents per drug, peaking 20 years after first instance) was observed for the Most Profitable group, which corresponded to data for patenting activity over time (Figure 5.7). This was followed by Priority Review (~75 patents per drug, peaking 17 years after first instance), NOC/c (~40 patents per drug, peaking ten years after first instance), and then PR-NOC (~25 patents per drug, peaking 8–9 years after first instance) groups. The fact that peak patenting for the Most Profitable group was earliest for patenting activity compared to all other groups analyzed and latest for peak patenting per drug is likely explained by the lack of regulatory lag for approval and post-market obligations and the accrual of an established market for Most Profitable drugs. On this basis, it is not surprising that the Priority Review group had the next fastest patenting per group cycle and that the two NOC/c groups had the fastest patenting cycles. Priority Review involves no additional post-market evidentiary obligations whereas NOC/c approvals do and therefore the market has time to solidify earlier. Thus the diminished and faster NOC/c and PR-NOC/c patenting per drug data simply reflect the ongoing nature of approval and patenting for these groups.

One of the most significant observations of the data in this chapter is that the results demonstrate empirically that firms are able to identify attractive drug candidates early in the approval process for intellectual property rights layering. At this point, firms begin the process of increasing the number of patent applications and granted patents, layering these patents on drugs going through the approval process (and, one assumes, numerous related drugs that are already approved and linked through product clusters), preparing to list patents on the patent register in a strategic manner, as well as ensuring patents are obtained that have broad classifications in order to to expand the boundary of legal protection afforded by the patent and linkage regulation regimes. This, in turn, allows firms to fill coffers with candidates for later NDS and SNDS submissions.

It is worth pointing out that the linkage regime in particular, operating in combination with the existing drug regulatory regime, has proven to be a highly flexible tool in the hands of sophisticated pharmaceutical firms. The combination of the speed of patent listing compared with patenting and the relatively low relevance requirement for listing has enabled pharmaceutical firms to rapidly identify attractive drug targets for legal protection even during the regulatory approval stage. This goal is supported by the large number of patents and patent classifications observed here and the wide berth in regulatory requirements for approval of NAS and SNDS drugs.

The group that best exemplifies the flexibility of the drug approval-drug patenting linkage is the combined PR-NOC/c group. This category represents perhaps the best bet of pharmaceutical sponsors in the high-risk stakes of drug development. It offers the most favorable balance of expedited review with minimally intrusive post-marketing obligations for therapeutic niches with known demand. Composed of the smallest number of drugs in the cohort, the characteristics of this group differed substantially for almost all metrics studied when the data were normalized. For example, while the PR-NOC/c group had by far the lowest number of drugs (n = 6) with the lowest number of patents (n = 379), listed patents (n = 11), and patent classifications (n = 502), when averaged out for the number of drugs per group each of these metrics was the highest, or next to the highest, among the groups. PR-NOC/c drugs had an average of 63 patents per drug (Table 5.3), 2% of which were listed on the patent register. The average number of patents was 56% greater than the next highest group, represented by Most Profitable drugs.

While 2% listed patents is lower than listing percentages for the other groups (Most Profitable, 5.96%; Priority Review, 4.34%; NOC/c, 5.94%), it is noteworthy that the average patent date for PR-NOC/c drugs was almost two years later than that for the cohort or Most Profitable groups (Table 5.3). As such, both conventional patent protection and linkage regulation protection would be extended by three to five years compared to other groups studied. An extra period of patent protection of this nature is not inconsiderable, as is now recognized in the context of both brand-name and generic first-mover status. The PR-NOC/c group also had the smallest drug approval to patenting/patent listing lag differential (Figure 5.9), with both 50th and 100th percentile patent listing occurring prior to the average date of drug approval. Therefore, the regulatory lag for PR-NOC/c drugs would be reduced correspondingly. Finally, PR-NOC/c drugs had 83.7 patent classifications per drug (Figure 5.11; Tables 5.4 and 5.5). Notwithstanding the smaller range of WHO ATC classifications compared to other groups (Figure 5.12), this would open a large patent pool to underpin future patent listing efforts to delay generic competition via linkage regulations as well as to support future follow-on drug development via the conventional patent system. The closest group in each of these metrics was the NOC/c group, which represents the group with the least amount of pre-market evidentiary requirements in exchange for expedited review compared to the PR-NOC/c group.

As illustrated in Figure 5.12, there were also differences in the profiles of WHO therapeutic classes between groups. Of particular interest is the observation that the requirements for (1) effective treatment, prevention, or diagnosis of a disease, (2) evidence of a significant increase in safety and efficacy or decrease in risk such that the overall risk-benefit profile is improved, and (3) examples offered by regulators of what constitutes a serious or life-threatening disease and a severely debilitating disease for NOC/c[36] and Priority Review[37] approvals appear to be very similar, despite substantial differences in therapeutic classification data for these groups (Figure 5.12). Data for Priority Review were well distributed throughout all 10 ATC classes with concentrations in the groups discussed above. By contrast, the distribution of classes for both the NOC/c and PR-NOC/c were highly curtailed and narrowly distributed among Antineoplastic and Immunomodulatory, Systemic Antiinfective, Nervous System and Musculo-Skeletal classifications. While one might assume that Most Profitable drugs differ from Priority Review and NOC/c groups due to the possibility that the most profitable and/or innovative drug development may occur outside of regulatory preferences or unmet medical need, there is no clear explanation for the observed differences between NOC/c and Priority Review groups at present. A partial explanation may be that trends for the two groups have reversed over the last decade, with a crossover point about 2005.[38]

5.4.4 Implications for global drug development and regulation

As pointed out in Chapter 4, while our study was based on domestic Canadian data, we argue that the results are significant within the global context of drug regulatory reform and innovation policy. First, almost all major pharmaceutical companies are headquartered in either the United States or the European Union.[39] Products in smaller markets such as Canada therefore reflect therapeutic product development and intellectual property strategies of multinational firms rather than domestic firms. Secondly, efforts have been underway for some time to harmonize the goals and mechanisms of drug regulation globally. Over the last decade, regulators in Canada have harmonized their regulatory approval requirements to parallel those of the American Food and Drug Administration (FDA) and its European counterpart (EMEA), a trend that will only gain traction as jurisdictions embrace the principles of lifecycle-based regulation.[40] Third, global systems of translational research and national science and technology policy are closely integrated and likewise mirror one another, in large part due to the success of the US biotechnology enterprise.[41] Fourth, while the 'product cluster' model of drug development is becoming increasingly entrenched globally over time, nations with pharmaceutical linkage regimes appear to present multinational pharmaceutical firms with the 'path of least resistance' to product-patent clusters. Fifth, qualitative trends in approval of new and follow-on drugs track one another fairly closely in most major jurisdictions, and the drug patents that we analyzed represent high-value drugs not only in Canada, but also in US and EU markets. Given that the already small number of multinational pharmaceutical corporations responsible for global drug innovation are doing so increasingly in partnership with drug regulators,[42] it is reasonable to speculate that drug development and regulation is steadily converging upon a risk management philosophy whereby critical benefit-risk calculations for product development are made based on legal incentives provided for by regulators.[43]

Our findings do not indicate abnormal behavior by pharmaceutical companies. Rather, the data lend themselves to the conclusions that the pharmaceutical industry has engaged in very effective intellectual property lobbying over the last two decades and that these lobbying efforts have increasingly informed the drug development strategies of multinational pharmaceutical companies. As acknowledged by the Supreme Court of Canada, it is perfectly acceptable that pharmaceutical firms avail themselves of loopholes that allow product evergreening after the original patent has expired under conditions where the government has made, and continues to make, such loopholes available.[44]

5.5 Summary and conclusions

The study reviewed in this chapter was designed to empirically investigate two related phenomena within the context of emerging linkage regime models of intellectual property protection. The first was to probe the linkage between drug approval and patent listing for high-value pharmaceuticals. While the patent regime has for decades been claimed by both pharmaceutical firms and regulators to be integral for innovative drug development, the role of drug approval-drug patenting linkage in this process is unclear. Indeed, a growing cache of empirical studies of the patenting behavior of large pharmaceutical firms suggests that these firms have become highly adept at leveraging legal and regulatory opportunities offered to them favoring low-risk high-reward drug products. Empirical evidence relating to drug approval-drug patenting linkage would therefore be valuable at a time when jurisdictions other than the US and Canada are contemplating bringing into force similar provisions. A second consideration was to address how certain characteristics of the existing regulatory approval scheme, such as the relatively low threshold for NAS status and approval via the SNDS stream and provisions relating to expedited approval for drugs, might be linked to firm patenting and patent listing patterns. Accordingly, we investigated patent and therapeutic classes preferred by firms in their efforts to support new and follow-on drug development. Of particular interest was to obtain objective data relating to the possibility that firms might be leveraging loopholes in the regulatory and legislative structure underpinning the linkage regime in favor of a paradoxical drug approval-drug patenting linkage, that is whether firms may be obtaining the greatest intellectual property protection for products with the least innovative value and smallest development costs.

Our analysis of drug approvals, drug patenting, and patent listing under the domestic linkage regulation regime demonstrates strong, increasing, and faster utilization of both traditional patent law and emerging linkage regulation regimes by pharmaceutical firms. There were a large number of patents, patent classifications, and therapeutic classes for every drug studied. Moreover, firms are listing a significant number of these patents in order to delay generic entry. The results also demonstrate that pharmaceutical companies are becoming increasingly efficient at both patenting and patent listing over time. Indeed, results such as those presented here suggest that the legal protection afforded by the combination of traditional patent law and novel linkage regulations creates an unprecedented legal mechanism that simultaneously protects existing high-value drug products from generic competition and allows for further follow-on drug development.

As discussed here and elsewhere,[45] there is a wide berth for the definition of a new active substance (NAS) under domestic food and drug law and the type of chemicals and uses allowed under the supplemental, or SNDS, drug approval stream. The definition of an NAS is important as it determines whether a drug will be classified as a 'first-in-class' or 'me-too' drug, with correlated market price differentials and regulatory preferences. Similarly, the specific combination of chemical structure and use dictates whether a drug is approved via either the 'new' or 'follow-on' NDS or SNDS approval streams. Of relevance to the present study, a broad range of patent classifications would support a range of high-reward low-risk product development strategies relating to both new and follow-on drug development.

Not surprisingly, the functional scope of patent classifications identified in this work was substantial, and encompassed a wide range of chemical, use, combination, process, and administration/delivery patents. Similarly, both patents and drugs in the cohort studied were directed to an equally broad scope of therapeutic classes, with particular concentrations in the areas of unmet medical need preferred by drug regulators and the marketplace. Combined, the broad scope of patent type and therapeutic classifications observed here have the potential to support a vast array of new and follow-on drugs, including those meeting the requirements of first-in-class drugs approved in the less onerous follow-on SNDS approval stream.

Finally, the evidence reported here suggests that the linkage regime provides a highly flexible tool in the hands of sophisticated pharmaceutical firms. The number and array of patent types, the speed of patent listing, the automatic injunction, and the low relevance requirement for listing combined with low evidentiary requirements for new (NAS) and follow-on (SNDS) drug development enable pharmaceutical firms to rapidly identify attractive drug targets for legal protection both during and after regulatory approval. This property of the linkage regulation regime is demonstrated most effectively by the unique patenting, patent listing, and patent classification of drugs receiving the PR-NOC/c designation. Similar trends were observed with NOC/c and Priority Review groups, but to a lesser extent.

Together, the results described thus far show that the combination of conventional patent law, emerging linkage regulation regime and existing drug approval framework provide an invaluable mechanism for multinational pharmaceutical firms to efficiently and effectively identify attractive new and follow-on drug candidates for market exclusivity. The linkage regulation regime in particular has proven to be an excellent vehicle for firms to obtain extended legal protection on drugs at all stages of development, including drugs about to come off patent protection, drugs moving through the regulatory approval stage, and drugs that are currently in development.

Notes

1. Monika Sawicka and Ron A. Bouchard, 'Empirical Analysis of Canadian Drug Approval Data 2001–2008: Are Pharmaceutical Players "Doing More With Less"?' 3 *McGill J.L. & Health* 87 (2009) [Sawicka and Bouchard (2009)].
2. For a detailed discussion of expedited review pathways in Canada, see Ron A. Bouchard and Monika Sawicka, 'The Mud and the Blood and the Beer: Canada's Progressive Licensing Framework for Drug Approval,' 3 *McGill J.L. & Health* 51, at 56–60 (2009) [Bouchard and Sawicka (2009)].
3. Health Canada, *Guidance for Industry: Priority Review of Drug Submissions* (2006) online: <http://www.hc-sc.gc.ca/dhp-mps/alt_formats/hpfb-dgpsa/pdf/prodpharma/priordr-eng.pdf> [Health Canada, Priority Review Guidance Document].
4. Ibid., at 1–2.
5. See Trudo Lemmens and Ron A. Bouchard, 'Regulation of Pharmaceuticals in Canada,' in Jocelyn Downie, Timothy Caulfield, and Colleen Flood (eds), *Canadian Health Law and Policy*, 3rd edn (LexisNexis, 2007), at 326, 328 [Lemmens and Bouchard (2007)].
6. NOC/c approvals are granted pursuant to s. C.08.004(1), in compliance with the conditions of use stipulated in s. C.08.002(1)(g), C.08.002(1)(h),

C.08.006(2)(b), and C.05.006(2)(a) of the Food and Drug Regulations, CRC, ch. 870 (2009) [Food and Drug Regulations].

7. Health Canada, *Guidance for Industry: Notice of Compliance with Conditions* (Public Works and Government Services Canada, 2007), online: http://www.hc-sc.gc.ca/dhp-mps/alt_formats/hpfb-dgpsa/pdf/prodpharma/noccg_accd-eng.pdf [Health Canada, *Notice of Compliance with Conditions*].
8. Health Canada, *Access to Therapeutic Products: The Regulatory Process in Canada – Target Review Times* (2006), online: <http://www.hc-sc.gc.ca/ahc-asc/pubs/hpfb-dgpsa/access-therapeutic_acces-therapeutique-eng.php#6.2>.
9. In particular, the Patent Summary includes the patent number, application number, English title, French title, and abstract, and the Patent Details include the patent's Canadian patent classification (CPC), international patent classification, inventors, owners, applicants, agent, date of issue, date of filing, the availability of a licence, the language of filing, Patent Cooperation Treaty (PCT) status, and application priority date.
10. For a discussion of evergreening in the context of US and Canadian linkage regulations, see Andrew A. Caffrey and Jonathan M. Rotter, 'Consumer Protection, Patents and Procedure: Generic Drug Market Entry and the Need to Reform the Hatch-Waxman Act,' 9 *Va. J.L. & Tech.* 1, 4–7 (2004) [Caffrey and Rotter (2004)]; Edward Hore, 'A Comparison of US and Canadian Laws as They Affect Generic Pharmaceutical Drug Entry, 55 *Food & Drug L.J.* 373 (1992).
11. Letter from E. Somers, Health Canada, on 'New Active Substance' (June 4, 1991), online: <http://www.hc-sc.gc.ca/dhp-mps/prodpharma/applic-demande/pol/nas_nsa_pol-eng.php> [Letter from E. Somers]; Health Canada NOC Database Terminology (October 1, 2004), online: <http://www.hc-sc.gc.ca/dhp-mps/prodpharma/notices-avis/noc-acc/term_noc_acc-eng.php> [Health Canada NOC Database Terminology].
12. Letter from E. Somers, *supra* note 11; See also Health Canada NOC Database Terminology, *supra* note 11.
13. Sawicka and Bouchard (2009), *supra* note 1.
14. Food and Drug Regulations, *supra* note 6, at s. C.08.003.
15. Ibid., at s. C.08.003(2). See Lemmens and Bouchard (2007), *supra* note 5, at 326.
16. According to ss. 4(2) and 4(3) of the NOC Regulations:

> (2) A patent on a patent list in relation to a new drug submission is eligible to be added to the register if the patent contains
> (a) a claim for the medicinal ingredient and the medicinal ingredient has been approved through the issuance of a notice of compliance in respect of the submission;
> (b) a claim for the formulation that contains the medicinal ingredient and the formulation has been approved through the issuance of a notice of compliance in respect of the submission;
> (c) a claim for the dosage form and the dosage form has been approved through the issuance of a notice of compliance in respect of the submission; or

(d) a claim for the use of the medicinal ingredient, and the use has been approved through the issuance of a notice of compliance in respect of the submission.

(3) A patent on a patent list in relation to a supplement to a new drug submission is eligible to be added to the register if the supplement is for a change in formulation, a change in dosage form or a change in use of the medicinal ingredient, and

(a) in the case of a change in formulation, the patent contains a claim for the changed formulation that has been approved through the issuance of a notice of compliance in respect of the supplement;

(b) in the case of a change in dosage form, the patent contains a claim for the changed dosage form that has been approved through the issuance of a notice of compliance in respect of the supplement; or

(c) in the case of a change in use of the medicinal ingredient, the patent contains a claim for the changed use of the medicinal ingredient that has been approved through the issuance of a notice of compliance in respect of the supplement.

(Regulations Respecting a Notice of Compliance Pertaining to Patented Medicines, SOR/93-133, ss. 4(2)–(3), online: <http://laws.justice.gc.ca/eng/SOR-93-133/ index.html> (last visited October 8, 2009).)

17. World Health Organization Collaborating Center for Drug Statistics Methodology, online: <http://www.whocc.no/atcddd/> (last visited March 1, 2010).

18. Sawicka and Bouchard (2009), *supra* note 1; Ron A. Bouchard et al., 'The Pas de Deux of Pharmaceutical Regulation and Innovation: Who's Leading Whom?' 24 *Berkeley Tech. L.J.* 1 (2009) [Bouchard, 'Regulations' (2009)].

19. Ibid.

20. Ibid., at 1496–7.

21. Beta, Burr, Burr (4P), Cauchy, Chi-Squared, Chi-Squared (2P), Dagum, Dagum (4P), Erlang, Erlang (3P), Error, Error Function, Exponential, Exponential (2P), Fatigue Life, Fatigue Life (3P), Frechet, Frechet (3P), GammaGamma (3P), Gen. Extreme Value, Gen. Gamma, Gen. Gamma (4P), Gen. Pareto, Gumbel Max, Gumbel Min, Hypersecant, Inv. Gaussian, Inv. Gaussian (3P), Johnson SB, Johnson SU, Kumaraswamy, Laplace, Levy, Levy (2P), Log-Gamma, Logistic, Log-Logistic, Log-Logistic (3P), Lognormal, Lognormal (3P), Log-Pearson 3, Nakagami, Normal, Pareto, Pareto 2, Pearson 5, Pearson 5 (3P), Pearson 6, Pearson 6 (4P), Pert, Power Function, Rayleigh, Rayleigh (2P), Reciprocal, Rice, Student's t, Triangular, Uniform, Weibull, Weibull (3P).

22. A significant difference, however, was that the rate constant for the second phase (1/0.1971 = 5.07 years) was only slightly faster than for the first phase (1/0.1772 = 5.64 years) when V is fixed. Indeed when the second epoch is broadened from 2001 to 2003 the rate constant in years was actually larger

(7.75 and 5.96 years) than that for the first epoch for both the four- and two-parameter tests. This result, which likely reflects an incomplete database towards the end of the test period, is discussed more fully in section 5.3.3 on limitations below.

23. See, generally, the 2006 amendments to the NOC Regulations, the accompanying 2006 RIAS, and the 2009 Guidance Document summarizing the jurisprudence and policy grounds supporting a specific relevance requirement for patent listing and the timing of patent listing relevant to a generic Notice of Allegation: Regulatory Impact Analysis Statement relating to the Patented Medicines (Notice of Compliance) Regulations issued April 3, 2009 [RIAS].
24. Federal Trade Commission, *Generic Drug Entry Prior To Patent Expiration: An FTC Study* (2002), online: <http://www.ftc.gov/os/2002/07/genericdrugstudy.pdf>. For discussion of evergreening under Hatch-Waxman, see, generally, Caffrey and Rotter (2004), *supra* note 10, at 13–14.
25. *Eli Lilly Canada* v. *Canada*, [2003] 3 FC 140 (Can.) [*Eli Lilly*].
26. *AstraZeneca Can. Inc.* v. *Canada*, [2006] 2 SCR 560 [*AstraZeneca*].
27. Celecoxib is a non-steroidal anti-inflammatory used in the treatment of osteoarthritis, rheumatoid arthritis, pain, menstruation, and colonic and rectal polyps. Marketed by Pfizer as Celebrex™, it is a selective noncompetitive inhibitor of cyclooxygenase-2 (COX-2) enzyme.
28. Bouchard, 'Regulations' (2009), *supra* note 18.
29. Health Canada NAS, *supra* note 11; Health Canada NOC Database Terminology, *supra* note 11.
30. IMS Health, *Canadian Pharmaceutical Industry Review* 64–5 (IMS Consulting 2008).
31. Bouchard, 'Regulations' (2009), *supra* note 18.
32. For a general discussion of how the data support a 'more with less' theme in pharmaceutical innovation, see, generally, Sawicka and Bouchard (2009), *supra* note 1.
33. See RIAS and Government Guidance Documents to this effect, RIAS, *supra* note 23. In *Biolyse Pharm. Corp.* v. *Bristol-Myers Squibb Co.*, [2005] SCC 26, at 47 and 156–7, the Supreme Court of Canada held that RIASs are proper evidence of legislative intent. At 156, Justice Binnie stated:

> It has long been established that the usage of admissible extrinsic sources regarding a provision's legislative history and its context of enactment could be examined. I held in *Francis* v. *Baker*, at para. 35, that '[p]roper statutory interpretation principles therefore require that all evidence of legislative intent be considered, provided that it is relevant and reliable.' Consequently, in order to confirm the purpose of the impugned regulation, the intended application of an amendment to the regulation or the meaning of the legislative language, it is useful to examine the RIAS, prepared as part of the regulatory process (see Sullivan, at pp. 499–500).

34. *C. Gaz.* Vol. 138, No. 50, December 11, 2004.
35. See Ron A. Bouchard, 'I'm Still Your Baby: Canada's Continuing Support of U.S. Linkage Regime for Pharmaceuticals' (2010), online: <http://papers.ssrn.com/sol3/papers.cfm?abstract_id = 1537988>.
36. Health Canada, *Notice of Compliance with Conditions*, *supra* note 7.
37. See also Health Canada, 'Priority Review of Drug Submissions' (2007), online: <http://www.hc-sc.gc.ca/dhp-mps/alt_formats/hpfb-dgpsa/pdf/prodpharma/noccg_accd-eng.pdf>.
38. Sawicka and Bouchard (2009), *supra* note 1.
39. Michele Boldrin and David K. Levine, *Against Intellectual Monopoly* (Cambridge University Press, 2008), at 241.
40. Hans-Georg Eichler et al., 'Balancing Early Market Access to New Drugs with the Need for Benefit/Risk Data: A Mounting Dilemma,' 7 *Nature Revs Drug Discovery* 818, 823–4 (2008); Bouchard and Sawicka (2009), *supra* note 2.
41. Sheila Jasanoff, 'The Life Sciences and the Rule of Law,' 319 *J. Mol. Biol.* 891 (2002).
42. See, generally, Mary E. Wiktorowicz, 'Emergent Patterns in the Regulation of Pharmaceuticals: Institutions and Interests in the United States, Canada, Britain, and France,' 28 *J. Health Pol., Pol'y & L.* 615 (2003).
43. Organization for Economic Cooperation and Development, typically referred to as the OECD. See, generally, online: <http://www.oecd.org/home/0,2987,en_2649_201185_1_1_1_1_1,00.html>.
44. *AstraZeneca*, *supra* note 26 at 39. Discussing the general relevance requirement articulated by the Federal Court of Appeal in *Eli Lilly*, *supra* note 25, Justice Binnie stated:

    > Given the evident (and entirely understandable) commercial strategy of the innovative drug companies to evergreen their products by adding bells and whistles to a pioneering product even after the original patent for that pioneering product has expired, the decision of the Federal Court of Appeal would reward evergreening even if the generic manufacturer (and thus the public) does not thereby derive any benefit from the subsequently listed patents.

45. Bouchard, 'Regulations' (2009), *supra* note 18.

6

Implications of empirical data: are pharmaceutical linkage regulations a success?*

Abstract: Canada's linkage regime for pharmaceuticals was brought in under intense political pressure specifically to balance effective patent enforcement over new and innovative drugs with the timely market entry of lower priced generic competitors. It has been almost two decades since the regulations were enacted and to date there has been little objective assessment as to whether the regulations have, in fact, stimulated innovation and timely generic entry. This chapter discusses the implications of the empirical data reviewed in Chapters 3–5 for the legal legitimacy of pharmaceutical linkage given the purpose and intent of this legislation noted above. To this end, the original policy intent of the linkage regime in Canada, that in the US, the 'patent-specific' analysis for linkage cases promulgated by the Supreme Court of Canada in its cases on linkage, and relevant principles of statutory interpretation are reviewed.

Keywords: pharmaceutical linkage, patent law, empirical analysis, public health policy, patent-specific analysis, statutory interpretation

The purpose of the present chapter is to probe the issue of whether the Canadian domestic linkage regime, typical of other global linkage regimes, is a success when gauged against its specific policy underpinnings. A second goal is to investigate the possibility that empirical evidence demonstrating that legislation may not be achieving its desired goal can support the conclusion that the legislation is invalid or in need of substantial amendment in order for it to remain *intra vires*. To achieve these objectives it is necessary to explore the original policy intent of the legislation in order to provide a legal benchmark against which to judge the operation of law.

---

* This chapter is based upon material in R.A. Bouchard, 'I'm Still Your Baby: Canada's Continuing Support of U.S. Linkage Regulations for Pharmaceuticals,' *Marquette Intellectual Property Law Review* 15(1): 79–146 (2011).

It is also necessary to canvass Supreme Court of Canada jurisprudence on pharmaceutical linkage to probe whether the court has laid out one or more first principles for interpretation of pharmaceutical linkage against the broader backdrop of patent law. Finally, it is important to determine whether there are aspects of statutory interpretation that illuminate an investigation into whether the NOC Regulations are meeting the stated goals of stimulating the development of new and innovative drugs and facilitating timely entry of generic drugs, and the degree to which this question may be properly assessed from a purposive legal perspective.

6.1 Introduction

One of the major promises made by the US pharmaceutical industry in the lead-up to both Bill C-22 and Bill C-91,[1] supported by domestic universities, was to inject billions of dollars into domestic research and development activities. This investment was specifically targeted towards the production of innovative therapeutic products. The Minister of Industry, Science and Technology, Michael Wilson, along with the Minister of Consumer and Corporate Affairs, Michael Blais, both equated intellectual property rights with pharmaceutical innovation and hailed the new regime as the beginnings of a new, more innovative nation.[2] Mr Wilson went further, declaring that the injection of millions of dollars into domestic research and development would enable Canada to transition into 'a world-class pharmaceutical industry ...'[3] Claims of this nature were made at the same time as the government was receiving evidence to the effect that amendments to its domestic patent laws would chill generic competition and cost Canadian consumers between CN $4 and $7 billion over a 15-year period,[4] and that the CN $500 million in research and development investment by multinational firms was actually composed in large part of substantial tax incentives ranging from 50% to 70%, depending on the province.[5]

Experience since the time when pharmaceutical linkage came into force in both the United States and Canada has shown that the legal definitions of 'research' and 'development' costs are highly controversial,[6] with industry critics claiming that marketing, advertising, opportunity, and other related costs are in fact driving this line item.[7] There is ample evidence demonstrating that the pharmaceutical industry will take whatever steps necessary to protect what it sees as confidential information relating to research and development expenditures,[8] even when the US Government Accountability Office (GAO) is doing the asking.[9] In light of uncertainties as to how much financial support foreign firms have, in fact, provided to domestic research and development activities, the remaining discussion focuses on the data we do have in hand, that is whether drugs approved following enactment of the NOC Regulations constitute new or follow-on drugs and the degree to which the legal link between drug approval and drug patenting under the NOC Regulations has provided for extended intellectual property protection that would not have occurred 'but for' the operation of the linkage regime.

The remaining sections of the chapter provide a brief historical overview of portions of the debate leading up to the enactment of the linkage regime, discussion of the original policy intent underpinning the regulations according to the federal government, a review of selected Supreme Court of Canada jurisprudence and principles of statutory interpretation that may be instructive when interpreting the broad purpose of the linkage regime, and, finally, a reinterpretation of the empirical data in Chapters 3–5 based on the above material. The goal of this chapter is to assess, in an evidence-based manner, the performance of the linkage regime in light of the empirical data reported above and the stated policy goals underpinning the NOC Regulations to stimulate the development of new and innovative drugs and facilitate timely market entry of generic drugs.

6.2 Debate preceding Bill C-91

As well described in the literature and case law, compulsory licensing of pharmaceuticals was introduced in Canada in 1923 and expanded yet again in 1969 to control increasing drug costs. In 1987, amendments to the Patent Act in the form of Bill C-22 limited compulsory licensing and created the Patented Medicine Prices Review Board (PMPRB) to ensure that the prices of patented pharmaceuticals were not excessive. The second, and more major, round of reforms came in 1993, at which time Bill C-91[10] eliminated compulsory licensing, harmonized patent protection of pharmaceuticals in Canada with other developed nations, and enacted the Patented Medicines (Notice of Compliance) Regulations. Not surprisingly, many of the issues subject to intense criticism and judicial review since then were also raised in the limited period of examination of Bill C-91, during the end of the 34th Session of Parliament in December 1992. These issues include: the impact of the bill on drug costs, domestic research and development investments, patent terms, job creation, and the trickle-down effects of increased public health costs. However, with one major exception, the debate was characterized by a significant lack of foresight about the extent to which the reforms would impact patent protection for pharmaceuticals and the regulatory mechanisms through which this change would be effected.

One of the primary points of contention in the Bill C-91 debate was investment of money by foreign multinationals into domestic research and development activities and the translation of this support into new and innovative products. The Minister of Industry, Science and Technology, the Minister of Consumer and Corporate Affairs, and almost all of the major provincial universities equated increased intellectual property protection with increased research, increased innovation, and increased national productivity.[11] In particular, extended patent rights were seen as the gateway to enhanced production of new and innovative technologies that could compete globally. Support of expanded patent protection by industry and government sectors is well known. Less known, however, was the role of the Canadian university system in this process. University advocates, including those with clear conflicts of interest, claimed that industry profits resulting from enhanced patent protection would create a better society for Canadians.[12] It was simply assumed by university advocates that increased intellectual property protection was positively related to increased innovation as well as increased therapeutic benefit to the public.

This sentiment was not unanimous among Legislative Committee members or witnesses appearing before the Committee. In particular, the Committee heard evidence from at least two major reports to the contrary that bear further scrutiny. A 1981 OECD study[13] noted that when governments with historically low levels of pharmaceutical research and development try to stimulate it through policy levers such as patent rights the results have been disappointing. The Eastman Commission[14] similarly noted that Canada lacks the fundamental resources to be a global force in pharmaceutical research and development. The Commission went further, stating that providing multinational firms with enhanced domestic patent rights would not increase domestic innovation, given long established research and development centers elsewhere.[15] As argued by one Committee member,[16] conclusions such as those of Eastman and the OECD were consistent with data from a federal study showing Bill C-22 had minimal impact on university research and development activity. Nevertheless, the Minister of Consumer and Corporate Affairs, Harvie André, in the lead up to Bill C-22, and Michael Wilson, the Minister of Industry, Science and Technology at the time Bill C-91 was debated, continued to assert that increased patent rights would enable Canada to innovate on a 'world scale' and to develop a 'world-class pharmaceutical industry ...'[17]

A point that resonates particularly well with the data reported in Chapter 3 was also raised by the Canadian Association of Consumers (CAC). The CAC expressed concern that patent reforms providing greater protection for me-too and line extension drugs would come at the cost of truly innovative drugs and innovative health research generally. Citing the Eastman report, the CAC noted that patent rights are not inalienable and are granted by governments cautiously with the specific purpose of stimulating an 'appropriate amount of innovation.'[18] However, the issue of including definitions of the desired level of innovation resulting from increased patent rights or even evidence-based output metrics for research and development investments was not taken up by many in the debate despite repeated calls for such outcomes by some participants in the hearings.[19]

Insightful comments were also made by the CAC on the potential ramifications of extended patent protection for the development of new and innovative drugs.[20] Milton Friedman was cited to the effect that patent monopolies too often provide strong incentives to shift research and development towards products like me-too drugs where patents are more easily granted, the key observation being that, as with patents granted by the Patent and Trademark Office,[21] drug regulators are in the routine and predictable habit of granting approvals on products with low innovative value. As used here, the phrase 'low innovative value' refers to follow-on drugs that have little or no therapeutic benefit over existing marketed drugs.

Indeed, the Committee heard evidence from an Industry, Science and Technology study[22] that indicated that 80% of clinical practitioners deemed domestic research and development to be in the service of me-too drugs. This observation accords with our data that nearly 60% of all drugs approved by Canadian regulators between 2001 and 2008 were me-too drugs.[23] It is also consistent with statements made by the Medical Directors at Pfizer and Squibb that as much as 75% of scientific research had been channeled into 'copycat drugs and unimportant combinations.'[24] Even Dr Eastman, while providing testimony before the Committee as Chair of the PMPRB, acknowledged that there is little therapeutic benefit to be gained from me-too and, particularly, line extension drugs.[25] This statement accords with the results of later studies conducted in Canada, France, and the United States,[26] including those in Chapters 3–5. Finally, the Committee heard testimony about the 'natural experiment' in Italy, where de novo institution of patent protections that were harmonious with those in the United States actually reduced national innovation and drove up the cost of drugs.[27] While we acknowledge room for debate in the interpretation of these studies, it is nevertheless clear that at the time the linkage regime came into force, there was significant evidence to suggest that increased patent rights would lead to neither enhanced innovation nor timely generic entry.

In retrospect, perhaps the most remarkable aspect of the debate leading up to the passage of Bill C-91 was that Section 4 of the Patent Act Amendment Act containing the linkage regulations was hardly debated at all, let alone noticed by most participants at the hearings. The original goal of the amendments was to allay concerns by brand-name drug manufacturers that generic firms might use the provisions of the legislation allowing generics to seek regulatory approval without being subject to infringement (the so-called 'early working' exception) to sell these products before the patent expired.

Misunderstandings of the purpose, procedures, and even existence of the linkage regulations were widespread. For example, the Committee heard testimony that only 16 drugs would be affected by the regulations.[28] Several policy-makers called as witnesses claimed they were not sure even why they were called to the proceedings,[29] stating on a number of occasions[30] that they lacked the qualifications to comment on Bill C-91 even though they were responsible for drafting related policy documents based on which more senior officials were testifying. Also common was the assertion that drugs that would be affected by the legislation were only associated with one patent, and thus it was only one patent extension that generics had to contend with when waiting for market entry. The most significant comments of this nature came from Dr Elizabeth Dickson, Director General, Chemical and Bio-Industries Branch, Department of Industry, Science and Technology. Dr Dickson testified that, 'I must explain that when a new medicine comes on the market there is *a main patent*. When *that main patent expires*, anyone may copy that product and bring it to market.'[31]

The general consensus at the hearings, included in testimony from the Canadian Health Collation,[32] Dr Dickson,[33] and Michael Wilson, Minister of Industry, Science and Technology,[34] was that patent reforms pursuant to Bill C-91 would increase market exclusivity for brand-name pharmaceuticals by only one to three years.

The lone voice of dissent was Dr Stephen Schondelmeyer, a US economist and pharmacologist who conducted an independent study on the potential impact of Bill C-91. It is not surprising an American would bring the most experienced voice to the table. Indeed, it is obvious from the language, concepts, and even the measurements he employed in his analysis that

Dr Schondelmeyer had several years of experience with the US Hatch-Waxman linkage regime prior to giving testimony relating to Bill C-91. In addition to predictions based on empirical data, the most important contribution made to the debate was introducing for the first time a focus on cumulative market exclusivity rather than on patent term per se:

> In fact, you may not realize that most pharmaceutical products have two, three, or even four patents that protect them, not just one patent. They'll have a patent on the chemical entity itself. There'll be a patent on the dosage form. There'll be a patent on the use of the product in some cases, and sometimes a patent on the process by which the pharmaceutical is made. *So one can't analyse [sic] the impact of this patent extension simply by looking at the extension of an individual patent. What you have to analyse [sic] is the effect of the combination of those patents that are extended and how much that extends the total market exclusivity of a given pharmaceutical.*[35]

Based on his study, Dr Schondelmeyer suggested that, in sharp contrast to the three years of market extension alluded to above, 33% of products affected by Bill C-91 would have increased market exclusivity by a term of ten years or more.[36] Moreover, due to increasingly harmful effects on innovation, the short-term effects would be far less onerous than the long-term effects, with the worst impact on innovation and extended market exclusivity being seen about ten years after Bill C-91 came into force.[37] As discussed in more detail below, this is consistent with the data presented in Chapters 3 and 5 showing steadily declining new drug development, steadily increasing follow-on innovation, and steadily increasing patent protection over the last decade, accompanied by increasing delays for generic entry. As noted above, Dr Dickson and Michael Wilson vigorously denied the importance of cumulative market exclusivity, maintaining that only one patent per drug prevented generic entry and that Bill C-91 would only increase exclusivity by a maximum of three years.

In addition to the strength of the US pharmaceutical lobby,[38] trade harmonization efforts in the context of GATT[39] and NAFTA,[40] pressures from Quebec politicians and lobbyists,[41] and concerns about incoming then-President-Elect Bill Clinton perhaps looking to a system of price control for pharmaceuticals not unlike that of the PMPRB,[42] another reason for the patent reforms of Bill C-22 and C-91 was provided by the CAC. In its testimony before the Parliamentary Committee on Bill C-91,[43] the group claimed that patent reforms such as those enshrined in Bill C-22 and Bill C-91 represented a naive effort by the federal government to attract research and development funds in competition with other global jurisdictions with more established research and development bases that were using their patent systems and tax bases in the same way. The CAC claimed that leveraging intellectual property strategy in this manner could not reasonably result in positive social welfare outcomes. Rather, the more likely result was that reforms of this nature would induce a flow of capital to nations who have taxpayers with the deepest pockets.[44] Instead of stimulating innovation, or even providing incentives for innovation, the net result is capital market protectionism by multinational pharmaceutical firms. It is here where the 'paradoxical drug approval-drug patenting linkage' described in our Northwestern study[45] is particularly relevant, as the evidence we obtained suggests that firms may be strongly targeting their drug development efforts towards products with the greatest patent protection and the least amount of innovation.

A related point, which accords well with later developed models of policy resistance[46] and policy failure[47] is the apparent failure of both legislators and policy-makers to at least anticipate some of the unintended consequences and feedback loops of rapidly pushing through widespread patent reforms based on a hitherto unexplored link between the goals and objects of industrial patent law with those of food and drug law:

> [A]s one involved in public policy, often the decisions we make quickly and without thorough evaluation are decisions that come back to haunt us. Most legislation is precipitated by some critical event that has occurred. We try to quickly develop legislation that responds to that critical event and then often find out after the fact that in addition to trying to solve the initial problem we have created a number of unintended consequences down the line that we have to go back and fix and correct.[48]

6.3 'Original policy intent'

Often courts are left without clear guidance by government, either before or after legislation or regulations come into force. Fortunately, the specific policy grounds underpinning the NOC Regulations have been articulated by the federal government in numerous government Regulatory Impact Analysis Statements (RIASs).[49] The Supreme Court of Canada has ruled that such documents constitute proper evidence of legislative intent, including in the context of litigation under the regulations.[50]

According to a series of RIAS documents over a period of approximately ten years, the 'original policy intent' in enacting the linkage regime was to balance patent enforcement *over new and innovative drugs* with the *timely* market entry of generic drugs. The two pillars of the regulations were to increase production of new and innovative drugs while getting older drugs genericized as quickly as possible. Importantly, the NOC Regulations were intended to operate in accordance with the established principles of patent law,[51] and to further the 'societal imperative' of developing new remedies to enhance public health.[52] The specific linkage between the goals and objectives of food and drug law with those of patent law is said to reaffirm the 'stability, predictability and competitiveness of Canada's pharmaceutical patent regime',[53] a link vetted by multinational pharmaceutical firms themselves before and after the Canadian linkage regime came into force.[54]

In the United States, where pharmaceutical linkage first came into force, the purpose of Hatch-Waxman was explicitly to balance the two competing policy objectives of inducing brand pharmaceutical firms to make the investments necessary to develop new and innovative drug products while also enabling competitors to bring cheaper, generic copies of those drugs to market as soon as possible.[55] As noted by Senator Hatch at the time the legislation came into force: 'The public receives the best of both worlds – cheaper drugs today and better drugs tomorrow.'[56] Therefore, in addition to stimulating pioneering drug development, a second major policy goal of linkage in the Unites States was to facilitate timely generic entry.[57] In its report on Hatch-Waxman, the Committee on the Judiciary was explicit as to what public policy grounds were involved in achieving the balance of these competing policy goals, stating that early generic availability would substantially assist in the reduction of health care costs for the poor, the under-insured,the elderly, and the government as a purchaser of prescription drugs. In addition, and given the regulatory nature of the industry involved, early-working allowing a shortening of the delay of generic entry was held not to unduly encroach on the patent rights of brand firms and to properly enhance competition between brand and generic firms.[58]

Hence the goal of linkage in both originating jurisdictions was to facilitate timely generic entry while also stimulating the development of new and innovative drugs.

What does it mean for a drug to be 'new and innovative'? When drafting the NOC Regulations, the federal government did not provide specific definitions for these terms (in RIAS documents or otherwise), nor did it provide a Preamble as one often finds preceding legislation. The implication is that the matter was left for the courts to adjudicate or that the government did not, or would not, say one way or the other.[59]

According to the *Oxford International Dictionary*,[60] the word 'innovate' evolved from the Latin *innovare* (1548), to make new. The term focuses on bringing forth something completely new, novel, or revolutionary into existence. The word 'new,' from the Greek *véos*, Latin *novus*, and Old English *néowe*, refers to something that did not exist before, something that is brought into existence for the first time, is fresh, and not previously known. Similarly, the word 'novel' (1475), from the French *nouveau* and Latin *novellum*, refers to something that is fresh, or of recent origin, of a new kind or nature that is hitherto unknown. Finally, the word 'revolutionary,' from Old French and late Middle English (1450), refers to an instance of great change in a particular thing that is rare, an overthrow of the established way of doing things.

The definition for each of these words is internally consistent and contains both qualitative and quantitative aspects that may be relevant to interpretation of the NOC Regulations. The former refers to the notion that an innovative product (to use the current vernacular) is one that has not appeared before its introduction into the marketplace in any *meaningful* manner, while the latter may be taken to imply that the product is not only the *first* of its kind in existence but represents a truly *revolutionary* product rather than an incremental advance over existing products.

As noted in our Berkeley study,[61] while the plain meaning of the terms new and innovation are straightforward, published definitions of what should constitute an innovative drug range are based largely on industry affiliation. At one end, industry supporters argue that a new and innovative drug is one that merely contains an NAS,[62] to the slightly more stringent requirements of either being directed to first-in-class therapies (irrespective of whether approval is directed to a new or follow-on drug)[63] or to follow-on drugs that nevertheless undergo priority review.[64] However, merely containing an NAS is an insufficient basis for designating a drug as pioneering or even as strongly innovative. This is because there is ample room in either definition for minor changes to previously approved medical ingredients, including salts, esters, solvates, polymorphs and enantiomers. A similar conclusion applies to drugs that are only directed to first-in-class therapies, as these can also be follow-on versions of previously marketed products containing slightly modified medical ingredients or directed to new uses within a therapeutic class. Similarly, where priority review need only be directed to drugs demonstrating moderate clinical improvement over existing therapies, it is also an insufficient proxy for strong innovation.

The most plausible definition is that a truly new and innovative drug is one approved via the new drug approval pathway, one that contains an NAS, one that undergoes some form of priority review, and one that is directed to a first-in-class therapy.[65] Only in combination do these requirements approach a reasonable definition for a truly breakthrough or pioneering technology that would constitute a new and innovative drug, such as that contemplated by the NOC Regulations.

The second policy goal underpinning the regulations is to facilitate the timely entry of generic drugs into the marketplace. The definition of 'timely' (1593), from the Old English adjective *tímlíce*, is to appear early, soon, quickly, or in good season.[66] Thus, when something appears in a timely manner it does so at a time that provides the greatest benefit to those for whom it appears. Given the public health goal of facilitating generic entry for cost-savings purposes (for individual consumers and institutional payers), one can reasonably assume the timeliness of generic entry refers to the earliest possible date of patent expiry pertaining to a new and innovative drug. This is consistent with the fact that the enabling section of the NOC Regulations is the infringement section pertaining to the early working provision. As noted in the June 17, 2006 RIAS:

> On one end of the balance lies subsection 55.2(1) of the *Patent Act*, better known as the 'early-working' exception. In the pharmaceutical industry, early-working allows second- and subsequent-entry drug manufacturers (typically generic drug companies) to use a *patented, innovative drug* for the purpose of seeking approval to market a competing version of that drug.[67]

As discussed in more detail below, however, the concept of early working did not,[68] and indeed should not,[69] refer to the working of *any* patent at *any* time. It was intended to refer to a specific patent on a specific drug about to come off patent protection so as to allow generic firms to prepare for timely market entry. A second element of this analysis is that a drug referred to in section 55.2(1) is not a new and innovative drug for the purposes of *all* time. It is a drug that is new and innovative at a particular time in history. The moment when this drug is no longer new or innovative, for example when it becomes the basis of SNDS submissions and follow-on drugs,[70] constitutes the moment in history when patents are no longer in relation to new and innovative drugs, and thus the moment that may reasonably trigger timely generic entry.

A time-sensitive definition of patent protection for drugs that are 'new and innovative' is consistent with policy debates preceding the coming into force of Hatch-Waxman in the United States. While acknowledging that multiple patents could be listed on the patent register, the Committee on Energy and Commerce, to whom the Hatch-Waxman amendment were referred by Congress, explicitly noted that the ability of brand firms to delay generic entry should be narrow both in scope and time, the proper time for generic entry being 'the expiration date of the valid patent covering the original product,' and that 'there should be no other direct or indirect method of extending patent term.'[71]

The Committee on the Judiciary, to whom Hatch-Waxman was also referred, acknowledged that FDA rules restricting generic entry prior to Hatch-Waxman 'had serious anti-competitive effects' and that the 'net result of these rules has been the practical extension of the monopoly position of the patent holder beyond the expiration of the patent.'[72] The Committee on the Judiciary went further regarding the multiple patent listing issue, stating that it 'accepted the rationale put forward by the Committee on Energy and Commerce concerning the need to avoid multiple patent term extensions' to the effect that 'the only patented product which experiences any substantial regulatory delay is the first product patent (or if there is no product patent, the first process patent).' As a result, the Committee concluded that any 'subsequent patents on approved drug products are frequently not the same magnitude of innovation as occurs with respect to the initial patent' and that 'on public policy and health policy grounds ... only the first patent on a drug-type product should be extended.'[73]

Thus there is substantial evidence in both Canada and the United States that the nexus between drug approval and patents should be narrow, both in scope and time.

In choosing the words 'the development of new and innovative drugs' to be one half of the balance linking patent law to food and drug law, federal governments in the United States and Canada articulated a clear public policy goal that pioneering drug development is desired in exchange for the 'unusual protections' afforded to the pharmaceutical industry by the linkage regime.[74] Similarly, in choosing the words 'timely market entry of their lower priced generic competitors' these governments articulated a second public policy goal of cost-savings,[75] triggered by the expiry of specific patents on specific drug forms that are no longer new and innovative.

Based on the foregoing argument, it is reasonable to conclude that the 'balance' sought to be effected by the NOC Regulations between food and drug law and patent law is not just a *qualitative* balance between two poles, but also a *quantitative* balance. The more reward there is on the private side of the ledger, the more there must be on the public side in order to maintain a valid legal equilibrium.

Our data indicate that generic market entry is substantially delayed by the linkage regime, and that rent-seeking behavior by brand-name pharmaceutical firms to leverage loopholes in the regime is passed on in the form of continued monopoly costs to the public. Put another way, the results of Chapters 3–5 reveal the fact that not only has the production of new and innovative drugs declined over the last decade, but also that the legal protection of drugs under the linkage regime has conversely increased compared to the protection afforded via conventional infringement grounds.

The data suggest that there are two components to the disequilibrium affected by the regulations 'in operation.' First is the increase in private rewards compared to neutral public value, and second is the delay in generic entry compared to a neutral private reward. Of note, the two components combine to produce a larger disequilibrium than either one alone.

An investigation into the qualitative and quantitative nature of the balancing of public and private benefits such as that described above is consistent with the quid pro quo of the traditional patent bargain and the fact that the enabling statute for the NOC Regulations is the Patent Act. With this in mind, the following section turns to the Supreme Court of Canada's 'patent-specific' analysis evidenced in its trilogy of cases on the NOC Regulations.

6.4 'Patent-specific' analysis

The qualitative and quantitative interpretation of the original policy intent advocated above supports a specific reading of the application of section 55.2 (infringement) to a narrow range of patents per drug rather than a general reading that would lay the groundwork for a broad and potentially indefinite extension of market exclusivity for already approved pharmaceuticals. The starting point for the analysis is the enabling statute. As noted by Driedger:

> It is not enough to ascertain the meaning of a regulation when read in light of its own object and the facts surrounding its making; it is also necessary to read the words conferring the power in the whole context of the authorizing statute. The intent of the statute transcends and governs the intent of the regulation.[76]

In its leading decisions on the linkage regime in *Biolyse* and *AstraZeneca*,[77] the Supreme Court of Canada narrowly constrained its analysis on drug submissions and patent listing within the terms of the Patent Act, expressly stipulating a patent-specific analysis rather than a broad inclusive analysis of drug submissions and patents supporting market exclusivity under the NOC Regulations.[78] The court held that while the balance sought is that between food and drug law and regulations and patent law and regulations,[79] the objects of patent legislation and policy take precedence when interpreting the broad ambit of the NOC Regulations. When analyzing cases under the NOC Regulations, courts are required to specifically consider the balance struck under the Patent Act whereby the public gives an inventor the right to monopoly protection of their invention in exchange for disclosure of socially valuable information.[80]

In *Biolyse*, the court held that when contemplating inventions in the field of patented medicines, we must be mindful of the fact that Parliament was concerned not only with the balance between inventors and potential users, but also 'that between protection of intellectual property on the one hand and, on the other hand, the desire to reduce health care costs while being fair to those whose ingenuity brought the drugs into existence in the first place.'[81] As a result, claims such as those by Industry Canada, that poor or otherwise inefficient working of the NOC Regulations resulting in evergreening of older products can be counterbalanced by the benefits of a patent regime that gives multinational firms confidence in Canada,[82] must be tempered by legal assessment of relevant evidence pertaining to the functioning of the regulations in light of legislative intent. This latter statement is consistent with amendments to the NOC Regulations specifically intended to limit evergreening through abuse of the automatic stay provision.[83]

If the public benefits of innovation are raised under the linkage regulations through the terms of the patent bargain,[84] then how much does one ask for in exchange for the unusual protections of the linkage regime? The term 'patent bargain' is usually used to refer to a grant of a limited patent monopoly in exchange for public disclosure of socially valuable knowledge.[85] In a public health context, where drug approval and drug patenting are linked, the essence of the patent bargain may be viewed as the exchange of extended patent protection for a socially beneficial level of pharmaceutical innovation that is proportional to the benefit to firms of extending market exclusivity. Thus the public expects, and should expect, something of substantial value in exchange for extended patent protection and monopoly pricing. In other words, there should be a strong functional legal nexus between public health policy and patent policy.

The social benefits of approval-patenting linkage are also implied by the obligation on courts to carefully scrutinize pharmaceutical patents to determine if they properly merit the grant of a monopoly privilege in light of the substantial public interest at stake,[86] as well as the observation that the linkage regulations are deemed to involve 'special enforcement provisions' that operate well beyond the purview of traditional patent law.[87] As stated in *Whirlpool*,[88] the bargain between patentee and public is in the interest of both sides only where the patentee receives a monopoly reward that is proportional to what it discloses to the public; a patentee who evergreens an invention via successive patents on uninventive additions prolongs its monopoly beyond what the public has agreed to pay.

Two cases in particular are instructive about how narrow the functional linkage between the rights of the inventor and those of the public in the context of the patent bargain should be. In *AstraZeneca* v. *Canada*, the Supreme Court held that the listing provisions of the NOC Regulations are linked only to a 'specific' drug submission rather than a general submission. The court held that a general listing provision would allow undue evergreening,[89] which would be inconsistent with the intent of Parliament in enacting the NOC Regulations. A broad interpretation of the listing provision was seen by the court to undermine the balance sought by Parliament between the objectives of food and drug law and patent law,[90] with the result that the public would not derive appropriate benefit from patent legislation – in this case from properly listed patents. The court stipulated that this scenario 'offends the "balance" inherent to the quid pro quo' in that the 'patentee takes too much in exchange for a weakly innovative invention.'[91]

In other words, the functional legal nexus between patent law and food and drug law was insufficiently narrow to support the extension of a patent monopoly on weakly innovative drugs via the linkage regime.

The court also held that ambiguity as to the specific intent of a regulation does not have to manifest itself in specific statutory text in order to be properly considered by the court. Rather, such ambiguity should be analyzed within the entire context of the legislation.[92] Importantly, the court overruled a general listing requirement notwithstanding the acceptable industrial strategy of firms to evergreen products by 'adding bells and whistles to a pioneering product even after the original patent for [the] pioneering product has expired.'[93] This result was based on the finding that an overly broad interpretation of the NOC Regulations was inconsistent with the narrow terms of Parliament's intent in enacting the regulations and offended the quid pro quo of the traditional patent bargain.

A similar result was obtained in *Biolyse* v. *Bristol-Myers Squibb* (BMS) again using a patent-specific analysis. Here the Supreme Court dealt with what constituted a brand-name versus a generic 'submission' and, thus, whether a second-entry firm needs to litigate all listed patents prior to market entry. BMS argued that a drug submission should be construed broadly to include all submissions, whereas Biolyse argued that the term should be interpreted narrowly. While the word 'submission' was seen to provide an entry into analysis of statutory language governing submissions, the court noted that the term submission was not specifically defined in the regulations. Under the terms of its earlier decision in *Bell ExpressVu*,[94] the court saw its duty to consider the entire context of the provision and enabling legislation before undertaking a specific analysis of the term.

Taking a purposive approach, the court held that the term submission should be analyzed in its narrow sense rather than a broad general sense. A general interpretation was seen to lead to the absurd result whereby a submission by one firm relevant to a medication encompassed all further submissions relating to that medication, thus allowing the original patentee to evergreen its product via ever diminishing minor improvements. This scenario was seen to push the regulations well beyond their stated purpose, stifle competition and innovation in the pharmaceutical industry, and yield a result at odds with legislative intent.[95] The section was held to be *ultra vires* based on breach of the quid pro quo such that the patentee could extend its monopoly far beyond what its skill and ingenuity contributed to the public. As with *AstraZeneca*, the court's decision was patent-specific and hinged on a narrow rather than general nexus between drug approval and drug patenting.

A strong lesson from *Biolyse* and *AstraZeneca* is that critical to analysis of whether pharmaceutical linkage is a success or failure in achieving its twin policy goals is the long-held exercise in patent jurisprudence to ensure the patent owner is not getting more of a monopoly than the public bargained for despite claims of the patentee (and its industry and government supporters) to the contrary.[96] Innumerable cases have been brought before the courts based more on imagined, or hypothetical, inventions rather than real ones. When only patent law is construed, the difference is whether or not the inventions satisfy the requirements set out in relevant patent legislation. This is not so with regard to the NOC Regulations, which provide for a *specific* legal and functional link among the drug approved, its relevant patents, and whether they are listed on the patent register. The unique nature of the interrelationship between the Food and Drug Act, the Food and Drugs Regulations, the Patent Act, and the

Patented Medicines (Notice of Compliance) Regulations was recognized in this regard by the federal government in its lengthy 2004 RIAS: 'Despite their seemingly competing policy objectives, it is important that neither instrument [Patent Act, NOC Regulations] be considered in isolation, as the intended policy can only be achieved when the two operate in a balanced fashion.'[97]

Based on the foregoing jurisprudence, it is plausible to argue that the interpretation of what constitutes sufficient grounds for the 'special protection' afforded by the NOC Regulations may be seen to differ from the threshold for patentability per se.

Indeed, the difference between real and imagined inventiveness has been previously recognized by regulators in the context of the NOC Regulations and used to negate the protection of the regulations for inventions where a patentee failed to demonstrate a strong connection between the invention sought to be protected and the product sought to be approved.[98] This suggests that the concept of early working should not refer to the working of *any* patent at *any* time. Rather, the early-working provision specifically, and hence the empirical outputs of the linkage regime more generally, should only encompass patents relating to a *specific* drug that is new and innovative for the first time in history. The early-working provision should not encompass patents that form the basis of SNDS submissions and follow-on drugs. Ironically, this approach was supported by the federal government in its testimony before the Parliamentary Committee on Bill C-91. That testimony stated that a new and innovative drug was said to have '[one] main patent' and 'w[h]en that main patent expires, anyone may copy that product and bring it to market.'[99] As discussed above, a similar conclusion was reached by both the Committee on Energy and Commerce and the Committee on the Judiciary at the time the originating Hatch-Waxman regime came into force.

In light of government reports and jurisprudence on topic, one can reasonably conclude that the linkage regime was never intended to act as a vehicle for the continuous evergreening of blockbuster products. At least with regard to Canadian law, pharmaceutical linkage was intended to provide for international harmonization of Canada's patent laws balanced by a narrow (patent-specific) exemption to the infringement section of the Patent Act in order to allow the early working of generic drugs prior to expiration of the main patent on a given drug. To paraphrase Justice Binnie in *Free World Trust*,[100] there is a high economic cost attached to taking an overly broad approach to assessing the nexus between drug approval and drug patenting. Continuing the analogy, we might also say that it is the proper policy of patent law to keep the legal nexus between the scope of patent protection and the scope of innovation narrowly construed rather than broadly construed, and to assess the integrity of this nexus in light of all relevant empirical evidence. Otherwise, as at issue in *Biolyse* and *AstraZeneca*, the pharmaceutical linkage regime may stifle innovation, operate beyond its stated purpose, and yield a result that is at odds with legislative intent.

6.5 Statutory interpretation

The purpose of this section is to raise the possibility that empirical evidence demonstrating that legislation does not achieve its ends can support the conclusion that the legislation is invalid or in need of substantial amendment in order for it to remain *intra vires*. An ancillary goal is to explore whether there are aspects of statutory interpretation that illuminate an investigation into whether the NOC Regulations are meeting the stated goals of stimulating the development of new and innovative drugs and facilitating timely entry of generic drugs, and the manner in which this question may be assessed from a purposive perspective.

According to the principles of purposive analysis reviewed by Hutchinson in the context of intellectual property,[101] the essence of ordinary language is paramount to the exercise of statutory interpretation. The ordinary language of a statute or regulation is informed contextually by the scheme and purpose as well as evidence of statutory intent.[102] Referred to as 'external context,'[103] the interface between original policy intent and the consequences thereof in the real world informed by the original policy intent refers to 'how the legislation works operationally.'[104] As a reminder, the twin policy goals underpinning the NOC Regulations are to stimulate the development of new and innovative drugs and to facilitate timely generic entry. In the present circumstances, the term external context could thus reasonably be assumed to encompass empirical evidence of the extent and manner in which the NOC Regulations affect (1) the production of new and innovative remedies and (2) the timely entry of generic remedies once the original product patent has expired. Considerations of external context are those which privilege the setting in which a law *operates*, i.e. empirically, as a response to a set of evolving institutions and relationships.[105]

The construction of law as a dynamic and adaptive (or maladaptive) system with multiple interconnected and interdependent nodes is consistent with arguments made on the potential impact of Bill C-91 by the Canadian

Association of Consumers (CAC) discussed in section 6.2 above. Of particular relevance, the CAC pointed out that in exchange for patent reforms including linkage Canada could possibly be contributing to capital market protectionism by multinational pharmaceutical firms, a likely preference by firms and regulators for low-level innovations (me-too and other follow-on drugs), as well as minimal positive social welfare outcomes given the preference for enhanced follow-on innovations. These concerns were echoed in the testimony of US-based economist Stephen Schondelmeyer who underscored the potential of pharmaceutical linkage to result in significantly enhanced market exclusivity periods and cautioned the Parliamentary Committee to think through the issue of unintended consequences when constructing a system of innovation where new drug development and generic entry are fundamentally tied to patents on older products.

The notion of the law as a complex system can also be seen in selected writings of Fuller and Dworkin to the extent that the purpose, indeed the validity, of the law may be ascertained by the evolving context in which it operates.[106] The notion that the law is 'alive' rather than stagnant draws strong parallels to legal and other social sciences scholarship demonstrating the law to be a dynamic complex adaptive system.[107] In such systems, the law-in-operation is strongly contingent on positive and negative feedback loops that impact on system performance,[108] including systems of intellectual property law and biomedical innovation.[109]

Another principle of statutory interpretation that may be particularly relevant to analysis of the linkage regime is that interpretation of legislative intent entails an understanding of what 'mischief' the statute or regulation was intended to remedy at the time it was enacted.[110] Review of the matters before the House of Commons Legislative Committee on Bill C-91 indicate a clear concern with stimulating the production of globally competitive innovative pharmaceutical technologies balanced by the cost considerations of promoting early generic entry. These goals are entirely consistent with the original policy intent underpinning the regulations enumerated in RIAS documents, ranging from 1993 to the present, to balance the production of new and innovative drugs with the timely entry of generic products. Important to the type of balancing function inherent in the NOC Regulations, Parliament is assumed to avoid promulgating laws and regulations that conflict with one another.[111] Implicit in both the purposive and mischief analyses is the recognition of *indeterminate* considerations when making law and public policy that cannot be predicted,[112] yet which nevertheless must be accounted for in later assessments of legislative purpose or effect.

When courts are presented with competing interpretations (i.e. general or specific; Patent Act or Food and Drugs Act; health policy v. industrial policy), the clear choice is one that accords most substantively with the legislative purpose and one that is consistent with an interpretation of a given statute or regulation as a 'workable whole.'[113] In other words, the law and policy of the legislation or regulation need to operate consistently with one another from an operational perspective. As noted by Fuller:

> The troublesome cases are in reality resolved not in advance by the legislator, but at the point of application. This means that in applying the statute the judge or police sergeant must be guided not simply by the words but also by some conception of what is fit and proper to come into the park; conceptions of this sort are implicit in the practices and attitudes of the society of which he is a member ... All this adds up to the conclusion that *an important part of the statute in question is not made by the legislator, but grows and develops as an implication of complex practices and attitudes which may themselves be in a state of development or change.*[114]

As implied in the passage from Fuller, the purpose and intent of a statute or regulation is not static. Rather, it represents a dynamic process of refining and clarifying means and ends through a system of positive and negative feedback loops.[115] In other words, the intent and meaning of legislation or regulation is how it operates 'in the lives of people affected by it,' not theoretically or hypothetically as an isolated idea or even goal. This, importantly, includes objective evidence of the operation of statutes and regulations such as empirical evidence of contextual operational efficiency.[116]

A final point, which has not escaped the notice of the Supreme Court of Canada[117] or the US Federal Circuit,[118] is that courts are not the only legal authorities deciding whether legislation or regulations are valid or invalid. When faced with growing evidence of the lack of success of any legal vehicle, it is the role of the legislature to learn and dynamically adapt to external signals relating to its original policy intent, and to decide *rationally* in an *evidence-based manner* whether to abandon either the law or the original policy intent given objective evidence of how a statute or regulation operates in the 'real world.' Where objective empirical evidence such as that reviewed from Chapters 3 to 5 shows that the vehicle is operating in contrast to its stated and dynamically interpreted goals, it may be *ultra vires*[119] or otherwise operating outside of its stated ambit.[120]

6.6 Revisiting the empirical data

In the discussion above, we saw that courts look favorably on evidence relating to how a statute or regulation operates in the real world, and that law can be viewed in the context of statutory interpretation as a dynamic legal construct that may or may not evolve away from its stated goal or purpose. What, then, is the evidence that the operation of linkage regulations is inconsistent with the intent of the federal government to encourage the development of, or even to simply protect patents relating to, new and innovative drugs? Indeed, there are two major sets of observations from our empirical work to suggest that the operation of the linkage regulations is inconsistent with the goal underpinning the linkage regime. The first set of observations relates to drug patenting and the specific levels of innovation supported by these patents. The second set of observations relates to how, in combination, drug approval, drug patenting, and the pharmaceutical linkage regime act in a coordinated manner to increase the effective period of market exclusivity to the detriment of timely generic entry.

First, we observed a time-dependent decrease in new drug development over a nearly ten-year period, well after the NOC Regulations came into force. This was accompanied by a concomitant increase, in some cases non-linear, in the development of follow-on drugs. The data reviewed above indicate that these trends have occurred seemingly independently of strong time-dependent trends in drug patenting, patent listing, and drug approvals, consistent with the principles of emerging lifecycle regulatory models of drug regulation. The results demonstrate that pharmaceutical firms, when they so desire, are capable of responding rapidly and strongly to regulatory incentives in the context of drug regulation, but that this responsiveness has not extended to increasing the production of new and innovative drugs. An additional observation is that when drug approval data are analyzed cumulatively, there is a vanishingly small fraction (1.87%) of brand-name drugs that are truly 'new and innovative.' It is difficult to believe that when Parliament stipulated that only patents on new and innovative drugs were to be protected via the new pharmaceutical linkage law it had this low level of innovation in mind. Here, it is important to bear in mind that, unlike other industries, incremental innovations that have little or no therapeutic value to individual patients may nevertheless be used as tools to extend the market exclusivity for blockbuster drugs with broad social value that would otherwise come off patent.

The second primary finding of our work is that operation of the NOC Regulations increases the effective period of patent protection by at least twofold beyond the normal period. As such, the evidence suggests that the linkage regulations are being used as more of a sword than a shield by pharmaceutical firms. The degree of protection offered is indiscriminate, and is not specific to high-value inventions. Indeed, the observation in both the US and Canada that up to 50–75% of listed patents are invalid or not infringed when litigated on the merits[121] supports the conclusion that the functional nexus between drug approval and drug patenting need only be very weak (i.e. general) to support a significant extension of the patent monopoly for drugs coming off patent protection under the NOC Regulations. This scenario is worsened by a weak relevance standard for patent listing,[122] particularly one that permits listing of multiple patents on follow-on drugs with little change in benefit : risk. Thus not only has the linkage regime not resulted in the development of new and innovative drugs, it has also failed to stimulate the 'timely market entry of generic drugs.' Therefore both limbs of the balance inherent in the original policy intent underpinning the linkage regime are offended.

Supporting the conclusion above is the finding that patenting of drugs by pharmaceutical firms has escalated substantially since the coming into force of the NOC Regulations, providing increasing fodder for the patent listing and automatic stay mechanisms under the regulations. Related to this is the finding that cumulative patenting and patent listing have converged strongly over time, and that the delay between drug approval and patent listing has declined to the point that the patent listing now seems a better proxy of drug development in Canada than patenting per se. Trends in new and follow-on drugs were not altered by the increasing application of the principles of lifecycle regulation, which, like the NOC Regulations, is also strongly premised on the production of new and innovative drug products in exchange for strong intellectual property and regulatory rights.[123] Thus, in the absence of a reward system that is proportional to the degree of innovation, lifecycle-based drug regulation is not likely to alter the profile of domestic drug development.

Findings from empirical studies such as those in Chapters 3–5 support the conclusion that the patterns for new and follow-on drugs may not be reflective, as claimed by industry and its supporters, of low-hanging fruit already being picked, or escalating costs of drug development. This does not mean that a significant fraction of the low-hanging fruit has not been picked or that drug development has not become more expensive over time. Rather, results demonstrating a time-gated and increasing focus by firms on follow-on drug development, and on broadening the scope and number of patents, patent type classifications, and therapeutic classifications supporting them, suggest that firms may be aiming *ex ante* at discrete legal targets provided for by law. In the absence of demonstrable intent by government otherwise, this would be of no concern. However, in both the United States and Canada, federal governments have in fact stated that the twin goals of pharmaceutical linkage are to provide strong patent protection for new and innovative drugs while also facilitating rapid generic entry, and that these goals are to be achieved in the form of a specific legal nexus between drug approval and drug patenting informed by legal and policy grounds underpinning the legislation.

Contrary to the original policy behind the NOC Regulations, brand-name firms appear to have decreased their innovative output following the coming into force of the linkage regime while at the same time engaging in increased evergreening of already appropriated technologies using the linkage regulations as the preferred vehicle for patent extension. The empirical data show that, at best, the linkage between patent law and food and drug law is general rather than specific in nature. This is indicative of a weak legal and functional nexus between the scope of innovation and scope of patent protection, thus raising the possibility that the NOC Regulations might, in principle, infringe the quid pro quo of the patent bargain and produce a result that is at odds with legislative intent.

Based on the data presented thus far, one can argue that both ends of the balancing function of the linkage regime (stimulating new and innovative drug development and facilitating timely entry of generic drugs) are operating poorly or at least very inefficiently. On the one hand, generic competition is being stifled owing to a twofold increase in the term of patent protection under the regulations on patents that are weakly relevant to the reference product and that are often invalid when litigated on the merits. On the other hand, strong intellectual property protection is consistently and increasingly being afforded under the regulations for patents that are not in relation to new and innovative drugs, including those with a paradoxical approval-patent linkage. As suggested earlier, this suggests that there are two components to the disequilibrium affected by the regulations 'in operation.' First, is the increase in private rewards compared to neutral public value, and second is the delay in generic entry compared to a neutral private reward? The two components combine to produce a larger disequilibrium than either one alone.

As explored more fully in the context of product clusters in Chapter 7, a related observation is that drug development by domestic firms over the last decade has been strongly focused on technology appropriation in jurisdictions with and without pharmaceutical linkage. This is ironic, as one of the major concerns of policy-makers in the early stages of development of the NOC Regulations was to 'thwart' appropriation by generic drug companies of innovative technologies propagated by brand-name drug companies,[124] typically articulated as 'rights piracy.' As discussed above, the term 'appropriation' is usually used to refer to a party's ability to capture profits generated from their own inventions or related inventions.

The data in Chapters 3–5 strongly suggest that not only are generic firms not unduly appropriating innovative technologies, but even if obtaining an NOC based on bioequivalence grounds could be construed as appropriation, generic firms are only following the lead of brand-name firms who are themselves focusing on follow-on approvals while at the same time decreasing new drug development activities. This led us to conclude in our McGill study[125] that the domestic limbs of multinational pharmaceutical companies are 'doing more with less.' As such, not just brand-name firms, but all forms of domestic pharmaceutical companies we studied over the course of nearly a decade are focusing a progressively greater share of their patenting and regulatory approval energy on appropriating, or extending the value of, existing technologies over time, presumably relying on the acquisition of pioneering biotechnology firms as their technologies crystallize through clinical trials.

Finally, the data in Chapters 3–5 have some meaningful implications for innovation theory in general, which holds that follow-on or incremental innovation is equally important to overall domestic productivity and prosperity as pioneering innovation. However, unlike other industries, follow-on innovations in the pharmaceutical sector often have little or no therapeutic benefit for the population at large compared to existing drug products. While this is obviously not true for all follow-on drugs, when the system is effectively gamed using existing loopholes in the law, the multiple patent listing provision in combination with weak evidentiary requirements for drug approval can be used to powerfully extend market exclusivity for blockbuster drugs in a manner that impacts drug pricing for both public and private payers. Patents on products within a cluster can be used for this purpose either by providing the basis for follow-on drug submissions or by providing a large pool for patent listing purposes. In either case, breakthrough innovation is diminished at the same time as the timely entry of generic products is delayed. Thus, as noted in Chapter 4, the social consequences of a regulatory preference for follow-on drugs may be much greater in the public health sector than other sectors of the economy.

6.7 Summary and conclusions

Our empirical investigation into the nexus between drug approval, drug patenting, patent listing, and litigation under the domestic Canadian linkage regime for pharmaceuticals has yielded a number of important observations. Primary among these is that the development, approval, and marketing of new and innovative breakthrough drugs have stagnated in favor of follow-on drug development. The number of truly innovative drugs is very low, representing about 1.87% of all brand-name submissions and 1.23% of total submissions. This trend has been ongoing for about decade and appears to have occurred independently of concomitant changes in firm patenting, patent listing, and patent litigation. The second primary observation is that operation of the linkage regime over the same time frame has resulted in a doubling of cumulative patent protection for blockbuster drugs, from an average term of 22 years to a term of 43 years. Extended patent protection under the NOC Regulations was associated with a substantial degree of litigation, often resulting in opposing decisions on validity or infringement at the same level of court. Unlike the US linkage regime, litigation in Canada is deemed to be judicial review in nature. Thus generic firms, while successful on issues of validity or infringement under linkage laws, remain vulnerable to a post hoc infringement action. There is little question as to whether these costs are passed on to consumers in the form of monopoly prices. Together the data show that the production of new and innovative drugs is low and decreasing over time, that domestic pharmaceutical companies are focused more on appropriating existing technologies than on breakthrough drug development, and that generic entry on high-value drugs is being increasingly delayed.

The empirical findings reviewed here are at odds with the intent of the federal government in enacting the NOC Regulations to stimulate the development of new and innovative drugs and facilitate the timely entry of generic drugs. Strong questions as to the validity of the NOC Regulations arise when a purposive patent-specific approach to interpreting the NOC Regulations is taken, as stipulated by the Supreme Court of Canada in its leading patent jurisprudence. Taking this approach to analysis of the linkage of drug approval and drug patenting in the specific infringement context of section 55.2(1) of Canada's Patent Act, one could argue that the concept of early working does not refer to the working of *any* patent at *any* time. As suggested by testimony by the federal government before the Legislative Committee on Bill C-91, the early-working provision was intended to refer to a specific patent on a specific drug so as to allow generic firms to prepare for timely market entry in relation to that drug and that patent. A second element of a patent-specific analysis is that a drug as referred to in section 55.2(1) is not a new and innovative drug for the purposes of *all* time. It is a drug that is new and innovative at a particular time in history. The moment when this drug is no longer new or innovative, for example when it becomes the basis of SNDS submissions and follow-on drugs, constitutes the moment in history when patents are no longer in relation to new and innovative drugs, and thus the moment which may reasonably trigger timely generic entry.

A similar conclusion may be drawn from the legal debate surrounding the coming into force of the US Hatch-Waxman regime, particularly with respect to influential reports from the Committee on Energy and Commerce and the Committee on the Judiciary preceding the legislation.

Relegating patents listed on the patent register only to specific drug submissions considered to be 'new and innovative' based on objective evidence such as that reviewd and proposed in Chapters 5 and 7 rather than in an arbitrary manner on all new (NDS) and follow-on (SNDS) submissions would be in line with the spirit of the regulations to encourage the development of new and innovative drugs and to facilitate the timely entry of generic alternatives. Amendment to the NOC Regulations in this manner would accord with the framework for the linkage regime put forward by the Canadian government in the lead-up to Bill C-91. It would also be consistent with the policy underpinning linkage as laid out by the Committee on Energy and Commerce and the Committee on the Judiciary in the United States in the lead-up to Hatch-Waxman. At the time both pieces of legislation came into force, the US and Canadian governments strongly asserted that linkage protection was aimed at a narrow range of patents on new and innovative drugs, and when that narrow range of patents expire, anyone in a position to copy that product can legally bring it to market. As discussed above in greater detail, the language used by both governments is consistent with the plain meaning of the terms 'new and innovative' and 'timely.'

In choosing the words 'the development of new and innovative drugs' to be one-half of the balance linking patent law to food and drug law, federal governments in the United States and Canada articulated a clear public policy goal that pioneering drug development is desired in exchange for the 'unusual protections' afforded to the pharmaceutical industry by the linkage regime. Similarly, in choosing the words 'timely market entry of their lower priced generic competitors' these governments articulated a second public policy goal of cost-savings, triggered by the expiry of specific patents on specific drug forms that are no longer new and innovative. Thus the balance sought to be effected by pharmaceutical linkage is not just a qualitative balance between poles, but also a quantitative balance. The more reward there is on the private side of the ledger, the more there must be on the public side in order to maintain a valid legal equilibrium.

The data in Chapters 3–5 demonstrate that, when analyzed in its 'real-world' context, the Canadian linkage regulations are not working either as intended by Parliament at the time the law was passed or even in a manner that is consistent with the goals and objectives of the federal government as articulated in later RIAS documents. Private firms are obtaining extended patent protection for weakly inventive products, while at the same time generic competition is markedly delayed. The result is that pharmaceutical firms are reaping the rewards of intellectual property protection at historically high levels in this country while the public (and institutional payers) is being deprived of reasonably priced pharmaceuticals.

In light of the principle of statutory interpretation that legislation should be understood and assessed objectively in the setting in which it operates, it is possible that the operation of the NOC Regulations as currently constituted breaches the quid pro quo of the traditional patent bargain from a patent-specific perspective. Based on the same reasoning and evidence one might conclude that the linkage regime does not rectify the mischief it was intended to remedy, and thus may yield a result that is at odds with legislative intent.

Finally, data such as those in Chapters 3–5 suggest that the blending of industrial and health policy goals may be ineffective and possibly counterproductive in terms of public health outcomes. Particularly worrisome is the potential for linkage loopholes permitting a 'paradoxical drug approval-drug patenting nexus,' whereby the largest degree of market exclusivity is provided on products with the least amount of innovation. A theory of how this may occur within the context of pharmaceutical linkage via the development of 'product clusters' is provided in Chapter 7.

There is no question that established and emerging drug regulatory regimes have the potential to increase the efficiency of public health provision by placing both new and innovative and older blockbuster remedies in clinical environments sooner. However, a growing body of evidence, including data reviewed here, seems to indicate that the efficacy of this approach can be weakened through inadequate monitoring and supervision, such that pharmaceutical firms perceive a higher incentive to exploit existing patented technologies in new ways rather than increasing the flow of new technologies. At a more general level, the data lend empirical substance to an emerging consensus that, in many circumstances, intellectual property rights may be an inhibitor of innovation in so far as this term is construed to yield the greatest social benefits for the public. The results may have important implications for innovation theory in general, the classical view of which holds that follow-on or incremental innovation is equally important to overall domestic productivity and prosperity as pioneering innovation. However, unlike other industries, follow-on innovations in the pharmaceutical sector often have little or no therapeutic benefit for the population at large compared to existing drug products. This is clear from the history of Bill C-22 and Bill C-91 reviewed above. While obviously not true for all follow-on drugs, when the system is effectively gamed (as it often is for high-value drugs), the multiple patent listing provision in combination with weak evidentiary requirements for the combination of patents and new and follow-on drug approval can be used to powerfully extend market exclusivity for blockbuster drugs in a manner that impacts drug pricing for both public and private payers. Thus the social consequences of a regulatory preference for follow-on drugs may be different in the public health sector than in other sectors of the economy.

It is concluded that policy and legislative incentives designed to stimulate innovation in the pharmaceutical industry have had the opposite effect, and that shifting to a lifecycle regulatory model is unlikely to alter this scenario absent effort to balance economic incentives for breakthrough and follow-on drug development. Importantly, the findings presented in this book do not suggest unusual behavior by pharmaceutical firms. Rather, the data point to the failure of policy incentives intended to induce the desired result, namely stimulating the development of new and pioneering drugs while also facilitating the timely entry of generic drugs and thus access to essential and affordable medicines.

As discussed in greater detail elsewhere,[126] it is possible that unintended consequences such as those reported here have come about, at least in part, as a result of the discrete system of legal checks and balances comprising the domestic linkage regime, particularly when the balance of 'pro-brand' and 'pro-generic' provisions in the Canadian system of linkage are compared to those employed in other jurisdictions.

Notes

1. Christopher Scott Harrison, 'Protection of Pharmaceuticals as Foreign Policy: The Canada-U.S. Trade Agreement and Bill C-22 Versus the North American Free Trade Agreement and Bill C-91,' 26 *N.C. J. Int'l L. & Com. Reg.* 457, 460 (2000–1) [Harrison (2000–1)], at 491.

2. *Minutes of Proceedings and Evidence of the Legislative Committee on Bill C-91*, 34: 8 Parliament of Canada, 8: 39–42 (December 1, 1992).
3. *Minutes of Proceedings and Evidence of the Legislative Committee on Bill C-91*, 34: 8 Parliament of Canada, 8: 30 (December 1, 1992).
4. *Minutes of Proceedings and Evidence of the Legislative Committee on Bill C-91*, 34: 7 Parliament of Canada, 7: 68–92 (December 1, 1992).
5. For a review of the evidence in front of the House of Commons in the context of Bills C-22 and C-91, see Harrison (2000–1), *supra* note 1, at 511–524, and Michael C. Jordan, 'The Politics of Drug Patenting in Canada,' 102 (August 2005) [Jordan (n.d.)] (unpublished MA thesis, University of Saskatchewan) (on file with the University of Saskatchewan, Electronic Thesis 7 Dissertation Project). In the parliamentary debate leading up to the enactment of Bill C-91, it was widely noted by several Members of Parliament that the CN $300–500 million figure had to be reduced in accordance with provincial tax incentives, which amounted to 55, 60, and 70 cents on the dollar in Alberta, Ontario, and Quebec, respectively (*Minutes of Proceedings and Evidence of the Legislative Committee on Bill C-91*, 34: 4 Parliament of Canada, 4: 14, 4: 39 (November 27, 1992) and ibid. at 34: 5 Parliament of Canada, 5: 38, 5: 40, 5: 91 (November 30, 1992)). During cross-examination, federal employees acknowledged that these figures were correct and that the calculations were intentionally left out of government reports on the topic leading to the hearings (ibid. at 34: 6 Parliament of Canada 6: 10 (November 30, 1992)).
6. For a detailed history of litigation over public disclosure of pharmaceutical R&D costs, see generally US Cong. Off. of Tech. Assessment, Pharmaceutical R&D: Costs, Risks, and Rewards 284–88 (1993) [Off. of Tech. Assessment]. The US Supreme Court, in the seminal *Bowsher* v. *Merck Co.* decision, held that pharmaceutical R&D and related costs constituted confidential information and, thus, that the federal government did not have the authority to compel disclosure of such information (460 US 824, 843 (1983)). For a more recent discussion of pharmaceutical R&D costs see US National Institute of Health, 'NIH Response to Conference Report Request for Plan to Ensure Taxpayer's Interests are Protected' (2001), online: <http://www.nih.gov/news/070101wyden.htm>. In Canada, data submitted by pharmaceutical companies are deemed to be 'commercially sensitive' and as such constitute confidential information under the Federal Access to Information Act (see RSC, 1985 c. A-1 20(6)). Under section 20(6), disclosure can only be made where it is in the public interest and relates to public health and safety. Health Canada will not, however, release information where public interest in disclosure is outweighed by financial loss or prejudice to the competitive position of the disclosing party (ibid.). See also North American Free Trade Agreement, U.S.-Can.-Mex., December 17, 1992, TS No. 2 (1994), 32 ILM 289 (between the Governments of Canada, Mexico, and the United States; entered into force January 1, 1994), at art. 1711; Trade Related Aspects of Intellectual Property (TRIPS) 1994, October 30, 1947, TS No. 27 (1947), 58 UNTS 187 (negotiated as part of the

Uruguay Round (1986–94) of the World Trade Organization's General Agreement on Tariffs and Trade (GATT)), at art. 39 (pertaining to data and market exclusivity, which deem commercially sensitive information to be confidential). See, generally, Regulatory Impact Analysis Statement, 138 C. *Gaz.* Pt. I, at 3712 n. 50 (2004) (Regulations Amending the Food and Drug Regulations [1390 – Data Protection]), as modified by Regulatory Impact Analysis Statement, 140 C. *Gaz.* Pt. I, at 1598 n. 24 (2006) (Regulations Amending the Food and Drug Regulations (Data Protection)).

7. See *Minutes of Proceedings and Evidence of the Legislative Committee on Bill C-91*, 34: 4 Parliament of Canada, 4: 12, 4: 20 (November 27, 1992) (testimony of the Canadian Medical Association) and ibid. at 34: 7 Parliament of Canada, 7A: 51 (December 1, 1992) (testimony from Green Shield). For a discussion of the role of marketing generally in Canada, see Trudo Lemmens and Ron A. Bouchard, 'Regulation of Pharmaceuticals in Canada,' in Jocelyn Downie, Timothy Caulfield, and Colleen Flood (eds), *Canadian Health Law and Policy*, 3rd edn (LexisNexis, 2007), at 311, 312.
8. Thomas O. McGarity and Sidney A. Shapiro, 'The Trade Secret Status of Health and Safety Testing Information: Reforming Agency Disclosure Policies,' 93 *Harv. L. Rev.* 837 (1980); Jeffery M. Drazen, 'Who Owns the Data in a Clinical Trial?' 8 *Sci. Eng. Ethics* 407 (2002).
9. Off. of Tech. Assessment, *supra* note 6, at 284–8.
10. Patent Act Amendment Act, SC 1992, c. 2 (Can.).
11. *Minutes of Proceedings and Evidence of the Legislative Committee on Bill C-91*, 34: 5 Parliament of Canada, 5: 8, 5: 114, 5: 116 (November 30, 1992) and ibid. at 34: 8 Parliament of Canada, 8: 24, 8: 28 (December 1, 1992) (testimony of Lorne Tyrell, UT, Group of 10, Minister Blais, and Minister Wilson).
12. See, for example, *Minutes of Proceedings and Evidence of the Legislative Committee on Bill C-91*, 34: 5 Parliament of Canada, 5: 20 (November 30, 1992) (testimony of Lorne Tyrrell, who himself was the recipient of substantial pharmaceutical funding, which helped to create a spin-out company from which he personally profited). The notion that pharmaceutical funds were 'vital' to the health of Canadian universities was supported by testimony from other university administrators, including the so-called 'Group of 10.' See, for example, ibid. at 34: 5 Parliament of Canada, 5: 116.
13. M.L. Burstall, J.H. Dunning, and A. Lake, *Multinational Enterprises, Governments and Technology: The Pharmaceutical Industry* (OECD, 1981) (cited in the Canadian Health Coalition and Medical Reform Group Brief, *Minutes of Proceedings and Evidence of the Legislative Committee on Bill C-91*, 34: 5 Parliament of Canada, 5A: 73, A5: 83 (November 30, 1992)).
14. Report of the Commission of Inquiry on the Pharmaceutical Industry (Supply and Services Canada 1985) (cited in *Minutes of Proceedings and Evidence of the Legislative Committee on Bill C-91*, 34: 5 Parliament of Canada, 5: 12 (November 30, 1992)).

15. This point was also raised by the Canadian Consumer Protection Agency in its submissions (cited in *Minutes of Proceedings and Evidence of the Legislative Committee on Bill C-91*, 34: 5 Parliament of Canada, 5: 41 (November 30, 1992)).
16. *Minutes of Proceedings and Evidence of the Legislative Committee on Bill C-91*, 34: 5 Parliament of Canada, 5: 12 (November 30, 1992) (testimony of Mr MacDonald (Dartmouth) citing a Canadian Industry, Science and Technology Report entitled 'Impact of Pharmaceutical Company Sponsored Research on Basic Research in Canadian Universities').
17. *Minutes of Proceedings and Evidence of the Legislative Committee on Bill C-91*, 34: 8 Parliament of Canada, 8: 30 (December 1, 1992) (testimony of Minister Wilson); *Minutes of Proceedings and Evidence of the Legislative Committee on Bill C-91*, 34: 5 Parliament of Canada, 5A: 73, 5A: 81 (November 30, 1992) (CHC Brief).
18. *Minutes of Proceedings and Evidence of the Legislative Committee on Bill C-91*, 34: 5 Parliament of Canada, 5: 60, 5A: 19, 5A: 20, 5A: 30 (November 30, 1992) (Canadian Association of Consumers, submissions and brief).
19. Both the Canadian Medical Association (CMA) and the Canadian Association of Consumers (CAC) requested that the federal government take an 'evidence-based' approach to assessing research and development costs and the impact of patent reforms on the costs and benefits of the public health system. *Minutes of Proceedings and Evidence of the Legislative Committee on Bill C-91*, 34: 5 Parliament of Canada, 5: 53 (November 30, 1992) (CAC); ibid. at 34: 4 Parliament of Canada, 4: 8, 4A: 18, 4: 10 (November 27, 1992) (CMA); Harrison (2000–1), *supra* note 1, at 526, concluding in his study of the political and economic factors underpinning Bill C-22 and Bill C-91 that 'one cannot persuasively argue that the Mulroney administration tied or linked this costly policy (repeal of compulsory licensing) to any tangible benefit.' Indeed, during the debate over the repeal of compulsory licensing and patent reforms in the lead up to TRIPS, NAFTA, and Bill C-22, proponents of increased patent protection were criticized for the lack of commitments by the pharmaceutical industry that would be 'measureable and enforceable' (ibid.). The Minister of Consumer and Corporate Affairs at the time, Harvie André, replied that output metrics were not necessary, saying instead '[w]e prefer carrots to whips. If it turns out that the donkey will not go with the carrot then maybe you will have to use the whip.' *Minutes of Proceedings and Evidence of the Legislative Committee on Bill C-22*, 33: 2 Parliament of Canada, 1: 11, 1545 (December 16, 1982) (cited in Jordan (n.d.), *supra* note 5, at 31–2).
20. *Minutes of Proceedings and Evidence of the Legislative Committee on Bill C-91*, 34: 5 Parliament of Canada, 5A: 30 (November 30, 1992).
21. Mark A. Lemley, 'Rational Ignorance at the Patent Office,' 95 *NW. U. L. Rev.* 1495, 1495 (2001).

22. CHC Brief, *Minutes of Proceedings and Evidence of the Legislative Committee on Bill C-91*, 34: 5 Parliament of Canada, 5A: 72, 5A: 83 (November 30, 1992) (citing K.M. Taylor, 'The Impact of the Pharmaceutical Industry's Clinical Research Programs on Medical Education, Practice and Researchers in Canada: A Discussion Paper,' in *Canadian Pharmaceutical Research and Development: Four Short-Term Studies* (Department of Industry, Science and Technology, 1991)).
23. Ron A. Bouchard, Jamil Sawani, Chris McLelland, Monika Sawicka, and Richard W. Hawkins, 'The Pas de Deux of Pharmaceutical Regulation and Innovation: Who's Leading Whom?' 24 *Berkeley Tech. L.J.* 1461, 1463 n. 2 (2009) [Bouchard et al. (2009)] , at 1491.
24. *Minutes of Proceedings and Evidence of the Legislative Committee on Bill C-91*, 34: 7 Parliament of Canada, 7: 20 (December 1, 1992).
25. *Minutes of Proceedings and Evidence of the Legislative Committee on Bill C-91*, 34: 7 Parliament of Canada, 7: 46 (December 1, 1992).
26. Patented Medicine Prices Review Board, *Annual Report 2000*, 24 (2001); Editorial, 'European and French Pharmaceutical Market Assessed by Prescrire in 2005: Mainly Bogus Innovation,' 30 *Farmacia Hospitalaria* 68 n. 2 (2006); 'Drugs in 2001: A Number of Ruses Unveiled,' 11 *Prescrire Int'l* 58, 58 (2002); Kenneth I. Kaitin et al., 'Therapeutic Ratings and End-of-Phase II Conferences: Initiatives to Accelerate the Availability of Important New Drugs,' 31 *J. Clinical Pharmacology* 17 (1991); Joel Lexchin, 'Intellectual Property Rights and the Canadian Pharmaceutical Marketplace: Where Do We Go From Here?' 35 *Int'l. J. Health Servs.* 237, 243 (2005); Domenico Motola et al., 'An Update on the First Decade of the European Centralized Procedure: How Many Innovative Drugs?' 62 *Brit. J. of Clinical Pharmacology* 610 n. 5 (2006); 'New Medicines in 2007: Regulatory Agencies and Policy Makers Leave Public Health in the Hands of the Pharmaceutical Industry,' 17 *Prescrire Int'l* 78 n. 94 (2008); Nat'l Inst. for Health Care Mgmt., *Changing Patterns of Pharmaceutical Innovation* 1, 7–14 (2002) [*Pharmaceutical Innovation* (2002)], at 7.
27. *Minutes of Proceedings and Evidence of the Legislative Committee on Bill C-91*, 34: 5 Parliament of Canada, 5: 134 (November 30, 1992) (Canadian Health Coalition); ibid. at 34: 7 Parliament of Canada, 7: 13 (members of Parliament) (December 1, 1992).
28. *Minutes of Proceedings and Evidence of the Legislative Committee on Bill C-91*, 34: 5 Parliament of Canada, 5: 126 (November 30, 1992) (comment made by a Vice President of Research from UBC).
29. *Minutes of Proceedings and Evidence of the Legislative Committee on Bill C-91*, 34: 6 Parliament of Canada, 6: 4 (November 30, 1992) (Mr David Blaker, Head, Risk Assessment and Management Section, Bureau of Drug Research, of National Health and Welfare).
30. *Minutes of Proceedings and Evidence of the Legislative Committee on Bill C-91*, 34: 6 Parliament of Canada, 6: 6–7, 6: 9–11 (November 30, 1992) (Mr Blaker).

Another witness, Mr Ross Duncan (Consumer Policy Branch, Department of Consumer and Corporate Affairs), testified that the only data he used to construct his report on the impact of Bill C-91 was data provided by the Pharmaceutical Manufacturers Association of Canada (PMAC) (ibid., at 6: 12).

31. *Minutes of Proceedings and Evidence of the Legislative Committee on Bill C-91*, 34: 8 Parliament of Canada, 8: 37 (December 1, 1992) (emphasis added).
32. *Minutes of Proceedings and Evidence of the Legislative Committee on Bill C-91*, 34: 5 Parliament of Canada, 5: 76, 5: 133 (November 30, 1992).
33. *Minutes of Proceedings and Evidence of the Legislative Committee on Bill C-91*, 34: 8 Parliament of Canada, 8: 40 (December 1, 1992).
34. Ibid.
35. *Minutes of Proceedings and Evidence of the Legislative Committee on Bill C-91*, 34: 7 Parliament of Canada, 7: 68 (December 1, 1992) (emphasis added).
36. *Minutes of Proceedings and Evidence of the Legislative Committee on Bill C-91*, 34: 7 Parliament of Canada, 7: 68, 7A: 111 (December 1, 1992).
37. *Minutes of Proceedings and Evidence of the Legislative Committee on Bill C-91*, 34: 7 Parliament of Canada, 7: 70 (December 1, 1992). Professor Schondelmeyer assessed the net cumulative savings to Canadians (individual consumers, hospitals, and insurance plans) from 1993 to 2010 would be CN $7 billion in constant 1993 dollars.
38. *Minutes of Proceedings and Evidence of the Legislative Committee on Bill C-91*, 34: 5 Parliament of Canada, 5: 42 (November 30, 1992) (Canadian Center for Policy Alternatives (CCPA)). The pharmaceutical industry was reportedly the second largest contributor to US election campaign funding. See, for example, 'How Health PACs Spend Millions to Influence Elections,' *Washington Post*, March 21, 1989, at 14 (cited in 34: 7 Parliament of Canada, 7A: 45 (December 1, 1992)).
39. *Minutes of Proceedings and Evidence of the Legislative Committee on Bill C-91*, 34: 5 Parliament of Canada, 5: 42 (November 30, 1992) (CCPA).
40. *Minutes of Proceedings and Evidence of the Legislative Committee on Bill C-91*, 34: 5 Parliament of Canada, 5: 49 (November 30, 1992).
41. For a first-hand view, see all nine volumes of *Minutes of Proceedings and Evidence of the Legislative Committee on Bill C-91*, 34 Parliament of Canada (1992). For an arm's length view, see generally Harrison (2000–1), *supra* note 1; Robert Tancer, 'Foreign Investment in North America and the Pharmaceutical Industry in Canada,' *Int'l Exec.*, March/April (1997), at 283.
42. *Minutes of Proceedings and Evidence of the Legislative Committee on Bill C-91*, 34: 5 Parliament of Canada, 5: 73 (November 30, 1992); ibid. at 34: 7 Parliament of Canada, 7: 18 (Karpoff), 7: 99 (Canadian Drug Manufacturers Association (CDMA)) (December 1, 1992). But see ibid. at 34: 8 Parliament of Canada, 8: 37 (December 1, 1992) (Minister Wilson) for a strong rebuttal of this argument. For a historical discussion of why President Clinton might

support price controls in the United States while seeking intellectual property privileges globally, see Harrison (2000–1), *supra* note 1, at 461, 522, 523, 526.

43. *Minutes of Proceedings and Evidence of the Legislative Committee on Bill C-91*, 34: 5 Parliament of Canada, 5: 54–57 (November 30, 1992).

44. As a reminder, between 50 and 75% of the proposed sum of CN $500 million that the pharmaceutical industry would invest in domestic research and development was composed of provincial tax breaks. This is particularly relevant given testimony by Dr Joel Lexchin before the C-91 Committee, *Minutes of Proceedings and Evidence of the Legislative Committee on Bill C-91*, 34: 5 Parliament of Canada, 5: 135 (November 30, 1992), that the majority of profits for provincial drug plans are due to savings from generic drugs. In addition to provincial tax savings, Canada is known to have one of the more generous Scientific Research and Experimental Development (SRED) tax credit programs (ibid.).

45. See *supra* section 6.3.

46. See, generally, John D. Sterman, 'All Models Are Wrong: Reflections on Becoming a Systems Scientist,' 18 *Sys. Dynamics Rev.* 501 n. 4 (2002).

47. See, generally, Barry Bozeman and Daniel Sarewitz, 'Public Values and Public Failure in US [*sic*] Science Policy,' 32 *Sci. and Pub. Pol'y* 119 n. 2 (2005); Barry Bozeman, 'Public-Value Failure: When Efficient Markets May Not Do,' 62 *Pub. Admin. Rev.* 145, 145 (2002).

48. *Minutes of Proceedings and Evidence of the Legislative Committee on Bill C-91*, 34: 7 Parliament of Canada, 7: 92 (December 1, 1992).

49. Evidence of legislative intent regarding balancing patent enforcement and generic entry can be found in early RIAS documents. See 138 *C. Gaz.* 50 Pt. I, 3714 (2004); 140 *C. Gaz.* 24 Pt. I, 1601 (2006); 142 *C. Gaz.* 13 Pt. II, 1390, 1588 (2008); Health Canada, Health Prods. and Food Branch, Guidance Document, Patented Medicines (Notice of Compliance) Regulations (2010), online: <http://www.hc-sc.gc.ca/dhp-mps/alt_formats/hpfb-dgpsa/pdf/prodpharma/applic-demande/guide-ld/postnoc_change_apresac/noc_pn_framework_ac_sa_cadre-eng.pdf>. An articulation of the government's pharmaceutical policy as it relates to the NOC Regulations can be found in the June 17, 2006 RIAS, which states:

> The Government's pharmaceutical patent policy seeks to balance effective patent enforcement over new and innovative drugs with the timely market entry of their lower-priced generic competitors. The current manner in which that balance is realized was established in 1993, with the enactment of Bill C-91, the Patent Act Amendment Act, 1992, SC 1993, c. 2. (140 *C. Gaz.* 24 Pt. I, 1611 (2006))

See, generally, 132 *C. Gaz.* 11 Pt. I, 553 (1998); 133 *C. Gaz.* 21 Pt. II, 2355 (1999). Evidence of legislative intent regarding the 'original policy intent' of encouraging development of new and innovative drugs can be found in both RIAS and related Guidance Document.

50. *Biolyse Pharma Corp.* v. *Bristol-Myers Squibb Co.*, [2005] 1 SCR 533, §§ 47, 156, 157 (Can.). Justice Binnie stated:

> It has long been established that the usage of admissible extrinsic sources regarding a provision's legislative history and its context of enactment could be examined. I held in *Francis v. Baker*, at para. 35, that '[p]roper statutory interpretation principles therefore require that all evidence of legislative intent be considered, provided that it is relevant and reliable.' Consequently, in order to confirm the purpose of the impugned regulation, the intended application of an amendment to the regulation or the meaning of the legislative language, it is useful to examine the RIAS, prepared as part of the regulatory process . . . (at § 156)

See Ruth Sullivan, *Sullivan and Driedger on the Construction of Statutes*, 4th edn (2002) [Sullivan (2002)], at 499–500.

51. *Biolyse*, [2005] 1 SCR at §§ 47, 156–7; *AstraZeneca Canada Inc.* v. *Canada (Minister of Health)*, [2006] 2 SCR 560 (Can.); *ratiopharm inc.* v. *Wyeth and Wyeth Canada*, [2007] FCA 264 (Can.).
52. 138 C. *Gaz.* 50 Pt. I. 3714 (2004).
53. 142 C. *Gaz.* 13 Pt. I, 1390 (2008).
54. In his 2003 testimony before the House of Commons Standing Committee on Industry, Science and Technology, the CEO of GlaxoSmithKline stipulated that the NOC Regulations ensured *balance* within Canada's patent regime and encouraged *innovation* into *new* therapies (Jordan (n.d.), *supra* note 5, at 66 (emphasis added)). For an example of pharmaceutical literature highlighting the importance of linkage regulations see Canada's Research-based Pharmaceutical Companies (Rx&D) Information Guide 2002, Section 2: Industry Issues (2002); AstraZeneca Can., 'The Patent Act & Linkage Regulations: Essential Tools for the Advancement of Medical Science in Canada' (2009), online: <http://www.astrazeneca.ca/documents/en/aboutus/PatentActLinkageRegulations.pdf>.
55. *Abbott Labs.* v. *Young*, 920 F.2d 984, 991 (DC Cir. 1990); HR Rep. No. 98-857, pt. 1, at 14–15 (1984); *Mylan Pharms., Inc.* v. *Thompson*, 268 F.3d 1323, 1326 (Fed. Cir. 2001).
56. Richard Epstein and Bruce Kuhlik, *Navigating the Anticommons for Pharmaceutical Patents: Steady the Course on Hatch-Waxman*, Univ. of Chi. L. & Econ. Working Paper No. 209, 2004, n. 24 (citing Congressional Record – Senate at 23764 (August 10, 1984).
57. Daniel R. Cahoy, 'Patent Fences and Constitutional Fence Posts: Property Barriers to Pharmaceutical Importation,' 15 *Fordham Intell. Prop. Media & Ent. L.J.* 623 (2005).
58. HR Rep. 98-857, pt. 2, at 25 (1984).
59. Both the Canadian Medical Association and the Consumers Association of Canada in their evidence before the Parliamentary Committee on Bill C-91 requested that government take an evidence-based approach to research and

development, and noted that no attempt was made by the government in the lead-up to Bill C-91 to empirically or objectively assess the potential impact of patent reforms on the costs and benefits to federal or provincial public health systems. See *supra* notes 5 and 55, for comments by the Minister of Consumer and Corporate Affairs that at the time Bills C-22 and C-91 were being implemented, suggest Parliament did know that it was possible to measure innovation and construct a national pharmaceutical policy with balanced incentives and rewards, deciding instead the preferable route was to eschew this approach in favor of a system with neither output metrics nor proportionality (Jordan (n.d.), *supra* note 5; Harrison (2000–1), *supra* note 1). See, generally, *Minutes of Proceedings and Evidence of the Legislative Committee on Bill C-91*, 34: 4 Parliament of Canada, 4: 8–10, 4A: 18 (November 27, 1992) and ibid. at 34: 5 Parliament of Canada, 5: 53 (November 30, 1992).

60. *Oxford International Dictionary of the English Language*, Unabridged (1958).
61. Bouchard et al. (2009), *supra* note 23, at 1508.
62. J.D. Kleinke, 'Commentary: Much Ado About a Good Thing,' 325 *BMJ* 1168, 1168 (2002).
63. See Fredric J. Cohen, Opinion, 'Macro Trends in Pharmaceutical Innovation,' 4 *Nature Rev. Drug Discovery*, January (2005) [Cohen (2005)], at 78; US Nat'l Res. Council, Prospectus for National Knowledge Assessment, Committee on Knowledge Assessment Office of International Affairs (1996).
64. Bouchard et al. (2009), *supra* note 23. See, for example, *Pharmaceutical Innovation* (2002), *supra* note 26.
65. Ibid.
66. *Oxford International Dictionary*, *supra* note 60.
67. 140 *C. Gaz.* Pt. I, at 1611 n. 24 (2006) (emphasis added).
68. During the parliamentary debates leading up to Bill C-91, it was clear that there would only be a small number of patents, indeed most often a single or *main* patent, to contend with in the early working scenario. See, generally, testimony on this point by the Director General, Chemical and Bio-Industries Branch, Department of Industry, Science and Technology, *Minutes of Proceedings and Evidence of the Legislative Committee on Bill C-91*, 34: 8 Parliament of Canada, 8: 37 (December 1, 1992) and testimony from Green Shield, ibid. at 34: 7 Parliament of Canada, 7: 27 (December 1, 1992).
69. For the reasons why it *should not* be discussed in the review of the Supreme Court of Canada's 'patent-specific' analysis, see the *Biolyse* and *AstraZeneca* cases.
70. For example, the conversion from a mesylate to besylate salt form, a dihydrate to monohydrate crystalline form, a tablet to capsule form, between different stereoisomers or enantiomeric forms, etc., with little or no change in bioavailability, pharmacokinetics, and therapeutic benefit.

71. House Report No. 98-857, Pt. 1 (1984). At 30, the Committee stated:

> Article 1, section 8, clause 8 of the constitution empowers Congress to grant exclusive rights to an inventor for a limited time. That limited time should be a definite time and, thereafter, immediate competition should be encouraged. For that reason, Title I of the bill permits the filing of abbreviated new drug applications before a patent expires and contemplates that the effective approval Date will be the expiration date of the valid patent covering the original Product. Other sections of title II permit the extension of the term of a patent for a definite time provided certain conditions are met. There should be no other direct or indirect method of extending patent term.

72. HR 98-857, Pt. 2, at 4 (1984).
73. Ibid., at 5–6.
74. The Federal Court of Canada, the Federal Court of Appeal, and the Supreme Court of Canada have repeatedly cited the language of the Supreme Court, which refers to the NOC Regulations as a 'draconian regime' in its first decision on topic. See *Merck Frosst Canada Inc.* v. *Canada (Minister of Nat'l Health & Welfare)*, [1998] 2 SCR 193, § 33 (Can.).
75. As noted by the Committee on the Judiciary in its influential report (HR Rep. 98-857, Pt. 2, at 25 (1984)), the public policy grounds achieved through early generic availability included: reduction of healthcare costs for the poor, the under-insured, the elderly, and the government as a purchaser of prescription drugs.
76. Elmer A. Driedger, *Construction of Statutes*, 2nd edn (1983), at 247. For discussion of Driedger's approach to statutory interpretation in the context of NOC Regulations analysis, see *Biolyse Pharma Corp.* v. *Bristol-Myers Squibb Co.*, [2005] 1 SCR 533 (Can.); *AstraZeneca Canada Inc.* v. *Canada (Minister of Health)*, [2006] 2 SCR 550, § 26 (Can.).
77. *Biolyse*, [2005] 1 SCR at § 26; *AstraZeneca*, [2006] 2 SCR at § 36.
78. *AstraZeneca*, [2006] 2 SCR at § 39. A 'patent-specific analysis' was recently confirmed by Health Canada in its 2009 Guidance Document relating to the NOC Regulations. Health Canada Guidance, *supra* note 49, at 26. In addition to acknowledging that a 'patent-specific analysis' is necessary when interpreting the NOC Regulations, the government further stated that only certain patents are 'eligible' for protection under the NOC Regulations, indicating that not all patents fall within the purview of the regulations (ibid., at 28). See also *AstraZeneca*, [2006] 2 SCR at § 39; *Ferring Inc.* v. *Canada (Minister of Health)*, [2008] 1 FCR 19, §§ 51–7 (Can.).
79. *AstraZeneca*, [2006] 2 SCR, at § 39.
80. *Biolyse*, [2005] 1 SCR, at 533.
81. *Biolyse*, [2005] 1 SCR, at 533, § 2.
82. 142 *C. Gaz.* 13 Pt. II, 1390, 1593 (2008). This is a similar statement to that found in all post-2004 RIAS documents that the NOC Regulations provide

'stability, predictability and competitiveness' to Canada's pharmaceutical patent regime. See, generally, 138 *C. Gaz.* 50 Pt. I, 3714 (2004); 140 *C. Gaz.* 24 Pt. I, 1601 (2006); 142 *C. Gaz.* 13 Pt. I, 1390, 1588 (2008).

83. See 132 *C. Gaz.* 11 Pt. I, 553 (1998); 133 *C. Gaz.* 21 Pt. II, 2355 (1999); 138 *C. Gaz.* 50 Pt. I, 3714 (2004); 140 *C. Gaz.* 24 Pt. I, 1601 (2006); 142 *C. Gaz.* 13 Pt. II, 1390, 1588 (2008).

84. Ron A. Bouchard, Richard W. Hawkins, Robert Clark, Ray Hagtvedt, and Jamil Sawani, 'Empirical Analysis of Drug Approval–Drug Patenting Linkage for High Value Pharmaceuticals,' 8 *NW. J. Tech. & Int. Prop.* 174 (2010) [Bouchard et al. (2010)].

85. *Graham* v. *John Deere Co.*, 383 US 1, 8 (1966); *KSR Int'l* v. *Teleflex, Inc.*, 550 US 398 (2007); *Whirlpool Corp.* v. *Camco, Inc.*, [2000] 2 SCR 1067 (Can.). For general discussion, see Ron A. Bouchard, '*KSR v. Teleflex* Part 1: Impact of U.S [*sic*] Supreme Court Patent Law on Canadian Intellectual Property and Regulatory Rights Landscape,' 15 *Health L.J.* 221 (2007) [Bouchard, '*KSR* Part 1' (2007)].

86. *Farbwerke Hoechst Aktiengesellschaft Vormals Meister Lucius & Bruning* v. *Comm'r of Patents* [1966] SCR 604 (Can.).

87. 140 *C. Gaz.* 24 Pt. I, 1598 (2006).

88. *Whirlpool*, [2000] 2 SCR at § 37 (Can.). See also *Free World Trust* v. *Électro Santé Inc.*, [2000] 2 SCR 1024, § 13 (Can.).

89. *AstraZeneca Canada Inc.* v. *Canada (Minister of Health)*, [2006] 2 SCR 550, § 23 (Can.).

90. Ibid., at § 39.

91. Ibid.

92. Ibid., at §§ 29–30.

93. Ibid., at § 39.

94. *Bell ExpressVu Ltd.* v. *Rex*, [2002] SCR 42, § 10 (Can.).

95. *Biolyse Pharma Corp.* v. *Bristol-Myers Squibb Co.*, [2005] 1 SCR 533, §§ 65–7 (Can.).

96. *Free World Trust* v. *Électro Santé Inc.*, [2000] 2 SCR 1024, § 42 (Can.).

97. 138 *C. Gaz.* 50 Pt. 1, 3712 (2004).

98. 140 *C. Gaz.* 24 Pt. 1, 1598, 1611–12 (2006). The government specifically stipulated that:

> [A] temporal connection between the invention sought to be protected and the product sought to be approved. This ensures that patents for inventions discovered after the existence of a product do not pre-empt generic competition on that product. Similarly, the relevance requirement limits the protection of the PM (NOC) Regulations to that which the innovator has invested time and money to test and have approved for sale. This prevents hypothetical innovation from impeding generic market entry and encourages innovators to bring their latest inventions to market. Finally, in only allowing patents to be listed which contain claims for the medicine or its use, the subject matter requirement makes it clear that innovations

> without direct therapeutic application, such as processes or intermediates, do not merit the special enforcement protection of the PM (NOC) Regulations. (Ibid., at 1612–13)

99. *Minutes of Proceedings and Evidence of the Legislative Committee on Bill C-91*, 34: 8 Parliament of Canada, 8: 37 (December 1, 1992).
100. *Free World Trust* v. *Électro Santé Inc.*, [2000] 2 SCR 1024, § 42 (Can.). The court states:

> The patent system is designed to advance research and development and to encourage broader economic activity. Achievement of these objectives is undermined however if competitors fear to tread in the vicinity of the patent because its scope lacks a reasonable measure of precision and certainty. A patent of uncertain scope becomes 'a public nuisance' . . .

R.C.A. Photophone, Ltd. v. *Gaumont-British Picture Corp.* (1936), 53 RPC 167, 195 (Eng. CA):

> Potential competitors are deterred from working in areas that are not in fact covered by the patent even though costly and protracted litigation (which in the case of patent disputes can be very costly and protracted indeed) might confirm that what the competitors propose to do is entirely lawful. Potential investment is lost or otherwise directed. Competition is 'chilled'. The patent owner is getting more of a monopoly than the public bargained for. There is a high economic cost attached to uncertainty and it is the proper policy of patent law to keep it to a minimum. (Ibid.)

101. See, generally, Cameron Hutchinson, 'Which *Kraft* of Statutory Interpretation? A Supreme Court of Canada Trilogy on Intellectual Property Law,' 46 *Alberta L. Rev.* 1 (2008) [Hutchinson (2008)].
102. Ibid., at 7.
103. Sullivan (2002), *supra* note 50.
104. Hutchinson (2008), *supra* note 101, at 7.
105. Ibid., at 7–8.
106. Ibid., at 27 (citing William N. Eskridge, Philip P. Frickey, and Elizabeth Garrett, *Legislation and Statutory Interpretation*, 2nd edn (Foundation Press, 2006), at 221–30), suggesting that statutes may evolve in ways contrary to or against the initial intent, allowing for an adaptive assessment of the validity of a law against contemporary evidence of its operation or functioning.
107. John H. Miller and Scott E. Page, *Complex Adaptive Systems: An Introduction to Computational Models of Social Life* (Princeton University Press, 2007):

> In a complicated world, the various elements that make up the system maintain a degree of independence from one another. Thus, removing one such element [which reduces the level of complication] does not fundamentally alter the system's behavior apart from that which directly resulted from the piece that was removed. Complexity arises when the dependencies among

> the elements become important. In such a system, removing one such element destroys system behavior to an extent that goes well beyond what is embodied by the particular element that is removed. Complexity is a deep property of a system, whereas complication is not. (p. 9)

108. Feedback interactions in complex systems have received increased attention in recent years. See, generally, Albert-Laszlo Barabási, *Linked: How Everything Is Connected to Everything Else and What It Means for Business, Science, and Everyday Life* (Plume, 2003) (investigating the role of feedback in biological and social networks, including corporations and living organisms, producing system fitness); James Gleick, *Chaos: Making a New Science* (Viking, 1987); John H. Holland, *Adaptation in Natural and Artificial Systems* (MIT Press, 1992) (1975) [Holland (1992)]; John H. Holland, *Hidden Order: How Adaptation Builds Complexity* (Addison-Wesley, 1995) [Holland (1995)]; Steven Johnson, *Emergence: The Connected Lives of Ants, Brains, Cities, and Software* (Scribner, 2001); Stuart Kauffman, *At Home in the Universe: The Search for the Laws of Self-Organization and Complexity* (Viking, 1995); Grégoire Nicolis and Ilya Prigogine, *Exploring Complexity: An Introduction* (W.H. Freeman, 1989); M. Mitchell Waldrop, *Complexity: The Emerging Science at the Edge of Order and Chaos* (Simon & Schuster, 1992); Brian W. Arthur, 'Positive Feedbacks in the Economy,' 262 *Sci. Am.* 92, 92–9 (1990).
109. Bouchard et al. (2009), *supra* note 23; Ron A. Bouchard, '*KSR v. Teleflex* Part 2: Impact of U.S [*sic*] Supreme Court Patent Law on Canadian and Global Systems-Based Innovation Ecologies,' 15 *Health L.J.* 247, 274 (2007); Ron A. Bouchard, 'Living Separate and Apart is Never Easy: Inventive Capacity of the PHOSITA as the Tie that Binds Obviousness and Inventiveness in Pharmaceutical Litigation,' 4 *Ottawa L. & Tech. J.* 1 (2007); Ron A. Bouchard, 'Reflections on the Value of Systems Models for Regulation of Medical Research and Product Development,' 17 *Health L. Rev.* 30, 32 (2008).
110. Hutchinson (2008), *supra* note 104, at 7–8 (citing Randal N. Graham, *Statutory Interpretation: Theory and Practice* (E. Montgomery Publications, 2001), 31).
111. Hutchinson (2008), *supra* note 104, at 7.
112. Ibid., at 21.
113. Lon L. Fuller, *Anatomy of the Law* (Praeger, 1968) [Fuller, *Anatomy* (1968)]; Lon L. Fuller, 'Positivism and Fidelity to Law – A Reply to Professor Hart,' 71 *Harv. L. Rev.* 630, 667 (1958) [Fuller, 'Fidelity' (1958)]. For a discussion of Fuller's work in the context of intellectual property litigation, see Hutchinson (2008), *supra* note 104, at 22–4.
114. See Fuller, *Anatomy* (1968), *supra* note 113, at 5 (emphasis added). As noted by Hutchinson, '[t]he process of interpreting a statute is not just drawing out what legislators put into it but adjusting the statute to the implicit demands and values of the society to which it is to be applied' (see Hutchinson (2008), *supra* note 104, at 24 n. 129). 'In this sense it may be said that no enacted law ever comes from its legislator wholly and fully "made"' (ibid.).

115. Hutchinson (2008), *supra* note 104, at 23 (referring to Fuller, 'Fidelity' (1958), *supra* note 113, at 668).
116. Hutchinson (2008), *supra* note 104.
117. Virtually every domestic legal commentator and lawyer writing or litigating this issue has referenced the *Merck* court's description of the NOC Regulations as 'draconian.' See *Merck Frosst Canada Inc.* v. *Canada* [1998] 2 SCR 193, § 33 (Can.).
118. *Roche Prods. Inc.* v. *Bolar Pharmaceutical Co.*, 733 F.2d 858 (EDNY 1984).
119. *Biolyse Pharma Corp.* v. *Bristol-Myers Squibb Co.*, [2005] 1 SCR 533 (Can.).
120. *AstraZeneca Canada Inc. v. Canada (Minister of Health)*, [2006] 2 SCR 550 (Can.).
121. Edward Hore, 'Patently Absurd: Evergreening of Pharmaceutical Patent Protection under the Patented Medicines (Notice of Compliance) Regulations of Canada's Patent Act' (2004), online: <http://www.canadiangenerics.ca/en/news/docs/patently_absurd_04.pdf>; Andrew A. Caffrey, III and Jonathan M. Rotter, 'Consumer Protection, Patents and Procedure: Generic Drug Market Entry and the Need to Reform the Hatch-Waxman Act,' 9 *Va. J.L. & Tech.* 1, 13, § 27 (2004); Edward Hore, 'A Comparison of U.S. and Canadian Laws as They Affect Generic Pharmaceutical Entry,' 55 *Food & Drug L.J.* 373 (1999–2000). For an update of these numbers, see, generally, *Pharmaceuticals: Analyzing Litigation Success Rates,* RBC Capital Markets, Industry Comment, January 15, 2010; C. Scott Hemphill and Mark A. Lemley, *Earning Exclusivity: Generic Drug Incentives and the Hatch-Waxman Act*, Stanford Law and Economics Olin Working Paper No. 405, Columbia Law and Economics Working Paper No. 391, 2011, available at <http://papers.ssrn.com/sol3/papers.cfm?abstract_id=1736822>. For a discussion of parallel rates of litigation and findings of invalidity in the EU, see European Commission Pharmaceutical Sector Inquiry Final Report, July 8, 2009 and the European Commission Pharmaceutical Sector Inquiry Preliminary Report, November 28, 2008.
122. 142 C. *Gaz.* 13 Pt. II, 1390 (2008) (clarifying judicial rulings on topic in 2006 by the Supreme Court of Canada in *AstraZeneca* and the Federal Court of Appeal in *Wyeth Canada* v. *ratiopharm, inc.*, [2008] 1 FCR 447 (Can.)).
123. Ron A. Bouchard and Monika Sawicka, 'The Mud and the Blood and the Beer: Canada's Progressive Licensing Framework for Drug Approval,' 3 *McGill J.L. & Health* 49, 51 (2009) [Bouchard and Sawicka (2009)].
124. *Biolyse Pharma Corp.* v. *Bristol-Myers Squibb Co.*, [2005] 1 SCR 533, § 45 (Can.) (citing *Apotex* Inc. v. Canada, [1994] 1 FC 742 (Can.), aff'd [1994] 3 SCR 1100 (Can.)).
125. See, generally, Bouchard and Sawicka (2009), *supra* note 123.
126. R.A. Bouchard, D. Cahoy, B. Domeij, G. Dutfield, T. Faunce, A. Hollis, P. Jones, F. Ali Khader, J. Lexchin, H. Nam, and J.L. Serrano, 'Structure-Function Analysis of Global Pharmaceutical Linkage Regulations,' *Minnesota Journal of Law, Science & Technology* 12(2): 1–60 (2011 in press).

7

Future directions: testable hypotheses and evolution toward global pharmaceutical linkage*

Abstract: This chapter wraps up the book by proposing a series of testable hypotheses based on findings up to this point and reviews the global evolution of pharmaceutical linkage. A cluster-based theory of drug development is developed based on our empirical observations gauged against loopholes in linkage laws that allow for the clustering of numerous drug products and related patents over time. The chapter ends with a description of the author's participation in a global study of pharmaceutical linkage. A major goal of this work is to investigate the structural and functional aspects of different systems of pharmaceutical linkage in different jurisdictions, and their relationship on the one hand to drug availability costs and expenditures, and incentives for innovation and protection of intellectual property rights on the other.

Keywords: cluster-based drug development, global pharmaceutical linkage, structure-function analysis

There are two aspects to the final chapter. The first is to propose a series of testable hypotheses for future empirical research regarding linkage-based drug development and the implications thereof for generic entry and access to essential medications. A second is to identify a framework for the analysis of global pharmaceutical linkage as these regimes exist independently and the manner in which they combine to form a global regulatory framework.

---

* This chapter is based upon material in R.A. Bouchard, 'I'm Still Your Baby: Canada's Continuing Support of U.S. Linkage Regulations for Pharmaceuticals,' *Marquette Intellectual Property Law Review* 15(1): 79–146 (2011).

First, a theory for linkage-based pharmaceutical innovation is developed, whereby discrete provisions in linkage laws allow for the development of 'product clusters.' These clusters are comprised of an evolving number of follow-on over time drugs centered on a single or small number of new and innovative drug(s). Products are surrounded by a constellation of patents which are interconnected between products by a combination of traditional infringement law and newer forms of linkage laws.

The second hypothesis is that changes in drug approval, patenting, patent listing, and other related metrics over time can be incorporated into a series of three-dimensional (3-D) spatio-temporal models. Models of this nature would allow for the visual identification and quantification of product clusters and the manner in which they evolve over time to chill generic entry.

A third hypothesis is proposed whereby the most innovative products are not associated with the greatest number of drug approvals, drug patents, or related chemical components, as currently anticipated under many theories of patenting. Rather, an alternative scenario is proposed where the most innovative drugs begin their lifecycle with very few associated approvals and related patents and grow only with vetting by regulators and the market over time into progressively larger and less innovative product clusters.

A fourth and related hypothesis is articulated whereby product clusters may, under certain conditions, yield a 'paradoxical drug approval-drug patenting linkage,' where the largest scope of market exclusivity (and hence delayed generic entry) is associated with the lowest degree of innovation.

The author is also participating in a global study of pharmaceutical linkage regulation. In the second portion of the chapter, a novel 'structure-function' framework for the analysis of global linkage regulations is outlined, along with potential lessons for jurisdictions that already have or are contemplating bringing in some form of pharmaceutical linkage.

7.1 Hypotheses regarding cluster-based drug development

7.1.1 Hypothesis I

The data, law and policy reviewed in this book demonstrate that pharmaceutical linkage creates a specific and empirically observable legal nexus between drug approval, drug patents, and patent litigation. As illustrated by the results reviewed in Chapters 3–5 above, the nature and scope of this nexus can profoundly shape market entry for brand-name and generic drugs, and thus access to essential medications. The scope of the legal nexus between patent law and food and drug law depends on at least four discrete mechanisms provided for by law: (1) the type of drug submission; (2) the type of drug patent; (3) the legal standard for patent listing; and (4) how many patents are listed on the patent register. As such, the nexus can be broad (weak) or narrow (specific). The lower the evidentiary standard for new or follow-on drug approval, the easier patents are to come by, the easier it is to list patents on the patent register, and the more patents that can be listed on the patent register, the weaker the legal nexus between approval and patenting.

The first testable hypothesis is that the discrete legal mechanisms underpinning the linkage regime as they operate in tandem with the evidentiary requirements for drug approval provide an excellent vehicle for the development of 'product clusters.' The cluster model grew out of our analysis of the convergent and linear patent tree methodologies used for analyzing multi-generational drug families such as those illustrated in Figures 7.1 and 7.2. As discussed below in the context of Figure 7.3, the patent tree analysis was modified to include not only a time element (Δ time)

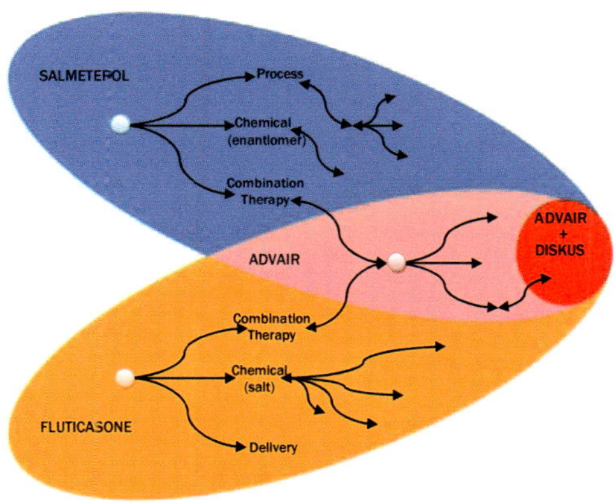

Figure 7.1 Example of convergent patent tree analysis for fourth-generation product Advair Diskus®.

Patents were identified using the specific and general search strings described in Chapter 5. In addition to quantifying patents per drug, the patent tree method allows assessment of how specific drugs evolve into related drug forms or (in this case) drug products representing combinations of known drugs. In addition, the analysis allows for identification of relevant patent types based on the classification nomenclature described in Chapters 2–4. Finally, the analysis is open to the inclusion of data relating to the type of patents granted to pharmaceutical companies (Chapter 5) as well as the listing of such patents on the patent register in order to prevent generic entry (Chapters 4–5).

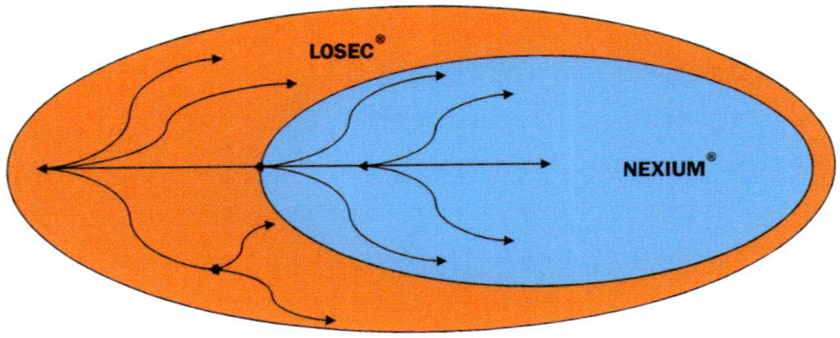

Figure 7.2 Example of linear patent tree analysis for second-generation product Nexium®.

Patents were identified using the same specific and general search strings and have the same advantages and properties as the 'convergent patent tree' illustrated in Figure 7.1.

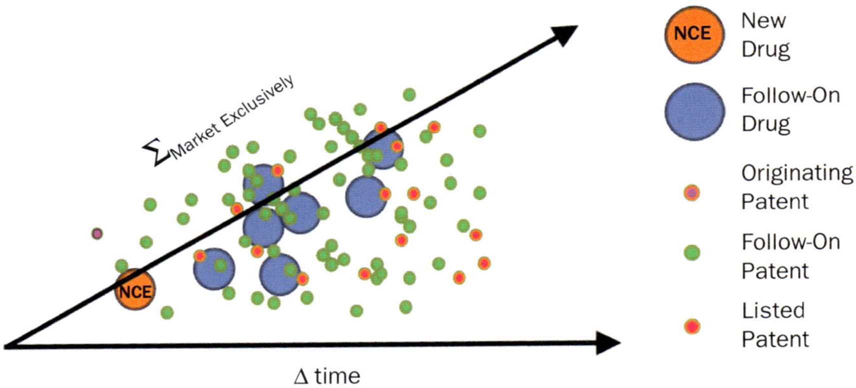

Figure 7.3 Hypothetical product cluster-based model of drug development.

Product clusters begin at some point in time with the first new and innovative drug (•; NCE) and associated originating patent (•). With time, and vetting by the market and regulators, further follow-on drug approvals (•) and patents (•) are granted within the cluster, and an increasing number of these patents are listed on the patent register (•). Listed patents can be used increasingly over time to prohibit generic entry not only on the originating new and innovative drug, but also on all drugs in the cluster that are deemed under law to be relevant to the originating drug.

but also a cumulative market exclusivity element ($\Sigma_{\text{Market Exclusivity}}$) and provision for listing patents on the patent register.

As illustrated in Figure 7.3, product clusters are hypothesized to be comprised of an expanding number of new and follow-on drugs over time centered on a single new and original drug. Products in the cluster are surrounded by a constellation of patents, all of which are interconnected between products within a given cluster through different forms of patent law. These patents serve two primary functions. First, they provide support for follow-on drug development within the cluster via traditional infringement law operating in tandem with food and drug laws. Second, via newer forms of linkage laws, they provide fodder for listing on the patent register in order to delay generic entry. Importantly, generic entry may be delayed not only for the original new and innovative drug, but also for all other follow-on drugs in the cluster for which the patents are deemed legally relevant.

The capacity of product clusters to delay generic entry is a *specific function* of patent law operating in conjunction with linkage law and food and drug law. The greater the number of patents granted, the greater the number of new and follow-on drugs approved, the greater the scope of patent classifications per patent, the greater the number of patents permitted to be listed on the patent register, and the lower the relevance standard for listing patents against a given reference product, the greater the ability of patents to support a long-term product cluster. It is expected of course that different clusters will have different spatio-temporal characteristics, for example whether they represent clustering within or between brand-name firms or whether there is a single or small number of truly new and innovative drugs per cluster. Having said this, the clustering effect of follow-on drugs and associated patents and listed patents over time remains a central theme.

Perhaps more importantly, our data suggest that it may be the *sum* of the interactions between multiple drugs and multiple patents in clusters over time that most effectively chills generic entry and increases public health costs. As noted by Kingston,[1] rational investment in a portfolio of relatively high-risk products becomes increasingly so in the pharmaceutical sector when the risk attaching to the portfolio as a whole is statistically lower than that of the more risky individual components. Such investments are even more attractive when patents are easier to come by and defend, and where drug development strategy is focused on rational drug design rather than drug screening. Patent portfiolios have also been described by Polk Wagner and Parchomovsky,[2] who observed that the right to exclude conferred by a collection of related patents under common control is essentially equivalent to the sum of individual patent rights.[3]

Our findings are consistent with the notion of patent portfolios, and extend the concept to include not only patents, but also multiple clusters of patents and related products and patent listing. Our data support the conclusion that such clusters arise as a function of food and drug law operating in conjunction with traditional patent law and newer forms of linkage laws. Similar observations have been made in the European Union where certain provisions in domestic patent laws and food and drug laws of Member States have been effectively gamed by brand firms to create a kind of 'ghost linkage' system of drug regulation.[4] Given that linkage allows firms to do formally (and up front) what they must expend greater time and resources to do informally (around the back end) in jurisdictions without linkage, it may be said that pharmaceutical linkage may well present the 'path of least resistance' to cluster-based drug development. This helps to understand why similar patent and drug development strategies are being leveraged in jurisdictions with and without linkage regimes; nations cannot simply opt out of effective linkage without going out of their way to ensure systems of ghost linkage are not permitted.

The convergence of results of this nature in Canada, the United States, the European Union and other nations suggests that cluster-based drug development has become an increasingly entrenched component of the global innovation landscape relating to pharmaceuticals. In this light, it would be valuable to develop an evidence-based model of innovation under linkage laws (as well as in jurisdictions with ghost linkage) that empirically identifies the scope of functional legal linkages between different drugs, patents, and listed patents in product clusters, and how these linkages combine (and re-combine) over time to potentially alter drug development, drug pricing and reimbursement, the timing of generic entry, and access to essential medications.

7.1.2 Hypothesis II

A major advantage of the product cluster model is that there is, in fact, considerable empirical evidence available for study, including the various types of new and follow-on drugs, patents, patent classifications, listed patents, related litigation, as well as the relation of these metrics to one another over time. This wide array of empirically observable metrics and the observation that they change over time sets up the possibility that, akin to the development of 3-D models of protein folding and X-ray crystallography, the data can be expressed in the form of 3-D spatio-temporal models. Analogous to models in the basic medical sciences, product cluster models should allow stakeholders such as politicians, law-makers, the judiciary, and scholars to first identify and then track the evolution of product clusters over time, with regard to both their structure and function. In this manner, 'rotational' 3-D cluster models would be particularly useful to enable visual and numerical quantification of the impact of clustering on drug development, generic entry, and access to essential medications in the same manner that one might look at a car from behind (highlighting the 'gas tank,' or original drug product and associated patent tandems) as well as from the side (from the rear to the front of the vehicle, underscoring how and when approvals, patents, and listed patents increase over time with market and regulator vetting).

In a best-case scenario, product clustering data could be paired with objective evidence of the level of innovation and social benefit associated with various follow-on drugs in the cluster, allowing for weighted algorithms to be created for pricing and reimbursement purposes. Such algorithms may also provide an evidence-based empirical indicator of the need by governments to fund high-risk research and development activities by pharmaceutical companies. As with any good tool, the knowledge gained from this type of analysis has the potential to help all relevant stakeholders in the public health arena in the exercise of their various mandates.

7.1.3 Hypothesis III

A third testable hypothesis emanating from the work reviewed in Chapters 3–5 relates to the evolution of product clusters over time, particularly with respect to the level of innovation associated with growing clusters of pharmaceutical products and patents. Up to this point in time the majority of pharmaceutical policies and certainly the lobbying efforts of multinational drug companies have been focused on the incentives provided for high-risk drug development in the form of patent rights. In order to assess innovation, most studies and government reports over the last two to three decades have employed methods for counting patents, prior art cites and related litigation statistics, but a coherent evidence-based model for qualifying intellectual property associated with pharmaceutical products has not yet been articulated.

Using data such as those described in Chapters 3 and 4, we have made strides towards developing a qualitative innovation index for pharmaceuticals.[5] The index reflects the drug development priorities identified by Canadian and other federal and regional drug regulators over the last decade. The index is also intended to reflect the height of the evidentiary hurdles over which brand and generic drug companies much step in order to successfully obtain regulatory approval for the various types of new and follow-on drug classes elaborated in Chapters 3–5.

One of the implications of our preliminary results is that the greatest number of drugs approved and patents associated with these drugs are in classes with very low levels of innovation (line extension drugs (SNDS), and in particular SNDS me-too drugs). This is not surprising given the data in Chapters 3 and 4, particularly the very low levels of truly innovative drugs described using the methodology developed in Chapter 4. What is surprising, however, is that the most innovative drugs have by far the lowest, rather than the highest, number of patents and related chemical components. Thus the greatest numbers of approvals and associated patents are awarded for the products with the lowest levels of innovation. Conversely, the lowest number of approvals and associated patents are associated with products with the highest innovation index values. This can be seen in the preliminary data for approvals for a cohort of 2,087 drugs presented in Figure 7.4. Data are represented by symbols, showing an exponential decline in the number of drugs approved in higher innovation index bins. The drugs clusters denoted 'on deck', 'at bat', and 'home run' represent a theoretical mock-up of how drug clusters grow in time from a spatio-temporal perspective. These results are somewhat surprising, as traditional patent theory would suggest that the greater the level of innovation associated with a given product, the greater should be its level of intellectual property protection and social development.

As noted above, the empirical results reviewed in this book taken in combination with theoretical and empirical studies conducted on drug and patent clusters in the United States and European Union suggest that cluster-based innovation may be an increasing feature of the innovation

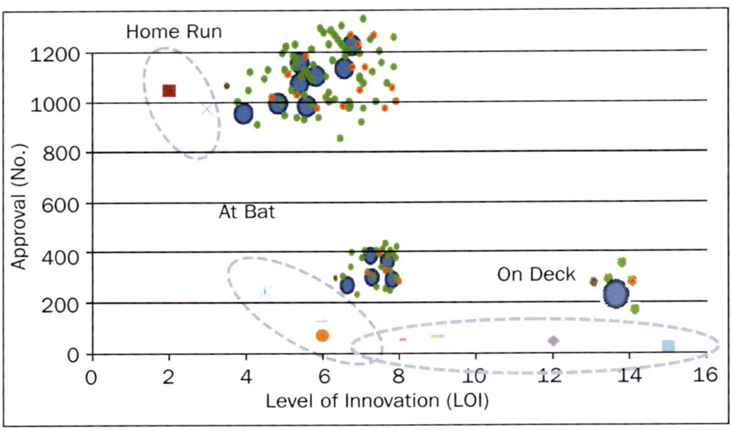

Figure 7.4 Hypothetical cluster-based drug development and hedging.

Product clusters are hypothesized to begin life at the most innovative end of the spectrum, with few patents and a small or negligible number of listed patents. Over time, and increased vetting by regulators and the market, the cluster expands to include more products, patents and listed patents but, as a whole becomes less and less innovative. The desired end point (the 'home run') is a substantial but low-level cluster with numerous products, patents and listed patents, and the widest scope of market exclusivity and cumulative patent protection. Prior to this point, clusters are 'at bat,' as they reach a critical state prior to moving into an expanded spatio-temporal state or merely 'on deck' as firms await critical regulator and market vetting.

landscape relating to pharmaceuticals. A primary characteristic of cluster-based drug development is that clusters must begin their spatio-temporal growth at some point in time. Given this necessity, a third testable hypothesis is to investigate whether, as illustrated in Figure 7.4, product clusters begin their life as single-drug products or small groupings at the most innovative end of the index and, with increased vetting of products in the cluster over time by regulators and the market, grow in scope to encompass an increasing number of products and patents. As this occurs, the cluster may be anticipated to 'swing up and to the left' of the innovation index, moving from a high level of innovation with a low number of patents and listed patents to first a moderate and then a much lower level of innovation but with greater spatio-temporal characteristics.

If borne out by empirical data, an emphasis by pharmaceutical firms on cluster-based product development would represent a comparatively risk-averse form of hedging by pharmaceutical firms, hence its identification with patent portfiolos rather than the high-risk/high-reward innovation that is desired by the public and presumably is at the heart of the patent bargain. As suggested in Chapter 5, we argue that the pharmaceutical linkage regime not only represents the path of least resistance to product clusters, but that this scenario has developed as a result of firms aiming *ex ante* at legal targets which provide the most return on investment rather than the most benefit to the public where the two do not coincide. The legal target is offered by the unique overlap between patent law and food and drug law in the form of pharmaceutical linkage, more specifically the iterative effect of the ease of obtaining (1) patents, (2) new and follow-on drug approvals, and (3) patent listing on the patent register.

7.1.4 Hypothesis IV

The fourth, and final, testable hypothesis is that product clusters may have particular relevance for loopholes within the linkage regime that allow for what was referred to in Chapter 5 as a 'paradoxical approval-patent linkage.' The paradoxical nature of the drug approval-drug patenting nexus refers to the situation where multiple line extensions occur within a cluster that in turn are allowed, via a combination of the multiple patent listing provision under linkage law and low evidentiary standard of approval for new and follow-on drugs under food and drug law, to extend market exclusivity not only on the original new drug form, but also on all other chemically related drug forms against which they may be listed on the patent register over time.

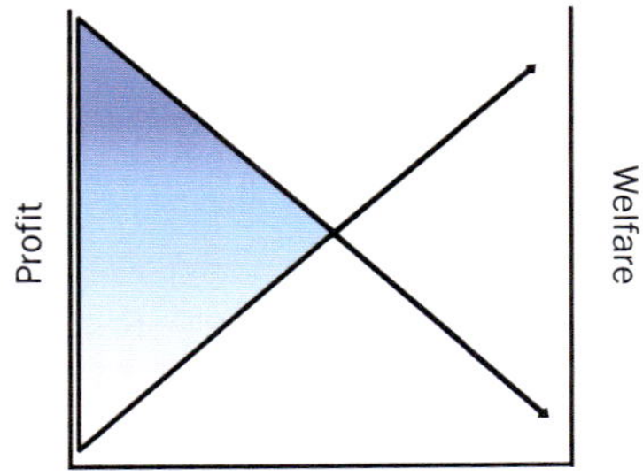

Figure 7.5 Paradoxical drug approval-drug patenting nexus.

Left and right axes represent increases (profit) and decreases (welfare) in firm profits and public welfare resulting from an increase in market exclusivity associated follow-on drug product clusters as the number of line extensions and cumulative patent protection for the product cluster increase. Both profit and public welfare are assumed for the sake of simplicity to change linearly from the origin. The upward arrow represents profit whereas the downward arrow represents public welfare. The graph indicates that increases in the duration of market exclusivity (and hence monopoly pricing) on drug clusters with little public welfare benefit yield an increasingly paradoxical relationship between the scope of patent protection per cluster and the degree of social benefit associated with that protection.

As illustrated in Figure 7.5, as the number of follow-on drugs in the cluster grows over time, so too does cumulative market exclusivity and innovator firm profit. The maximum point of inefficiency occurs when the product cluster has a very long duration of cumulative market exclusivity with little or no therapeutic benefit to the larger population compared with the original pioneering drug on which the cluster is based. This is referred to as the most 'paradoxical' drug approval-drug patenting nexus from a public policy perspective because the two goals of pharmaceutical linkage are to increase the production of new and innovative drugs and to facilitate timely generic entry. Both goals are frustrated with increased market exclusivity on poorly innovative clusters. Any move away from the point where the special provisions of pharmaceutical linkage to provide enhanced intellectual property protection for older blockbuster drugs is no longer balanced by a proportional benefit to society under the patent bargain is thus deemed to be paradoxical.[6] There is some analogy here to the dead weight loss problem for pharmaceutical products that are largely the result of publicly funded medical research conducted by university researchers.[7] Given that empirical data are only beginning to be reported, this clustering effect may present a more substantial barrier to generic entry than previously recognized, and it is not clear whether generics are being adequately compensated for taking on the risk of litigation.

An important element of empirical work on product clusters as described here and elsewhere will be to assess clustering data before and after critical amendments to linkage laws, such as those aimed at reducing the automatic stay from many to one per reference product and narrowing the scope of listable patents from those generally on a marketed drug to those only relevant to the specific drug submission against which they are listed. This will allow law-makers and other stakeholders to assess the legal, economic, and public policy efficacy of discrete law reform efforts.

7.2 Globalization of pharmaceutical linkage

As noted at the outset in Chapter 1, prompt and affordable access to essential medicines is a significant component of most domestic and global models of public health. The availability and costs of new and generic drugs is a function of traditional patent law incentives and emerging linkage regulations.[8] Patent law is a well described,[9] if controversial,[10] 'policy lever' for stimulating the development of new drugs.[11] As discussed throughout this book, linkage regulations tie generic drug availability to existing drug patents by connecting approval to the resolution of patent validity or infringement,[12] potentially resulting in long and costly litigation.[13] While the patent system has been in operation for about 500 years,[14] the linkage regime has only been in existence for about 25 years following the passage of the Hatch-Waxman Act in the United States in 1984[15] and the Canadian NOC Regulations in 1993.[16] Importantly, the objective of linkage in both originating jurisdictions was to balance the competing policy goals of stimulating the development of new and innovative drugs and the timely entry of generic drugs.[17]

Based on the above, we see that, especially when compared to the patent system, the linkage regime represents a novel and emerging intellectual property paradigm for protecting pharmaceutical inventions. Even so, by 2011, we are witnessing the rapid spread of the linkage regime on a global level. This is due to the rapidly escalating growth in the number of multilateral and bilateral free trade agreements with the US.[18] These agreements often require participating nations to incorporate linkage and other intellectual property provisions in exchange for preferential trade terms.[19] As many such agreements are negotiated outside the purview of the World Trade Organization (WTO) and provide stronger intellectual property protection for drugs than does TRIPS, they are often referred to as 'TRIPS-Plus.'[20] Suggestive of the strength of the multinational pharmaceutical lobby, the European Commission (EC) has recently reported numerous instances where member nations have attempted to institute pharmaceutical linkage regimes even though EU law prohibits this form of intellectual property law.[21]

The implications of pharmaceutical linkage for global public health are immense. As reviewed in Chapters 3–5 and section 7.1 above, there is growing empirical evidence to suggest that pharmaceutical linkage can substantially extend cumulative patent terms for high-value drugs. These results are consistent with early predictions of the impact of linkage by Schondelmeyer,[22] based on his work with the originating US regime.[23] An additional concern is that the extension of market exclusivity on brand-name drugs occurs even though up to 50–75% of the patents challenged on the merits may be invalid or not infringed by the generic equivalent.[24] Pharmaceutical linkage creates a conflicting system where governments with linkage regimes that limit the timely appearance of generics also depend on these firms to produce cost-savings and limit the growth in pharmaceutical expenditures.[25] A related issue is that costs of prolonged litigation are known to be passed on to consumers,[26] with differential costs to governments and the public in accordance with their system of drug reimbursement,[27] public health,[28] public-private discourse,[29] and health equity.[30]

Considerations such as the foregoing must, of course, be balanced against the widely accepted need for innovative drugs in developed and developing nations, the presumption favoring the validity of patents in most developed nations,[31] as well as the notion in law that if the state grants a party an exclusive right, it cannot grant another party permission to invade that right without just cause. For this reason the twin policy goals underpinning linkage are said to be 'competing' in nature.

In addition to shaping the marketplace for brand-name and generic drugs, intellectual property protection for pharmaceuticals, including linkage, has become a controversial cog in the global machine of providing individuals with essential medications, in developed[32] as well as in developing[33] nations. Canada, like many developed nations, has attempted to play a key role in the global effort to provide underserved populations with essential medications through its Access to Medicines Regime,[34] but with less success than anticipated.[35] Moreover, and perhaps more importantly, up to this point effort has been focused primarily on the limits of traditional patent law,[36] with emerging forms of patent and other regulatory protection receiving considerably less attention. A related observation is that while the concept of pharmaceutical linkage is relatively new compared to the patent system, there is already significant pressure to broaden it beyond drug approval to include linkage between patent rights and other regulatory aspects of drug approval and marketing.[37]

One of the major implications of the empirical research reviewed from Chapters 3–5 is that inclusion of linkage in a nation's basket of international trade obligations may present a more expansive notion of patent protection for drug products than previously recognized, particularly when gauged against the relatively narrow nexus originally envisaged between drug patents and the marketed products against which they are listed.[38] For example, the EC Pharmaceutical Sector Inquiry[39] has articulated a broad definition of pharmaceutical linkage, including linkage of patent status to the following: formal legal proceedings between parties, patent settlements, interventions before national drug regulators regarding market approval, drug pricing, and reimbursement.[40] An evolving landscape such as this raises the question of whether the pharmaceutical industry is using linkage as an emerging stepping-stone in its efforts to control the movement of drugs across international borders. Moreover, a growing number of legal disputes have been reported whereby countries without linkage regulations have attempted to import or export drugs where shipments are seized by other nations alleging that these shipments are in violation of domestic patent laws linked to international trade instruments,[41] such as TRIPS or other FTAs.[42]

Owing to the confluence of the events reviewed above over time, linkage regulations in respect to therapeutic products have quietly emerged as a key driver of public health costs and medical product regulation on the global stage, both for developed and developing nations.

The author is a member of a global network of intellectual property and health policy scholars, economists, and practicing lawyers , who have come together to study global pharmaceutical linkage regulation.[43] When the group began its work, the obvious question to ask was, what should the focus be of future research on pharmaceutical linkage as it evolves over time from its North American roots? We noted with interest that the study of structure-function relationships in living systems, at both the micro and macro levels, has served the life sciences especially well over the last century. Structure-function analyses in the life sciences have led to numerous key insights into molecular, cellular, tissue, organ, and whole-body functioning over the last half-century. For example, structure-function studies have yielded detailed descriptions of drug, chemical, and hormonal receptors, cell membrane and intracellular constituents, second messenger systems, and chemical and hormonal mediation of intra- and inter-organ function. More recently, functional imaging techniques have revealed a remarkable degree of brain plasticity in the context of congenital and acquired disease states, including under circumstances where dysfunction was previously thought to be permanent.

As demonstrated by pioneering work in general systems theory and systems biology over the last half century, the interaction between structural and functional elements in a system is bi-directional, that is not only does structure influence function, but function also influences structure. As discussed further below, this occurs through various feedback mechanisms. The structure-function paradigm applies fundamentally to law in two ways: first, because governments have specific legal and policy goals in mind when drafting law and regulations, and these goals are expressed in the form of discrete legal and regulatory language; second, because policy goals and the statutory language employed by governments and administrative bodies are reviewable by the courts in judicial review and other proceedings and are often revisited by governments in the context of their law reform efforts.

The rapid spread of pharmaceutical linkage worldwide offers a unique and time-sensitive opportunity to carry out empirical work on the system as it evolves globally from its original locus in North America. A major goal of our work on global pharmaceutical linkage will be to investigate the structural and functional aspects of different systems of linkage regulations, and their relationship on the one hand to drug availability costs, and expenditures, and incentives for innovation and protection of intellectual property rights on the other.

As in other complex political and economic systems,[44] the pharmaceutical linkage system is assumed to have structural and functional characteristics that can be identified and measured, and which in turn can serve as appropriate benchmarks to assess the performance of the system relative to its goals and objectives. Key decision-makers, pharmaceutical firms, the courts, patent counsel, consumers, and other actors are assumed to interact in domestic and global networks through reasonably well defined channels of communication.[45] As in other complex political and economic systems,[46] this network is assumed to have structural and functional characteristics that can be identified and measured, and which in turn serve as appropriate benchmarks to assess the performance of the system relative to its goals and objectives.

The specific basket of legal checks and balances in a given linkage regime is pivotal, as it determines not only how a complex system of pharmaceutical regulation begins operating *de novo* following the coming into force of law, but also how it evolves over time to yield demonstrable empirical results. It has been previously shown, for example, that the behavior of dynamic legal systems,[47] including how systems learn, self-regulate, and adapt and grow,[48] is strongly influenced by positive and negative feedback.[49] Positive feedback is feedback that results in growth or amplification of a particular process or group of related processes whereas negative feedback results in a tamping or slowing of a particular process or group of processes. Studies of complex social, biological, and technological systems have shown that the unintended consequences resulting from feedback have the potential to force a system away from operating at or near the point of efficiency.[50]

The term 'structural' is used to refer to the broad administrative, legal, and policy attributes of the linkage regime in differing jurisdictions as these represent the initial starting conditions for the operation of local linkage regimes. The initial starting conditions, as in dynamical physical systems,[51] represent the sum of the political, economic, and public policy conditions that together form the 'take-off' point for a new law and the conditions in which it begins to operate. The structural aspect also encompasses the specific legal mechanisms that drive the operation of linkage regimes in various jurisdictions. Identifying the structural attributes and mechanisms of individual linkage systems is important, as they provide the benchmark from which to assess the successes and failures of each system in operation and their potential to combine to form a global regulatory regime.

Our work thus far has identified a number of important structural aspects of pharmaceutical linkage, including: assessment in each jurisdiction of the original policy intent underpinning the linkage regime; the manner in which public health policy and economic policy is perceived by governments and the courts to converge or diverge through the linkage vector; the legal checks and balances found within the linkage regime designed specifically to maintain balance between the interests of brand and generic firms; the provisions in addition to linkage that were included in enabling legislation; and the growing expansion of the linkage concept beyond the drug approval-drug patenting nexus to encompass that between patenting and international trade mechanisms as well as how pharmaceutical linkage is in the process of informing the construction of new laws pertaining to follow-on biologics.

By contrast, the term 'functional' is used to refer to the outputs of the regulations in each jurisdiction as well as how they functionally interact across borders to operate as a global regulatory regime. The functional aspects of a system reflect the behavior of the system as it evolves with time away from the initial starting conditions.[52] The functional aspects identified for study include: the impact of linkage regulations on the development of new and innovative drugs; the manner in which this is balanced by the timely entry of generic drugs; the degree to which market exclusivity is or can be extended solely by operation of the linkage regime; how brand firms use the linkage system in order to extend market exclusivity on high-value drugs; the costs to consumers or other payers of extended exclusivity; the costs of extended exclusivity based on patents that are ultimately found to be invalid or not infringed; the impact of differing mechanisms of regulatory oversight on drug pricing and reimbursement; and the role of empirical studies for the legitimacy of linkage regulations.

A significant advantage of a global approach to studying pharmaceutical linkage is that investigating linkage in different jurisdictions allows for both an investigation of the structural and functional characteristics of local linkage regimes with different initial starting conditions and different legal mechanisms of operation, and the identification of general rules of linkage as the different national forms of linkage interact and influence global pharmaceutical regulation. The former provides a *descriptive* mechanism for assessing the successes and failures of different regimes, while the latter provides a *prescriptive* approach for key decision-makers to revise, institute, or abolish linkage regulations according to the goals and objectives of differing nations.

Different economic, public health and political systems are expected to present a different set of initial starting conditions not only for the *de novo* operation of linkage regulations in each jurisdiction as they come into force, but also for the manner in which these systems evolve, grow, and adapt to changing conditions over time. Indeed, our research suggests substantial differences between jurisdictions in this regard and that these differences may be fundamentally responsible for the opposition of certain nations to pharmaceutical linkage and the varying degrees of success of those employing them in achieving the twin policy goals of linkage to encourage the development of innovative drugs while also facilitating the timely entry of generic drugs and access to essential medications.

Notes

1. William Kingston, 'Intellectual Property's Problems: How Far Is the US Constitution to Blame?' *Intellectual Property Quarterly* 4, 315–41 (2002).
2. R. Polk Wagner and Gideon Parchomovsky, 'Patent Portfolios,' 154 *University of Pennsylvania Law Review* 1 (2005).
3. Ibid., at 5–6 and 33.
4. *European Commission Pharmaceutical Sector Inquiry*, Final Rep. (EC) July 8, 2009, at 23 [EC Final Rep. (2009)].
5. R.A. Bouchard, 'Qualifying Intellectual Property II: A Novel Innovation Index for Pharmaceutical Products,' 29 *Santa Clara Computer and High Technology Law Journal* 1, 1–78 (in press July 2011); R.A. Bouchard, 'Qualifying Intellectual Property I: Harmonized Measurement of New and Follow-On Drug Approvals, Patents and Chemical Components,' 18 *Boston University Journal of Science and Technology Law* 1, 1–63 (in press July 2011).

6. Ron A. Bouchard, 'I'm Still Your Baby: Canada's Continuing Support of U.S. Linkage Regulations for Pharmaceuticals,' 15(1) *Marquette Intellectual Property Law Review* 1–52 (2011); R.A. Bouchard, D. Cahoy, B. Domeij, G. Dutfield, T. Faunce, A. Hollis, P. Jones, F. Ali Khader, J. Lexchin, H. Nam, and J.L. Serrano, 'Structure-Function Analysis of Global Pharmaceutical Linkage Regulations,' 12 *Minn. J.L. Sci. & Tech.* 2, 397–461 (2011) [Bouchard et al. (2011)]; Andrew A. Caffrey and Jonathan M. Rotter, 'Consumer Protection, Patents and Procedure: Generic Drug Market Entry and the Need to Reform the Hatch-Waxman Act,' 9 *Va. J.L. & Tech.* 1, 4–7 (2004); Mathew Avery, 'Continuing Abuse of the Hatch-Waxman Act by Pharmaceutical Holders and the Failure of the 2003 Amendments,' 60 *Hastings L.J.* 171 (2008–9) [Avery (2008–9)].
7. Ron A. Bouchard and Trudo Lemmens, 'Privatizing Biomedical Research – A Third Way,' 26 *Nature Biotechnology* 31 (2008).
8. For an account of the relationship between patents and drug discovery, development, and marketing from the earliest days of the industry to the present, see, generally, Graham Dutfield, *Intellectual Property Rights and the Life Science Industries: Past, Present and Future*, 2nd edn (World Scientific, 2009).
9. See, generally, Bengt Domeij, *Pharmaceutical Patents in Europe* (Kluwer Law International, 2000); Bengt Domeij, 'Initial and Follow-on Pharmaceutical Inventions in Europe,' in Ove Granstrand (ed.), *Economics, Law and Intellectual Property* (Kluwer Law International, 2003), at 177–98. See also Kenneth Arrow, 'Economic Welfare and the Allocation of Resources for Innovation,' in *The Rate and Direction of Inventive Activity* (UMI, 1962), at 609–26; David Vaver, *Intellectual Property Rights: Critical Concepts in Law* (Routledge, 2006); Dan L. Burk and Mark A. Lemley, 'Policy Levers in Patent Law,' 89 *Va. L. Rev.* 1575 (2003); Robert P. Merges and Richard R. Nelson, 'On the Complex Economics of Patent Scope,' 90 *Colum. L. Rev.* 839 (1990).
10. See, generally, Sheldon Krimsky, *Science in the Private Interest: Has the Lure of Profits Corrupted Biomedical Research?* (Rowman & Littlefield, 2003); Michele Boldrin and David K. Levine, *Against Intellectual Monopoly* (Cambridge University Press, 2008), at 192–6 (finding only 'weak or no evidence' that IP protection increases innovation); Adam B. Jaffe, 'The U.S. Patent System in Transition: Policy Innovation and the Innovation Process,' 29 *Res. Pol'y* 531 (2000); Roberto Mazzoleni and Richard R. Nelson, 'The Benefits and Costs of Strong Patent Protection: A Contribution to the Current Debate,' 27 *Res. Pol'y* 273, 280 (1998); Marcia Angell, *The Truth About the Drug Companies: How They Deceive Us and What to Do About It* (Random House, 2004) [Angell (2004)]; Kevin Outterson, 'Pharmaceutical Arbitrage: Balancing Access and Innovation in International Prescription Drug Markets,' 5 *Yale J. Health Pol'y L. & Ethics* 193 (2005); Michele Boldrin and David K. Levine, *The Economics of Ideas and Intellectual Property*, Staff Report 357 (Federal Reserve Bank of Minneapolis, February 2005) [Boldrin and Levine, *Economics of Ideas* (2005)], at 102; Keith Pavitt, 'Proceedings of the National

Academy of Sciences of the United States of America National Policies for Technical Change: Where Are the Increasing Returns to Economic Research?' 93 *Proc. Nat'l Acad. Sci.* 126 (1996).

11. Ron A. Bouchard, 'Should Scientific Research in the Lead-Up to Invention Vitiate Obviousness Under the Patented Medicines (Notice of Compliance) Regulations: To Test or Not to Test?' 6 *Can. J.L. & Tech.* 1, 1–27 (2007); Ron A. Bouchard, 'Living Separate and Apart is Never Easy: Inventive Capacity of the PHOSITA as the Tie that Binds Obviousness and Inventiveness in Pharmaceutical Litigation,' 4 *Ottawa L. & Tech. J.* 1 (2007); Ron A. Bouchard, '*KSR v. Teleflex* Part 1: Impact of U.S [*sic*] Supreme Court Patent Law on Canadian Intellectual Property and Regulatory Rights Landscape,' 15 *Health L.J.* 221 (2007), at 222–46; Thomas Faunce and Joel Lexchin, '"Linkage" Pharmaceutical Evergreening in Canada and Australia,' *4 Austl. and N.Z. Health Pol'y* 1, 8 (2007); Paul Jones, '*KSR* and the Supreme Court: The Silence is Deafening,' 53 *Antitrust Bulletin* 849 (2008).
12. For a review of Canadian linkage regulations, see Chapter 2. See also Ron A. Bouchard, Richard W. Hawkins, Robert Clark, Ray Hagtvedt, and Jamil Sawani, 'Empirical Analysis of Drug Approval–Drug Patenting Linkage for High Value Pharmaceuticals,' 8 *NW. J. Tech. & Int. Prop.* 174 (2010) [Bouchard et al. (2010)], at 174–227; Ron A. Bouchard, Jamil Sawani, Chris McLelland, Monika Sawicka, and Richard W. Hawkins, 'The Pas de Deux of Pharmaceutical Regulation and Innovation: Who's Leading Whom?' 24 *Berkeley Tech. L.J.* 1461, 1463 n. 2 (2009) [Bouchard et al. (2009)]; Monika Sawicka and Ron A. Bouchard, 'Empirical Analysis of Canadian Drug Approval Data 2001–2008: Are Pharmaceutical Players "Doing More With Less"?' 3 *McGill J.L. & Health* 85 (2009); Joel Lexchin, 'After Compulsory Licensing: Coming Issues in Canadian Pharmaceutical Policy and Politics,' 40 *Health Pol'y* 69 (1997).
13. Boldrin and Levine (2005), *supra* note 10, at 102.
14. Jean O. Lanjouw and William Jack, Brief: 'Trading Up: How Much Should Poor Countries Pay to Support Pharmaceutical Innovation?' 4 *Ctr. for Global Dev.* 1, 1–8 (2004).
15. 21 USC § 355(j)(7)(A) (2006) (establishing a list of 'Approved Drug Products with Therapeutic Equivalence' commonly known as the 'Orange Book'). For a description of US linkage laws, see Gerald Mossinghoff, 'Overview of the Hatch-Waxman Act and Its Impact on the Drug Development Process,' 54 *Food & Drug L.J.* 187–94 (1999); Andrew A. Caffrey, III and Jonathan M. Rotter, 'Consumer Protection, Patents and Procedure: Generic Drug Market Entry and the Need to Reform the Hatch-Waxman Act,' 9 *Va. J.L. & Tech.* 1, 13, § 27 (2004) [Caffrey and Rotter (2004)], at 4–7; Rebecca S. Eisenberg, 'Patents, Product Exclusivity, and Information Dissemination: How Law Directs Biopharmaceutical Research and Development,' 72 *Fordham L. Rev.* 477, 483 (2003); Jeremy Bulow, 'The Gaming of Pharmaceutical Patents,' 4 *Innovation Pol'y and the Economy: Nat'l Bureau of Econ. Res.* (2004) [Bulow

(2004)]; Richard Epstein and Bruce Kuhlik, *Navigating the Anticommons for Pharmaceutical Patents: Steady the Course on Hatch-Waxman*, n. 24 (Univ. of Chi. L. & Econ., Working Paper No. 209, 2004) (citing Congressional Record – Senate at 23764 (August 10, 1984); Avery (2008–9), *supra* note 6.

16. Patented Medicines (Notice of Compliance) Regulations SOR/1993-133 (Can.). For early descriptions of Canadian linkage law, see, for example, Robert Tancer, 'Foreign Investment in North America and the Pharmaceutical Industry in Canada,' *The Int'l Exec.*, March/April 1997, at 283; Christopher Scott Harrison, 'Protection of Pharmaceuticals as Foreign Policy: The Canada-U.S. Trade Agreement and Bill C-22 Versus the North American Free Trade Agreement and Bill C-91,' 26 *N.C. J. Int'l L. & Com. Reg.* 457, 460 (2000–1) [Harrison, 'Protection' (2000–1)]; Edward Hore, 'Patently Absurd: Evergreening of Pharmaceutical Patent Protection Under the Patented Medicines (Notice of Compliance) Regulations of Canada's Patent Act (2004) [Hore (2004)], online: <http://www.canadiangenerics.ca/en/news/docs/patently_absurd_04.pdf>.
17. Avery (2008–9), *supra* note 6; Bouchard et al. (2010), *supra* note 12.
18. Carlos María Correa, 'Implications of Bilateral Free Trade Agreements on Access to Medicines,' 84 *Bull. of the World Health Org.* (2006) [Correa (2006)], 399–404; Judit Rius Sanjuan, 'Patent-Registration Linkage,' Discussion Paper – No. 2 (Consumer Project on Tech.), April 3, 2006, at 1, online: <http://www.cptech.org/publications/CPTechDPNo2Linkage.pdf>; *Overview on Patent Linkage*, Consulting Report (Finston Consulting, LLC) August 7, 2006, at 1, online: <http://www.finstonconsulting.com/version03/files/Overview.pdf> (UK Consulting Report).
19. Tomas Alured Faunce, 'Global Intellectual Property Protection for Innovative Pharmaceuticals: Challenges for Bioethics and Health Law,' in *Globalisation and Health* (2006), 87–108; Tomas Alured Faunce and Kathy Shats, 'Bilateral Trade Agreements as Drivers of National and Transnational Benefit from Health Technology Policy: Implications of Recent US Deals for Australian Negotiations with China and India,' 62 *Austl. J. of Int'l Aff.* 196–213 (2008).
20. Correa, *supra* note 18, at 401.
21. EC Final Rep. (2009), *supra* note 4, at 23. This theme is developed extensively in the European Commission Pharmaceutical Sector Inquiry Preliminary Report. See *European Commission Pharmaceutical Sector Inquiry*, Preliminary Rep. (EPO) October 3, 2008, at 14, 113 [EC Preliminary Rep. (2008)].
22. Dr Stephen Schondelmeyer, a pharmacologist and health economist, gave evidence before the House of Commons to the effect that it is not the term of single patents that mattered most, but rather how patents add cumulatively to extend market exclusivity, a claim the government at the time vigorously denied. Compare the testimony of Dr Stephen Schondelmeyer (Professor, University of Minnesota) and Dr Elizabeth Dickson (Director General, Chemical and Bio-Industries Branch, Department of Industry, Science and Technology), *Minutes of Proceedings and Evidence of the Legislative Committee*

on Bill C-91, 34: 7 Parliament of Canada, 7: 65–7: 96 (December 1, 1992); ibid. at 34: 8 Parliament of Canada, 8: 37–8: 40 (December 1, 1992).

23. Lara J. Glasgow, 'Stretching the Limits of Intellectual Property Rights: Has the Pharmaceutical Industry Gone Too Far?,' 41 *Idea* 227, 233 n. 27 (2001) (citing the Gale Group, 'Intellectual Property Rules: A Delicate Balancing Act for Drug Development,' 23 *Chain Drug Rev.* RX13 (2001)).
24. *Generic Drug Entry Prior to Patent Expiration*, FTC Study (Fed. Trade Comm'n), July 2002, online: <http://www.ftc.gov/os/2002/07/generic drugstudy. pdf>. See Hore, *supra* note 16; Caffrey and Rotter (2004), *supra* note 15, at 40 n. 293. It should be noted, however, that these data are now somewhat old, and require updating in both the United States and Canada following amendments to the respective linkage regimes over the last half decade.
25. EC Preliminary Rep. (2008), *supra* note 21, at 314. The European Commission states:

    > Originator companies may also litigate against pricing and reimbursement bodies, claiming patent infringement, irregularities in the generic registration file or concerns about bioequivalence or non-compliance of the promotional material. However, as described in Chapter C.2.5., when the interventions before the marketing authorisation [*sic*] authorities lead to litigation, originator companies lose most of the cases, which suggest that the arguments submitted against the generic product could not be substantiated.

26. Boldrin and Levine (2008), *supra* note 10; Boldrin and Levine, *Economics of Ideas* (2005), *supra* note 10; Bulow (2004), *supra* note 15.
27. Colleen Flood, Mark Stabile, and Carolyn Tuohy (eds), *Exploring Social Insurance: Can a Dose of Europe Cure Canadian Health Care Finance?* (McGill-Queen's University Press, 2008); Colleen Flood, Mark Stabile, and Carolyn Tuohy (eds), *Canadian Health Law and Policy*, 3rd edn (LexisNexis, 2007); Colleen Flood (ed.), *Just Medicare: What's In, What's Out, How We Decide* (University of Toronto Press, 2006); Colleen Flood, Kent Roach, and Lorne Sossin (eds), *Access to Care, Access to Justice: The Legal Debate Over Private Health Insurance in Canada* (University of Toronto Press, 2005).
28. Philip J. Hilts, *Protecting America's Health: The FDA, Business, and One Hundred Years of Regulation* (Knopf, 2003); Jerry Avorn, *Powerful Medicines: The Benefits, Risks, and Costs of Prescription Drugs* (Knopf, 2004); Angell (2004), *supra* note 10; Jay S. Cohen, *Over Dose: The Case Against the Drug Companies* (Tarcher, 2001); Ray Moynihan and Alan Cassels, *Selling Sickness: How the World's Biggest Pharmaceutical Companies Are Turning Us All into Patients* (Nation Books, 2005).
29. Mary E. Wiktorowicz, 'Emergent Patterns in the Regulation of Pharmaceuticals: Institutions and Interests in the United States, Canada, Britain, and France,' 28 *J. Health Pol. Pol'y & L.* 615, 620 (2003).
30. See World Health Organization, *Integrating Intellectual Property Rights and Development Policy*, Report (2006); Eric Noehrenberg, 'Report of the

Commission on Intellectual Property Rights, Innovation and Public Health: An Industry Perspective,' 84 *Bull. of the World Health Org.*, May 2006, at 419; Emmanuel Hassan, Ohid Yaqub, and Stephanie Diepeveen, *Intellectual Property and Developing Countries* (Rand Corp., 2010); Kevin Outterson, 'Should Access to Medicines and TRIPS Flexibilities Be Limited to Specific Diseases?,' 34 *Am. J.L. & Med.* 279, 279–301 (2008). See, generally, Trudo Lemmens, 'Leopards in the Temple: Restoring Scientific Integrity to the Commercialized Research Scene,' 32 *J.L. Med. & Ethics* 641 (2004); Trudo Lemmens, 'Piercing the Veil of Corporate Secrecy about Clinical Trials,' *Hastings Ctr. Rep.* (2004) 14; E. Richard Gold, 'The Reach of Patent Law and Institutional Competence,' 1 *Ottawa L. & Tech. J.* 263 (2004).

31. For a critique of the presumption of validity in patent law, see Mark A. Lemley and Douglas Lichtman, 'Rethinking Patent Law's Presumption of Validity,' 60 *Stan. L. Rev.* 45 (2007).
32. Aaron S. Kesselheim and Jeffery Avorn, 'Biomedical Patents and the Public's Health: Is There a Role for Eminent Domain?' 295 *JAMA* 434, 434–7 (2006).
33. World Health Organization, *Public Health: Innovation and Intellectual Property Rights*, Rep. of the Comm'n on Intell. Prop. Rights, Innovation and Pub. Health (WHO, April 25, 2006); Graham Dutfield, 'Delivering Drugs to the Poor: Will the TRIPS Amendment Help?' 34 *Am. J. L. & Med.* 107–24 (2008); Aaron Kesselheim, 'Think Globally, Prescribe Locally: How Rational Pharmaceutical Policy in the U.S. Can Improve Global Access to Essential Medicines,' 34 *Am. J. L. & Med.* 125, 125–39 (2008).
34. Canada's Access to Medicines Regime was established by the Government of Canada. It allows Canada to enact *compulsory licences*, despite provisions in the Patent Act to the contrary, to export *essential medicines* to countries without capacity to manufacture the same. The popular front for this effort was the 2004 Act to amend the Patent Act and the Food and Drugs Act, also known as the Jean Chrétien Pledge to Africa Act. For more information see Canada's Access to Medicines Regime, online: <http://www.camr-rcam.gc.ca/index_e.html> (last visited October 18, 2010).
35. Jillian Clare Kohler et al., 'Canada's Access to Medicines Regime: Promise or Failure of Humanitarian Effort?' 5 *Healthcare Pol'y* 40, 40–8 (2010).
36. Peter Drahos, 'Intellectual Property and Pharmaceutical Markets: A Nodal Governance Approach,' 77 *Temp. L. Rev.* 401, 401–24 (2004) [Drahos (2004)]; Jillian Clare Cohen, Patricia Illingworth, and Udo Schulenk (eds), *The Power of Pills: Social, Ethical and Legal Issues in Drug Development, Marketing and Pricing* (Pluto, 2006).
37. EC Final Rep., *supra* note 4; EC Preliminary Rep., *supra* note 21.
38. Caffrey and Rotter (2004), *supra* note 15; Hore (2004), *supra* note 16; Bouchard et al. (2009), *supra* note 12.
39. EC Final Rep., *supra* note 4. In the Executive Summary, the EC states that:

> The Commission will continue to strictly enforce the applicable Community law and, for instance, act against patent linkage, as according to

> Community legislation, marketing authorisation [*sic*] bodies cannot take the patent status of the originator medicine into account when deciding on marketing authorisations [*sic*] of generic medicines. (Ibid., at 23)

In the 2008 Preliminary Report, the EC stated more specifically that patent linkage is considered unlawful under Regulation (EC) No. 726/2004 and Directive (EC) No. 2001/83 (EC Preliminary Rep., *supra* note 21, at 14). Further elaboration is provided to the effect that:

> Patent linkage refers to the practice of linking the granting of MA, the pricing and reimbursement status or any regulatory approval for a generic medicinal product, to the status of a patent (application) for the originator reference product. Under EU law, it is not allowed to link marketing authorisation [*sic*] to the patent status of the originator reference product. Article 81 of the Regulation and Article 126 of the Directive provide that authorisation [*sic*] to market a medicinal product shall not be refused, suspended or revoked except on the grounds set out in the Regulation and the Directive. Since the status of a patent (application) is not included in the grounds set out in the Regulation and in the Directive, it cannot be used as an argument for refusing, suspending or revoking MA. (Ibid., at 113–14)

40. Preliminary Rep., *supra* note 21, at 22–3. The report states:

> Interventions before regulatory bodies (marketing authorisation [sic] authorities and pricing and reimbursement bodies) appear to be a standard tool in originator companies' toolbox. Although contacting the health authorities may address legitimate concerns, it can also be used to delay or block the marketing authorisation [*sic*] or the pricing or reimbursement status of the generic product. In particular, by suggesting that the generic product is less efficient or safe or is not equivalent, raising patent infringement issues concerning the generic product in question and alleging that any decision favourable [*sic*] to the generic company would make the authorities liable to patent infringement damages (patent linkage), originator companies gain time and can create delays in granting marketing approval for the generic product and its entry into the market. (Ibid., at 314)

41. See North American Free Trade Agreement, U.S.-Can.-Mex., December 17, 1992, TS No. 2 (1994), 32 ILM 289 (between the Governments of Canada, Mexico, and the United States; entered into force January 1, 1994); Trade Related Aspects of Intellectual Property (TRIPS) 1994, October 30, 1947, TS No. 27 (1947), 58 UNTS 187 (negotiated as part of the Uruguay Round (1986–1994) of the World Trade Organization's General Agreement on Tariffs and Trade (GATT).
42. For example, a 2008 shipment of the anti-HIV drug Abacavir was confiscated by Dutch customs authorities. The shipment was from an Indian company bound for Nigeria. It was paid for by UNITAID, the drug purchase arm of the WHO, and was meant to be distributed by the William J. Clinton Foundation.

See, for example, 'Posting of GenericIPguy to Indian Patent Oppositions: Abacavir Hemisulfate' – Indian pre grant opposition documents, online: <http://indianpatentoppositions.blogspot.com/2007/11/abacavir-hemisulfate-indian-pre-grant.html> (last visited November 21, 2007); EUR-Lex – 32003R1383-EN, online: <http://eur-lex.europa.eu/LexUriServ/LexUriServ.do?uri=CELEX:32003R1383:EN:HTML> (last visited October 18, 2010).

43. Bouchard et al. (2011), *supra* note 6.
44. Neil E. Harrison (ed.), *Complexity in World Politics: Concepts and Methods of a New Paradigm* (SUNY Press, 2006) [Harrison, *Complexity* (2006)]; Robert Jervis, *System Effects: Complexity in Political and Social Life* (Princeton University Press, 1997) [Jervis (1997)]; Barry Bozeman and Daniel Sarewitz, 'Public Values and Public Failure in US Science Policy,' 32 *Science and Public Policy* 119 (2005) [Bozeman and Sarewitz (2005)]; Barry Bozeman, 'Public Value Failure: When Efficient Markets May Not Do,' 62 *Public Administration Review* 145 (2002) [Bozeman (2002)]; John D. Sterman, 'All Models Are Wrong: Reflections on Becoming a Systems Scientist,' 18 *System Dynamics Review* 501 (2002) [Sterman (2002)].
45. Drahos (2004), *supra* note 36.
46. Harrison, 'Protection' (2000–1), *supra* note 16; Jervis (1997), *supra* note 44, at 87 (noting that 'the interactions in the system may alter the meaning of the yardstick'); Bozeman and Sarewitz (2005), *supra* note 44; Bozeman (2002), *supra* note 44; Sterman (2002), *supra* note 44, at 501 n. 4.
47. Neil E. Harrison, 'Thinking About the World We Make,' in Harrison, *Complexity* (2006), *supra* note 44; Jervis (1997), *supra* note 44.
48. See, for example, J.B. Ruhl, 'The Fitness of Law: Using Complexity Theory to Describe the Evolution of Law and Society and Its Practical Meaning for Democracy,' 49 *Vand. L. Rev.* 1407 (1996); J.B. Ruhl, 'Regulation by Adaptive Management: Is It Possible?' 7 *Minn. J.L. Sci. & Tech.* 21 (2005–6).
49. Feedback interactions in complex systems have received increased attention in recent years. See, generally, Albert-Laszlo Barabási, *Linked: How Everything Is Connected to Everything Else and What It Means for Business, Science, and Everyday Life* (Plume, 2003) [Barabási (2003)]; James Gleick, *Chaos: Making a New Science* (Viking, 1987) [Gleick (1987)]; John H. Holland, *Adaptation in Natural and Artificial Systems* (MIT Press, 1992) (1975) [Holland (1992)]; John H. Holland, *Hidden Order: How Adaptation Builds Complexity* (Addison-Wesley, 1995) [Holland (1995)]; Steven Johnson, *Emergence: The Connected Lives of Ants, Brains, Cities, and Software* (Scribner, 2001) [Johnson (2001)]; Stuart Kauffman, *At Home in the Universe: The Search for the Laws of Self-Organization and Complexity* (Viking, 1995) [Kaufmann (1995)]; Grégoire Nicolis and Ilya Prigogine, *Exploring Complexity: An Introduction* (W.H. Freeman, 1989) [Nicolis and Prigogine (1989)]; M. Mitchell Waldrop, *Complexity: The Emerging Science at the Edge of Order and Chaos* (Simon & Schuster, 1992) [Waldrop (1992)]; Brian W. Arthur, 'Positive Feedbacks in the Economy,' 262 *Sci. Am.* 92, 92–9 (1990) [Arthur (1990)].

50. See, for example, Robert M. May et al., 'Complex Systems: Ecology for Bankers,' 451 *Nature* 893 (2008). For a look at the role of feedback in policy failure, see, generally, Jervis (1997), *supra* note 44; Harrison, *Complexity* (2006), *supra* note 44; Bozeman (2002), *supra* note 44; Bozeman and Sarewitz (2005), *supra* note 44; and Sterman (2002), *supra* note 44.
51. See, generally, Barabási (2003), *supra* note 49; Gleick (1987), *supra* note 49; Holland (1992), *supra* note 49; Holland (1995), *supra* note 49; Johnson (2001), *supra* note 49; Kauffman (1995), *supra* note 49; Nicolis and Prigogine (1989), *supra* note 49; Waldrop (1992), *supra* note 49; Arthur (1990), *supra* note 49, at 92–9.
52. Harrison, *Complexity* (2006), *supra* note 44; Jervis (1997), *supra* note 44; see also Clifford Shearing and Jennifer Wood, 'Nodal Governance, Democracy, and the New "Denizens,"' 30 *J.L. & Soc'y* 400, 401–6 (2003); Les Johnston and Clifford Shearing, *Governing Security: Explorations in Policing and Justice* (2003), ch. 8, 138; Scott Burris, 'Governance, Microgovernance and Health,' 77 *Temp. L. Rev.* 335, 357 (2004); Drahos (2004), *supra* note 36.

Index